The Valley of

Jack London

Alpha Editions

This edition published in 2024

ISBN : 9789362928016

Design and Setting By
Alpha Editions
www.alphaedis.com
Email - info@alphaedis.com

Contents

BOOK I

CHAPTER 1

"You hear me, Saxon? Come on along. What if it is the Bricklayers? I'll have gentlemen friends there, and so'll you. The Al Vista band'll be along, an' you know it plays heavenly. An' you just love dancin'——"

Twenty feet away, a stout, elderly woman interrupted the girl's persuasions. The elderly woman's back was turned, and the back--loose, bulging, and misshapen—began a convulsive heaving.

"Gawd!" she cried out. "O Gawd!"

She flung wild glances, like those of an entrapped animal, up and down the big whitewashed room that panted with heat and that was thickly humid with the steam that sizzled from the damp cloth under the irons of the many ironers. From the girls and women near her, all swinging irons steadily but at high pace, came quick glances, and labor efficiency suffered to the extent of a score of suspended or inadequate movements. The elderly woman's cry had caused a tremor of money-loss to pass among the piece-work ironers of fancy starch.

She gripped herself and her iron with a visible effort, and dabbed futilely at the frail, frilled garment on the board under her hand.

"I thought she'd got'em again—didn't you?" the girl said.

"It's a shame, a woman of her age, and... condition," Saxon answered, as she frilled a lace ruffle with a hot fluting-iron. Her movements were delicate, safe, and swift, and though her face was wan with fatigue and exhausting heat, there was no slackening in her pace.

"An' her with seven, an' two of 'em in reform school," the girl at the next board sniffed sympathetic agreement. "But you just got to come to Weasel Park to-morrow, Saxon. The Bricklayers' is always lively—tugs-of-war, fat-man races, real Irish jiggin', an'... an' everything. An' the floor of the pavilion's swell."

But the elderly woman brought another interruption. She dropped her iron on the shirtwaist, clutched at the board, fumbled it, caved in at the knees and hips, and like a half-empty sack collapsed on the floor, her long shriek rising in the pent room to the acrid smell of scorching cloth. The women at the boards near to her scrambled, first, to the hot iron to save the cloth, and then to her, while the forewoman hurried belligerently down the aisle. The women farther away continued unsteadily at their work, losing movements to the extent of a minute's set-back to the totality of the efficiency of the fancy-starch room.

"Enough to kill a dog," the girl muttered, thumping her iron down on its rest with reckless determination. "Workin' girls' life ain't what it's cracked up. Me to quit—that's what I'm comin' to."

"Mary!" Saxon uttered the other's name with a reproach so profound that she was compelled to rest her own iron for emphasis and so lose a dozen movements.

Mary flashed a half-frightened look across.

"I didn't mean it, Saxon," she whimpered. "Honest, I didn't. I wouldn't never go that way. But I leave it to you, if a day like this don't get on anybody's nerves. Listen to that!"

The stricken woman, on her back, drumming her heels on the floor, was shrieking persistently and monotonously, like a mechanical siren. Two women, clutching her under the arms, were dragging her down the aisle. She drummed and shrieked the length of it. The door opened, and a vast, muffled roar of machinery burst in; and in the roar of it the drumming and the shrieking were drowned ere the door swung shut. Remained of the episode only the scorch of cloth drifting ominously through the air.

"It's sickenin'," said Mary.

And thereafter, for a long time, the many irons rose and fell, the pace of the room in no wise diminished; while the forewoman strode the aisles with a threatening eye for incipient breakdown and hysteria. Occasionally an ironer lost the stride for an instant, gasped or sighed, then caught it up again with weary determination. The long summer day waned, but not the heat, and under the raw flare of electric light the work went on.

By nine o'clock the first women began to go home. The mountain of fancy starch had been demolished—all save the few remnants, here and there, on the boards, where the ironers still labored.

Saxon finished ahead of Mary, at whose board she paused on the way out.

"Saturday night an' another week gone," Mary said mournfully, her young cheeks pallid and hollowed, her black eyes blue-shadowed and tired. "What d'you think you've made, Saxon?"

"Twelve and a quarter," was the answer, just touched with pride. "And I'd a-made more if it wasn't for that fake bunch of starchers."

"My! I got to pass it to you," Mary congratulated. "You're a sure fierce hustler—just eat it up. Me—I've only ten an' a half, an' for a hard week... See you on the nine-forty. Sure now. We can just fool around until the dancin' begins. A lot of my gentlemen friends'll be there in the afternoon."

Two blocks from the laundry, where an arc-light showed a gang of toughs on the corner, Saxon quickened her pace. Unconsciously her face set and hardened as she passed. She did not catch the words of the muttered comment, but the rough laughter it raised made her guess and warmed her checks with resentful blood. Three blocks more, turning once to left and once to right, she walked on through the night that was already growing cool. On either side were workingmen's houses, of weathered wood, the ancient paint grimed with the dust of years, conspicuous only for cheapness and ugliness.

Dark it was, but she made no mistake, the familiar sag and screeching reproach of the front gate welcome under her hand. She went along the narrow walk to the rear, avoided the missing step without thinking about it, and entered the kitchen, where a solitary gas-jet flickered. She turned it up to the best of its flame. It was a small room, not disorderly, because of lack of furnishings to disorder it. The plaster, discolored by the steam of many wash-days, was crisscrossed with cracks from the big earthquake of the previous spring. The floor was ridged, wide-cracked, and uneven, and in front of the stove it was worn through and repaired with a five-gallon oil-can hammered flat and double. A sink, a dirty roller-towel, several chairs, and a wooden table completed the picture.

An apple-core crunched under her foot as she drew a chair to the table. On the frayed oilcloth, a supper waited. She attempted the cold beans, thick with grease, but gave them up, and buttered a slice of bread.

The rickety house shook to a heavy, prideless tread, and through the inner door came Sarah, middle-aged, lop-breasted, hair-tousled, her face lined with care and fat petulance.

"Huh, it's you," she grunted a greeting. "I just couldn't keep things warm. Such a day! I near died of the heat. An' little Henry cut his lip awful. The doctor had to put four stitches in it."

Sarah came over and stood mountainously by the table.

"What's the matter with them beans?" she challenged.

"Nothing, only..." Saxon caught her breath and avoided the threatened outburst. "Only I'm not hungry. It's been so hot all day. It was terrible in the laundry."

Recklessly she took a mouthful of the cold tea that had been steeped so long that it was like acid in her mouth, and recklessly, under the eye of her sister-in-law, she swallowed it and the rest of the cupful. She wiped her mouth on her handkerchief and got up.

"I guess I'll go to bed."

"Wonder you ain't out to a dance," Sarah sniffed. "Funny, ain't it, you come home so dead tired every night, an' yet any night in the week you can get out an' dance unearthly hours."

Saxon started to speak, suppressed herself with tightened lips, then lost control and blazed out. "Wasn't you ever young?"

Without waiting for reply, she turned to her bedroom, which opened directly off the kitchen. It was a small room, eight by twelve, and the earthquake had left its marks upon the plaster. A bed and chair of cheap pine and a very ancient chest of drawers constituted the furniture. Saxon had known this chest of drawers all her life. The vision of it was woven into her earliest recollections. She knew it had crossed the plains with her people in a prairie schooner. It was of solid mahogany. One end was cracked and dented from the capsize of the wagon in Rock Canyon. A bullet-hole, plugged, in the face of the top drawer, told of the fight with the Indians at Little Meadow. Of these happenings her mother had told her; also had she told that the chest had come with the family originally from England in a day even earlier than the day on which George Washington was born.

Above the chest of drawers, on the wall, hung a small looking-glass. Thrust under the molding were photographs of young men and women, and of picnic groups wherein the young men, with hats rakishly on the backs of their heads, encircled the girls with their arms. Farther along on the wall were a colored calendar and numerous colored advertisements and sketches torn out of magazines. Most of these sketches were of horses. From the gas-fixture hung a tangled bunch of well-scribbled dance programs.

Saxon started to take off her hat, but suddenly sat down on the bed. She sobbed softly, with considered repression, but the weak-latched door swung noiselessly open, and she was startled by her sister-in-law's voice.

"NOW what's the matter with you? If you didn't like them beans—"

"No, no," Saxon explained hurriedly. "I'm just tired, that's all, and my feet hurt. I wasn't hungry, Sarah. I'm just beat out."

"If you took care of this house," came the retort, "an' cooked an' baked, an' washed, an' put up with what I put up, you'd have something to be beat out about. You've got a snap, you have. But just wait." Sarah broke off to cackle gloatingly. "Just wait, that's all, an' you'll be fool enough to get married some day, like me, an' then you'll get yours—an' it'll be brats, an' brats, an' brats, an' no more dancin', an' silk stockin's, an' three pairs of shoes at one time. You've got a cinch--nobody to think of but your own precious self—an' a lot of young hoodlums makin' eyes at you an' tellin' you how beautiful your eyes are. Huh! Some fine day you'll tie up to one of 'em, an' then, mebbe, on occasion, you'll wear black eyes for a change."

"Don't say that, Sarah," Saxon protested. "My brother never laid hands on you. You know that."

"No more he didn't. He never had the gumption. Just the same, he's better stock than that tough crowd you run with, if he can't make a livin' an' keep his wife in three pairs of shoes. Just the same he's oodles better'n your bunch of hoodlums that no decent woman'd wipe her one pair of shoes on. How you've missed trouble this long is beyond me. Mebbe the younger generation is wiser in such things—I don't know. But I do know that a young woman that has three pairs of shoes ain't thinkin' of anything but her own enjoyment, an' she's goin' to get hers, I can tell her that much. When I was a girl there wasn't such doin's. My mother'd taken the hide off me if I done the things you do. An' she was right, just as everything in the world is wrong now. Look at your brother, a-runnin' around to socialist meetin's, an' chewin' hot air, an' diggin' up extra strike dues to the union that means so much bread out of the mouths of his children, instead of makin' good with his bosses. Why, the dues he pays would keep me in seventeen pairs of shoes if I was nannygoat enough to want 'em. Some day, mark my words, he'll get his time, an' then what'll we do? What'll I do, with five mouths to feed an' nothin' comin' in?"

She stopped, out of breath but seething with the tirade yet to come.

"Oh, Sarah, please won't you shut the door?" Saxon pleaded.

The door slammed violently, and Saxon, ere she fell to crying again, could hear her sister-in-law lumbering about the kitchen and talking loudly to herself.

CHAPTER II

Each bought her own ticket at the entrance to Weasel Park. And each, as she laid her half-dollar down, was distinctly aware of how many pieces of fancy starch were represented by the coin. It was too early for the crowd, but bricklayers and their families, laden with huge lunch-baskets and armfuls of babies, were already going in—a healthy, husky race of workmen, well-paid and robustly fed. And with them, here and there, undisguised by their decent American clothing, smaller in bulk and stature, weazened not alone by age but by the pinch of lean years and early hardship, were grandfathers and mothers who had patently first seen the light of day on old Irish soil. Their faces showed content and pride as they limped along with this lusty progeny of theirs that had fed on better food.

Not with these did Mary and Saxon belong. They knew them not, had no acquaintances among them. It did not matter whether the festival were Irish, German, or Slavonian; whether the picnic was the Bricklayers', the Brewers', or the Butchers'. They, the girls, were of the dancing crowd that swelled by a certain constant percentage the gate receipts of all the picnics.

They strolled about among the booths where peanuts were grinding and popcorn was roasting in preparation for the day, and went on and inspected the dance floor of the pavilion. Saxon, clinging to an imaginary partner, essayed a few steps of the dip-waltz. Mary clapped her hands.

"My!" she cried. "You're just swell! An' them stockin's is peaches."

Saxon smiled with appreciation, pointed out her foot, velvet-slippered with high Cuban heels, and slightly lifted the tight black skirt, exposing a trim ankle and delicate swell of calf, the white flesh gleaming through the thinnest and flimsiest of fifty-cent black silk stockings. She was slender, not tall, yet the due round lines of womanhood were hers. On her white shirtwaist was a pleated jabot of cheap lace, caught with a large novelty pin of imitation coral. Over the shirtwaist was a natty jacket, elbow-sleeved, and to the elbows she wore gloves of imitation suede. The one essentially natural touch about her appearance was the few curls, strangers to curling-irons, that escaped from under the little naughty hat of black velvet pulled low over the eyes.

Mary's dark eyes flashed with joy at the sight, and with a swift little run she caught the other girl in her arms and kissed her in a breast-crushing embrace. She released her, blushing at her own extravagance.

"You look good to me," she cried, in extenuation. "If I was a man I couldn't keep my hands off you. I'd eat you, I sure would."

They went out of the pavilion hand in hand, and on through the sunshine they strolled, swinging hands gaily, reacting exuberantly from the week of deadening toil. They hung over the railing of the bear-pit, shivering at the huge and lonely denizen, and passed quickly on to ten minutes of laughter at the monkey cage. Crossing the grounds, they looked down into the little race track on the bed of a natural amphitheater where the early afternoon games were to take place. After that they explored the woods, threaded by countless paths, ever opening out in new surprises of green-painted rustic tables and benches in leafy nooks, many of which were already pre-empted by family parties. On a grassy slope, tree-surrounded, they spread a newspaper and sat down on the short grass already tawny-dry under the California sun. Half were they minded to do this because of the grateful indolence after six days of insistent motion, half in conservation for the hours of dancing to come.

"Bert Wanhope'll be sure to come," Mary chattered. "An' he said he was going to bring Billy Roberts—'Big Bill,' all the fellows call him. He's just a big boy, but he's awfully tough. He's a prizefighter, an' all the girls run after him. I'm afraid of him. He ain't quick in talkin'. He's more like that big bear we saw. Brr-rf! Brr-rf!—bite your head off, just like that. He ain't really a prize-fighter. He's a teamster—belongs to the union. Drives for Coberly and Morrison. But sometimes he fights in the clubs. Most of the fellows are scared of him. He's got a bad temper, an' he'd just as soon hit a fellow as eat, just like that. You won't like him, but he's a swell dancer. He's heavy, you know, an' he just slides and glides around. You wanta have a dance with'm anyway. He's a good spender, too. Never pinches. But my!—he's got one temper."

The talk wandered on, a monologue on Mary's part, that centered always on Bert Wanhope.

"You and he are pretty thick," Saxon ventured.

"I'd marry'm to-morrow," Mary flashed out impulsively. Then her face went bleakly forlorn, hard almost in its helpless pathos. "Only, he never asks me. He's..." Her pause was broken by sudden passion. "You watch out for him, Saxon, if he ever comes foolin' around you. He's no good. Just the same, I'd marry him to-morrow. He'll never get me any other way." Her mouth opened, but instead of speaking she drew a long sigh. "It's a funny world, ain't it?" she added. "More like a scream. And all the stars are worlds, too. I wonder where God hides. Bert Wanhope says there ain't no God. But he's just terrible. He says the most terrible things. I believe in God. Don't you? What do you think about God, Saxon?"

Saxon shrugged her shoulders and laughed.

"But if we do wrong we get ours, don't we?" Mary persisted. "That's what they all say, except Bert. He says he don't care what he does, he'll never get his, because when he dies he's dead, an' when he's dead he'd like to see any one put anything across on him that'd wake him up. Ain't he terrible, though? But it's all so funny. Sometimes I get scared when I think God's keepin' an eye on me all the time. Do you think he knows what I'm sayin' now? What do you think he looks like, anyway?"

"I don't know," Saxon answered. "He's just a funny proposition."

"Oh!" the other gasped.

"He IS, just the same, from what all people say of him," Saxon went on stoutly. "My brother thinks he looks like Abraham Lincoln. Sarah thinks he has whiskers."

"An' I never think of him with his hair parted," Mary confessed, daring the thought and shivering with apprehension. "He just couldn't have his hair parted. THAT'D be funny."

"You know that little, wrinkly Mexican that sells wire puzzles?" Saxon queried. "Well, God somehow always reminds me of him."

Mary laughed outright.

"Now that IS funny. I never thought of him like that. How do you make it out?"

"Well, just like the little Mexican, he seems to spend his time peddling puzzles. He passes a puzzle out to everybody, and they spend all their lives tryin' to work it out. They all get stuck. I can't work mine out. I don't know where to start. And look at the puzzle he passed Sarah. And she's part of Tom's puzzle, and she only makes his worse. And they all, an' everybody I know—you, too—are part of my puzzle."

"Mebbe the puzzles is all right," Mary considered. "But God don't look like that yellow little Greaser. THAT I won't fall for. God don't look like anybody. Don't you remember on the wall at the Salvation Army it says 'God is a spirit'?"

"That's another one of his puzzles, I guess, because nobody knows what a spirit looks like."

"That's right, too." Mary shuddered with reminiscent fear. "Whenever I try to think of God as a spirit, I can see Hen Miller all wrapped up in a sheet an' runnin' us girls. We didn't know, an' it scared the life out of us. Little Maggie Murphy fainted dead away, and Beatrice Peralta fell an' scratched her face horrible. When I think of a spirit all I can see is a white sheet runnin' in the dark. Just the same, God don't look like a Mexican, an' he don't wear his hair parted."

A strain of music from the dancing pavilion brought both girls scrambling to their feet.

"We can get a couple of dances in before we eat," Mary proposed. "An' then it'll be afternoon an' all the fellows 'll be here. Most of them are pinchers—that's why they don't come early, so as to get out of taking the girls to dinner. But Bert's free with his money, an' so is Billy. If we can beat the other girls to it, they'll take us to the restaurant. Come on, hurry, Saxon."

There were few couples on the floor when they arrived at the pavilion, and the two girls essayed the first waltz together.

"There's Bert now," Saxon whispered, as they came around the second time.

"Don't take any notice of them," Mary whispered back. "We'll just keep on goin'. They needn't think we're chasin' after them."

But Saxon noted the heightened color in the other's cheek, and felt her quicker breathing.

"Did you see that other one?" Mary asked, as she backed Saxon in a long slide across the far end of the pavilion. "That was Billy Roberts. Bert said he'd come. He'll take you to dinner, and Bert'll take me. It's goin' to be a swell day, you'll see. My! I only wish the music'll hold out till we can get back to the other end."

Down the floor they danced, on man-trapping and dinner-getting intent, two fresh young things that undeniably danced well and that were delightfully surprised when the music stranded them perilously near to their desire.

Bert and Mary addressed each other by their given names, but to Saxon Bert was "Mr. Wanhope," though he called her by her first name. The only introduction was of Saxon and Billy Roberts. Mary carried it off with a flurry of nervous carelessness.

"Mr. Robert—Miss Brown. She's my best friend. Her first name's Saxon. Ain't it a scream of a name?"

"Sounds good to me," Billy retorted, hat off and hand extended. "Pleased to meet you, Miss Brown."

As their hands clasped and she felt the teamster callouses on his palm, her quick eyes saw a score of things. About all that he saw was her eyes, and then it was with a vague impression that they were blue. Not till later in the day did he realize that they were gray. She, on the contrary, saw his eyes as they really were—deep blue, wide, and handsome in a sullen-boyish way. She saw that they were straight-looking, and she liked them, as she had liked the glimpse she had caught of his hand, and as she liked the contact of his hand itself. Then, too, but not sharply, she had perceived the short, square-set nose, the rosiness of cheek, and the firm, short upper lip, ere delight centered her flash of gaze on the well-modeled, large clean mouth where red lips smiled clear of the white, enviable teeth. A BOY, A GREAT BIG MAN-BOY, was her thought; and, as they smiled at each other and their hands slipped apart, she was startled by a glimpse of his hair—short and crisp and sandy, hinting almost of palest gold save that it was too flaxen to hint of gold at all.

So blond was he that she was reminded of stage-types she had seen, such as Ole Olson and Yon Yonson; but there resemblance ceased. It was a matter of color only, for the eyes were dark-lashed and -browed, and were cloudy with temperament rather than staring a child-gaze of wonder, and the suit of smooth brown cloth had been made by a tailor. Saxon appraised the suit on the instant, and her secret judgment was NOT A CENT LESS THAN FIFTY DOLLARS. Further, he had none of the awkwardness of the Scandinavian immigrant. On the contrary, he was one of those rare individuals that radiate muscular grace through the ungraceful man-garments of civilization. Every movement was supple, slow, and apparently considered. This she did not see nor analyze. She saw only a clothed man with grace of carriage and movement. She felt, rather than perceived, the calm and certitude of all the muscular play of him, and she felt, too, the promise of easement and rest that was especially grateful and craved-for by one who had incessantly, for six days and at top-speed, ironed fancy starch. As the touch of his hand had been good, so, to her, this subtler feel of all of him, body and mind, was good.

As he took her program and skirmished and joked after the way of young men, she realized the immediacy of delight she had taken in him. Never in her life had she been so affected by any man. She wondered to herself: IS THIS THE MAN?

He danced beautifully. The joy was hers that good dancers take when they have found a good dancer for a partner. The grace of those slow-moving, certain muscles of his accorded perfectly with the rhythm of the music. There was never doubt, never a betrayal of indecision. She glanced at Bert, dancing "tough" with Mary, caroming down the long floor with more than one collision with the increasing couples. Graceful himself in his slender, tall, lean-stomached way, Bert was accounted a good dancer; yet Saxon did not remember ever having danced with him with keen pleasure. Just a hit of a jerk spoiled his dancing—a jerk that did not occur, usually, but that always impended. There was something spasmodic in his mind. He was too quick, or he continually threatened to be too quick. He always seemed just on the verge of overrunning the time. It was disquieting. He made for unrest.

"You're a dream of a dancer," Billy Roberts was saying. "I've heard lots of the fellows talk about your dancing."

"I love it," she answered.

But from the way she said it he sensed her reluctance to speak, and danced on in silence, while she warmed with the appreciation of a woman for gentle consideration. Gentle consideration was a thing rarely encountered in the life she lived. IS THIS THE MAN? She remembered Mary's "I'd marry him to-morrow," and caught herself speculating on marrying Billy Roberts by the next day—if he asked her.

With eyes that dreamily desired to close, she moved on in the arms of this masterful, guiding pressure. A PRIZE-FIGHTER! She experienced a thrill of wickedness as she thought of what Sarah would say could she see her now. Only he wasn't a prizefighter, but a teamster.

Came an abrupt lengthening of step, the guiding pressure grew more compelling, and she was caught up and carried along, though her velvet-shod feet never left the floor. Then came the sudden control down to the shorter step again, and she felt herself being held slightly from him so that he might look into her face and laugh with her in joy at the exploit. At the end, as the band slowed in the last bars, they, too, slowed, their dance fading with the music in a lengthening glide that ceased with the last lingering tone.

"We're sure cut out for each other when it comes to dancin'," he said, as they made their way to rejoin the other couple.

"It was a dream," she replied.

So low was her voice that he bent to hear, and saw the flush in her cheeks that seemed communicated to her eyes, which were softly warm and sensuous. He took the program from her and gravely and gigantically wrote his name across all the length of it.

"An' now it's no good," he dared. "Ain't no need for it."

He tore it across and tossed it aside.

"Me for you, Saxon, for the next," was Bert's greeting, as they came up. "You take Mary for the next whirl, Bill."

"Nothin' doin', Bo," was the retort. "Me an' Saxon's framed up to last the day."

"Watch out for him, Saxon," Mary warned facetiously. "He's liable to get a crush on you."

"I guess I know a good thing when I see it," Billy responded gallantly.

"And so do I," Saxon aided and abetted.

"I'd 'a' known you if I'd seen you in the dark," Billy added.

Mary regarded them with mock alarm, and Bert said good-naturedly:

"All I got to say is you ain't wastin' any time gettin' together. Just the same, if you can spare a few minutes from each other after a couple more whirls, Mary an' me'd be complimented to have your presence at dinner."

"Just like that," chimed Mary.

"Quit your kiddin'," Billy laughed back, turning his head to look into Saxon's eyes. "Don't listen to 'em. They're grouched because they got to dance together. Bert's a rotten dancer, and Mary ain't so much. Come on, there she goes. See you after two more dances."

CHAPTER III

They had dinner in the open-air, tree-walled dining-room, and Saxon noted that it was Billy who paid the reckoning for the four. They knew many of the young men and women at the other tables, and greetings and fun flew back and forth. Bert was very possessive with Mary, almost roughly so, resting his hand on hers, catching and holding it, and, once, forcibly slipping off her two rings and refusing to return them for a long while. At times, when he put his arm around her waist, Mary promptly disengaged it; and at other times, with elaborate obliviousness that deceived no one, she allowed it to remain.

And Saxon, talking little but studying Billy Roberts very intently, was satisfied that there would be an utter difference in the way he would do such things... if ever he would do them. Anyway, he'd never paw a girl as Bert and lots of the other fellows did. She measured the breadth of Billy's heavy shoulders.

"Why do they call you 'Big' Bill?" she asked. "You're not so very tall."

"Nope," he agreed. "I'm only five feet eight an' three-quarters. I guess it must be my weight."

"He fights at a hundred an' eighty," Bert interjected.

"Oh, cut it," Billy said quickly, a cloud-rift of displeasure showing in his eyes. "I ain't a fighter. I ain't fought in six months. I've quit it. It don't pay."

"Yon got two hundred the night you put the Frisco Slasher to the bad," Bert urged proudly.

"Cut it. Cut it now.—Say, Saxon, you ain't so big yourself, are you? But you're built just right if anybody should ask you. You're round an' slender at the same time. I bet I can guess your weight."

"Everybody guesses over it," she warned, while inwardly she was puzzled that she should at the same time be glad and regretful that he did not fight any more.

"Not me," he was saying. "I'm a wooz at weight-guessin'. Just you watch me." He regarded her critically, and it was patent that warm approval played its little rivalry with the judgment of his gaze. "Wait a minute."

He reached over to her and felt her arm at the biceps. The pressure of the encircling fingers was firm and honest, and Saxon thrilled to it. There was magic in this man-boy. She would have known only irritation had Bert or any other man felt her arm. But this man! IS HE THE MAN? she was questioning, when he voiced his conclusion.

"Your clothes don't weigh more'n seven pounds. And seven from—hum—say one hundred an' twenty-three—one hundred an' sixteen is your stripped weight."

But at the penultimate word, Mary cried out with sharp reproof:

"Why, Billy Roberts, people don't talk about such things."

He looked at her with slow-growing, uncomprehending surprise.

"What things?" he demanded finally.

"There you go again! You ought to be ashamed of yourself. Look! You've got Saxon blushing!"

"I am not," Saxon denied indignantly.

"An' if you keep on, Mary, you'll have me blushing," Billy growled. "I guess I know what's right an' what ain't. It ain't what a guy says, but what he thinks. An' I'm thinkin' right, an' Saxon knows it. An' she an' I ain't thinkin' what you're thinkin' at all."

"Oh! Oh!" Mary cried. "You're gettin' worse an' worse. I never think such things."

"Whoa, Mary! Back up!" Bert checked her peremptorily. "You're in the wrong stall. Billy never makes mistakes like that."

"But he needn't be so raw," she persisted.

"Come on, Mary, an' be good, an' cut that stuff," was Billy's dismissal of her, as he turned to Saxon. "How near did I come to it?"

"One hundred and twenty-two," she answered, looking deliberately at Mary. "One twenty two with my clothes."

Billy burst into hearty laughter, in which Bert joined.

"I don't care," Mary protested, "You're terrible, both of you—an' you, too, Saxon. I'd never a-thought it of you."

"Listen to me, kid," Bert began soothingly, as his arm slipped around her waist.

But in the false excitement she had worked herself into, Mary rudely repulsed the arm, and then, fearing that she had wounded her lover's feelings, she took advantage of the teasing and banter to recover her good humor. His arm was permitted to return, and with heads bent together, they talked in whispers.

Billy discreetly began to make conversation with Saxon.

"Say, you know, your name is a funny one. I never heard it tagged on anybody before. But it's all right. I like it."

"My mother gave it to me. She was educated, and knew all kinds of words. She was always reading books, almost until she died. And she wrote lots and lots. I've got some of her poetry published in a San Jose newspaper long ago. The Saxons were a race of people—she told me all about them when I was a little girl. They were wild, like Indians, only they were white. And they had blue eyes, and yellow hair, and they were awful fighters."

As she talked, Billy followed her solemnly, his eyes steadily turned on hers.

"Never heard of them," he confessed. "Did they live anywhere around here?"

She laughed.

"No. They lived in England. They were the first English, and you know the Americans came from the English. We're Saxons, you an' me, an' Mary, an' Bert, and all the Americans that are real Americans, you know, and not Dagoes and Japs and such."

"My folks lived in America a long time," Billy said slowly, digesting the information she had given and relating himself to it. "Anyway, my mother's folks did. They crossed to Maine hundreds of years ago."

"My father was 'State of Maine," she broke in, with a little gurgle of joy. "And my mother was born in Ohio, or where Ohio is now. She used to call it the Great Western Reserve. What was your father?"

"Don't know." Billy shrugged his shoulders. "He didn't know himself. Nobody ever knew, though he was American, all right, all right."

"His name's regular old American," Saxon suggested. "There's a big English general right now whose name is Roberts. I've read it in the papers."

"But Roberts wasn't my father's name. He never knew what his name was. Roberts was the name of a gold-miner who adopted him. You see, it was this way. When they was Indian-fightin' up there with the Modoc Indians, a lot of the miners an' settlers took a hand. Roberts was captain of one outfit, and once, after a fight, they took a lot of prisoners—squaws, an' kids an' babies. An' one of the kids was my father. They figured he was about five years old. He didn't know nothin' but Indian."

Saxon clapped her hands, and her eyes sparkled: "He'd been captured on an Indian raid!"

"That's the way they figured it," Billy nodded. "They recollected a wagon-train of Oregon settlers that'd been killed by the Modocs four years before.

Roberts adopted him, and that's why I don't know his real name. But you can bank on it, he crossed the plains just the same."

"So did my father," Saxon said proudly.

"An' my mother, too," Billy added, pride touching his own voice. "Anyway, she came pretty close to crossin' the plains, because she was born in a wagon on the River Platte on the way out."

"My mother, too," said Saxon. "She was eight years old, an' she walked most of the way after the oxen began to give out."

Billy thrust out his hand.

"Put her there, kid," he said. "We're just like old friends, what with the same kind of folks behind us."

With shining eyes, Saxon extended her hand to his, and gravely they shook.

"Isn't it wonderful?" she murmured. "We're both old American stock. And if you aren't a Saxon there never was one—your hair, your eyes, your skin, everything. And you're a fighter, too."

"I guess all our old folks was fighters when it comes to that. It come natural to 'em, an' dog-gone it, they just had to fight or they'd never come through."

"What are you two talkin' about?" Mary broke in upon them.

"They're thicker'n mush in no time," Bert girded. "You'd think they'd known each other a week already."

"Oh, we knew each other longer than that," Saxon returned. "Before ever we were born our folks were walkin' across the plains together."

"When your folks was waitin' for the railroad to be built an' all the Indians killed off before they dasted to start for California," was Billy's way of proclaiming the new alliance. "We're the real goods, Saxon an' me, if anybody should ride up on a buzz-wagon an' ask you."

"Oh, I don't know," Mary boasted with quiet petulance. "My father stayed behind to fight in the Civil War. He was a drummer-boy. That's why he didn't come to California until afterward."

"And my father went back to fight in the Civil War," Saxon said.

"And mine, too," said Billy.

They looked at each other gleefully. Again they had found a new contact.

"Well, they're all dead, ain't they?" was Bert's saturnine comment. "There ain't no difference dyin' in battle or in the poorhouse. The thing is they're deado. I wouldn't care a rap if my father'd been hanged. It's all the same in a thousand years. This braggin' about folks makes me tired. Besides, my father couldn't a-fought. He wasn't born till two years after the war. Just the same, two of my uncles were killed at Gettysburg. Guess we done our share."

"Just like that," Mary applauded.

Bert's arm went around her waist again.

"We're here, ain't we?" he said. "An' that's what counts. The dead are dead, an' you can bet your sweet life they just keep on stayin' dead."

Mary put her hand over his mouth and began to chide him for his awfulness, whereupon he kissed the palm of her hand and put his head closer to hers.

The merry clatter of dishes was increasing as the dining-room filled up. Here and there voices were raised in snatches of song. There were shrill squeals and screams and bursts of heavier male laughter as the everlasting skirmishing between the young men and girls played on. Among some of the men the signs of drink were already manifest. At a near table girls were calling out to Billy. And Saxon, the sense of temporary possession already strong on her, noted with jealous eyes that he was a favorite and desired object to them.

"Ain't they awful?" Mary voiced her disapproval. "They got a nerve. I know who they are. No respectable girl 'd have a thing to do with them. Listen to that!"

"Oh, you Bill, you," one of them, a buxom young brunette, was calling. "Hope you ain't forgotten me, Bill."

"Oh, you chicken," he called back gallantly.

Saxon flattered herself that he showed vexation, and she conceived an immense dislike for the brunette.

"Goin' to dance?" the latter called.

"Mebbe," he answered, and turned abruptly to Saxon. "Say, we old Americans oughta stick together, don't you think? They ain't many of us left. The country's fillin' up with all kinds of foreigners."

He talked on steadily, in a low, confidential voice, head close to hers, as advertisement to the other girl that he was occupied.

From the next table on the opposite side, a young man had singled out Saxon. His dress was tough. His companions, male and female, were tough. His face was inflamed, his eyes touched with wildness.

"Hey, you!" he called. "You with the velvet slippers. Me for you."

The girl beside him put her arm around his neck and tried to hush him, and through the mufflement of her embrace they could hear him gurgling:

"I tell you she's some goods. Watch me go across an' win her from them cheap skates."

"Butchertown hoodlums," Mary sniffed.

Saxon's eyes encountered the eyes of the girl, who glared hatred across at her. And in Billy's eyes she saw moody anger smouldering. The eyes were more sullen, more handsome than ever, and clouds and veils and lights and shadows shifted and deepened in the blue of them until they gave her a sense of unfathomable depth. He had stopped talking, and he made no effort to talk.

"Don't start a rough house, Bill," Bert cautioned. "They're from across the bay an' they don't know you, that's all."

Bert stood up suddenly, stepped over to the other table, whispered briefly, and came back. Every face at the table was turned on Billy. The offender arose brokenly, shook off the detaining hand of his girl, and came over. He was a large man, with a hard, malignant face and bitter eyes. Also, he was a subdued man.

"You're Big Bill Roberts," he said thickly, clinging to the table as he reeled. "I take my hat off to you. I apologize. I admire your taste in skirts, an' take it from me that's a compliment; but I didn't know who you was. If I'd knowed you was Bill Roberts there wouldn't been a peep from my fly-trap. D'ye get me? I apologize. Will you shake hands?"

Gruffly, Billy said, "It's all right—forget it, sport;" and sullenly he shook hands and with a slow, massive movement thrust the other back toward his own table.

Saxon was glowing. Here was a man, a protector, something to lean against, of whom even the Butchertown toughs were afraid as soon as his name was mentioned.

CHAPTER IV

After dinner there were two dances in the pavilion, and then the band led the way to the race track for the games. The dancers followed, and all through the grounds the picnic parties left their tables to join in. Five thousand packed the grassy slopes of the amphitheater and swarmed inside the race track. Here, first of the events, the men were lining up for a tug of war. The contest was between the Oakland Bricklayers and the San Francisco Bricklayers, and the picked braves, huge and heavy, were taking their positions along the rope. They kicked heel-holds in the soft earth, rubbed their hands with the soil from underfoot, and laughed and joked with the crowd that surged about them.

The judges and watchers struggled vainly to keep back this crowd of relatives and friends. The Celtic blood was up, and the Celtic faction spirit ran high. The air was filled with cries of cheer, advice, warning, and threat. Many elected to leave the side of their own team and go to the side of the other team with the intention of circumventing foul play. There were as many women as men among the jostling supporters. The dust from the trampling, scuffling feet rose in the air, and Mary gasped and coughed and begged Bert to take her away. But he, the imp in him elated with the prospect of trouble, insisted on urging in closer. Saxon clung to Billy, who slowly and methodically elbowed and shouldered a way for her.

"No place for a girl," he grumbled, looking down at her with a masked expression of absent-mindedness, while his elbow powerfully crushed on the ribs of a big Irishman who gave room. "Things'll break loose when they start pullin'. They's been too much drink, an' you know what the Micks are for a rough house."

Saxon was very much out of place among these large-bodied men and women. She seemed very small and childlike, delicate and fragile, a creature from another race. Only Billy's skilled bulk and muscle saved her. He was continually glancing from face to face of the women and always returning to study her face, nor was she unaware of the contrast he was making.

Some excitement occurred a score of feet away from them, and to the sound of exclamations and blows a surge ran through the crowd. A large man, wedged sidewise in the jam, was shoved against Saxon, crushing her closely against Billy, who reached across to the man's shoulder with a massive thrust that was not so slow as usual. An involuntary grunt came from the victim, who turned his head, showing sun-reddened blond skin and unmistakable angry Irish eyes.

"What's eatin' yeh?" he snarled.

"Get off your foot; you're standin' on it," was Billy's contemptuous reply, emphasized by an increase of thrust.

The Irishman grunted again and made a frantic struggle to twist his body around, but the wedging bodies on either side held him in a vise.

"I'll break yer ugly face for yeh in a minute," he announced in wrath-thick tones.

Then his own face underwent transformation. The snarl left the lips, and the angry eyes grew genial.

"An' sure an' it's yerself," he said. "I didn't know it was yeh a-shovin'. I seen yeh lick the Terrible Swede, if yeh WAS robbed on the decision."

"No, you didn't, Bo," Billy answered pleasantly. "You saw me take a good beatin' that night. The decision was all right."

The Irishman was now beaming. He had endeavored to pay a compliment with a lie, and the prompt repudiation of the lie served only to increase his hero-worship.

"Sure, an' a bad beatin' it was," he acknowledged, "but yeh showed the grit of a bunch of wildcats. Soon as I can get me arm free I'm goin' to shake yeh by the hand an' help yeh aise yer young lady."

Frustrated in the struggle to get the crowd back, the referee fired his revolver in the air, and the tug-of-war was on. Pandemonium broke loose. Saxon, protected by the two big men, was near enough to the front to see much that ensued. The men on the rope pulled and strained till their faces were red with effort and their joints crackled. The rope was new, and, as their hands slipped, their wives and daughters sprang in, scooping up the earth in double handfuls and pouring it on the rope and the hands of their men to give them better grip.

A stout, middle-aged woman, carried beyond herself by the passion of the contest, seized the rope and pulled beside her husband, encouraged him with loud cries. A watcher from the opposing team dragged her screaming away and was dropped like a steer by an ear-blow from a partisan from the woman's team. He, in turn, went down, and brawny women joined with their men in the battle. Vainly the judges and watchers begged, pleaded, yelled, and swung with their fists. Men, as well as women, were springing in to the rope and pulling. No longer was it team against team, but all Oakland against all San Francisco, festooned with a free-for-all fight. Hands overlaid hands two and three deep in the struggle to grasp the rope. And hands that found no holds, doubled into bunches of knuckles that impacted on the jaws of the watchers who strove to tear hand-holds from the rope.

Bert yelped with joy, while Mary clung to him, mad with fear. Close to the rope the fighters were going down and being trampled. The dust arose in clouds, while from beyond, all around, unable to get into the battle, could be heard the shrill and impotent rage-screams and rage-yells of women and men.

"Dirty work, dirty work," Billy muttered over and over; and, though he saw much that occurred, assisted by the friendly Irishman he was coolly and safely working Saxon back out of the melee.

At last the break came. The losing team, accompanied by its host of volunteers, was dragged in a rush over the ground and disappeared under the avalanche of battling forms of the onlookers.

Leaving Saxon under the protection of the Irishman in an outer eddy of calm, Billy plunged back into the mix-up. Several minutes later he emerged with the missing couple—Bert bleeding from a blow on the ear, but hilarious, and Mary rumpled and hysterical.

"This ain't sport," she kept repeating. "It's a shame, a dirty shame."

"We got to get outa this," Billy said. "The fun's only commenced."

"Aw, wait," Bert begged. "It's worth eight dollars. It's cheap at any price. I ain't seen so many black eyes and bloody noses in a month of Sundays."

"Well, go on back an' enjoy yourself," Billy commended. "I'll take the girls up there on the side hill where we can look on. But I won't give much for your good looks if some of them Micks lands on you."

The trouble was over in an amazingly short time, for from the judges' stand beside the track the announcer was bellowing the start of the boys' foot-race; and Bert, disappointed, joined Billy and the two girls on the hillside looking down upon the track.

There were boys' races and girls' races, races of young women and old women, of fat men and fat women, sack races and three-legged races, and the contestants strove around the small track through a Bedlam of cheering supporters. The tug-of-war was already forgotten, and good nature reigned again.

Five young men toed the mark, crouching with fingertips to the ground and waiting the starter's revolver-shot. Three were in their stocking-feet, and the remaining two wore spiked running-shoes.

"Young men's race," Bert read from the program. "An' only one prize— twenty-five dollars. See the red-head with the spikes—the one next to the outside. San Francisco's set on him winning. He's their crack, an' there's a lot of bets up."

"Who's goin' to win?" Mary deferred to Billy's superior athletic knowledge.

"How can I tell!" he answered. "I never saw any of 'em before. But they all look good to me. May the best one win, that's all."

The revolver was fired, and the five runners were off and away. Three were outdistanced at the start. Redhead led, with a black-haired young man at his shoulder, and it was plain that the race lay between these two. Halfway around, the black-haired one took the lead in a spurt that was intended to last to the finish. Ten feet he gained, nor could Red-head cut it down an inch.

"The boy's a streak," Billy commented. "He ain't tryin' his hardest, an' Red-head's just bustin' himself."

Still ten feet in the lead, the black-haired one breasted the tape in a hubbub of cheers. Yet yells of disapproval could be distinguished. Bert hugged himself with joy.

"Mm-mm," he gloated. "Ain't Frisco sore? Watch out for fireworks now. See! He's bein' challenged. The judges ain't payin' him the money. An' he's got a gang behind him. Oh! Oh! Oh! Ain't had so much fun since my old woman broke her leg!"

"Why don't they pay him, Billy?" Saxon asked. "He won."

"The Frisco bunch is challengin' him for a professional," Billy elucidated. "That's what they're all beefin' about. But it ain't right. They all ran for that money, so they're all professional."

The crowd surged and argued and roared in front of the judges' stand. The stand was a rickety, two-story affair, the second story open at the front, and here the judges could be seen debating as heatedly as the crowd beneath them.

"There she starts!" Bert cried. "Oh, you rough-house!"

The black-haired racer, backed by a dozen supporters, was climbing the outside stairs to the judges.

"The purse-holder's his friend," Billy said. "See, he's paid him, an' some of the judges is willin' an' some are beefin'. An' now that other gang's going up—they're Redhead's." He turned to Saxon with a reassuring smile. "We're well out of it this time. There's goin' to be rough stuff down there in a minute."

"The judges are tryin' to make him give the money back," Bert explained. "An' if he don't the other gang'll take it away from him. See! They're reachin' for it now."

High above his head, the winner held the roll of paper containing the twenty-five silver dollars. His gang, around him, was shouldering back those who tried to seize the money. No blows had been struck yet, but the struggle increased until the frail structure shook and swayed. From the crowd beneath the winner was variously addressed: "Give it back, you dog!" "Hang on to it, Tim!" "You won fair, Timmy!" "Give it back, you dirty robber!" Abuse unprintable as well as friendly advice was hurled at him.

The struggle grew more violent. Tim's supporters strove to hold him off the floor so that his hand would still be above the grasping hands that shot up. Once, for an instant, his arm was jerked down. Again it went up. But evidently the paper had broken, and with a last desperate effort, before he went down, Tim flung the coin out in a silvery shower upon the heads of the crowd beneath. Then ensued a weary period of arguing and quarreling.

"I wish they'd finish, so as we could get back to the dancin'," Mary complained. "This ain't no fun."

Slowly and painfully the judges' stand was cleared, and an announcer,

stepping to the front of the stand, spread his arms appealing for

silence. The angry clamor died down.

"The judges have decided," he shouted, "that this day of good

fellowship an' brotherhood—"

"Hear! Hear!" Many of the cooler heads applauded. "That's the stuff!" "No fightin'!" "No hard feelin's!"

"An' therefore," the announcer became audible again, "the judges have decided to put up another purse of twenty-five dollars an' run the race over again!"

"An' Tim?" bellowed scores of throats. "What about Tim?" "He's been robbed!" "The judges is rotten!"

Again the announcer stilled the tumult with his arm appeal.

"The judges have decided, for the sake of good feelin', that Timothy McManus will also run. If he wins, the money's his."

"Now wouldn't that jar you?" Billy grumbled disgustedly. "If Tim's eligible now, he was eligible the first time. An' if he was eligible the first time, then the money was his."

"Red-head'll bust himself wide open this time," Bert jubilated.

"An' so will Tim," Billy rejoined. "You can bet he's mad clean through, and he'll let out the links he was holdin' in last time."

Another quarter of an hour was spent in clearing the track of the excited crowd, and this time only Tim and Red-head toed the mark. The other three young men had abandoned the contest.

The leap of Tim, at the report of the revolver, put him a clean yard in the lead.

"I guess he's professional, all right, all right," Billy remarked. "An' just look at him go!"

Half-way around, Tim led by fifty feet, and, running swiftly, maintaining the same lead, he came down the homestretch an easy winner. When directly beneath the group on the hillside, the incredible and unthinkable happened. Standing close to the inside edge of the track was a dapper young man with a light switch cane. He was distinctly out of place in such a gathering, for upon him was no ear-mark of the working class. Afterward, Bert was of the opinion that he looked like a swell dancing master, while Billy called him "the dude."

So far as Timothy McManus was concerned, the dapper young man was destiny; for as Tim passed him, the young man, with utmost deliberation, thrust his cane between Tim's flying legs. Tim sailed through the air in a headlong pitch, struck spread-eagled on his face, and plowed along in a cloud of dust.

There was an instant of vast and gasping silence. The young man, too, seemed petrified by the ghastliness of his deed. It took an appreciable interval of time for him, as well as for the onlookers, to realize what he had done. They recovered first, and from a thousand throats the wild Irish yell went up. Red-head won the race without a cheer. The storm center had shifted to the young man with the cane. After the yell, he had one moment of indecision; then he turned and darted up the track.

"Go it, sport!" Bert cheered, waving his hat in the air. "You're the goods for me! Who'd a-thought it? Who'd a-thought it? Say!—wouldn't it, now? Just wouldn't it?"

"Phew! He's a streak himself," Billy admired. "But what did he do it for? He's no bricklayer."

Like a frightened rabbit, the mad roar at his heels, the young man tore up the track to an open space on the hillside, up which he clawed and disappeared among the trees. Behind him toiled a hundred vengeful runners.

"It's too bad he's missing the rest of it," Billy said. "Look at 'em goin' to it."

Bert was beside himself. He leaped up and down and cried continuously.

"Look at 'em! Look at 'em! Look at 'em!"

The Oakland faction was outraged. Twice had its favorite runner been jobbed out of the race. This last was only another vile trick of the Frisco faction. So Oakland doubled its brawny fists and swung into San Francisco for blood. And San Francisco, consciously innocent, was no less willing to join issues. To be charged with such a crime was no less monstrous than the crime itself. Besides, for too many tedious hours had the Irish heroically suppressed themselves. Five thousands of them exploded into joyous battle. The women joined with them. The whole amphitheater was filled with the conflict. There were rallies, retreats, charges, and counter-charges. Weaker groups were forced fighting up the hillsides. Other groups, bested, fled among the trees to carry on guerrilla warfare, emerging in sudden dashes to overwhelm isolated enemies. Half a dozen special policemen, hired by the Weasel Park management, received an impartial trouncing from both sides.

"Nobody's the friend of a policeman," Bert chortled, dabbing his handkerchief to his injured ear, which still bled.

The bushes crackled behind him, and he sprang aside to let the locked forms of two men go by, rolling over and over down the hill, each striking when uppermost, and followed by a screaming woman who rained blows on the one who was patently not of her clan.

The judges, in the second story of the stand, valiantly withstood a fierce assault until the frail structure toppled to the ground in splinters.

"What's that woman doing?" Saxon asked, calling attention to an elderly woman beneath them on the track, who had sat down and was pulling from her foot an elastic-sided shoe of generous dimensions.

"Goin' swimming," Bert chuckled, as the stocking followed.

They watched, fascinated. The shoe was pulled on again over the bare foot. Then the woman slipped a rock the size of her fist into the stocking, and, brandishing this ancient and horrible weapon, lumbered into the nearest fray.

"Oh!—Oh!—Oh!" Bert screamed, with every blow she struck. "Hey, old flannel-mouth! Watch out! You'll get yours in a second. Oh! Oh! A peach! Did you see it? Hurray for the old lady! Look at her tearin' into 'em! Watch out, old girl!... Ah-h-h."

His voice died away regretfully, as the one with the stocking, whose hair had been clutched from behind by another Amazon, was whirled about in a dizzy semicircle.

Vainly Mary clung to his arm, shaking him back and forth and remonstrating.

"Can't you be sensible?" she cried. "It's awful! I tell you it's awful!"

But Bert was irrepressible.

"Go it, old girl!" he encouraged. "You win! Me for you every time! Now's your chance! Swat! Oh! My! A peach! A peach!"

"It's the biggest rough-house I ever saw," Billy confided to Saxon. "It sure takes the Micks to mix it. But what did that dude wanta do it for? That's what gets me. He wasn't a bricklayer—not even a workingman—just a regular sissy dude that didn't know a livin' soul in the grounds. But if he wanted to raise a rough-house he certainly done it. Look at 'em. They're fightin' everywhere."

He broke into sudden laughter, so hearty that the tears came into his eyes.

"What is it?" Saxon asked, anxious not to miss anything.

"It's that dude," Billy explained between gusts. "What did he wanta do it for? That's what gets my goat. What'd he wanta do it for?"

There was more crashing in the brush, and two women erupted upon the scene, one in flight, the other pursuing. Almost ere they could realize it, the little group found itself merged in the astounding conflict that covered, if not the face of creation, at least all the visible landscape of Weasel Park.

The fleeing woman stumbled in rounding the end of a picnic bench, and would have been caught had she not seized Mary's arm to recover balance, and then flung Mary full into the arms of the woman who pursued. This woman, largely built, middle-aged, and too irate to comprehend, clutched Mary's hair by one hand and lifted the other to smack her. Before the blow could fall, Billy had seized both the woman's wrists.

"Come on, old girl, cut it out," he said appeasingly. "You're in wrong. She ain't done nothin'."

Then the woman did a strange thing. Making no resistance, but maintaining her hold on the girl's hair, she stood still and calmly began to scream. The scream was hideously compounded of fright and fear. Yet in her face was neither fright nor fear. She regarded Billy coolly and appraisingly, as if to see how he took it—her scream merely the cry to the clan for help.

"Aw, shut up, you battleax!" Bert vociferated, trying to drag her off by the shoulders.

The result was that the four rocked back and forth, while the woman calmly went on screaming. The scream became touched with triumph as more crashing was heard in the brush.

Saxon saw Billy's slow eyes glint suddenly to the hardness of steel, and at the same time she saw him put pressure on his wrist-holds. The woman released her grip on Mary and was shoved back and free. Then the first man of the rescue was upon them. He did not pause to inquire into the merits of the affair. It was sufficient that he saw the woman reeling away from Billy and screaming with pain that was largely feigned.

"It's all a mistake," Billy cried hurriedly. "We apologize, sport—"

The Irishman swung ponderously. Billy ducked, cutting his apology short, and as the sledge-like fist passed over his head, he drove his left to the other's jaw. The big Irishman toppled over sidewise and sprawled on the edge of the slope. Half-scrambled back to his feet and out of balance, he was caught by Bert's fist, and this time went clawing down the slope that was slippery with short, dry grass. Bert was redoubtable. "That for you, old girl—my compliments," was his cry, as he shoved the woman over the edge on to the treacherous slope. Three more men were emerging from the brush.

In the meantime, Billy had put Saxon in behind the protection of the picnic table. Mary, who was hysterical, had evinced a desire to cling to him, and he had sent her sliding across the top of the table to Saxon.

"Come on, you flannel-mouths!" Bert yelled at the newcomers, himself swept away by passion, his black eyes flashing wildly, his dark face inflamed by the too-ready blood. "Come on, you cheap skates! Talk about Gettysburg. We'll show you all the Americans ain't dead yet!"

"Shut your trap—we don't want a scrap with the girls here," Billy growled harshly, holding his position in front of the table. He turned to the three rescuers, who were bewildered by the lack of anything visible to rescue. "Go on, sports. We don't want a row. You're in wrong. They ain't nothin' doin' in the fight line. We don't wanta fight—d'ye get me?"

They still hesitated, and Billy might have succeeded in avoiding trouble had not the man who had gone down the bank chosen that unfortunate moment to reappear, crawling groggily on hands and knees and showing a bleeding face. Again Bert reached him and sent him downslope, and the other three, with wild yells, sprang in on Billy, who punched, shifted position, ducked and punched, and shifted again ere he struck the third time. His blows were clean and hard, scientifically delivered, with the weight of his body behind.

Saxon, looking on, saw his eyes and learned more about him. She was frightened, but clear-seeing, and she was startled by the disappearance of all depth of light and shadow in his eyes. They showed surface only—a hard, bright surface, almost glazed, devoid of all expression save deadly seriousness. Bert's eyes showed madness. The eyes of the Irishmen were angry and serious, and yet not all serious. There was a wayward gleam in them, as if they enjoyed the fracas. But in Billy's eyes was no enjoyment. It was as if he had certain work to do and had doggedly settled down to do it.

Scarcely more expression did she note in the face, though there was nothing in common between it and the one she had seen all day. The boyishness had vanished. This face was mature in a terrifying, ageless way. There was no anger in it, nor was it even pitiless. It seemed to have glazed as hard and passionlessly as his eyes. Something came to her of her wonderful mother's tales of the ancient Saxons, and he seemed to her one of those Saxons, and she caught a glimpse, on the well of her consciousness, of a long, dark boat, with a prow like the beak of a bird of prey, and of huge, half-naked men, wing-helmeted, and one of their faces, it seemed to her, was his face. She did not reason this. She felt it, and visioned it as by an unthinkable clairvoyance, and gasped, for the flurry of war was over. It had lasted only seconds, Bert was dancing on the edge of the slippery slope and mocking the vanquished who had slid impotently to the bottom. But Billy took charge.

"Come on, you girls," he commanded. "Get onto yourself, Bert. We got to get outa this. We can't fight an army."

He led the retreat, holding Saxon's arm, and Bert, giggling and jubilant, brought up the rear with an indignant Mary who protested vainly in his unheeding ears.

For a hundred yards they ran and twisted through the trees, and then, no signs of pursuit appearing, they slowed down to a dignified saunter. Bert, the trouble-seeker, pricked his ears to the muffled sound of blows and sobs, and stepped aside to investigate.

"Oh! look what I've found!" he called.

They joined him on the edge of a dry ditch and looked down. In the bottom were two men, strays from the fight, grappled together and still fighting. They were weeping out of sheer fatigue and helplessness, and the blows they only occasionally struck were open-handed and ineffectual.

"Hey, you, sport—throw sand in his eyes," Bert counseled. "That's it, blind him an' he's your'n."

"Stop that!" Billy shouted at the man, who was following instructions, "Or I'll come down there an' beat you up myself. It's all over—d'ye get me? It's all over an' everybody's friends. Shake an' make up. The drinks are on both of you. That's right—here, gimme your hand an' I'll pull you out."

They left them shaking hands and brushing each other's clothes.

"It soon will be over," Billy grinned to Saxon. "I know 'em. Fight's fun with them. An' this big scrap's made the day a howlin' success. What did I tell you!—look over at that table there."

A group of disheveled men and women, still breathing heavily, were shaking hands all around.

"Come on, let's dance," Mary pleaded, urging them in the direction of the pavilion.

All over the park the warring bricklayers were shaking hands and making up, while the open-air bars were crowded with the drinkers.

Saxon walked very close to Billy. She was proud of him. He could fight, and he could avoid trouble. In all that had occurred he had striven to avoid trouble. And, also, consideration for her and Mary had been uppermost in his mind.

"You are brave," she said to him.

"It's like takin' candy from a baby," he disclaimed. "They only rough-house. They don't know boxin'. They're wide open, an' all you gotta do is hit 'em. It ain't real fightin', you know." With a troubled, boyish look in his eyes, he stared at his bruised knuckles. "An' I'll have to drive team to-morrow with 'em," he lamented. "Which ain't fun, I'm tellin' you, when they stiffen up."

CHAPTER V

At eight o'clock the Al Vista band played "Home, Sweet Home," and, following the hurried rush through the twilight to the picnic train, the four managed to get double seats facing each other. When the aisles and platforms were packed by the hilarious crowd, the train pulled out for the short run from the suburbs into Oakland. All the car was singing a score of songs at once, and Bert, his head pillowed on Mary's breast with her arms around him, started "On the Banks of the Wabash." And he sang the song through, undeterred by the bedlam of two general fights, one on the adjacent platform, the other at the opposite end of the car, both of which were finally subdued by special policemen to the screams of women and the crash of glass.

Billy sang a lugubrious song of many stanzas about a cowboy, the refrain of which was, "Bury me out on the lone pr-rairie."

"That's one you never heard before; my father used to sing it," he told Saxon, who was glad that it was ended.

She had discovered the first flaw in him. He was tonedeaf. Not once had he been on the key.

"I don't sing often," he added.

"You bet your sweet life he don't," Bert exclaimed. "His friends'd kill him if he did."

"They all make fun of my singin'," he complained to Saxon. "Honest, now, do you find it as rotten as all that?"

"It's... it's maybe flat a bit," she admitted reluctantly.

"It don't sound flat to me," he protested. "It's a regular josh on me. I'll bet Bert put you up to it. You sing something now, Saxon. I bet you sing good. I can tell it from lookin' at you."

She began "When the Harvest Days Are Over." Bert and Mary joined in; but when Billy attempted to add his voice he was dissuaded by a shin-kick from Bert. Saxon sang in a clear, true soprano, thin but sweet, and she was aware that she was singing to Billy.

"Now THAT is singing what is," he proclaimed, when she had finished. "Sing it again. Aw, go on. You do it just right. It's great."

His hand slipped to hers and gathered it in, and as she sang again she felt the tide of his strength flood warmingly through her.

"Look at 'em holdin' hands," Bert jeered. "Just a-holdin' hands like they was afraid. Look at Mary an' me. Come on an' kick in, you cold-feets. Get together. If you don't, it'll look suspicious. I got my suspicions already. You're framin' somethin' up."

There was no mistaking his innuendo, and Saxon felt her cheeks flaming.

"Get onto yourself, Bert," Billy reproved.

"Shut up!" Mary added the weight of her indignation. "You're awfully raw, Bert Wanhope, an' I won't have anything more to do with you—there!"

She withdrew her arms and shoved him away, only to receive him

forgivingly half a dozen seconds afterward.

"Come on, the four of us," Bert went on irrepressibly. "The

night's young. Let's make a time of it—Pabst's Cafe first, and then

some. What you say, Bill? What you say, Saxon? Mary's game."

Saxon waited and wondered, half sick with apprehension of this man beside her whom she had known so short a time.

"Nope," he said slowly. "I gotta get up to a hard day's work to-morrow, and I guess the girls has got to, too."

Saxon forgave him his tone-deafness. Here was the kind of man she always had known existed. It was for some such man that she had waited. She was twenty-two, and her first marriage offer had come when she was sixteen. The last had occurred only the month before, from the foreman of the washing-room, and he had been good and kind, but not young. But this one beside her—he was strong and kind and good, and YOUNG. She was too young herself not to desire youth. There would have been rest from fancy starch with the foreman, but there would have been no warmth. But this man beside her.... She caught herself on the verge involuntarily of pressing his hand that held hers.

"No, Bert, don't tease; he's right," Mary was saying. "We've got to get some sleep. It's fancy starch to-morrow, and all day on our feet."

It came to Saxon with a chill pang that she was surely older than Billy. She stole glances at the smoothness of his face, and the essential boyishness of him, so much desired, shocked her. Of course he would marry some girl years younger than himself, than herself. How old was he? Could it be that he was too young for her? As he seemed to grow inaccessible, she was drawn toward him more compellingly. He was so strong, so gentle. She lived over the events of the day. There was no flaw there. He had considered her and Mary, always. And he had torn the program up and danced only with her. Surely he had liked her, or he would not have done it.

She slightly moved her hand in his and felt the harsh contact of his teamster callouses. The sensation was exquisite. He, too, moved his hand, to accommodate the shift of hers, and she waited fearfully. She did not want him to prove like other men, and she could have hated him had he dared to take advantage of that slight movement of her fingers and put his arm around her. He did not, and she flamed toward him. There was fineness in him. He was neither rattle-brained, like Bert, nor coarse like other men she had encountered. For she had had experiences, not nice, and she had been made to suffer by the lack of what was termed chivalry, though she, in turn, lacked that word to describe what she divined and desired.

And he was a prizefighter. The thought of it almost made her gasp. Yet he answered not at all to her conception of a prizefighter. But, then, he wasn't a prizefighter. He had said he was not. She resolved to ask him about it some time if... if he took her out again. Yet there was little doubt of that, for when a man danced with one girl a whole day he did not drop her immediately. Almost she hoped that he was a prizefighter. There was a delicious tickle of wickedness about it. Prizefighters were such terrible and mysterious men. In so far as they were out of the ordinary and were not mere common workingmen such as carpenters and laundrymen, they represented romance. Power also they represented. They did not work for bosses, but spectacularly and magnificently, with their own might, grappled with the great world and wrung splendid living from its reluctant hands. Some of them even owned automobiles and traveled with a retinue of trainers and servants. Perhaps it had been only Billy's modesty that made him say he had quit fighting. And yet, there were the callouses on his hands. That showed he had quit.

CHAPTER VI

They said good-bye at the gate. Billy betrayed awkwardness that was sweet to Saxon. He was not one of the take-it-for-granted young men. There was a pause, while she feigned desire to go into the house, yet waited in secret eagerness for the words she wanted him to say.

"When am I goin' to see you again?" he asked, holding her hand in his.

She laughed consentingly.

"I live 'way up in East Oakland," he explained. "You know there's where the stable is, an' most of our teaming is done in that section, so I don't knock around down this way much. But, say—" His hand tightened on hers. "We just gotta dance together some more. I'll tell you, the Orindore Club has its dance Wednesday. If you haven't a date—have you?"

"No," she said.

"Then Wednesday. What time'll I come for you?"

And when they had arranged the details, and he had agreed that she should dance some of the dances with the other fellows, and said good night again, his hand closed more tightly on hers and drew her toward him. She resisted slightly, but honestly. It was the custom, but she felt she ought not for fear he might misunderstand. And yet she wanted to kiss him as she had never wanted to kiss a man. When it came, her face upturned to his, she realized that on his part it was an honest kiss. There hinted nothing behind it. Rugged and kind as himself, it was virginal almost, and betrayed no long practice in the art of saying good-bye. All men were not brutes after all, was her thought.

"Good night," she murmured; the gate screeched under her hand; and she hurried along the narrow walk that led around to the corner of the house.

"Wednesday," he called softly.

"Wednesday," she answered.

But in the shadow of the narrow alley between the two houses she stood still and pleasured in the ring of his foot falls down the cement sidewalk. Not until they had quite died away did she go on. She crept up the back stairs and across the kitchen to her room, registering her thanksgiving that Sarah was asleep.

She lighted the gas, and, as she removed the little velvet hat, she felt her lips still tingling with the kiss. Yet it had meant nothing. It was the way of the young men. They all did it. But their good-night kisses had never tingled, while this one tingled in her brain as well as on her lip. What was it? What did it mean? With a sudden impulse she looked at herself in the glass. The eyes were happy and bright. The color that tinted her cheeks so easily was in them and glowing. It was a pretty reflection, and she smiled, partly in joy, partly in appreciation, and the smile grew at sight of the even rows of strong white teeth. Why shouldn't Billy like that face? was her unvoiced query. Other men had liked it. Other men did like it. Even the other girls admitted she was a good-looker. Charley Long certainly liked it from the way he made life miserable for her.

She glanced aside to the rim of the looking-glass where his photograph was wedged, shuddered, and made a moue of distaste. There was cruelty in those eyes, and brutishness. He was a brute. For a year, now, he had bullied her. Other fellows were afraid to go with her. He warned them off. She had been forced into almost slavery to his attentions. She remembered the young bookkeeper at the laundry—not a workingman, but a soft-handed, soft-voiced gentleman—whom Charley had beaten up at the corner because he had been bold enough to come to take her to the theater. And she had been helpless. For his own sake she had never dared accept another invitation to go out with him.

And now, Wednesday night, she was going with Billy. Billy! Her heart leaped. There would be trouble, but Billy would save her from him. She'd like to see him try and beat Billy up.

With a quick movement, she jerked the photograph from its niche and threw it face down upon the chest of drawers. It fell beside a small square case of dark and tarnished leather. With a feeling as of profanation she again seized the offending photograph and flung it across the room into a corner. At the same time she picked up the leather case. Springing it open, she gazed at the daguerreotype of a worn little woman with steady gray eyes and a hopeful, pathetic mouth. Opposite, on the velvet lining, done in gold lettering, was, CARLTON FROM DAISY. She read it reverently, for it represented the father she had never known, and the mother she had so little known, though she could never forget that those wise sad eyes were gray.

Despite lack of conventional religion, Saxon's nature was deeply religious. Her thoughts of God were vague and nebulous, and there she was frankly puzzled. She could not vision God. Here, in the daguerreotype, was the concrete; much she had grasped from it, and always there seemed an infinite more to grasp. She did not go to church. This was her high altar and holy of holies. She came to it in trouble, in loneliness, for counsel, divination, and comfort. In so far as she found herself different from the girls of her acquaintance, she quested here to try to identify her characteristics in the pictured face. Her mother had been different from other women, too. This, forsooth, meant to her what God meant to others. To this she strove to be true, and not to hurt nor vex. And how little she really knew of her mother, and of how much was conjecture and surmise, she was unaware; for it was through many years she had erected this mother-myth.

Yet was it all myth? She resented the doubt with quick jealousy, and, opening the bottom drawer of the chest, drew forth a battered portfolio. Out rolled manuscripts, faded and worn, and arose a faint far scent of sweet-kept age. The writing was delicate and curled, with the quaint fineness of half a century before. She read a stanza to herself:

"Sweet as a wind-lute's airy strains Your gentle muse has learned to sing, And California's boundless plains Prolong the soft notes echoing."

She wondered, for the thousandth time, what a windlute was; yet much of beauty, much of beyondness, she sensed of this dimly remembered beautiful mother of hers. She communed a while, then unrolled a second manuscript. "To C. B.," it read. To Carlton Brown, she knew, to her father, a love-poem from her mother. Saxon pondered the opening lines:

"I have stolen away from the crowd in the groves, Where the nude statues stand, and the leaves point and shiver At ivy-crowned Bacchus, the Queen of the Loves, Pandora and Psyche, struck voiceless forever."

This, too, was beyond her. But she breathed the beauty of it. Bacchus, and Pandora and Psyche—talismans to conjure with! But alas! the necromancy was her mother's. Strange, meaningless words that meant so much! Her marvelous mother had known their meaning. Saxon spelled the three words aloud, letter by letter, for she did not dare their pronunciation; and in her consciousness glimmered august connotations, profound and unthinkable. Her mind stumbled and halted on the star-bright and dazzling boundaries of a world beyond her world in which her mother had roamed at will. Again and again, solemnly, she went over the four lines. They were radiance and light to the world, haunted with phantoms of pain and unrest, in which she had her being. There, hidden among those cryptic singing lines, was the clue. If she could only grasp it, all would be made clear. Of this she was sublimely confident. She would understand Sarah's sharp tongue, her unhappy brother, the cruelty of Charley Long, the justness of the bookkeeper's beating, the day-long, month-long, year-long toil at the ironing-board.

She skipped a stanza that she knew was hopelessly beyond her, and tried again:

"The dusk of the greenhouse is luminous yet

With quivers of opal and tremors of gold;

For the sun is at rest, and the light from the west,

Like delicate wine that is mellow and old,

"Flushes faintly the brow of a naiad that stands In the spray of a fountain, whose seed-amethysts Tremble lightly a moment on bosom and hands, Then dip in their basin from bosom and wrists."

"It's beautiful, just beautiful," she sighed. And then, appalled at the length of all the poem, at the volume of the mystery, she rolled the manuscript and put it away. Again she dipped in the drawer, seeking the clue among the cherished fragments of her mother's hidden soul.

This time it was a small package, wrapped in tissue paper and tied with ribbon. She opened it carefully, with the deep gravity and circumstance of a priest before an altar. Appeared a little red-satin Spanish girdle, whale-boned like a tiny corset, pointed, the pioneer finery of a frontier woman who had crossed the plains. It was hand-made after the California-Spanish model of forgotten days. The very whalebone had been home-shaped of the raw material from the whaleships traded for in hides and tallow. The black lace trimming her mother had made. The triple edging of black velvet strips— her mother's hands had sewn the stitches.

Saxon dreamed over it in a maze of incoherent thought. This was concrete. This she understood. This she worshiped as man-created gods have been worshiped on less tangible evidence of their sojourn on earth.

Twenty-two inches it measured around. She knew it out of many verifications. She stood up and put it about her waist. This was part of the ritual. It almost met. In places it did meet. Without her dress it would meet everywhere as it had met on her mother. Closest of all, this survival of old California-Ventura days brought Saxon in touch. Hers was her mother's form. Physically, she was like her mother. Her grit, her ability to turn off work that was such an amazement to others, were her mother's. Just so had her mother been an amazement to her generation—her mother, the toy-like creature, the smallest and the youngest of the strapping pioneer brood, who nevertheless had mothered the brood. Always it had been her wisdom that was sought, even by the brothers and sisters a dozen years her senior. Daisy, it was, who had put her tiny foot down and commanded the removal from the fever flatlands of Colusa to the healthy mountains of Ventura; who had backed the savage old Indian-fighter of a father into a corner and fought the entire family that Vila might marry the man of her choice; who had flown in the face of the family and of community morality and demanded the divorce of Laura from her criminally weak husband; and who on the other hand, had held the branches of the family together when only misunderstanding and weak humanness threatened to drive them apart.

The peacemaker and the warrior! All the old tales trooped before Saxon's eyes. They were sharp with detail, for she had visioned them many times, though their content was of things she had never seen. So far as details were concerned, they were her own creation, for she had never seen an ox, a wild Indian, nor a prairie schooner. Yet, palpitating and real, shimmering in the sun-flashed dust of ten thousand hoofs, she saw pass, from East to West, across a continent, the great hegira of the land-hungry Anglo-Saxon. It was part and fiber of her. She had been nursed on its traditions and its facts from the lips of those who had taken part. Clearly she saw the long wagon-train, the lean, gaunt men who walked before, the youths goading the lowing oxen that fell and were goaded to their feet to fall again. And through it all, a flying shuttle, weaving the golden dazzling thread of personality, moved the form of her little, indomitable mother, eight years old, and nine ere the great traverse was ended, a necromancer and a law-giver, willing her way, and the way and the willing always good and right.

Saxon saw Punch, the little, rough-coated Skye-terrier with the honest eyes (who had plodded for weary months), gone lame and abandoned; she saw Daisy, the chit of a child, hide Punch in the wagon. She saw the savage old worried father discover the added burden of the several pounds to the dying oxen. She saw his wrath, as he held Punch by the scruff of the neck. And she saw Daisy, between the muzzle of the long-barreled rifle and the little dog. And she saw Daisy thereafter, through days of alkali and heat, walking, stumbling, in the dust of the wagons, the little sick dog, like a baby, in her arms.

But most vivid of all, Saxon saw the fight at Little Meadow—and Daisy, dressed as for a gala day, in white, a ribbon sash about her waist, ribbons and a round-comb in her hair, in her hands small water-pails, step forth into the sunshine on the flower-grown open ground from the wagon circle, wheels interlocked, where the wounded screamed their delirium and babbled of flowing fountains, and go on, through the sunshine and the wonder-inhibition of the bullet-dealing Indians, a hundred yards to the waterhole and back again.

Saxon kissed the little, red satin Spanish girdle passionately, and wrapped it up in haste, with dewy eyes, abandoning the mystery and godhead of mother and all the strange enigma of living.

In bed, she projected against her closed eyelids the few rich scenes of her mother that her child-memory retained. It was her favorite way of wooing sleep. She had done it all her life—sunk into the death-blackness of sleep with her mother limned to the last on her fading consciousness. But this mother was not the Daisy of the plains nor of the daguerreotype. They had been before Saxon's time. This that she saw nightly was an older mother, broken with insomnia and brave with sorrow, who crept, always crept, a pale, frail creature, gentle and unfaltering, dying from lack of sleep, living by will, and by will refraining from going mad, who, nevertheless, could not will sleep, and whom not even the whole tribe of doctors could make sleep. Crept—always she crept, about the house, from weary bed to weary chair and back again through long days and weeks of torment, never complaining, though her unfailing smile was twisted with pain, and the wise gray eyes, still wise and gray, were grown unutterably larger and profoundly deep.

But on this night Saxon did not win to sleep quickly; the little creeping mother came and went; and in the intervals the face of Billy, with the cloud-drifted, sullen, handsome eyes, burned against her eyelids. And once again, as sleep welled up to smother her, she put to herself the question IS THIS THE MAN?

CHAPTER VII

The work in the ironing-room slipped off, but the three days until Wednesday night were very long. She hummed over the fancy starch that flew under the iron at an astounding rate.

"I can't see how you do it," Mary admired. "You'll make thirteen or fourteen this week at that rate."

Saxon laughed, and in the steam from the iron she saw dancing golden letters that spelled WEDNESDAY.

"What do you think of Billy?" Mary asked.

"I like him," was the frank answer.

"Well, don't let it go farther than that."

"I will if I want to," Saxon retorted gaily.

"Better not," came the warning. "You'll only make trouble for yourself. He ain't marryin'. Many a girl's found that out. They just throw themselves at his head, too."

"I'm not going to throw myself at him, or any other man."

"Just thought I'd tell you," Mary concluded. "A word to the wise."

Saxon had become grave.

"He's not... not..." she began, than looked the significance of the question she could not complete.

"Oh, nothin' like that—though there's nothin' to stop him. He's straight, all right, all right. But he just won't fall for anything in skirts. He dances, an' runs around, an' has a good time, an' beyond that—nitsky. A lot of 'em's got fooled on him. I bet you there's a dozen girls in love with him right now. An' he just goes on turnin' 'em down. There was Lily Sanderson—you know her. You seen her at that Slavonic picnic last summer at Shellmound—that tall, nice-lookin' blonde that was with Butch Willows?"

"Yes, I remember her," Saxon said. "What about her?"

"Well, she'd been runnin' with Butch Willows pretty steady, an' just because she could dance, Billy dances a lot with her. Butch ain't afraid of nothin'. He wades right in for a showdown, an' nails Billy outside, before everybody, an' reads the riot act. An' Billy listens in that slow, sleepy way of his, an' Butch gets hotter an' hotter, an' everybody expects a scrap.

"An' then Billy says to Butch, 'Are you done?' 'Yes,' Butch says; 'I've said my say, an' what are you goin' to do about it?' An' Billy says—an' what d'ye think he said, with everybody lookin' on an' Butch with blood in his eye? Well, he said, 'I guess nothin', Butch.' Just like that. Butch was that surprised you could knocked him over with a feather. 'An' never dance with her no more?' he says. 'Not if you say I can't, Butch,' Billy says. Just like that.

"Well, you know, any other man to take water the way he did from Butch— why, everybody'd despise him. But not Billy. You see, he can afford to. He's got a rep as a fighter, an' when he just stood back 'an' let Butch have his way, everybody knew he wasn't scared, or backin' down, or anything. He didn't care a rap for Lily Sanderson, that was all, an' anybody could see she was just crazy after him."

The telling of this episode caused Saxon no little worry. Hers was the average woman's pride, but in the matter of man-conquering prowess she was not unduly conceited. Billy had enjoyed her dancing, and she wondered if that were all. If Charley Long bullied up to him would he let her go as he had let Lily Sanderson go? He was not a marrying man; nor could Saxon blind her eyes to the fact that he was eminently marriageable. No wonder the girls ran after him. And he was a man-subduer as well as a woman-subduer. Men liked him. Bert Wanhope seemed actually to love him. She remembered the Butchertown tough in the dining-room at Weasel Park who had come over to the table to apologize, and the Irishman at the tug-of-war who had abandoned all thought of fighting with him the moment he learned his identity.

A very much spoiled young man was a thought that flitted frequently through Saxon's mind; and each time she condemned it as ungenerous. He was gentle in that tantalizing slow way of his. Despite his strength, he did not walk rough-shod over others. There was the affair with Lily Sanderson. Saxon analysed it again and again. He had not cared for the girl, and he had immediately stepped from between her and Butch. It was just the thing that Bert, out of sheer wickedness and love of trouble, would not have done. There would have been a fight, hard feelings, Butch turned into an enemy, and nothing profited to Lily. But Billy had done the right thing—done it slowly and imperturbably and with the least hurt to everybody. All of which made him more desirable to Saxon and less possible.

She bought another pair of silk stockings that she had hesitated at for weeks, and on Tuesday night sewed and drowsed wearily over a new shirtwaist and earned complaint from Sarah concerning her extravagant use of gas.

Wednesday night, at the Orindore dance, was not all undiluted pleasure. It was shameless the way the girls made up to Billy, and, at times, Saxon found his easy consideration for them almost irritating. Yet she was compelled to acknowledge to herself that he hurt none of the other fellows' feelings in the way the girls hurt hers. They all but asked him outright to dance with them, and little of their open pursuit of him escaped her eyes. She resolved that she would not be guilty of throwing herself at him, and withheld dance after dance, and yet was secretly and thrillingly aware that she was pursuing the right tactics. She deliberately demonstrated that she was desirable to other men, as he involuntarily demonstrated his own desirableness to the women.

Her happiness came when he coolly overrode her objections and insisted on two dances more than she had allotted him. And she was pleased, as well as angered, when she chanced to overhear two of the strapping young cannery girls. "The way that little sawed-off is monopolizin' him," said one. And the other: "You'd think she might have the good taste to run after somebody of her own age." "Cradle-snatcher," was the final sting that sent the angry blood into Saxon's cheeks as the two girls moved away, unaware that they had been overheard.

Billy saw her home, kissed her at the gate, and got her consent to go with him to the dance at Germania Hall on Friday night.

"I wasn't thinkin' of goin'," he said. "But if you'll say the word... Bert's goin' to be there."

Next day, at the ironing boards, Mary told her that she and Bert were dated for Germania Hall.

"Are you goin'?" Mary asked.

Saxon nodded.

"Billy Roberts?"

The nod was repeated, and Mary, with suspended iron, gave her a long and curious look.

"Say, an' what if Charley Long butts in?"

Saxon shrugged her shoulders.

They ironed swiftly and silently for a quarter of an hour.

"Well," Mary decided, "if he does butt in maybe he'll get his. I'd like to see him get it—the big stiff! It all depends how Billy feels—about you, I mean."

"I'm no Lily Sanderson," Saxon answered indignantly. "I'll never give Billy Roberts a chance to turn me down."

"You will, if Charley Long butts in. Take it from me, Saxon, he ain't no gentleman. Look what he done to Mr. Moody. That was a awful beatin'. An' Mr. Moody only a quiet little man that wouldn't harm a fly. Well, he won't find Billy Roberts a sissy by a long shot."

That night, outside the laundry entrance, Saxon found Charley Long waiting. As he stepped forward to greet her and walk alongside, she felt the sickening palpitation that he had so thoroughly taught her to know. The blood ebbed from her face with the apprehension and fear his appearance caused. She was afraid of the rough bulk of the man; of the heavy brown eyes, dominant and confident; of the big blacksmith-hands and the thick strong fingers with the hair-pads on the back to every first joint. He was unlovely to the eye, and he was unlovely to all her finer sensibilities. It was not his strength itself, but the quality of it and the misuse of it, that affronted her. The beating he had given the gentle Mr. Moody had meant half-hours of horror to her afterward. Always did the memory of it come to her accompanied by a shudder. And yet, without shock, she had seen Billy fight at Weasel Park in the same primitive man-animal way. But it had been different. She recognized, but could not analyze, the difference. She was aware only of the brutishness of this man's hands and mind.

"You're lookin' white an' all beat to a frazzle," he was saying. "Why don't you cut the work? You got to some time, anyway. You can't lose me, kid."

"I wish I could," she replied.

He laughed with harsh joviality. "Nothin' to it, Saxon. You're just cut out to be Mrs. Long, an' you're sure goin' to be."

"I wish I was as certain about all things as you are," she said with mild sarcasm that missed.

"Take it from me," he went on, "there's just one thing you can be certain of—an' that is that I am certain." He was pleased with the cleverness of his idea and laughed approvingly. "When I go after anything I get it, an' if anything gets in between it gets hurt. D'ye get that? It's me for you, an' that's all there is to it, so you might as well make up your mind and go to workin' in my home instead of the laundry. Why, it's a snap. There wouldn't be much to do. I make good money, an' you wouldn't want for anything. You know, I just washed up from work an' skinned over here to tell it to you once more, so you wouldn't forget. I ain't ate yet, an' that shows how much I think of you."

"You'd better go and eat then," she advised, though she knew the futility of attempting to get rid of him.

She scarcely heard what he said. It had come upon her suddenly that she was very tired and very small and very weak alongside this colossus of a man. Would he dog her always? she asked despairingly, and seemed to glimpse a vision of all her future life stretched out before her, with always the form and face of the burly blacksmith pursuing her.

"Come on, kid, an' kick in," he continued. "It's the good old summer time, an' that's the time to get married."

"But I'm not going to marry you," she protested. "I've told you a thousand times already."

"Aw, forget it. You want to get them ideas out of your think-box. Of course, you're goin' to marry me. It's a pipe. An' I'll tell you another pipe. You an' me's goin' acrost to Frisco Friday night. There's goin' to be big doin's with the Horseshoers."

"Only I'm not," she contradicted.

"Oh, yes you are," he asserted with absolute assurance. "We'll catch the last boat back, an' you'll have one fine time. An' I'll put you next to some of the good dancers. Oh, I ain't a pincher, an' I know you like dancin'."

"But I tell you I can't," she reiterated.

He shot a glance of suspicion at her from under the black thatch of brows that met above his nose and were as one brow.

"Why can't you?"

"A date," she said.

"Who's the bloke?"

"None of your business, Charley Long. I've got a date, that's all."

"I'll make it my business. Remember that lah-de-dah bookkeeper rummy? Well, just keep on rememberin' him an' what he got."

"I wish you'd leave me alone," she pleaded resentfully. "Can't you be kind just for once?"

The blacksmith laughed unpleasantly.

"If any rummy thinks he can butt in on you an' me, he'll learn different, an' I'm the little boy that'll learn 'm.—Friday night, eh? Where?"

"I won't tell you."

"Where?" he repeated.

Her lips were drawn in tight silence, and in her cheeks were little angry spots of blood.

"Huh!—As if I couldn't guess! Germania Hall. Well, I'll be there, an' I'll take you home afterward. D'ye get that? An' you'd better tell the rummy to beat it unless you want to see 'm get his face hurt."

Saxon, hurt as a prideful woman can be hurt by cavalier treatment, was tempted to cry out the name and prowess of her new-found protector. And then came fear. This was a big man, and Billy was only a boy. That was the way he affected her. She remembered her first impression of his hands and glanced quickly at the hands of the man beside her. They seemed twice as large as Billy's, and the mats of hair seemed to advertise a terrible strength. No, Billy could not fight this big brute. He must not. And then to Saxon came a wicked little hope that by the mysterious and unthinkable ability that prizefighters possessed, Billy might be able to whip this bully and rid her of him. With the next glance doubt came again, for her eye dwelt on the blacksmith's broad shoulders, the cloth of the coat muscle-wrinkled and the sleeves bulging above the biceps.

"If you lay a hand on anybody I'm going with again——" she began.

"Why, they'll get hurt, of course," Long grinned. "And they'll deserve it, too. Any rummy that comes between a fellow an' his girl ought to get hurt."

"But I'm not your girl, and all your saying so doesn't make it so."

"That's right, get mad," he approved. "I like you for that, too. You've got spunk an' fight. I like to see it. It's what a man needs in his wife—and not these fat cows of women. They're the dead ones. Now you're a live one, all wool, a yard long and a yard wide."

She stopped before the house and put her hand on the gate.

"Good-bye," she said. "I'm going in."

"Come on out afterward for a run to Idora Park," he suggested.

"No, I'm not feeling good, and I'm going straight to bed as soon as I eat supper."

"Huh!" he sneered. "Gettin' in shape for the fling to-morrow night, eh?"

With an impatient movement she opened the gate and stepped inside.

"I've given it to you straight," he went on. "If you don't go with me to-morrow night somebody'll get hurt."

"I hope it will be you," she cried vindictively.

He laughed as he threw his head back, stretched his big chest, and half-lifted his heavy arms. The action reminded her disgustingly of a great ape she had once seen in a circus.

"Well, good-bye," he said. "See you to-morrow night at Germania Hall."

"I haven't told you it was Germania Hall."

"And you haven't told me it wasn't. All the same, I'll be there. And I'll take you home, too. Be sure an' keep plenty of round dances open fer me. That's right. Get mad. It makes you look fine."

CHAPTER VIII

The music stopped at the end of the waltz, leaving Billy and Saxon at the big entrance doorway of the ballroom. Her hand rested lightly on his arm, and they were promenading on to find seats, when Charley Long, evidently just arrived, thrust his way in front of them.

"So you're the buttinsky, eh?" he demanded, his face malignant with passion and menace.

"Who?—me?" Billy queried gently. "Some mistake, sport. I never butt in."

"You're goin' to get your head beaten off if you don't make yourself scarce pretty lively."

"I wouldn't want that to happen for the world," Billy drawled. "Come on, Saxon. This neighborhood's unhealthy for us."

He started to go on with her, but Long thrust in front again.

"You're too fresh to keep, young fellow," he snarled. "You need saltin' down. D'ye get me?"

Billy scratched his head, on his face exaggerated puzzlement.

"No, I don't get you," he said. "Now just what was it you said?"

But the big blacksmith turned contemptuously away from him to Saxon.

"Come here, you. Let's see your program."

"Do you want to dance with him?" Billy asked.

She shook her head.

"Sorry, sport, nothin' doin'," Billy said, again making to start on.

For the third time the blacksmith blocked the way.

"Get off your foot," said Billy. "You're standin' on it."

Long all but sprang upon him, his hands clenched, one arm just starting back for the punch while at the same instant shoulders and chest were coming forward. But he restrained himself at sight of Billy's unstartled body and cold and cloudy eyes. He had made no move of mind or muscle. It was as if he were unaware of the threatened attack. All of which constituted a new thing in Long's experience.

"Maybe you don't know who I am," he bullied.

"Yep, I do," Billy answered airily. "You're a record-breaker at rough-housin'." (Here Long's face showed pleasure.) "You ought to have the Police

Gazette diamond belt for rough-housin' baby buggies'. I guess there ain't a one you're afraid to tackle."

"Leave 'm alone, Charley," advised one of the young men who had crowded about them. "He's Bill Roberts, the fighter. You know'm. Big Bill."

"I don't care if he's Jim Jeffries. He can't butt in on me this way."

Nevertheless it was noticeable, even to Saxon, that the fire had gone out of his fierceness. Billy's name seemed to have a quieting effect on obstreperous males.

"Do you know him?" Billy asked her.

She signified yes with her eyes, though it seemed she must cry out a thousand things against this man who so steadfastly persecuted her. Billy turned to the blacksmith.

"Look here, sport, you don't want trouble with me. I've got your number. Besides, what do we want to fight for? Hasn't she got a say so in the matter?"

"No, she hasn't. This is my affair an' yourn."

Billy shook his head slowly. "No; you're in wrong. I think she has a say in the matter."

"Well, say it then," Long snarled at Saxon, "who're you goin' to go with?—me or him? Let's get it settled."

For reply, Saxon reached her free hand over to the hand that rested on Billy's arm.

"Nuff said," was Billy's remark.

Long glared at Saxon, then transferred the glare to her protector.

"I've a good mind to mix it with you anyway," Long gritted through his teeth.

Saxon was elated as they started to move away. Lily Sanderson's fate had not been hers, and her wonderful man-boy, without the threat of a blow, slow of speech and imperturbable, had conquered the big blacksmith.

"He's forced himself upon me all the time," she whispered to Billy. "He's tried to run me, and beaten up every man that came near me. I never want to see him again."

Billy halted immediately. Long, who was reluctantly moving to get out of the way, also halted.

"She says she don't want anything more to do with you," Billy said to him. "An' what she says goes. If I get a whisper any time that you've been botherin' her, I'll attend to your case. D'ye get that?"

Long glowered and remained silent.

"D'ye get that?" Billy repeated, more imperatively.

A growl of assent came from the blacksmith

"All right, then. See you remember it. An' now get outa the way or I'll walk over you."

Long slunk back, muttering inarticulate threats, and Saxon moved on as in a dream. Charley Long had taken water. He had been afraid of this smooth-skinned, blue-eyed boy. She was quit of him—something no other man had dared attempt for her. And Billy had liked her better than Lily Sanderson.

Twice Saxon tried to tell Billy the details of her acquaintance with Long, but each time was put off.

"I don't care a rap about it," Billy said the second time. "You're here, ain't you?"

But she insisted, and when, worked up and angry by the recital, she had finished, he patted her hand soothingly.

"It's all right, Saxon," he said. "He's just a big stiff. I took his measure as soon as I looked at him. He won't bother you again. I know his kind. He's a dog. Roughhouse? He couldn't rough-house a milk wagon."

"But how do you do it?" she asked breathlessly. "Why are men so afraid of you? You're just wonderful."

He smiled in an embarrassed way and changed the subject.

"Say," he said, "I like your teeth. They're so white an' regular, an' not big, an' not dinky little baby's teeth either. They're ... they're just right, an' they fit you. I never seen such fine teeth on a girl yet. D'ye know, honest, they kind of make me hungry when I look at 'em. They're good enough to eat."

At midnight, leaving the insatiable Bert and Mary still dancing, Billy and Saxon started for home. It was on his suggestion that they left early, and he felt called upon to explain.

"It's one thing the fightin' game's taught me," he said. "To take care of myself. A fellow can't work all day and dance all night and keep in condition. It's the same way with drinkin'—an' not that I'm a little tin angel. I know what it is. I've been soused to the guards an' all the rest of it. I like my beer—big schooners of it; but I don't drink all I want of it. I've tried, but it don't pay. Take that big stiff to-night that butted in on us. He ought to had my number. He's a dog anyway, but besides he had beer bloat. I sized that up the first rattle, an' that's the difference about who takes the other fellow's number. Condition, that's what it is."

"But he is so big," Saxon protested. "Why, his fists are twice as big as yours."

"That don't mean anything. What counts is what's behind the fists. He'd turn loose like a buckin' bronco. If I couldn't drop him at the start, all I'd do is to keep away, smother up, an' wait. An' all of a sudden he'd blow up—go all to pieces, you know, wind, heart, everything, and then I'd have him where I wanted him. And the point is he knows it, too."

"You're the first prizefighter I ever knew," Saxon said, after a pause.

"I'm not any more," he disclaimed hastily. "That's one thing the fightin' game taught me—to leave it alone. It don't pay. A fellow trains as fine as silk—till he's all silk, his skin, everything, and he's fit to live for a hundred years; an' then he climbs through the ropes for a hard twenty rounds with some tough customer that's just as good as he is, and in those twenty rounds he frazzles out all his silk an' blows in a year of his life. Yes, sometimes he blows in five years of it, or cuts it in half, or uses up all of it. I've watched 'em. I've seen fellows strong as bulls fight a hard battle and die inside the year of consumption, or kidney disease, or anything else. Now what's the good of it? Money can't buy what they throw away. That's why I quit the game and went back to drivin' team. I got my silk, an' I'm goin' to keep it, that's all."

"It must make you feel proud to know you are the master of other men," she said softly, aware herself of pride in the strength and skill of him.

"It does," he admitted frankly. "I'm glad I went into the game—just as glad as I am that I pulled out of it…. Yep, it's taught me a lot—to keep my eyes open an' my head cool. Oh, I've got a temper, a peach of a temper. I get scared of myself sometimes. I used to be always breakin' loose. But the fightin' taught me to keep down the steam an' not do things I'd be sorry for afterward."

"Why, you're the sweetest, easiest tempered man I know," she interjected.

"Don't you believe it. Just watch me, and sometime you'll see me break out that bad that I won't know what I'm doin' myself. Oh, I'm a holy terror when I get started!"

This tacit promise of continued acquaintance gave Saxon a little joy-thrill.

"Say," he said, as they neared her neighborhood, "what are you doin' next Sunday?"

"Nothing. No plans at all."

"Well, suppose you an' me go buggy-riding all day out in the hills?"

She did not answer immediately, and for the moment she was seeing the nightmare vision of her last buggy-ride; of her fear and her leap from the buggy; and of the long miles and the stumbling through the darkness in thin-soled shoes that bruised her feet on every rock. And then it came to her with a great swell of joy that this man beside her was not such a man.

"I love horses," she said. "I almost love them better than I do dancing, only I don't know anything about them. My father rode a great roan war-horse. He was a captain of cavalry, you know. I never saw him, but somehow I always can see him on that big horse, with a sash around his waist and his sword at his side. My brother George has the sword now, but Tom—he's the brother I live with says it is mine because it wasn't his father's. You see, they're only my half-brothers. I was the only child by my mother's second marriage. That was her real marriage—her love-marriage, I mean."

Saxon ceased abruptly, embarrassed by her own garrulity; and yet the impulse was strong to tell this young man all about herself, and it seemed to her that these far memories were a large part of her.

"Go on an' tell me about it," Billy urged. "I like to hear about the old people of the old days. My people was along in there, too, an' somehow I think it was a better world to live in than now. Things was more sensible and natural. I don't exactly say what I mean. But it's like this: I don't understand life to-day. There's the labor unions an' employers' associations, an' strikes', an' hard times, an' huntin' for jobs, an' all the rest. Things wasn't like that in the old days. Everybody farmed, an' shot their meat, an' got enough to eat, an' took care of their old folks. But now it's all a mix-up that I can't understand. Mebbe I'm a fool, I don't know. But, anyway, go ahead an' tell us about your mother."

"Well, you see, when she was only a young woman she and Captain Brown fell in love. He was a soldier then, before the war. And he was ordered East for the war when she was away nursing her sister Laura. And then came the news that he was killed at Shiloh. And she married a man who had loved her for years and years. He was a boy in the same wagon-train coming across the plains. She liked him, but she didn't love him. And afterward came the news that my father wasn't killed after all. So it made her very sad, but it did not spoil her life. She was a good mother and a good wife and all that, but she was always sad, and sweet, and gentle, and I think her voice was the most beautiful in the world."

"She was game, all right," Billy approved.

"And my father never married. He loved her all the time. I've got a lovely poem home that she wrote to him. It's just wonderful, and it sings like music. Well, long, long afterward her husband died, and then she and my father made their love marriage. They didn't get married until 1882, and she was pretty well along."

More she told him, as they stood by the gate, and Saxon tried to think that the good-bye kiss was a trifle longer than just ordinary.

"How about nine o'clock?" he queried across the gate. "Don't bother about lunch or anything. I'll fix all that up. You just be ready at nine."

CHAPTER IX

Sunday morning Saxon was beforehand in getting ready, and on her return to the kitchen from her second journey to peep through the front windows, Sarah began her customary attack.

"It's a shame an' a disgrace the way some people can afford silk stockings," she began. "Look at me, a-toilin' and a-stewin' day an' night, and I never get silk stockings—nor shoes, three pairs of them all at one time. But there's a just God in heaven, and there'll be some mighty big surprises for some when the end comes and folks get passed out what's comin' to them."

Tom, smoking his pipe and cuddling his youngest-born on his knees, dropped an eyelid surreptitiously on his cheek in token that Sarah was in a tantrum. Saxon devoted herself to tying a ribbon in the hair of one of the little girls. Sarah lumbered heavily about the kitchen, washing and putting away the breakfast dishes. She straightened her back from the sink with a groan and glared at Saxon with fresh hostility.

"You ain't sayin' anything, eh? An' why don't you? Because I guess you still got some natural shame in you a-runnin' with a prizefighter. Oh, I've heard about your goings-on with Bill Roberts. A nice specimen he is. But just you wait till Charley Long gets his hands on him, that's all."

"Oh, I don't know," Tom intervened. "Bill Roberts is a pretty good boy from what I hear."

Saxon smiled with superior knowledge, and Sarah, catching her, was infuriated.

"Why don't you marry Charley Long? He's crazy for you, and he ain't a drinkin' man."

"I guess he gets outside his share of beer," Saxon retorted.

"That's right," her brother supplemented. "An' I know for a fact that he keeps a keg in the house all the time as well."

"Maybe you've been guzzling from it," Sarah snapped.

"Maybe I have," Tom said, wiping his mouth reminiscently with the back of his hand.

"Well, he can afford to keep a keg in the house if he wants to," she returned to the attack, which now was directed at her husband as well. "He pays his bills, and he certainly makes good money—better than most men, anyway."

"An' he hasn't a wife an' children to watch out for," Tom said.

"Nor everlastin' dues to unions that don't do him no good."

"Oh, yes, he has," Tom urged genially. "Blamed little he'd work in that shop, or any other shop in Oakland, if he didn't keep in good standing with the Blacksmiths. You don't understand labor conditions, Sarah. The unions have got to stick, if the men aren't to starve to death."

"Oh, of course not," Sarah sniffed. "I don't understand anything. I ain't got a mind. I'm a fool, an' you tell me so right before the children." She turned savagely on her eldest, who startled and shrank away. "Willie, your mother is a fool. Do you get that? Your father says she's a fool—says it right before her face and yourn. She's just a plain fool. Next he'll be sayin' she's crazy an' puttin' her away in the asylum. An' how will you like that, Willie? How will you like to see your mother in a straitjacket an' a padded cell, shut out from the light of the sun an' beaten like a nigger before the war, Willie, beaten an' clubbed like a regular black nigger? That's the kind of a father you've got, Willie. Think of it, Willie, in a padded cell, the mother that bore you, with the lunatics screechin' an' screamin' all around, an' the quick-lime eatin' into the dead bodies of them that's beaten to death by the cruel wardens—"

She continued tirelessly, painting with pessimistic strokes the growing black future her husband was meditating for her, while the boy, fearful of some vague, incomprehensible catastrophe, began to weep silently, with a pendulous, trembling underlip. Saxon, for the moment, lost control of herself.

"Oh, for heaven's sake, can't we be together five minutes without quarreling?" she blazed.

Sarah broke off from asylum conjurations and turned upon her sister-in-law.

"Who's quarreling? Can't I open my head without bein' jumped on by the two of you?"

Saxon shrugged her shoulders despairingly, and Sarah swung about on her husband.

"Seein' you love your sister so much better than your wife, why did you want to marry me, that's borne your children for you, an' slaved for you, an' toiled for you, an' worked her fingernails off for you, with no thanks, an 'insultin' me before the children, an' sayin' I'm crazy to their faces. An' what have you ever did for me? That's what I want to know—me, that's cooked for you, an' washed your stinkin' clothes, and fixed your socks, an' sat up nights with your brats when they was ailin'. Look at that!"

She thrust out a shapeless, swollen foot, encased in a monstrous, untended shoe, the dry, raw leather of which showed white on the edges of bulging cracks.

"Look at that! That's what I say. Look at that!" Her voice was persistently rising and at the same time growing throaty. "The only shoes I got. Me. Your wife. Ain't you ashamed? Where are my three pairs? Look at that stockin'."

Speech failed her, and she sat down suddenly on a chair at the table, glaring unutterable malevolence and misery. She arose with the abrupt stiffness of an automaton, poured herself a cup of cold coffee, and in the same jerky way sat down again. As if too hot for her lips, she filled her saucer with the greasy-looking, nondescript fluid, and continued her set glare, her breast rising and falling with staccato, mechanical movement.

"Now, Sarah, be c'am, be c'am," Tom pleaded anxiously.

In response, slowly, with utmost deliberation, as if the destiny of empires rested on the certitude of her act, she turned the saucer of coffee upside down on the table. She lifted her right hand, slowly, hugely, and in the same slow, huge way landed the open palm with a sounding slap on Tom's astounded cheek. Immediately thereafter she raised her voice in the shrill, hoarse, monotonous madness of hysteria, sat down on the floor, and rocked back and forth in the throes of an abysmal grief.

Willie's silent weeping turned to noise, and the two little girls, with the fresh ribbons in their hair, joined him. Tom's face was drawn and white, though the smitten cheek still blazed, and Saxon wanted to put her arms comfortingly around him, yet dared not. He bent over his wife.

"Sarah, you ain't feelin' well. Let me put you to bed, and I'll finish tidying up."

"Don't touch me!—don't touch me!" she screamed, jerking violently away from him.

"Take the children out in the yard, Tom, for a walk, anything—get them away," Saxon said. She was sick, and white, and trembling. "Go, Tom, please, please. There's your hat. I'll take care of her. I know just how."

Left to herself, Saxon worked with frantic haste, assuming the calm she did not possess, but which she must impart to the screaming bedlamite upon the floor. The light frame house leaked the noise hideously, and Saxon knew that the houses on either side were hearing, and the street itself and the houses across the street. Her fear was that Billy should arrive in the midst of it. Further, she was incensed, violated. Every fiber rebelled, almost in a nausea; yet she maintained cool control and stroked Sarah's forehead and hair with slow, soothing movements. Soon, with one arm around her, she managed to win the first diminution in the strident, atrocious, unceasing scream. A few minutes later, sobbing heavily, the elder woman lay in bed, across her forehead and eyes a wet-pack of towel for easement of the headache she and Saxon tacitly accepted as substitute for the brain-storm.

When a clatter of hoofs came down the street and stopped, Saxon was able to slip to the front door and wave her hand to Billy. In the kitchen she found Tom waiting in sad anxiousness.

"It's all right," she said. "Billy Roberts has come, and I've got to go. You go in and sit beside her for a while, and maybe she'll go to sleep. But don't rush her. Let her have her own way. If she'll let you take her hand, why do it. Try it, anyway. But first of all, as an opener and just as a matter of course, start wetting the towel over her eyes."

He was a kindly, easy-going man; but, after the way of a large percentage of the Western stock, he was undemonstrative. He nodded, turned toward the door to obey, and paused irresolutely. The look he gave back to Saxon was almost dog-like in gratitude and all-brotherly in love. She felt it, and in spirit leapt toward it.

"It's all right—everything's all right," she cried hastily.

Tom shook his head.

"No, it ain't. It's a shame, a blamed shame, that's what it is." He shrugged his shoulders. "Oh, I don't care for myself. But it's for you. You got your life before you yet, little kid sister. You'll get old, and all that means, fast enough. But it's a bad start for a day off. The thing for you to do is to forget all this, and skin out with your fellow, an' have a good time." In the open door, his hand on the knob to close it after him, he halted a second time. A spasm contracted his brow. "Hell! Think of it! Sarah and I used to go buggy-riding once on a time. And I guess she had her three pairs of shoes, too. Can you beat it?"

In her bedroom Saxon completed her dressing, for an instant stepping upon a chair so as to glimpse critically in the small wall-mirror the hang of her ready-made linen skirt. This, and the jacket, she had altered to fit, and she had double-stitched the seams to achieve the coveted tailored effect. Still on the chair, all in the moment of quick clear-seeing, she drew the skirt tightly back and raised it. The sight was good to her, nor did she under-appraise the lines of the slender ankle above the low tan tie nor did she under-appraise the delicate yet mature swell of calf outlined in the fresh brown of a new cotton stocking. Down from the chair, she pinned on a firm sailor hat of white straw with a brown ribbon around the crown that matched her ribbon belt. She rubbed her cheeks quickly and fiercely to bring back the color Sarah had driven out of them, and delayed a moment longer to put on her tan lisle-thread gloves. Once, in the fashion-page of a Sunday supplement, she had read that no lady ever put on her gloves after she left the door.

With a resolute self-grip, as she crossed the parlor and passed the door to Sarah's bedroom, through the thin wood of which came elephantine moanings and low slubberings, she steeled herself to keep the color in her cheeks and the brightness in her eyes. And so well did she succeed that Billy never dreamed that the radiant, live young thing, tripping lightly down the steps to him, had just come from a bout with soul-sickening hysteria and madness.

To her, in the bright sun, Billy's blondness was startling. His cheeks, smooth as a girl's, were touched with color. The blue eyes seemed more cloudily blue than usual, and the crisp, sandy hair hinted more than ever of the pale straw-gold that was not there. Never had she seen him quite so royally young. As he smiled to greet her, with a slow white flash of teeth from between red lips, she caught again the promise of easement and rest. Fresh from the shattering chaos of her sister-in-law's mind, Billy's tremendous calm was especially satisfying, and Saxon mentally laughed to scorn the terrible temper he had charged to himself.

She had been buggy-riding before, but always behind one horse, jaded, and livery, in a top-buggy, heavy and dingy, such as livery stables rent because of sturdy unbreakableness. But here stood two horses, head-tossing and restless, shouting in every high-light glint of their satin, golden-sorrel coats that they had never been rented out in all their glorious young lives. Between them was a pole inconceivably slender, on them were harnesses preposterously string-like and fragile. And Billy belonged here, by elemental right, a part of them and of it, a master-part and a component, along with the spidery-delicate, narrow-boxed, wide- and yellow-wheeled, rubber-tired rig, efficient and capable, as different as he was different from the other man who had taken her out behind stolid, lumbering horses. He held the reins in one hand, yet, with low, steady voice, confident and assuring, held the nervous young animals more by the will and the spirit of him.

It was no time for lingering. With the quick glance and fore-knowledge of a woman, Saxon saw, not merely the curious children clustering about, but the peering of adult faces from open doors and windows, and past window-shades lifted up or held aside. With his free hand, Billy drew back the linen robe and helped her to a place beside him. The high-backed, luxuriously upholstered seat of brown leather gave her a sense of great comfort; yet even greater, it seemed to her, was the nearness and comfort of the man himself and of his body.

"How d'ye like 'em?" he asked, changing the reins to both hands and chirruping the horses, which went out with a jerk in an immediacy of action that was new to her. "They're the boss's, you know. Couldn't rent animals like them. He lets me take them out for exercise sometimes. If they ain't exercised regular they're a handful.—Look at King, there, prancin'. Some style, eh? Some style! The other one's the real goods, though. Prince is his name. Got to have some bit on him to hold'm.—Ah! Would you?—Did you see'm, Saxon? Some horse! Some horse!"

From behind came the admiring cheer of the neighborhood children, and Saxon, with a sigh of content, knew that the happy day had at last begun.

CHAPTER X

"I don't know horses," Saxon said. "I've never been on one's back, and the only ones I've tried to drive were single, and lame, or almost falling down, or something. But I'm not afraid of horses. I just love them. I was born loving them, I guess."

Billy threw an admiring, appreciative glance at her.

"That's the stuff. That's what I like in a woman—grit. Some of the girls I've had out—well, take it from me, they made me sick. Oh, I'm hep to 'em. Nervous, an' trembly, an' screechy, an' wabbly. I reckon they come out on my account an' not for the ponies. But me for the brave kid that likes the ponies. You're the real goods, Saxon, honest to God you are. Why, I can talk like a streak with you. The rest of 'em make me sick. I'm like a clam. They don't know nothin', an' they're that scared all the time—well, I guess you get me."

"You have to be born to love horses, maybe," she answered. "Maybe it's because I always think of my father on his roan war-horse that makes me love horses. But, anyway, I do. When I was a little girl I was drawing horses all the time. My mother always encouraged me. I've a scrapbook mostly filled with horses I drew when I was little. Do you know, Billy, sometimes I dream I actually own a horse, all my own. And lots of times I dream I'm on a horse's back, or driving him."

"I'll let you drive 'em, after a while, when they've worked their edge off. They're pullin' now.—There, put your hands in front of mine—take hold tight. Feel that? Sure you feel it. An' you ain't feelin' it all by a long shot. I don't dast slack, you bein' such a lightweight."

Her eyes sparkled as she felt the apportioned pull of the mouths of the beautiful, live things; and he, looking at her, sparkled with her in her delight.

"What's the good of a woman if she can't keep up with a man?" he broke out enthusiastically.

"People that like the same things always get along best together," she answered, with a triteness that concealed the joy that was hers at being so spontaneously in touch with him.

"Why, Saxon, I've fought battles, good ones, frazzlin' my silk away to beat the band before whisky-soaked, smokin' audiences of rotten fight-fans, that just made me sick clean through. An' them, that couldn't take just one stiff jolt or hook to jaw or stomach, a-cheerin' me an' yellin' for blood. Blood, mind you! An' them without the blood of a shrimp in their bodies. Why, honest, now, I'd sooner fight before an audience of one—you for instance, or anybody I liked. It'd do me proud. But them sickenin', sap-headed stiffs, with the grit of rabbits and the silk of mangy ky-yi's, a-cheerin' me—ME! Can you blame me for quittin' the dirty game?—Why, I'd sooner fight before broke-down old plugs of work-horses that's candidates for chicken-meat, than before them rotten bunches of stiffs with nothin' thicker'n water in their veins, an' Contra Costa water at that when the rains is heavy on the hills."

"I... I didn't know prizefighting was like that," she faltered, as she released her hold on the lines and sank back again beside him.

"It ain't the fightin', it's the fight-crowds," he defended with instant jealousy. "Of course, fightin' hurts a young fellow because it frazzles the silk outa him an' all that. But it's the low-lifers in the audience that gets me. Why the good things they say to me, the praise an' that, is insulting. Do you get me? It makes me cheap. Think of it—booze-guzzlin' stiffs that 'd be afraid to mix it with a sick cat, not fit to hold the coat of any decent man, think of them a-standin' up on their hind legs an' yellin' an' cheerin' me—ME!"

"Ha! ha! What d'ye think of that? Ain't he a rogue?"

A big bulldog, sliding obliquely and silently across the street, unconcerned with the team he was avoiding, had passed so close that Prince, baring his teeth like a stallion, plunged his head down against reins and check in an effort to seize the dog.

"Now he's some fighter, that Prince. An' he's natural. He didn't make that reach just for some low-lifer to yell'm on. He just done it outa pure cussedness and himself. That's clean. That's right. Because it's natural. But them fight-fans! Honest to God, Saxon...."

And Saxon, glimpsing him sidewise, as he watched the horses and their way on the Sunday morning streets, checking them back suddenly and swerving to avoid two boys coasting across street on a toy wagon, saw in him deeps and intensities, all the magic connotations of temperament, the glimmer and hint of rages profound, bleaknesses as cold and far as the stars, savagery as keen as a wolf's and clean as a stallion's, wrath as implacable as a destroying angel's, and youth that was fire and life beyond time and place. She was awed and fascinated, with the hunger of woman bridging the vastness to him, daring to love him with arms and breast that ached to him, murmuring to herself and through all the halls of her soul, "You dear, you dear."

"Honest to God, Saxon," he took up the broken thread, "they's times when I've hated them, when I wanted to jump over the ropes and wade into them, knock-down and drag-out, an' show'm what fightin' was. Take that night with Billy Murphy. Billy Murphy!—if you only knew him. My friend. As clean an' game a boy as ever jumped inside the ropes to take the decision. Him! We went to the Durant School together. We grew up chums. His fight was my fight. My trouble was his trouble. We both took to the fightin' game. They matched us. Not the first time. Twice we'd fought draws. Once the decision was his; once it was mine. The fifth fight of two lovin' men that just loved each other. He's three years older'n me. He's a wife and two or three kids, an' I know them, too. And he's my friend. Get it?

"I'm ten pounds heavier—but with heavyweights that 's all right. He can't time an' distance as good as me, an' I can keep set better, too. But he's cleverer an' quicker. I never was quick like him. We both can take punishment, an' we're both two-handed, a wallop in all our fists. I know the kick of his, an' he knows my kick, an' we're both real respectful. And we're even-matched. Two draws, and a decision to each. Honest, I ain't any kind of a hunch who's goin' to win, we're that even.

"Now, the fight.—You ain't squeamish, are you?"

"No, no," she cried. "I'd just love to hear—you are so wonderful."

He took the praise with a clear, unwavering look, and without hint of acknowledgment.

"We go along—six rounds—seven rounds—eight rounds; an' honors even. I've been timin' his rushes an' straight-leftin' him, an' meetin' his duck with a wicked little right upper-cut, an' he's shaken me on the jaw an' walloped my ears till my head's all singin' an' buzzin'. An' everything lovely with both of us, with a noise like a draw decision in sight. Twenty rounds is the distance, you know.

"An' then his bad luck comes. We're just mixin' into a clinch that ain't arrived yet, when he shoots a short hook to my head—his left, an' a real hay-maker if it reaches my jaw. I make a forward duck, not quick enough, an' he lands bingo on the side of my head. Honest to God, Saxon, it's that heavy I see some stars. But it don't hurt an' ain't serious, that high up where the bone's thick. An' right there he finishes himself, for his bad thumb, which I've known since he first got it as a kid fightin' in the sandlot at Watts Tract—he smashes that thumb right there, on my hard head, back into the socket with an out-twist, an' all the old cords that'd never got strong gets theirs again. I didn't mean it. A dirty trick, fair in the game, though, to make a guy smash his hand on your head. But not between friends. I couldn't a-done that to Bill Murphy for a million dollars. It was a accident, just because I was slow, because I was born slow.

"The hurt of it! Honest, Saxon, you don't know what hurt is till you've got a old hurt like that hurt again. What can Billy Murphy do but slow down? He's got to. He ain't fightin' two-handed any more. He knows it; I know it; The referee knows it; but nobody else. He goes on a-moving that left of his like it's all right. But it ain't. It's hurtin' him like a knife dug into him. He don't dast strike a real blow with that left of his. But it hurts, anyway. Just to move it or not move it hurts, an' every little dab-feint that I'm too wise to guard, knowin' there's no weight behind, why them little dab-touches on that poor thumb goes right to the heart of him, an' hurts worse than a thousand boils or a thousand knockouts—just hurts all over again, an' worse, each time an' touch.

"Now suppose he an' me was boxin' for fun, out in the back yard, an' he hurts his thumb that way, why we'd have the gloves off in a jiffy an' I'd be putting cold compresses on that poor thumb of his an' bandagin' it that tight to keep the inflammation down. But no. This is a fight for fight-fans that's paid their admission for blood, an' blood they're goin' to get. They ain't men. They're wolves.

"He has to go easy, now, an' I ain't a-forcin' him none. I'm all shot to pieces. I don't know what to do. So I slow down, an' the fans get hep to it. 'Why don't you fight?' they begin to yell; 'Fake! Fake!' 'Why don't you kiss'm?' 'Lovin' cup for yours, Bill Roberts!' an' that sort of bunk.

"'Fight!' says the referee to me, low an' savage. 'Fight, or I'll disqualify you—you, Bill, I mean you.' An' this to me, with a touch on the shoulder so they's no mistakin'.

"It ain't pretty. It ain't right. D'ye know what we was fightin' for? A hundred bucks. Think of it! An' the game is we got to do our best to put our man down for the count because of the fans has bet on us. Sweet, ain't it? Well, that's my last fight. It finishes me deado. Never again for yours truly.

"'Quit,' I says to Billy Murphy in a clinch; 'for the love of God, Bill, quit.' An' he says back, in a whisper, 'I can't, Bill—you know that.'

"An' then the referee drags us apart, an' a lot of the fans begins to hoot an' boo.

"'Now kick in, damn you, Bill Roberts, an' finish'm' the referee says to me, an' I tell'm to go to hell as Bill an' me flop into the next clinch, not hittin', an' Bill touches his thumb again, an' I see the pain shoot across his face. Game? That good boy's the limit. An' to look into the eyes of a brave man that's sick with pain, an' love 'm, an' see love in them eyes of his, an' then have to go on givin' 'm pain—call that sport? I can't see it. But the crowd's got its money on us. We don't count. We've sold ourselves for a hundred bucks, an' we gotta deliver the goods.

"Let me tell you, Saxon, honest to God, that was one of the times I wanted to go through the ropes an' drop them fans a-yellin' for blood an' show 'em what blood is.

"'For God's sake finish me, Bill,' Bill says to me in that clinch; 'put her over an' I'll fall for it, but I can't lay down.'

"D'ye want to know? I cry there, right in the ring, in that clinch. The weeps for me. 'I can't do it, Bill,' I whisper back, hangin' onto'm like a brother an' the referee ragin' an' draggin' at us to get us apart, an' all the wolves in the house snarlin'.

"'You got 'm!' the audience is yellin'. 'Go in an' finish 'm!' 'The hay for him, Bill; put her across to the jaw an' see 'm fall!'

"'You got to, Bill, or you're a dog,' Bill says, lookin' love at me in his eyes as the referee's grip untangles us clear.

"An' them wolves of fans yellin': 'Fake! Fake! Fake!' like that, an' keepin' it up.

"Well, I done it. They's only that way out. I done it. By God, I done it. I had to. I feint for 'm, draw his left, duck to the right past it, takin' it across my shoulder, an come up with my right to his jaw. An' he knows the trick. He's hep. He's beaten me to it an' blocked it with his shoulder a thousan' times. But this time he don't. He keeps himself wide open on purpose. Blim! It lands. He's dead in the air, an' he goes down sideways, strikin' his face first on the rosin-canvas an' then layin' dead, his head twisted under 'm till you'd a-thought his neck was broke. ME—I did that for a hundred bucks an' a bunch of stiffs I'd be ashamed to wipe my feet on. An' then I pick Bill up in my arms an' carry'm to his corner, an' help bring'm around. Well, they ain't no kick comin'. They pay their money an' they get their blood, an' a knockout. An' a better man than them, that I love, layin' there dead to the world with a skinned face on the mat."

For a moment he was still, gazing straight before him at the horses, his face hard and angry. He sighed, looked at Saxon, and smiled.

"An' I quit the game right there. An' Billy Murphy's laughed at me for it. He still follows it. A side-line, you know, because he works at a good trade. But once in a while, when the house needs paintin', or the doctor bills are up, or his oldest kid wants a bicycle, he jumps out an' makes fifty or a hundred bucks before some of the clubs. I want you to meet him when it comes handy. He's some boy I'm tellin' you. But it did make me sick that night."

Again the harshness and anger were in his face, and Saxon amazed herself by doing unconsciously what women higher in the social scale have done with deliberate sincerity. Her hand went out impulsively to his holding the lines, resting on top of it for a moment with quick, firm pressure. Her reward was a smile from lips and eyes, as his face turned toward her.

"Gee!" he exclaimed. "I never talk a streak like this to anybody. I just hold my hush an' keep my thinks to myself. But, somehow, I guess it's funny, I kind of have a feelin' I want to make good with you. An' that's why I'm tellin' you my thinks. Anybody can dance."

The way led uptown, past the City Hall and the Fourteenth Street skyscrapers, and out Broadway to Mountain View. Turning to the right at the cemetery, they climbed the Piedmont Heights to Blair Park and plunged into the green coolness of Jack Hayes Canyon. Saxon could not suppress her surprise and joy at the quickness with which they covered the ground.

"They are beautiful," she said. "I never dreamed I'd ever ride behind horses like them. I'm afraid I'll wake up now and find it's a dream. You know, I dream horses all the time. I'd give anything to own one some time."

"It's funny, ain't it?" Billy answered. "I like horses that way. The boss says I'm a wooz at horses. An' I know he's a dub. He don't know the first thing. An' yet he owns two hundred big heavy draughts besides this light drivin' pair, an' I don't own one."

"Yet God makes the horses," Saxon said.

"It's a sure thing the boss don't. Then how does he have so many?—two hundred of 'em, I'm tellin' you. He thinks he likes horses. Honest to God, Saxon, he don't like all his horses as much as I like the last hair on the last tail of the scrubbiest of the bunch. Yet they're his. Wouldn't it jar you?"

"Wouldn't it?" Saxon laughed appreciatively. "I just love fancy shirtwaists, an' I spent my life ironing some of the beautifullest I've ever seen. It's funny, an' it isn't fair."

Billy gritted his teeth in another of his rages.

"An' the way some of them women gets their shirtwaists. It makes me sick, thinkin' of you ironin' 'em. You know what I mean, Saxon. They ain't no use wastin' words over it. You know. I know. Everybody knows. An' it's a hell of a world if men an' women sometimes can't talk to each other about such things." His manner was almost apologetic yet it was defiantly and assertively right. "I never talk this way to other girls. They'd think I'm workin up to designs on 'em. They make me sick the way they're always lookin' for them designs. But you're different. I can talk to you that way. I know I've got to. It's the square thing. You're like Billy Murphy, or any other man a man can talk to."

She sighed with a great happiness, and looked at him with unconscious, love-shining eyes.

"It's the same way with me," she said. "The fellows I've run with I've never dared let talk about such things, because I knew they'd take advantage of it. Why, all the time, with them, I've a feeling that we're cheating and lying to each other, playing a game like at a masquerade ball." She paused for a moment, hesitant and debating, then went on in a queer low voice. "I haven't been asleep. I've seen... and heard. I've had my chances, when I was that tired of the laundry I'd have done almost anything. I could have got those fancy shirtwaists... an' all the rest... and maybe a horse to ride. There was a bank cashier... married, too, if you please. He talked to me straight out. I didn't count, you know. I wasn't a girl, with a girl's feelings, or anything. I was nobody. It was just like a business talk. I learned about men from him. He told me what he'd do. He..."

Her voice died away in sadness, and in the silence she could hear Billy grit his teeth.

"You can't tell me," he cried. "I know. It's a dirty world—an unfair, lousy world. I can't make it out. They's no squareness in it.—Women, with the best that's in 'em, bought an' sold like horses. I don't understand women that way. I don't understand men that way. I can't see how a man gets anything but cheated when he buys such things. It's funny, ain't it? Take my boss an' his horses. He owns women, too. He might a-owned you, just because he's got the price. An', Saxon, you was made for fancy shirtwaists an' all that, but, honest to God, I can't see you payin' for them that way. It'd be a crime—"

He broke off abruptly and reined in the horses. Around a sharp turn, speeding down the grade upon them, had appeared an automobile. With slamming of brakes it was brought to a stop, while the faces of the occupants took new lease of interest of life and stared at the young man and woman in the light rig that barred the way. Billy held up his hand.

"Take the outside, sport," he said to the chauffeur.

"Nothin' doin', kiddo," came the answer, as the chauffeur measured with hard, wise eyes the crumbling edge of the road and the downfall of the outside bank.

"Then we camp," Billy announced cheerfully. "I know the rules of the road. These animals ain't automobile broke altogether, an' if you think I'm goin' to have 'em shy off the grade you got another guess comin'."

A confusion of injured protestation arose from those that sat in the car.

"You needn't be a road-hog because you're a Rube," said the chauffeur. "We ain't a-goin' to hurt your horses. Pull out so we can pass. If you don't..."

"That'll do you, sport," was Billy's retort. "You can't talk that way to yours truly. I got your number an' your tag, my son. You're standin' on your foot.

- 66 -

Back up the grade an' get off of it. Stop on the outside at the first pssin'-place an' we'll pass you. You've got the juice. Throw on the reverse."

After a nervous consultation, the chauffeur obeyed, and the car backed up the hill and out of sight around the turn.

"Them cheap skates," Billy sneered to Saxon, "with a couple of gallons of gasoline an' the price of a machine a-thinkin' they own the roads your folks an' my folks made."

"Talkin' all night about it?" came the chauffeur's voice from around the bend. "Get a move on. You can pass."

"Get off your foot," Billy retorted contemptuously. "I'm a-comin' when I'm ready to come, an' if you ain't given room enough I'll go clean over you an' your load of chicken meat."

He slightly slacked the reins on the restless, head-tossing animals, and without need of chirrup they took the weight of the light vehicle and passed up the hill and apprehensively on the inside of the purring machine.

"Where was we?" Billy queried, as the clear road showed in front. "Yep, take my boss. Why should he own two hundred horses, an' women, an' the rest, an' you an' me own nothin'?"

"You own your silk, Billy," she said softly.

"An' you yours. Yet we sell it to 'em like it was cloth across the counter at so much a yard. I guess you're hep to what a few more years in the laundry'll do to you. Take me. I'm sellin' my silk slow every day I work. See that little finger?" He shifted the reins to one hand for a moment and held up the free hand for inspection. "I can't straighten it like the others, an' it's growin'. I never put it out fightin'. The teamin's done it. That's silk gone across the counter, that's all. Ever see a old four-horse teamster's hands? They look like claws they're that crippled an' twisted."

"Things weren't like that in the old days when our folks crossed the plains," she answered. "They might a-got their fingers twisted, but they owned the best goin' in the way of horses and such."

"Sure. They worked for themselves. They twisted their fingers for themselves. But I'm twistin' my fingers for my boss. Why, d'ye know, Saxon, his hands is soft as a woman's that's never done any work. Yet he owns the horses an' the stables, an' never does a tap of work, an' I manage to scratch my meal-ticket an' my clothes. It's got my goat the way things is run. An' who runs 'em that way? That's what I want to know. Times has changed. Who changed 'em?"

"God didn't."

"You bet your life he didn't. An' that's another thing that gets me. Who's God anyway? If he's runnin' things—an' what good is he if he ain't?—then why does he let my boss, an' men like that cashier you mentioned, why does he let them own the horses, an' buy the women, the nice little girls that oughta be lovin' their own husbands, an' havin' children they're not ashamed of, an' just bein' happy accordin' to their nature?"

CHAPTER XI

The horses, resting frequently and lathered by the work, had climbed the steep grade of the old road to Moraga Valley, and on the divide of the Contra Costa hills the way descended sharply through the green and sunny stillness of Redwood Canyon.

"Say, ain't it swell?" Billy queried, with a wave of his hand indicating the circled tree-groups, the trickle of unseen water, and the summer hum of bees.

"I love it," Saxon affirmed. "It makes me want to live in the country, and I never have."

"Me, too, Saxon. I've never lived in the country in my life—an' all my folks was country folks."

"No cities then. Everybody lived in the country."

"I guess you're right," he nodded. "They just had to live in the country."

There was no brake on the light carriage, and Billy became absorbed in managing his team down the steep, winding road. Saxon leaned back, eyes closed, with a feeling of ineffable rest. Time and again he shot glances at her closed eyes.

"What's the matter?" he asked finally, in mild alarm. "You ain't sick?"

"It's so beautiful I'm afraid to look," she answered. "It's so brave it hurts."

"BRAVE?—now that's funny."

"Isn't it? But it just makes me feel that way. It's brave. Now the houses and streets and things in the city aren't brave. But this is. I don't know why. It just is."

"By golly, I think you're right," he exclaimed. "It strikes me that way, now you speak of it. They ain't no games or tricks here, no cheatin' an' no lyin'. Them trees just stand up natural an' strong an' clean like young boys their first time in the ring before they've learned its rottenness an' how to double-cross an' lay down to the bettin' odds an' the fight-fans. Yep; it is brave. Say, Saxon, you see things, don't you?" His pause was almost wistful, and he looked at her and studied her with a caressing softness that ran through her in resurgent thrills. "D'ye know, I'd just like you to see me fight some time—a real fight, with something doin' every moment. I'd be proud to death to do it for you. An' I'd sure fight some with you lookin' on an' understandin'. That'd be a fight what is, take it from me. An' that's funny, too. I never wanted to fight before a woman in my life. They squeal and screech an' don't understand. But you'd understand. It's dead open an' shut you would."

A little later, swinging along the flat of the valley, through the little clearings of the farmers and the ripe grain-stretches golden in the sunshine, Billy turned to Saxon again.

"Say, you've ben in love with fellows, lots of times. Tell me about it. What's it like?"

She shook her head slowly.

"I only thought I was in love—and not many times, either—"

"Many times!" he cried.

"Not really ever," she assured him, secretly exultant at his unconscious jealousy. "I never was really in love. If I had been I'd be married now. You see, I couldn't see anything else to it but to marry a man if I loved him."

"But suppose he didn't love you?"

"Oh, I don't know," she smiled, half with facetiousness and half with certainty and pride. "I think I could make him love me."

"I guess you sure could," Billy proclaimed enthusiastically.

"The trouble is," she went on, "the men that loved me I never cared for that way.—Oh, look!"

A cottontail rabbit had scuttled across the road, and a tiny dust cloud lingered like smoke, marking the way of his flight. At the next turn a dozen quail exploded into the air from under the noses of the horses. Billy and Saxon exclaimed in mutual delight.

"Gee," he muttered, "I almost wisht I'd ben born a farmer. Folks wasn't made to live in cities."

"Not our kind, at least," she agreed. Followed a pause and a long sigh. "It's all so beautiful. It would be a dream just to live all your life in it. I'd like to be an Indian squaw sometimes."

Several times Billy checked himself on the verge of speech.

"About those fellows you thought you was in love with," he said finally. "You ain't told me, yet."

"You want to know?" she asked. "They didn't amount to anything."

"Of course I want to know. Go ahead. Fire away."

"Well, first there was Al Stanley—"

"What did he do for a livin'?" Billy demanded, almost as with authority.

"He was a gambler."

Billy's face abruptly stiffened, and she could see his eyes cloudy with doubt in the quick glance he flung at her.

"Oh, it was all right," she laughed. "I was only eight years old. You see, I'm beginning at the beginning. It was after my mother died and when I was adopted by Cady. He kept a hotel and saloon. It was down in Los Angeles. Just a small hotel. Workingmen, just common laborers, mostly, and some railroad men, stopped at it, and I guess Al Stanley got his share of their wages. He was so handsome and so quiet and soft-spoken. And he had the nicest eyes and the softest, cleanest hands. I can see them now. He played with me sometimes, in the afternoon, and gave me candy and little presents. He used to sleep most of the day. I didn't know why, then. I thought he was a fairy prince in disguise. And then he got killed, right in the bar-room, but first he killed the man that killed him. So that was the end of that love affair.

"Next was after the asylum, when I was thirteen and living with my brother—I've lived with him ever since. He was a boy that drove a bakery wagon. Almost every morning, on the way to school, I used to pass him. He would come driving down Wood Street and turn in on Twelfth. Maybe it was because he drove a horse that attracted me. Anyway, I must have loved him for a couple of months. Then he lost his job, or something, for another boy drove the wagon. And we'd never even spoken to each other.

"Then there was a bookkeeper when I was sixteen. I seem to run to bookkeepers. It was a bookkeeper at the laundry that Charley Long beat up. This other one was when I was working in Hickmeyer's Cannery. He had soft hands, too. But I quickly got all I wanted of him. He was... well, anyway, he had ideas like your boss. And I never really did love him, truly and honest, Billy. I felt from the first that he wasn't just right. And when I was working in the paper-box factory I thought I loved a clerk in Kahn's Emporium— you know, on Eleventh and Washington. He was all right. That was the trouble with him. He was too much all right. He didn't have any life in him, any go. He wanted to marry me, though. But somehow I couldn't see it. That shows I didn't love him. He was narrow-chested and skinny, and his hands were always cold and fishy. But my! he could dress—just like he came out of a bandbox. He said he was going to drown himself, and all kinds of things, but I broke with him just the same.

"And after that... well, there isn't any after that. I must have got particular, I guess, but I didn't see anybody I could love. It seemed more like a game with the men I met, or a fight. And we never fought fair on either side. Seemed as if we always had cards up our sleeves. We weren't honest or outspoken, but instead it seemed as if we were trying to take advantage of each other. Charley Long was honest, though. And so was that bank cashier. And even they made me have the fight feeling harder than ever. All of them always made me feel I had to take care of myself. They wouldn't. That was sure."

She stopped and looked with interest at the clean profile of his face as he watched and guided the horses. He looked at her inquiringly, and her eyes laughed lazily into his as she stretched her arms.

"That's all," she concluded. "I've told you everything, which I've never done before to any one. And it's your turn now."

"Not much of a turn, Saxon. I've never cared for girls—that is, not enough to want to marry 'em. I always liked men better—fellows like Billy Murphy. Besides, I guess I was too interested in trainin' an' fightin' to bother with women much. Why, Saxon, honest, while I ain't ben altogether good—you understand what I mean—just the same I ain't never talked love to a girl in my life. They was no call to."

"The girls have loved you just the same," she teased, while in her heart was a curious elation at his virginal confession.

He devoted himself to the horses.

"Lots of them," she urged.

Still he did not reply.

"Now, haven't they?"

"Well, it wasn't my fault," he said slowly. "If they wanted to look sideways at me it was up to them. And it was up to me to sidestep if I wanted to, wasn't it? You've no idea, Saxon, how a prizefighter is run after. Why, sometimes it's seemed to me that girls an' women ain't got an ounce of natural shame in their make-up. Oh, I was never afraid of them, believe muh, but I didn't hanker after 'em. A man's a fool that'd let them kind get his goat.
"

"Maybe you haven't got love in you," she challenged.

"Maybe I haven't," was his discouraging reply. "Anyway, I don't see myself lovin' a girl that runs after me. It's all right for Charley-boys, but a man that is a man don't like bein' chased by women."

"My mother always said that love was the greatest thing in the world," Saxon argued. "She wrote poems about it, too. Some of them were published in the San Jose Mercury."

"What do you think about it?"

"Oh, I don't know," she baffled, meeting his eyes with another lazy smile. "All I know is it's pretty good to be alive a day like this."

"On a trip like this—you bet it is," he added promptly.

At one o'clock Billy turned off the road and drove into an open space among the trees.

"Here's where we eat," he announced. "I thought it'd be better to have a lunch by ourselves than stop at one of these roadside dinner counters. An' now, just to make everything safe an' comfortable, I'm goin' to unharness the horses. We got lots of time. You can get the lunch basket out an' spread it on the lap-robe."

As Saxon unpacked the basket she was appalled at his extravagance. She spread an amazing array of ham and chicken sandwiches, crab salad, hard-boiled eggs, pickled pigs' feet, ripe olives and dill pickles, Swiss cheese, salted almonds, oranges and bananas, and several pint bottles of beer. It was the quantity as well as the variety that bothered her. It had the appearance of a reckless attempt to buy out a whole delicatessen shop.

"You oughtn't to blow yourself that way," she reproved him as he sat down beside her. "Why it's enough for half a dozen bricklayers."

"It's all right, isn't it?"

"Yes," she acknowledged. "But that's the trouble. It's too much so."

"Then it's all right," he concluded. "I always believe in havin' plenty. Have some beer to wash the dust away before we begin? Watch out for the glasses. I gotta return them."

Later, the meal finished, he lay on his back, smoking a cigarette, and questioned her about her earlier history. She had been telling him of her life in her brother's house, where she paid four dollars and a half a week board. At fifteen she had graduated from grammar school and gone to work in the jute mills for four dollars a week, three of which she had paid to Sarah.

"How about that saloonkeeper?" Billy asked. "How come it he adopted you?"

She shrugged her shoulders. "I don't know, except that all my relatives were hard up. It seemed they just couldn't get on. They managed to scratch a lean living for themselves, and that was all. Cady—he was the saloonkeeper—had been a soldier in my father's company, and he always swore by Captain Kit, which was their nickname for him. My father had kept the surgeons from amputating his leg in the war, and he never forgot it. He was making money in the hotel and saloon, and I found out afterward he helped out a lot to pay the doctors and to bury my mother alongside of father. I was to go to Uncle Will—that was my mother's wish; but there had been fighting up in the Ventura Mountains where his ranch was, and men had been killed. It was about fences and cattlemen or something, and anyway he was in jail a long time, and when he got his freedom the lawyers had got his ranch. He was an old man, then, and broken, and his wife took sick, and he got a job as night watchman for forty dollars a month. So he couldn't do anything for me, and Cady adopted me.

"Cady was a good man, if he did run a saloon. His wife was a big, handsome-looking woman. I don't think she was all right... and I've heard so since. But she was good to me. I don't care what they say about her, or what she was. She was awful good to me. After he died, she went altogether bad, and so I went into the orphan asylum. It wasn't any too good there, and I had three years of it. And then Tom had married and settled down to steady work, and he took me out to live with him. And—well, I've been working pretty steady ever since."

She gazed sadly away across the fields until her eyes came to rest on a fence bright-splashed with poppies at its base. Billy, who from his supine position had been looking up at her, studying and pleasuring in the pointed oval of her woman's face, reached his hand out slowly as he murmured:

"You poor little kid."

His hand closed sympathetically on her bare forearm, and as she looked down to greet his eyes she saw in them surprise and delight.

"Say, ain't your skin cool though," he said. "Now me, I'm always warm. Feel my hand."

It was warmly moist, and she noted microscopic beads of sweat on his forehead and clean-shaven upper lip.

"My, but you are sweaty."

She bent to him and with her handkerchief dabbed his lip and forehead dry, then dried his palms.

"I breathe through my skin, I guess," he explained. "The wise guys in the trainin' camps and gyms say it's a good sign for health. But somehow I'm sweatin' more than usual now. Funny, ain't it?"

She had been forced to unclasp his hand from her arm in order to dry it, and when she finished, it returned to its old position.

"But, say, ain't your skin cool," he repeated with renewed wonder. "Soft as velvet, too, an' smooth as silk. It feels great."

Gently explorative, he slid his hand from wrist to elbow and came to rest half way back. Tired and languid from the morning in the sun, she found herself thrilling to his touch and half-dreamily deciding that here was a man she could love, hands and all.

"Now I've taken the cool all out of that spot." He did not look up to her, and she could see the roguish smile that curled on his lips. "So I guess I'll try another."

He shifted his hand along her arm with soft sensuousness, and she, looking down at his lips, remembered the long tingling they had given hers the first time they had met.

"Go on and talk," he urged, after a delicious five minutes of silence. "I like to watch your lips talking. It's funny, but every move they make looks like a tickly kiss."

Greatly she wanted to stay where she was. Instead, she said:

"If I talk, you won't like what I say."

"Go on," he insisted. "You can't say anything I won't like."

"Well, there's some poppies over there by the fence I want to pick. And then it's time for us to be going."

"I lose," he laughed. "But you made twenty-five tickle kisses just the same. I counted 'em. I'll tell you what: you sing 'When the Harvest Days Are Over,' and let me have your other cool arm while you're doin' it, and then we'll go."

She sang looking down into his eyes, which were centered, not on hers, but on her lips. When she finished, she slipped his hands from her arms and got up. He was about to start for the horses, when she held her jacket out to him. Despite the independence natural to a girl who earned her own living, she had an innate love of the little services and finenesses; and, also, she remembered from her childhood the talk by the pioneer women of the courtesy and attendance of the caballeros of the Spanish-California days.

Sunset greeted them when, after a wide circle to the east and south, they cleared the divide of the Contra Costa hills and began dropping down the long grade that led past Redwood Peak to Fruitvale. Beneath them stretched the flatlands to the bay, checkerboarded into fields and broken by the towns of Elmhurst, San Leandro, and Haywards. The smoke of Oakland filled the western sky with haze and murk, while beyond, across the bay, they could see the first winking lights of San Francisco.

Darkness was on them, and Billy had become curiously silent. For half an hour he had given no recognition of her existence save once, when the chill evening wind caused him to tuck the robe tightly about her and himself. Half a dozen times Saxon found herself on the verge of the remark, "What's on your mind?" but each time let it remain unuttered. She sat very close to him.

The warmth of their bodies intermingled, and she was aware of a great restfulness and content.

"Say, Saxon," he began abruptly. "It's no use my holdin' it in any longer. It's ben in my mouth all day, ever since lunch. What's the matter with you an' me gettin' married?"

She knew, very quietly and very gladly, that he meant it. Instinctively she was impelled to hold off, to make him woo her, to make herself more desirably valuable ere she yielded. Further, her woman's sensitiveness and pride were offended. She had never dreamed of so forthright and bald a proposal from the man to whom she would give herself. The simplicity and directness of Billy's proposal constituted almost a hurt. On the other hand she wanted him so much—how much she had not realized until now, when he had so unexpectedly made himself accessible.

"Well you gotta say something, Saxon. Hand it to me, good or bad; but anyway hand it to me. An' just take into consideration that I love you. Why, I love you like the very devil, Saxon. I must, because I'm askin' you to marry me, an' I never asked any girl that before."

Another silence fell, and Saxon found herself dwelling on the warmth, tingling now, under the lap-robe. When she realized whither her thoughts led, she blushed guiltily in the darkness.

"How old are you, Billy?" she questioned, with a suddenness and irrelevance as disconcerting as his first words had been.

"Twenty-two," he answered.

"I am twenty-four."

"As if I didn't know. When you left the orphan asylum and how old you were, how long you worked in the jute mills, the cannery, the paper-box factory, the laundry—maybe you think I can't do addition. I knew how old you was, even to your birthday."

"That doesn't change the fact that I'm two years older."

"What of it? If it counted for anything, I wouldn't be lovin' you, would I? Your mother was dead right. Love's the big stuff. It's what counts. Don't you see? I just love you, an' I gotta have you. It's natural, I guess; and I've always found with horses, dogs, and other folks, that what's natural is right. There's no gettin' away from it, Saxon; I gotta have you, an' I'm just hopin' hard you gotta have me. Maybe my hands ain't soft like bookkeepers' an' clerks, but they can work for you, an' fight like Sam Hill for you, and, Saxon, they can love you."

The old sex antagonism which she had always experienced with men seemed to have vanished. She had no sense of being on the defensive. This was no game. It was what she had been looking for and dreaming about. Before Billy she was defenseless, and there was an all-satisfaction in the knowledge. She could deny him nothing. Not even if he proved to be like the others. And out of the greatness of the thought rose a greater thought—he would not so prove himself.

She did not speak. Instead, in a glow of spirit and flesh, she reached out to his left hand and gently tried to remove it from the rein. He did not understand; but when she persisted he shifted the rein to his right and let her have her will with the other hand. Her head bent over it, and she kissed the teamster callouses.

For the moment he was stunned.

"You mean it?" he stammered.

For reply, she kissed the hand again and murmured:

"I love your hands, Billy. To me they are the most beautiful hands in the world, and it would take hours of talking to tell you all they mean to me."

"Whoa!" he called to the horses.

He pulled them in to a standstill, soothed them with his voice, and made the reins fast around the whip. Then he turned to her with arms around her and lips to lips.

"Oh, Billy, I'll make you a good wife," she sobbed, when the kiss was broken.

He kissed her wet eyes and found her lips again.

"Now you know what I was thinkin' and why I was sweatin' when we was eatin' lunch. Just seemed I couldn't hold in much longer from tellin' you. Why, you know, you looked good to me from the first moment I spotted you."

"And I think I loved you from that first day, too, Billy. And I was so proud of you all that day, you were so kind and gentle, and so strong, and the way the men all respected you and the girls all wanted you, and the way you fought those three Irishmen when I was behind the picnic table. I couldn't love or marry a man I wasn't proud of, and I'm so proud of you, so proud."

"Not half as much as I am right now of myself," he answered, "for having won you. It's too good to be true. Maybe the alarm clock'll go off and wake me up in a couple of minutes. Well, anyway, if it does, I'm goin' to make the best of them two minutes first. Watch out I don't eat you, I'm that hungry for you."

He smothered her in an embrace, holding her so tightly to him that it almost hurt. After what was to her an age-long period of bliss, his arms relaxed and he seemed to make an effort to draw himself together.

"An' the clock ain't gone off yet," he whispered against her cheek. "And it's a dark night, an' there's Fruitvale right ahead, an' if there ain't King and Prince standin' still in the middle of the road. I never thought the time'd come when I wouldn't want to take the ribbons on a fine pair of horses. But this is that time. I just can't let go of you, and I've gotta some time to-night. It hurts worse'n poison, but here goes."

He restored her to herself, tucked the disarranged robe about her, and chirruped to the impatient team.

Half an hour later he called "Whoa!"

"I know I'm awake now, but I don't know but maybe I dreamed all the rest, and I just want to make sure."

And again he made the reins fast and took her in his arms.

CHAPTER XII

The days flew by for Saxon. She worked on steadily at the laundry, even doing more overtime than usual, and all her free waking hours were devoted to preparations for the great change and to Billy. He had proved himself God's own impetuous lover by insisting on getting married the next day after the proposal, and then by resolutely refusing to compromise on more than a week's delay.

"Why wait?" he demanded. "We're not gettin' any younger so far as I can notice, an' think of all we lose every day we wait."

In the end, he gave in to a month, which was well, for in two weeks he was transferred, with half a dozen other drivers, to work from the big stables of Corberly and Morrison in West Oakland. House-hunting in the other end of town ceased, and on Pine Street, between Fifth and Fourth, and in immediate proximity to the great Southern Pacific railroad yards, Billy and Saxon rented a neat cottage of four small rooms for ten dollars a month.

"Dog-cheap is what I call it, when I think of the small rooms I've ben soaked for," was Billy's judgment. "Look at the one I got now, not as big as the smallest here, an' me payin' six dollars a month for it."

"But it's furnished," Saxon reminded him. "You see, that makes a difference."

But Billy didn't see.

"I ain't much of a scholar, Saxon, but I know simple arithmetic; I've soaked my watch when I was hard up, and I can calculate interest. How much do you figure it will cost to furnish the house, carpets on the floor, linoleum on the kitchen, and all?"

"We can do it nicely for three hundred dollars," she answered. "I've been thinking it over and I'm sure we can do it for that."

"Three hundred," he muttered, wrinkling his brows with concentration. "Three hundred, say at six per cent.—that'd be six cents on the dollar, sixty cents on ten dollars, six dollars on the hundred, on three hundred eighteen dollars. Say—I'm a bear at multiplyin' by ten. Now divide eighteen by twelve, that'd be a dollar an' a half a month interest." He stopped, satisfied that he had proved his contention. Then his face quickened with a fresh thought. "Hold on! That ain't all. That'd be the interest on the furniture for four rooms. Divide by four. What's a dollar an' a half divided by four?"

"Four into fifteen, three times and three to carry," Saxon recited glibly. "Four into thirty is seven, twenty-eight, two to carry; and two-fourths is one-half. There you are."

"Gee! You're the real bear at figures." He hesitated. "I didn't follow you. How much did you say it was?"

"Thirty-seven and a half cents."

"Ah, ha! Now we'll see how much I've ben gouged for my one room. Ten dollars a month for four rooms is two an' a half for one. Add thirty-seven an' a half cents interest on furniture, an' that makes two dollars an' eighty-seven an' a half cents. Subtract from six dollars...."

"Three dollars and twelve and a half cents," she supplied quickly.

"There we are! Three dollars an' twelve an' a half cents I'm jiggered out of on the room I'm rentin'. Say! Bein' married is like savin' money, ain't it?"

"But furniture wears out, Billy."

"By golly, I never thought of that. It ought to be figured, too. Anyway, we've got a snap here, and next Saturday afternoon you've gotta get off from the laundry so as we can go an' buy our furniture. I saw Salinger's last night. I give'm fifty down, and the rest installment plan, ten dollars a month. In twenty-five months the furniture's ourn. An' remember, Saxon, you wanta buy everything you want, no matter how much it costs. No scrimpin' on what's for you an' me. Get me?"

She nodded, with no betrayal on her face of the myriad secret economies that filled her mind. A hint of moisture glistened in her eyes.

"You're so good to me, Billy," she murmured, as she came to him and was met inside his arms.

"So you've gone an' done it," Mary commented, one morning in the laundry. They had not been at work ten minutes ere her eye had glimpsed the topaz ring on the third finger of Saxon's left hand. "Who's the lucky one? Charley Long or Billy Roberts?"

"Billy," was the answer.

"Huh! Takin' a young boy to raise, eh?"

Saxon showed that the stab had gone home, and Mary was all contrition.

"Can't you take a josh? I'm glad to death at the news. Billy's a awful good man, and I'm glad to see you get him. There ain't many like him knockin' 'round, an' they ain't to be had for the askin'. An' you're both lucky. You was just made for each other, an' you'll make him a better wife than any girl I know. When is it to be?"

Going home from the laundry a few days later, Saxon encountered Charley Long. He blocked the sidewalk, and compelled speech with her.

"So you're runnin' with a prizefighter," he sneered. "A blind man can see your finish."

For the first time she was unafraid of this big-bodied, black-browed man with the hairy-matted hands and fingers. She held up her left hand.

"See that? It's something, with all your strength, that you could never put on my finger. Billy Roberts put it on inside a week. He got your number, Charley Long, and at the same time he got me."

"Skiddoo for you," Long retorted. "Twenty-three's your number."

"He's not like you," Saxon went on. "He's a man, every bit of him, a fine, clean man."

Long laughed hoarsely.

"He's got your goat all right."

"And yours," she flashed back.

"I could tell you things about him. Saxon, straight, he ain't no good. If I was to tell you—"

"You'd better get out of my way," she interrupted, "or I'll tell him, and you know what you'll get, you great big bully."

Long shuffled uneasily, then reluctantly stepped aside.

"You're a caution," he said, half admiringly.

"So's Billy Roberts," she laughed, and continued on her way. After half a dozen steps she stopped. "Say," she called.

The big blacksmith turned toward her with eagerness.

"About a block back," she said, "I saw a man with hip disease. You might go and beat him up."

Of one extravagance Saxon was guilty in the course of the brief engagement period. A full day's wages she spent in the purchase of half a dozen cabinet photographs of herself. Billy had insisted that life was unendurable could he not look upon her semblance the last thing when he went to bed at night and the first thing when he got up in the morning. In return, his photographs, one conventional and one in the stripped fighting costume of the ring, ornamented her looking glass. It was while gazing at the latter that she was reminded of her wonderful mother's tales of the ancient Saxons and sea-foragers of the English coasts. From the chest of drawers that had crossed the plains she drew forth another of her several precious heirlooms—a scrap-book of her mother's in which was pasted much of the fugitive newspaper verse of pioneer California days. Also, there were copies of paintings and old wood engravings from the magazines of a generation and more before.

Saxon ran the pages with familiar fingers and stopped at the picture she was seeking. Between bold headlands of rock and under a gray cloud-blown sky, a dozen boats, long and lean and dark, beaked like monstrous birds, were landing on a foam-whitened beach of sand. The men in the boats, half naked, huge-muscled and fair-haired, wore winged helmets. In their hands were swords and spears, and they were leaping, waist-deep, into the sea-wash and wading ashore. Opposed to them, contesting the landing, were skin-clad savages, unlike Indians, however, who clustered on the beach or waded into the water to their knees. The first blows were being struck, and here and there the bodies of the dead and wounded rolled in the surf. One fair-haired invader lay across the gunwale of a boat, the manner of his death told by the arrow that transfixed his breast. In the air, leaping past him into the water, sword in hand, was Billy. There was no mistaking it. The striking blondness, the face, the eyes, the mouth were the same. The very expression on the face was what had been on Billy's the day of the picnic when he faced the three wild Irishmen.

Somewhere out of the ruck of those warring races had emerged Billy's ancestors, and hers, was her afterthought, as she closed the book and put it back in the drawer. And some of those ancestors had made this ancient and battered chest of drawers which had crossed the salt ocean and the plains and been pierced by a bullet in the fight with the Indians at Little Meadow. Almost, it seemed, she could visualize the women who had kept their pretties and their family homespun in its drawers—the women of those wandering generations who were grandmothers and greater great grandmothers of her own mother. Well, she sighed, it was a good stock to be born of, a hard-working, hard-fighting stock. She fell to wondering what her life would have been like had she been born a Chinese woman, or an Italian woman like those she saw, head-shawled or bareheaded, squat, ungainly and swarthy, who carried great loads of driftwood on their heads up from the beach. Then she laughed at her foolishness, remembered Billy and the four-roomed cottage on Pine Street, and went to bed with her mind filled for the hundredth time with the details of the furniture.

CHAPTER XIII

"Our cattle were all played out," Saxon was saying, "and winter was so near that we couldn't dare try to cross the Great American Desert, so our train stopped in Salt Lake City that winter. The Mormons hadn't got bad yet, and they were good to us."

"You talk as though you were there," Bert commented.

"My mother was," Saxon answered proudly. "She was nine years old that winter."

They were seated around the table in the kitchen of the little Pine Street cottage, making a cold lunch of sandwiches, tamales, and bottled beer. It being Sunday, the four were free from work, and they had come early, to work harder than on any week day, washing walls and windows, scrubbing floors, laying carpets and linoleum, hanging curtains, setting up the stove, putting the kitchen utensils and dishes away, and placing the furniture.

"Go on with the story, Saxon," Mary begged. "I'm just dyin' to hear. And Bert, you just shut up and listen."

"Well, that winter was when Del Hancock showed up. He was Kentucky born, but he'd been in the West for years. He was a scout, like Kit Carson, and he knew him well. Many's a time Kit Carson and he slept under the same blankets. They were together to California and Oregon with General Fremont. Well, Del Hancock was passing on his way through Salt Lake, going I don't know where to raise a company of Rocky Mountain trappers to go after beaver some new place he knew about. He was a handsome man. He wore his hair long like in pictures, and had a silk sash around his waist he'd learned to wear in California from the Spanish, and two revolvers in his belt. Any woman 'd fall in love with him first sight. Well, he saw Sadie, who was my mother's oldest sister, and I guess she looked good to him, for he stopped right there in Salt Lake and didn't go a step. He was a great Indian fighter, too, and I heard my Aunt Villa say, when I was a little girl, that he had the blackest, brightest eyes, and that the way he looked was like an eagle. He'd fought duels, too, the way they did in those days, and he wasn't afraid of anything.

"Sadie was a beauty, and she flirted with him and drove him crazy. Maybe she wasn't sure of her own mind, I don't know. But I do know that she didn't give in as easy as I did to Billy. Finally, he couldn't stand it any more. He rode up that night on horseback, wild as could be. 'Sadie,' he said, 'if you don't promise to marry me to-morrow, I'll shoot myself to-night right back of the corral.' And he'd have done it, too, and Sadie knew it, and said she would. Didn't they make love fast in those days?"

"Oh, I don't know," Mary sniffed. "A week after you first laid eyes on Billy you was engaged. Did Billy say he was going to shoot himself back of the laundry if you turned him down?"

"I didn't give him a chance," Saxon confessed. "Anyway Del Hancock and Aunt Sadie got married next day. And they were very happy afterward, only she died. And after that he was killed, with General Custer and all the rest, by the Indians. He was an old man by then, but I guess he got his share of Indians before they got him. Men like him always died fighting, and they took their dead with them. I used to know Al Stanley when I was a little girl. He was a gambler, but he was game. A railroad man shot him in the back when he was sitting at a table. That shot killed him, too. He died in about two seconds. But before he died he'd pulled his gun and put three bullets into the man that killed him."

"I don't like fightin'," Mary protested. "It makes me nervous. Bert gives me the willies the way he's always lookin' for trouble. There ain't no sense in it."

"And I wouldn't give a snap of my fingers for a man without fighting spirit," Saxon answered. "Why, we wouldn't be here to-day if it wasn't for the fighting spirit of our people before us."

"You've got the real goods of a fighter in Billy," Bert assured her; "a yard long and a yard wide and genuine A Number One, long-fleeced wool. Billy's a Mohegan with a scalp-lock, that's what he is. And when he gets his mad up it's a case of get out from under or something will fall on you—hard."

"Just like that," Mary added.

Billy, who had taken no part in the conversation, got up, glanced into the bedroom off the kitchen, went into the parlor and the bedroom off the parlor, then returned and stood gazing with puzzled brows into the kitchen bedroom.

"What's eatin' you, old man," Bert queried. "You look as though you'd lost something or was markin' a three-way ticket. What you got on your chest? Cough it up."

"Why, I'm just thinkin' where in Sam Hill's the bed an' stuff for the back bedroom."

"There isn't any," Saxon explained. "We didn't order any."

"Then I'll see about it to-morrow."

"What d'ye want another bed for?" asked Bert. "Ain't one bed enough for the two of you?"

"You shut up, Bert!" Mary cried. "Don't get raw."

"Whoa, Mary!" Bert grinned. "Back up. You're in the wrong stall as usual."

"We don't need that room," Saxon was saying to Billy. "And so I didn't plan any furniture. That money went to buy better carpets and a better stove."

Billy came over to her, lifted her from the chair, and seated himself with her on his knees.

"That's right, little girl. I'm glad you did. The best for us every time. And to-morrow night I want you to run up with me to Salinger's an' pick out a good bedroom set an' carpet for that room. And it must be good. Nothin' snide."

"It will cost fifty dollars," she objected.

"That's right," he nodded. "Make it cost fifty dollars and not a cent less. We're goin' to have the best. And what's the good of an empty room? It'd make the house look cheap. Why, I go around now, seein' this little nest just as it grows an' softens, day by day, from the day we paid the cash money down an' nailed the keys. Why, almost every moment I'm drivin' the horses, all day long, I just keep on seein' this nest. And when we're married, I'll go on seein' it. And I want to see it complete. If that room'd be bare-floored an' empty, I'd see nothin' but it and its bare floor all day long. I'd be cheated. The house'd be a lie. Look at them curtains you put up in it, Saxon. That's to make believe to the neighbors that it's furnished. Saxon, them curtains are lyin' about that room, makin' a noise for every one to hear that that room's furnished. Nitsky for us. I'm goin' to see that them curtains tell the truth."

"You might rent it," Bert suggested. "You're close to the railroad yards, and it's only two blocks to a restaurant."

"Not on your life. I ain't marryin' Saxon to take in lodgers. If I can't take care of her, d'ye know what I'll do? Go down to Long Wharf, say 'Here goes nothin',' an' jump into the bay with a stone tied to my neck. Ain't I right, Saxon?"

It was contrary to her prudent judgment, but it fanned her pride. She threw her arms around her lover's neck, and said, ere she kissed him:

"You're the boss, Billy. What you say goes, and always will go."

"Listen to that!" Bert gibed to Mary. "That's the stuff. Saxon's onto her job."

"I guess we'll talk things over together first before ever I do anything," Billy was saying to Saxon.

"Listen to that," Mary triumphed. "You bet the man that marries me'll have to talk things over first."

"Billy's only givin' her hot air," Bert plagued. "They all do it before they're married."

Mary sniffed contemptuously.

"I'll bet Saxon leads him around by the nose. And I'm goin' to say, loud an' strong, that I'll lead the man around by the nose that marries me."

"Not if you love him," Saxon interposed.

"All the more reason," Mary pursued.

Bert assumed an expression and attitude of mournful dejection.

"Now you see why me an' Mary don't get married," he said. "I'm some big Indian myself, an' I'll be everlastingly jiggerooed if I put up for a wigwam I can't be boss of."

"And I'm no squaw," Mary retaliated, "an' I wouldn't marry a big buck Indian if all the rest of the men in the world was dead."

"Well this big buck Indian ain't asked you yet."

"He knows what he'd get if he did."

"And after that maybe he'll think twice before he does ask you."

Saxon, intent on diverting the conversation into pleasanter channels, clapped her hands as if with sudden recollection.

"Oh! I forgot! I want to show you something." From her purse she drew a slender ring of plain gold and passed it around. "My mother's wedding ring. I've worn it around my neck always, like a locket. I cried for it so in the orphan asylum that the matron gave it back for me to wear. And now, just to think, after next Tuesday I'll be wearing it on my finger. Look, Billy, see the engraving on the inside."

"C to D, 1879," he read.

"Carlton to Daisy—Carlton was my father's first name. And now, Billy, you've got to get it engraved for you and me."

Mary was all eagerness and delight.

"Oh, it's fine," she cried. "W to S, 1907."

Billy considered a moment.

"No, that wouldn't be right, because I'm not giving it to Saxon."

"I'll tell you what," Saxon said. "W and S."

"Nope." Billy shook his head. "S and W, because you come first with me."

"If I come first with you, you come first with us. Billy, dear, I insist on W and S."

"You see," Mary said to Bert. "Having her own way and leading him by the nose already."

Saxon acknowledged the sting.

"Anyway you want, Billy," she surrendered. His arms tightened about her.

"We'll talk it over first, I guess."

CHAPTER XIV

Sarah was conservative. Worse, she had crystallized at the end of her love-time with the coming of her first child. After that she was as set in her ways as plaster in a mold. Her mold was the prejudices and notions of her girlhood and the house she lived in. So habitual was she that any change in the customary round assumed the proportions of a revolution. Tom had gone through many of these revolutions, three of them when he moved house. Then his stamina broke, and he never moved house again.

So it was that Saxon had held back the announcement of her approaching marriage until it was unavoidable. She expected a scene, and she got it.

"A prizefighter, a hoodlum, a plug-ugly," Sarah sneered, after she had exhausted herself of all calamitous forecasts of her own future and the future of her children in the absence of Saxon's weekly four dollars and a half. "I don't know what your mother'd thought if she lived to see the day when you took up with a tough like Bill Roberts. Bill! Why, your mother was too refined to associate with a man that was called Bill. And all I can say is you can say good-bye to silk stockings and your three pair of shoes. It won't be long before you'll think yourself lucky to go sloppin' around in Congress gaiters and cotton stockin's two pair for a quarter."

"Oh, I'm not afraid of Billy not being able to keep me in all kinds of shoes," Saxon retorted with a proud toss of her head.

"You don't know what you're talkin' about." Sarah paused to laugh in mirthless discordance. "Watch for the babies to come. They come faster than wages raise these days."

"But we're not going to have any babies... that is, at first. Not until after the furniture is all paid for anyway."

"Wise in your generation, eh? In my days girls were more modest than to know anything about disgraceful subjects."

"As babies?" Saxon queried, with a touch of gentle malice.

"Yes, as babies."

"The first I knew that babies were disgraceful. Why, Sarah, you, with your five, how disgraceful you have been. Billy and I have decided not to be half as disgraceful. We're only going to have two—a boy and a girl."

Tom chuckled, but held the peace by hiding his face in his coffee cup. Sarah, though checked by this flank attack, was herself an old hand in the art. So temporary was the setback that she scarcely paused ere hurling her assault from a new angle.

"An' marryin' so quick, all of a sudden, eh? If that ain't suspicious, nothin' is. I don't know what young women's comin' to. They ain't decent, I tell you. They ain't decent. That's what comes of Sunday dancin' an' all the rest. Young women nowadays are like a lot of animals. Such fast an' looseness I never saw...."

Saxon was white with anger, but while Sarah wandered on in her diatribe, Tom managed to wink privily and prodigiously at his sister and to implore her to help in keeping the peace.

"It's all right, kid sister," he comforted Saxon when they were alone. "There's no use talkin' to Sarah. Bill Roberts is a good boy. I know a lot about him. It does you proud to get him for a husband. You're bound to be happy with him..." His voice sank, and his face seemed suddenly to be very old and tired as he went on anxiously. "Take warning from Sarah. Don't nag. Whatever you do, don't nag. Don't give him a perpetual-motion line of chin. Kind of let him talk once in a while. Men have some horse sense, though Sarah don't know it. Why, Sarah actually loves me, though she don't make a noise like it. The thing for you is to love your husband, and, by thunder, to make a noise of lovin' him, too. And then you can kid him into doing 'most anything you want. Let him have his way once in a while, and he'll let you have yourn. But you just go on lovin' him, and leanin' on his judgement—he's no fool—and you'll be all hunky-dory. I'm scared from goin' wrong, what of Sarah. But I'd sooner be loved into not going wrong."

"Oh, I'll do it, Tom," Saxon nodded, smiling through the tears his sympathy had brought into her eyes. "And on top of it I'm going to do something else, I'm going to make Billy love me and just keep on loving me. And then I won't have to kid him into doing some of the things I want. He'll do them because he loves me, you see."

"You got the right idea, Saxon. Stick with it, an' you'll win out."

Later, when she had put on her hat to start for the laundry, she found Tom waiting for her at the corner.

"An', Saxon," he said, hastily and haltingly, "you won't take anything I've said... you know... —about Sarah... as bein' in any way disloyal to her? She's a good woman, an' faithful. An' her life ain't so easy by a long shot. I'd bite out my tongue before I'd say anything against her. I guess all folks have their troubles. It's hell to be poor, ain't it?"

"You've been awful good to me, Tom. I can never forget it. And I know Sarah means right. She does do her best."

"I won't be able to give you a wedding present," her brother ventured apologetically. "Sarah won't hear of it. Says we didn't get none from my folks when we got married. But I got something for you just the same. A surprise. You'd never guess it."

Saxon waited.

"When you told me you was goin' to get married, I just happened to think of it, an' I wrote to brother George, askin' him for it for you. An' by thunder he sent it by express. I didn't tell you because I didn't know but maybe he'd sold it. He did sell the silver spurs. He needed the money, I guess. But the other, I had it sent to the shop so as not to bother Sarah, an' I sneaked it in last night an' hid it in the woodshed."

"Oh, it is something of my father's! What is it? Oh, what is it?"

"His army sword."

"The one he wore on his roan war horse! Oh, Tom, you couldn't give me a better present. Let's go back now. I want to see it. We can slip in the back way. Sarah's washing in the kitchen, and she won't begin hanging out for an hour."

"I spoke to Sarah about lettin' you take the old chest of drawers that was your mother's," Tom whispered, as they stole along the narrow alley between the houses. "Only she got on her high horse. Said that Daisy was as much my mother as yourn, even if we did have different fathers, and that the chest had always belonged in Daisy's family and not Captain Kit's, an' that it was mine, an' what was mine she had some say-so about."

"It's all right," Saxon reassured him. "She sold it to me last night. She was waiting up for me when I got home with fire in her eye."

"Yep, she was on the warpath all day after I mentioned it. How much did you give her for it?"

"Six dollars."

"Robbery—it ain't worth it," Tom groaned. "It's all cracked at one end and as old as the hills."

"I'd have given ten dollars for it. I'd have given 'most anything for it, Tom. It was mother's, you know. I remember it in her room when she was still alive."

In the woodshed Tom resurrected the hidden treasure and took off the wrapping paper. Appeared a rusty, steel-scabbarded saber of the heavy type carried by cavalry officers in Civil War days. It was attached to a moth-eaten sash of thick-woven crimson silk from which hung heavy silk tassels. Saxon almost seized it from her brother in her eagerness. She drew forth the blade and pressed her lips to the steel.

It was her last day at the laundry. She was to quit work that evening for good. And the next afternoon, at five, she and Billy were to go before a justice of the peace and be married. Bert and Mary were to be the witnesses, and after that the four were to go to a private room in Barnum's Restaurant for the wedding supper. That over, Bert and Mary would proceed to a dance at Myrtle Hall, while Billy and Saxon would take the Eighth Street car to Seventh and Pine. Honeymoons are infrequent in the working class. The next morning Billy must be at the stable at his regular hour to drive his team out.

All the women in the fancy starch room knew it was Saxon's last day. Many exulted for her, and not a few were envious of her, in that she had won a husband and to freedom from the suffocating slavery of the ironing board. Much of bantering she endured; such was the fate of every girl who married out of the fancy starch room. But Saxon was too happy to be hurt by the teasing, a great deal of which was gross, but all of which was good-natured.

In the steam that arose from under her iron, and on the surfaces of the dainty lawns and muslins that flew under her hands, she kept visioning herself in the Pine Street cottage; and steadily she hummed under her breath her paraphrase of the latest popular song:

"And when I work, and when I work, I'll always work for Billy."

By three in the afternoon the strain of the piece-workers in the humid, heated room grew tense. Elderly women gasped and sighed; the color went out of the cheeks of the young women, their faces became drawn and dark circles formed under their eyes; but all held on with weary, unabated speed. The tireless, vigilant forewoman kept a sharp lookout for incipient hysteria, and once led a narrow-chested, stoop-shouldered young thing out of the place in time to prevent a collapse.

Saxon was startled by the wildest scream of terror she had ever heard. The tense thread of human resolution snapped; wills and nerves broke down, and a hundred women suspended their irons or dropped them. It was Mary who had screamed so terribly, and Saxon saw a strange black animal flapping great claw-like wings and nestling on Mary's shoulder. With the scream, Mary crouched down, and the strange creature, darting into the air, fluttered full into the startled face of a woman at the next board. This woman promptly screamed and fainted. Into the air again, the flying thing darted hither and thither, while the shrieking, shrinking women threw up their arms, tried to run away along the aisles, or cowered under their ironing boards.

"It's only a bat!" the forewoman shouted. She was furious. "Ain't you ever seen a bat? It won't eat you!"

But they were ghetto people, and were not to be quieted. Some woman who could not see the cause of the uproar, out of her overwrought apprehension raised the cry of fire and precipitated the panic rush for the doors. All of them were screaming the stupid, soul-sickening high note of terror, drowning the forewoman's voice. Saxon had been merely startled at first, but the screaming panic broke her grip on herself and swept her away. Though she did not scream, she fled with the rest. When this horde of crazed women debouched on the next department, those who worked there joined in the stampede to escape from they knew not what danger. In ten minutes the laundry was deserted, save for a few men wandering about with hand grenades in futile search for the cause of the disturbance.

The forewoman was stout, but indomitable. Swept along half the length of an aisle by the terror-stricken women, she had broken her way back through the rout and quickly caught the light-blinded visitant in a clothes basket.

"Maybe I don't know what God looks like, but take it from me I've seen a tintype of the devil," Mary gurgled, emotionally fluttering back and forth between laughter and tears.

But Saxon was angry with herself, for she had been as frightened as the rest in that wild flight for out-of-doors.

"We're a lot of fools," she said. "It was only a bat. I've heard about them. They live in the country. They wouldn't hurt a fly. They can't see in the daytime. That was what was the matter with this one. It was only a bat."

"Huh, you can't string me," Mary replied. "It was the devil." She sobbed a moment, and then laughed hysterically again. "Did you see Mrs. Bergstrom faint? And it only touched her in the face. Why, it was on my shoulder and touching my bare neck like the hand of a corpse. And I didn't faint." She laughed again. "I guess, maybe, I was too scared to faint."

"Come on back," Saxon urged. "We've lost half an hour."

"Not me. I'm goin' home after that, if they fire me. I couldn't iron for sour apples now, I'm that shaky."

One woman had broken a leg, another an arm, and a number nursed milder bruises and bruises. No bullying nor entreating of the forewoman could persuade the women to return to work. They were too upset and nervous, and only here and there could one be found brave enough to re-enter the building for the hats and lunch baskets of the others. Saxon was one of the handful that returned and worked till six o'clock.

CHAPTER XV

"Why, Bert!—you're squiffed!" Mary cried reproachfully.

The four were at the table in the private room at Barnum's. The wedding supper, simple enough, but seemingly too expensive to Saxon, had been eaten. Bert, in his hand a glass of California red wine, which the management supplied for fifty cents a bottle, was on his feet endeavoring a speech. His face was flushed; his black eyes were feverishly bright.

"You've ben drinkin' before you met me," Mary continued. "I can see it stickin' out all over you."

"Consult an oculist, my dear," he replied. "Bertram is himself to-night. An' he is here, arisin' to his feet to give the glad hand to his old pal. Bill, old man, here's to you. It's how-de-do an' good-bye, I guess. You're a married man now, Bill, an' you got to keep regular hours. No more runnin' around with the boys. You gotta take care of yourself, an' get your life insured, an' take out an accident policy, an' join a buildin' an' loan society, an' a buryin' association—"

"Now you shut up, Bert," Mary broke in. "You don't talk about buryin's at weddings. You oughta be ashamed of yourself."

"Whoa, Mary! Back up! I said what I said because I meant it. I ain't thinkin' what Mary thinks. What I was thinkin'.... Let me tell you what I was thinkin'. I said buryin' association, didn't I? Well, it was not with the idea of castin' gloom over this merry gatherin'. Far be it...."

He was so evidently seeking a way out of his predicament, that Mary tossed her head triumphantly. This acted as a spur to his reeling wits.

"Let me tell you why," he went on. "Because, Bill, you got such an all-fired pretty wife, that's why. All the fellows is crazy over her, an' when they get to runnin' after her, what'll you be doin'? You'll be gettin' busy. And then won't you need a buryin' association to bury 'em? I just guess yes. That was the compliment to your good taste in skirts I was tryin' to come across with when Mary butted in."

His glittering eyes rested for a moment in bantering triumph on Mary.

"Who says I'm squiffed? Me? Not on your life. I'm seein' all things in a clear white light. An' I see Bill there, my old friend Bill. An' I don't see two Bills. I see only one. Bill was never two-faced in his life. Bill, old man, when I look at you there in the married harness, I'm sorry—" He ceased abruptly and turned on Mary. "Now don't go up in the air, old girl. I'm onto my job. My grandfather was a state senator, and he could spiel graceful an' pleasin' till the cows come home. So can I.—Bill, when I look at you, I'm sorry. I repeat,

I'm sorry." He glared challengingly at Mary. "For myself when I look at you an' know all the happiness you got a hammerlock on. Take it from me, you're a wise guy, bless the women. You've started well. Keep it up. Marry 'em all, bless 'em. Bill, here's to you. You're a Mohegan with a scalplock. An' you got a squaw that is some squaw, take it from me. Minnehaha, here's to you—to the two of you—an' to the papooses, too, gosh-dang them!"

He drained the glass suddenly and collapsed in his chair, blinking his eyes across at the wedded couple while tears trickled unheeded down his cheeks. Mary's hand went out soothingly to his, completing his break-down.

"By God, I got a right to cry," he sobbed. "I'm losin' my best friend, ain't I? It'll never be the same again never. When I think of the fun, an' scrapes, an' good times Bill an' me has had together, I could darn near hate you, Saxon, sittin' there with your hand in his."

"Cheer up, Bert," she laughed gently. "Look at whose hand you are holding."

"Aw, it's only one of his cryin' jags," Mary said, with a harshness that her free hand belied as it caressed his hair with soothing strokes. "Buck up, Bert. Everything's all right. And now it's up to Bill to say something after your dandy spiel."

Bert recovered himself quickly with another glass of wine.

"Kick in, Bill," he cried. "It's your turn now."

"I'm no hotair artist," Billy grumbled. "What'll I say, Saxon? They ain't no use tellin' 'em how happy we are. They know that."

"Tell them we're always going to be happy," she said. "And thank them for all their good wishes, and we both wish them the same. And we're always going to be together, like old times, the four of us. And tell them they're invited down to 507 Pine Street next Sunday for Sunday dinner.—And, Mary, if you want to come Saturday night you can sleep in the spare bedroom."

"You've told'm yourself, better'n I could." Billy clapped his hands. "You did yourself proud, an' I guess they ain't much to add to it, but just the same I'm goin' to pass them a hot one."

He stood up, his hand on his glass. His clear blue eyes under the dark brows and framed by the dark lashes, seemed a deeper blue, and accentuated the blondness of hair and skin. The smooth cheeks were rosy—not with wine, for it was only his second glass—but with health and joy. Saxon, looking up at him, thrilled with pride in him, he was so well-dressed, so strong, so handsome, so clean-looking—her man-boy. And she was aware of pride in herself, in her woman's desirableness that had won for her so wonderful a lover.

"Well, Bert an' Mary, here you are at Saxon's and my wedding supper. We're just goin' to take all your good wishes to heart, we wish you the same back, and when we say it we mean more than you think we mean. Saxon an' I believe in tit for tat. So we're wishin' for the day when the table is turned clear around an' we're sittin' as guests at your weddin' supper. And then, when you come to Sunday dinner, you can both stop Saturday night in the spare bedroom. I guess I was wised up when I furnished it, eh?"

"I never thought it of you, Billy!" Mary exclaimed. "You're every bit as raw as Bert. But just the same..."

There was a rush of moisture to her eyes. Her voice faltered and broke. She smiled through her tears at them, then turned to look at Bert, who put his arm around her and gathered her on to his knees.

When they left the restaurant, the four walked to Eighth and Broadway, where they stopped beside the electric car. Bert and Billy were awkward and silent, oppressed by a strange aloofness. But Mary embraced Saxon with fond anxiousness.

"It's all right, dear," Mary whispered. "Don't be scared. It's all right. Think of all the other women in the world."

The conductor clanged the gong, and the two couples separated in a sudden hubbub of farewell.

"Oh, you Mohegan!" Bert called after, as the car got under way. "Oh, you Minnehaha!"

"Remember what I said," was Mary's parting to Saxon.

The car stopped at Seventh and Pine, the terminus of the line. It was only a little over two blocks to the cottage. On the front steps Billy took the key from his pocket.

"Funny, isn't it?" he said, as the key turned in the lock. "You an' me. Just you an' me."

While he lighted the lamp in the parlor, Saxon was taking off her hat. He went into the bedroom and lighted the lamp there, then turned back and stood in the doorway. Saxon, still unaccountably fumbling with her hatpins, stole a glance at him. He held out his arms.

"Now," he said.

She came to him, and in his arms he could feel her trembling.

BOOK II

CHAPTER I

The first evening after the marriage night Saxon met Billy at the door as he came up the front steps. After their embrace, and as they crossed the parlor hand in hand toward the kitchen, he filled his lungs through his nostrils with audible satisfaction.

"My, but this house smells good, Saxon! It ain't the coffee—I can smell that, too. It's the whole house. It smells... well, it just smells good to me, that's all."

He washed and dried himself at the sink, while she heated the frying pan on the front hole of the stove with the lid off. As he wiped his hands he watched her keenly, and cried out with approbation as she dropped the steak in the frying pan.

"Where'd you learn to cook steak on a dry, hot pan? It's the only way, but darn few women seem to know about it."

As she took the cover off a second frying pan and stirred the savory contents with a kitchen knife, he came behind her, passed his arms under her arm-pits with down-drooping hands upon her breasts, and bent his head over her shoulder till cheek touched cheek.

"Um-um-um-m-m! Fried potatoes with onions like mother used to make. Me for them. Don't they smell good, though! Um-um-m-m-m!"

The pressure of his hands relaxed, and his cheek slid caressingly past hers as he started to release her. Then his hands closed down again. She felt his lips on her hair and heard his advertised inhalation of delight.

"Um-um-m-m-m! Don't you smell good—yourself, though! I never understood what they meant when they said a girl was sweet. I know, now. And you're the sweetest I ever knew."

His joy was boundless. When he returned from combing his hair in the bedroom and sat down at the small table opposite her, he paused with knife and fork in hand.

"Say, bein' married is a whole lot more than it's cracked up to be by most married folks. Honest to God, Saxon, we can show 'em a few. We can give 'em cards and spades an' little casino an' win out on big casino and the aces. I've got but one kick comin'."

The instant apprehension in her eyes provoked a chuckle from him.

"An' that is that we didn't get married quick enough. Just think. I've lost a whole week of this."

Her eyes shone with gratitude and happiness, and in her heart she solemnly pledged herself that never in all their married life would it be otherwise.

Supper finished, she cleared the table and began washing the dishes at the sink. When he evinced the intention of wiping them, she caught him by the lapels of the coat and backed him into a chair.

"You'll sit right there, if you know what's good for you. Now be good and mind what I say. Also, you will smoke a cigarette.—No; you're not going to watch me. There's the morning paper beside you. And if you don't hurry to read it, I'll be through these dishes before you've started."

As he smoked and read, she continually glanced across at him from her work. One thing more, she thought—slippers; and then the picture of comfort and content would be complete.

Several minutes later Billy put the paper aside with a sigh.

"It's no use," he complained. "I can't read."

"What's the matter?" she teased. "Eyes weak?"

"Nope. They're sore, and there's only one thing to do 'em any good, an' that's lookin' at you."

"All right, then, baby Billy; I'll be through in a jiffy."

When she had washed the dish towel and scalded out the sink, she took off her kitchen apron, came to him, and kissed first one eye and then the other.

"How are they now. Cured?"

"They feel some better already."

She repeated the treatment.

"And now?"

"Still better."

"And now?"

"Almost well."

After he had adjudged them well, he ouched and informed her that there was still some hurt in the right eye.

In the course of treating it, she cried out as in pain. Billy was all alarm.

"What is it? What hurt you?"

"My eyes. They're hurting like sixty."

And Billy became physician for a while and she the patient. When the cure was accomplished, she led him into the parlor, where, by the open window, they succeeded in occupying the same Morris chair. It was the most expensive comfort in the house. It had cost seven dollars and a half, and, though it was grander than anything she had dreamed of possessing, the extravagance of it had worried her in a half-guilty way all day.

The salt chill of the air that is the blessing of all the bay cities after the sun goes down crept in about them. They heard the switch engines puffing in the railroad yards, and the rumbling thunder of the Seventh Street local slowing down in its run from the Mole to stop at West Oakland station. From the street came the noise of children playing in the summer night, and from the steps of the house next door the low voices of gossiping housewives.

"Can you beat it?" Billy murmured. "When I think of that six-dollar furnished room of mine, it makes me sick to think what I was missin' all the time. But there's one satisfaction. If I'd changed it sooner I wouldn't a-had you. You see, I didn't know you existed only until a couple of weeks ago."

His hand crept along her bare forearm and up and partly under the elbow-sleeve.

"Your skin's so cool," he said. "It ain't cold; it's cool. It feels good to the hand."

"Pretty soon you'll be calling me your cold-storage baby," she laughed.

"And your voice is cool," he went on. "It gives me the feeling just as your hand does when you rest it on my forehead. It's funny. I can't explain it. But your voice just goes all through me, cool and fine. It's like a wind of coolness—just right. It's like the first of the sea-breeze settin' in in the afternoon after a scorchin' hot morning. An' sometimes, when you talk low, it sounds round and sweet like the 'cello in the Macdonough Theater orchestra. And it never goes high up, or sharp, or squeaky, or scratchy, like some women's voices when they're mad, or fresh, or excited, till they remind me of a bum phonograph record. Why, your voice, it just goes through me till I'm all trembling—like with the everlastin' cool of it. It's -- it's straight delicious. I guess angels in heaven, if they is any, must have voices like that."

After a few minutes, in which, so inexpressible was her happiness that she could only pass her hand through his hair and cling to him, he broke out again.

"I'll tell you what you remind me of. Did you ever see a thoroughbred mare, all shinin' in the sun, with hair like satin an' skin so thin an' tender that the least touch of the whip leaves a mark—all fine nerves, an' delicate an' sensitive, that'll kill the toughest bronco when it comes to endurance an' that can strain a tendon in a flash or catch death-of-cold without a blanket for a night? I wanta tell you they ain't many beautifuler sights in this world. An' they're that fine-strung, an' sensitive, an' delicate. You gotta handle 'em right-side up, glass, with care. Well, that's what you remind me of. And I'm goin' to make it my job to see you get handled an' gentled in the same way. You're as different from other women as that kind of a mare is from scrub work-horse mares. You're a thoroughbred. You're clean-cut an' spirited, an' your lines...

"Say, d'ye know you've got some figure? Well, you have. Talk about Annette Kellerman. You can give her cards and spades. She's Australian, an' you're American, only your figure ain't. You're different. You're nifty—I don't know how to explain it. Other women ain't built like you. You belong in some other country. You're Frenchy, that's what. You're built like a French woman an' more than that—the way you walk, move, stand up or sit down, or don't do anything."

And he, who had never been out of California, or, for that matter, had never slept a night away from his birthtown of Oakland, was right in his judgment. She was a flower of Anglo-Saxon stock, a rarity in the exceptional smallness and fineness of hand and foot and bone and grace of flesh and carriage— some throw-back across the face of time to the foraying Norman-French that had intermingled with the sturdy Saxon breed.

"And in the way you carry your clothes. They belong to you. They seem just as much part of you as the cool of your voice and skin. They're always all right an' couldn't be better. An' you know, a fellow kind of likes to be seen taggin' around with a woman like you, that wears her clothes like a dream, an' hear the other fellows say: 'Who's Bill's new skirt? She's a peach, ain't she? Wouldn't I like to win her, though.' And all that sort of talk."

And Saxon, her cheek pressed to his, knew that she was paid in full for all her midnight sewings and the torturing hours of drowsy stitching when her head nodded with the weariness of the day's toil, while she recreated for herself filched ideas from the dainty garments that had steamed under her passing iron.

"Say, Saxon, I got a new name for you. You're my Tonic Kid. That's what you are, the Tonic Kid."

"And you'll never get tired of me?" she queried.

"Tired? Why we was made for each other."

"Isn't it wonderful, our meeting, Billy? We might never have met. It was just by accident that we did."

"We was born lucky," he proclaimed. "That's a cinch."

"Maybe it was more than luck," she ventured.

"Sure. It just had to be. It was fate. Nothing could a-kept us apart."

They sat on in a silence that was quick with unuttered love, till she felt him slowly draw her more closely and his lips come near to her ear as they whispered: "What do you say we go to bed?"

Many evenings they spent like this, varied with an occasional dance, with trips to the Orpheum and to Bell's Theater, or to the moving picture shows, or to the Friday night band concerts in City Hall Park. Often, on Sunday, she prepared a lunch, and he drove her out into the hills behind Prince and King, whom Billy's employer was still glad to have him exercise.

Each morning Saxon was called by the alarm clock. The first morning he had insisted upon getting up with her and building the fire in the kitchen stove. She gave in the first morning, but after that she laid the fire in the evening, so that all that was required was the touching of a match to it. And in bed she compelled him to remain for a last little doze ere she called him for breakfast. For the first several weeks she prepared his lunch for him. Then, for a week, he came down to dinner. After that he was compelled to take his lunch with him. It depended on how far distant the teaming was done.

"You're not starting right with a man," Mary cautioned. "You wait on him hand and foot. You'll spoil him if you don't watch out. It's him that ought to be waitin' on you."

"He's the bread-winner," Saxon replied. "He works harder than I, and I've got more time than I know what to do with—time to burn. Besides, I want to wait on him because I love to, and because... well, anyway, I want to."

CHAPTER II

Despite the fastidiousness of her housekeeping, Saxon, once she had systematized it, found time and to spare on her hands. Especially during the periods in which her husband carried his lunch and there was no midday meal to prepare, she had a number of hours each day to herself. Trained for years to the routine of factory and laundry work, she could not abide this unaccustomed idleness. She could not bear to sit and do nothing, while she could not pay calls on her girlhood friends, for they still worked in factory and laundry. Nor was she acquainted with the wives of the neighborhood, save for one strange old woman who lived in the house next door and with whom Saxon had exchanged snatches of conversation over the backyard division fence.

One time-consuming diversion of which Saxon took advantage was free and unlimited baths. In the orphan asylum and in Sarah's house she had been used to but one bath a week. As she grew to womanhood she had attempted more frequent baths. But the effort proved disastrous, arousing, first, Sarah's derision, and next, her wrath. Sarah had crystallized in the era of the weekly Saturday night bath, and any increase in this cleansing function was regarded by her as putting on airs and as an insinuation against her own cleanliness. Also, it was an extravagant misuse of fuel, and occasioned extra towels in the family wash. But now, in Billy's house, with her own stove, her own tub and towels and soap, and no one to say her nay, Saxon was guilty of a daily orgy. True, it was only a common washtub that she placed on the kitchen floor and filled by hand; but it was a luxury that had taken her twenty-four years to achieve. It was from the strange woman next door that Saxon received a hint, dropped in casual conversation, of what proved the culminating joy of bathing. A simple thing—a few drops of druggist's ammonia in the water; but Saxon had never heard of it before.

She was destined to learn much from the strange woman. The acquaintance had begun one day when Saxon, in the back yard, was hanging out a couple of corset covers and several pieces of her finest undergarments. The woman leaning on the rail of her back porch, had caught her eye, and nodded, as it seemed to Saxon, half to her and half to the underlinen on the line.

"You're newly married, aren't you?" the woman asked. "I'm Mrs. Higgins. I prefer my first name, which is Mercedes."

"And I'm Mrs. Roberts," Saxon replied, thrilling to the newness of the designation on her tongue. "My first name is Saxon."

"Strange name for a Yankee woman," the other commented.

"Oh, but I'm not Yankee," Saxon exclaimed. "I'm Californian."

"La la," laughed Mercedes Higgins. "I forgot I was in America. In other lands all Americans are called Yankees. It is true that you are newly married?"

Saxon nodded with a happy sigh. Mercedes sighed, too.

"Oh, you happy, soft, beautiful young thing. I could envy you to hatred—you with all the man-world ripe to be twisted about your pretty little fingers. And you don't realize your fortune. No one does until it's too late."

Saxon was puzzled and disturbed, though she answered readily:

"Oh, but I do know how lucky I am. I have the finest man in the world."

Mercedes Higgins sighed again and changed the subject. She nodded her head at the garments.

"I see you like pretty things. It is good judgment for a young woman. They're the bait for men—half the weapons in the battle. They win men, and they hold men—" She broke off to demand almost fiercely: "And you, you would keep your husband?—always, always—if you can?"

"I intend to. I will make him love me always and always."

Saxon ceased, troubled and surprised that she should be so intimate with a stranger.

"'Tis a queer thing, this love of men," Mercedes said. "And a failing of all women is it to believe they know men like books. And with breaking hearts, die they do, most women, out of their ignorance of men and still foolishly believing they know all about them. Oh, la la, the little fools. And so you say, little new-married woman, that you will make your man love you always and always? And so they all say it, knowing men and the queerness of men's love the way they think they do. Easier it is to win the capital prize in the Little Louisiana, but the little new-married women never know it until too late. But you—you have begun well. Stay by your pretties and your looks. 'Twas so you won your man, 'tis so you'll hold him. But that is not all. Some time I will talk with you and tell what few women trouble to know, what few women ever come to know.—Saxon!—'tis a strong, handsome name for a woman. But you don't look it. Oh, I've watched you. French you are, with a Frenchiness beyond dispute. Tell Mr. Roberts I congratulate him on his good taste."

She paused, her hand on the knob of her kitchen door.

"And come and see me some time. You will never be sorry. I can teach you much. Come in the afternoon. My man is night watchman in the yards and sleeps of mornings. He's sleeping now."

Saxon went into the house puzzling and pondering. Anything but ordinary was this lean, dark-skinned woman, with the face withered as if scorched in great heats, and the eyes, large and black, that flashed and flamed with advertisement of an unquenched inner conflagration. Old she was—Saxon caught herself debating anywhere between fifty and seventy; and her hair, which had once been blackest black, was streaked plentifully with gray. Especially noteworthy to Saxon was her speech. Good English it was, better than that to which Saxon was accustomed. Yet the woman was not American. On the other hand, she had no perceptible accent. Rather were her words touched by a foreignness so elusive that Saxon could not analyze nor place it.

"Uh, huh," Billy said, when she had told him that evening of the day's event. "So SHE'S Mrs. Higgins? He's a watchman. He's got only one arm. Old Higgins an' her—a funny bunch, the two of them. The people's scared of her—some of 'em. The Dagoes an' some of the old Irish dames thinks she's a witch. Won't have a thing to do with her. Bert was tellin' me about it. Why, Saxon, d'ye know, some of 'em believe if she was to get mad at 'em, or didn't like their mugs, or anything, that all she's got to do is look at 'em an' they'll curl up their toes an' croak. One of the fellows that works at the stable—you've seen 'm—Henderson—he lives around the corner on Fifth—he says she's bughouse."

"Oh, I don't know," Saxon defended her new acquaintance. "She may be crazy, but she says the same thing you're always saying. She says my form is not American but French."

"Then I take my hat off to her," Billy responded. "No wheels in her head if she says that. Take it from me, she's a wise gazabo."

"And she speaks good English, Billy, like a school teacher, like what I guess my mother used to speak. She's educated."

"She ain't no fool, or she wouldn't a-sized you up the way she did."

"She told me to congratulate you on your good taste in marrying me," Saxon laughed.

"She did, eh? Then give her my love. Me for her, because she knows a good thing when she sees it, an' she ought to be congratulating you on your good taste in me."

It was on another day that Mercedes Higgins nodded, half to Saxon, and half to the dainty women's things Saxon was hanging on the line.

"I've been worrying over your washing, little new-wife," was her greeting.

"Oh, but I've worked in the laundry for years," Saxon said quickly.

Mercedes sneered scornfully.

"Steam laundry. That's business, and it's stupid. Only common things should go to a steam laundry. That is their punishment for being common. But the pretties! the dainties! the flimsies!—la la, my dear, their washing is an art. It requires wisdom, genius, and discretion fine as the clothes are fine. I will give you a recipe for homemade soap. It will not harden the texture. It will give whiteness, and softness, and life. You can wear them long, and fine white clothes are to be loved a long time. Oh, fine washing is a refinement, an art. It is to be done as an artist paints a picture, or writes a poem, with love, holily, a true sacrament of beauty.

"I shall teach you better ways, my dear, better ways than you Yankees know. I shall teach you new pretties." She nodded her head to Saxon's underlinen on the line. "I see you make little laces. I know all laces—the Belgian, the Maltese, the Mechlin—oh, the many, many loves of laces! I shall teach you some of the simpler ones so that you can make them for yourself, for your brave man you are to make love you always and always."

On her first visit to Mercedes Higgins, Saxon received the recipe for home-made soap and her head was filled with a minutiae of instruction in the art of fine washing. Further, she was fascinated and excited by all the newness and strangeness of the withered old woman who blew upon her the breath of wider lands and seas beyond the horizon.

"You are Spanish?" Saxon ventured.

"No, and yes, and neither, and more. My father was Irish, my mother Peruvian-Spanish. 'Tis after her I took, in color and looks. In other ways after my father, the blue-eyed Celt with the fairy song on his tongue and the restless feet that stole the rest of him away to far-wandering. And the feet of him that he lent me have led me away on as wide far roads as ever his led him."

Saxon remembered her school geography, and with her mind's eye she saw a certain outline map of a continent with jiggly wavering parallel lines that denoted coast.

"Oh," she cried, "then you are South American."

Mercedes shrugged her shoulders.

"I had to be born somewhere. It was a great ranch, my mother's. You could put all Oakland in one of its smallest pastures."

Mercedes Higgins sighed cheerfully and for the time was lost in retrospection. Saxon was curious to hear more about this woman who must have lived much as the Spanish-Californians had lived in the old days.

"You received a good education," she said tentatively. "Your English is perfect."

"Ah, the English came afterward, and not in school. But, as it goes, yes, a good education in all things but the most important—men. That, too, came afterward. And little my mother dreamed—she was a grand lady, what you call a cattle-queen—little she dreamed my fine education was to fit me in the end for a night watchman's wife." She laughed genuinely at the grotesqueness of the idea. "Night watchman, laborers, why, we had hundreds, yes, thousands that toiled for us. The peons—they are like what you call slaves, almost, and the cowboys, who could ride two hundred miles between side and side of the ranch. And in the big house servants beyond remembering or counting. La la, in my mother's house were many servants."

Mercedes Higgins was voluble as a Greek, and wandered on in reminiscence.

"But our servants were lazy and dirty. The Chinese are the servants par excellence. So are the Japanese, when you find a good one, but not so good as the Chinese. The Japanese maidservants are pretty and merry, but you never know the moment they'll leave you. The Hindoos are not strong, but very obedient. They look upon sahibs and memsahibs as gods! I was a memsahib—which means woman. I once had a Russian cook who always spat in the soup for luck. It was very funny. But we put up with it. It was the custom."

"How you must have traveled to have such strange servants!" Saxon encouraged.

The old woman laughed corroboration.

"And the strangest of all, down in the South Seas, black slaves, little kinky-haired cannibals with bones through their noses. When they did not mind, or when they stole, they were tied up to a cocoanut palm behind the compound and lashed with whips of rhinoceros hide. They were from an island of cannibals and head-hunters, and they never cried out. It was their pride. There was little Vibi, only twelve years old—he waited on me—and when his back was cut in shreds and I wept over him, he would only laugh and say, 'Short time little bit I take 'm head belong big fella white marster.' That was Bruce Anstey, the Englishman who whipped him. But little Vibi never got the head. He ran away and the bushmen cut off his own head and ate every bit of him."

Saxon chilled, and her face was grave; but Mercedes Higgins rattled on.

"Ah, those were wild, gay, savage days. Would you believe it, my dear, in three years those Englishmen of the plantation drank up oceans of champagne and Scotch whisky and dropped thirty thousand pounds on the adventure. Not dollars—pounds, which means one hundred and fifty thousand dollars. They were princes while it lasted. It was splendid, glorious. It was mad, mad. I sold half my beautiful jewels in New Zealand before I got started again. Bruce Anstey blew out his brains at the end. Roger went mate on a trader with a black crew, for eight pounds a month. And Jack Gilbraith—he was the rarest of them all. His people were wealthy and titled, and he went home to England and sold cat's meat, sat around their big house till they gave him more money to start a rubber plantation in the East Indies somewhere, on Sumatra, I think—or was it New Guinea?"

And Saxon, back in her own kitchen and preparing supper for Billy, wondered what lusts and rapacities had led the old, burnt-faced woman from the big Peruvian ranch, through all the world, to West Oakland and Barry Higgins. Old Barry was not the sort who would fling away his share of one hundred and fifty thousand dollars, much less ever attain to such opulence. Besides, she had mentioned the names of other men, but not his.

Much more Mercedes had talked, in snatches and fragments. There seemed no great country nor city of the old world or the new in which she had not been. She had even been in Klondike, ten years before, in a half-dozen flashing sentences picturing the fur-clad, be-moccasined miners sowing the barroom floors with thousands of dollars' worth of gold dust. Always, so it seemed to Saxon, Mrs. Higgins had been with men to whom money was as water.

CHAPTER III

Saxon, brooding over her problem of retaining Billy's love, of never staling the freshness of their feeling for each other and of never descending from the heights which at present they were treading, felt herself impelled toward Mrs. Higgins. SHE knew; surely she must know. Had she not hinted knowledge beyond ordinary women's knowledge?

Several weeks went by, during which Saxon was often with her. But Mrs. Higgins talked of all other matters, taught Saxon the making of certain simple laces, and instructed her in the arts of washing and of marketing. And then, one afternoon, Saxon found Mrs. Higgins more voluble than usual, with words, clean-uttered, that rippled and tripped in their haste to escape. Her eyes were flaming. So flamed her face. Her words were flames. There was a smell of liquor in the air and Saxon knew that the old woman had been drinking. Nervous and frightened, at the same time fascinated, Saxon hemstitched a linen handkerchief intended for Billy and listened to Mercedes' wild flow of speech.

"Listen, my dear. I shall tell you about the world of men. Do not be stupid like all your people, who think me foolish and a witch with the evil eye. Ha! ha! When I think of silly Maggie Donahue pulling the shawl across her baby's face when we pass each other on the sidewalk! A witch I have been, 'tis true, but my witchery was with men. Oh, I am wise, very wise, my dear. I shall tell you of women's ways with men, and of men's ways with women, the best of them and the worst of them. Of the brute that is in all men, of the queerness of them that breaks the hearts of stupid women who do not understand. And all women are stupid. I am not stupid. La la, listen.

"I am an old woman. And like a woman, I'll not tell you how old I am. Yet can I hold men. Yet would I hold men, toothless and a hundred, my nose touching my chin. Not the young men. They were mine in my young days. But the old men, as befits my years. And well for me the power is mine. In all this world I am without kin or cash. Only have I wisdom and memories— memories that are ashes, but royal ashes, jeweled ashes. Old women, such as I, starve and shiver, or accept the pauper's dole and the pauper's shroud. Not I. I hold my man. True, 'tis only Barry Higgins—old Barry, heavy, an ox, but a male man, my dear, and queer as all men are queer. 'Tis true, he has one arm." She shrugged her shoulders. "A compensation. He cannot beat me, and old bones are tender when the round flesh thins to strings.

"But when I think of my wild young lovers, princes, mad with the madness of youth! I have lived. It is enough. I regret nothing. And with old Barry I have my surety of a bite to eat and a place by the fire. And why? Because I know men, and shall never lose my cunning to hold them. 'Tis bitter sweet, the knowledge of them, more sweet than bitter—men and men and men! Not stupid dolts, nor fat bourgeois swine of business men, but men of temperament, of flame and fire; madmen, maybe, but a lawless, royal race of madmen.

"Little wife-woman, you must learn. Variety! There lies the magic. 'Tis the golden key. 'Tis the toy that amuses. Without it in the wife, the man is a Turk; with it, he is her slave, and faithful. A wife must be many wives. If you would have your husband's love you must be all women to him. You must be ever new, with the dew of newness ever sparkling, a flower that never blooms to the fulness that fades. You must be a garden of flowers, ever new, ever fresh, ever different. And in your garden the man must never pluck the last of your posies.

"Listen, little wife-woman. In the garden of love is a snake. It is the commonplace. Stamp on its head, or it will destroy the garden. Remember the name. Commonplace. Never be too intimate. Men only seem gross. Women are more gross than men.—No, do not argue, little new-wife. You are an infant woman. Women are less delicate than men. Do I not know? Of their own husbands they will relate the most intimate love-secrets to other women. Men never do this of their wives. Explain it. There is only one way. In all things of love women are less delicate. It is their mistake. It is the father and the mother of the commonplace, and it is the commonplace, like a loathsome slug, that beslimes and destroys love.

"Be delicate, little wife-woman. Never be without your veil, without many veils. Veil yourself in a thousand veils, all shimmering and glittering with costly textures and precious jewels. Never let the last veil be drawn. Against the morrow array yourself with more veils, ever more veils, veils without end. Yet the many veils must not seem many. Each veil must seem the only one between you and your hungry lover who will have nothing less than all of you. Each time he must seem to get all, to tear aside the last veil that hides you. He must think so. It must not be so. Then there will be no satiety, for on the morrow he will find another last veil that has escaped him.

"Remember, each veil must seem the last and only one. Always you must seem to abandon all to his arms; always you must reserve more that on the morrow and on all the morrows you may abandon. Of such is variety, surprise, so that your man's pursuit will be everlasting, so that his eyes will look to you for newness, and not to other women. It was the freshness and the newness of your beauty and you, the mystery of you, that won your man. When a man has plucked and smelled all the sweetness of a flower, he looks for other flowers. It is his queerness. You must ever remain a flower almost plucked yet never plucked, stored with vats of sweet unbroached though ever broached.

"Stupid women, and all are stupid, think the first winning of the man the final victory. Then they settle down and grow fat, and stale, and dead, and heartbroken. Alas, they are so stupid. But you, little infant-woman with your first victory, you must make your love-life an unending chain of victories. Each day you must win your man again. And when you have won the last victory, when you can find no more to win, then ends love. Finis is written, and your man wanders in strange gardens. Remember, love must be kept insatiable. It must have an appetite knife-edged and never satisfied. You must feed your lover well, ah, very well, most well; give, give, yet send him away hungry to come back to you for more."

Mrs. Higgins stood up suddenly and crossed out of the room. Saxon had not failed to note the litheness and grace in that lean and withered body. She watched for Mrs. Higgins' return, and knew that the litheness and grace had not been imagined.

"Scarcely have I told you the first letter in love's alphabet," said Mercedes Higgins, as she reseated herself.

In her hands was a tiny instrument, beautifully grained and richly brown, which resembled a guitar save that it bore four strings. She swept them back and forth with rhythmic forefinger and lifted a voice, thin and mellow, in a fashion of melody that was strange, and in a foreign tongue, warm-voweled, all-voweled, and love-exciting. Softly throbbing, voice and strings arose on sensuous crests of song, died away to whisperings and caresses, drifted through love-dusks and twilights, or swelled again to love-cries barbarically imperious in which were woven plaintive calls and madnesses of invitation and promise. It went through Saxon until she was as this instrument, swept with passional strains. It seemed to her a dream, and almost was she dizzy, when Mercedes Higgins ceased.

"If your man had clasped the last of you, and if all of you were known to him as an old story, yet, did you sing that one song, as I have sung it, yet would his arms again go out to you and his eyes grow warm with the old mad lights. Do you see? Do you understand, little wife-woman?"

Saxon could only nod, her lips too dry for speech.

"The golden koa, the king of woods," Mercedes was crooning over the instrument. "The ukulele—that is what the Hawaiians call it, which means, my dear, the jumping flea. They are golden-fleshed, the Hawaiians, a race of lovers, all in the warm cool of the tropic night where the trade winds blow."

Again she struck the strings. She sang in another language, which Saxon deemed must be French. It was a gayly-devilish lilt, tripping and tickling. Her large eyes at times grew larger and wilder, and again narrowed in enticement and wickedness. When she ended, she looked to Saxon for a verdict.

"I don't like that one so well," Saxon said.

Mercedes shrugged her shoulders.

"They all have their worth, little infant-woman with so much to learn. There are times when men may be won with wine. There are times when men may be won with the wine of song, so queer they are. La la, so many ways, so many ways. There are your pretties, my dear, your dainties. They are magic nets. No fisherman upon the sea ever tangled fish more successfully than we women with our flimsies. You are on the right path. I have seen men enmeshed by a corset cover no prettier, no daintier, than these of yours I have seen on the line.

"I have called the washing of fine linen an art. But it is not for itself alone. The greatest of the arts is the conquering of men. Love is the sum of all the arts, as it is the reason for their existence. Listen. In all times and ages have been women, great wise women. They did not need to be beautiful. Greater than all woman's beauty was their wisdom. Princes and potentates bowed down before them. Nations battled over them. Empires crashed because of them. Religions were founded on them. Aphrodite, Astarte, the worships of the night—listen, infant-woman, of the great women who conquered worlds of men."

And thereafter Saxon listened, in a maze, to what almost seemed a wild farrago, save that the strange meaningless phrases were fraught with dim, mysterious significance. She caught glimmerings of profounds inexpressible and unthinkable that hinted connotations lawless and terrible. The woman's speech was a lava rush, scorching and searing; and Saxon's cheeks, and forehead, and neck burned with a blush that continuously increased. She trembled with fear, suffered qualms of nausea, thought sometimes that she would faint, so madly reeled her brain; yet she could not tear herself away, and sat on and on, her sewing forgotten on her lap, staring with inward sight upon a nightmare vision beyond all imagining. At last, when it seemed she could endure no more, and while she was wetting her dry lips to cry out in protest, Mercedes ceased.

"And here endeth the first lesson," she said quite calmly, then laughed with a laughter that was tantalizing and tormenting. "What is the matter? You are not shocked?"

"I am frightened," Saxon quavered huskily, with a half-sob of nervousness. "You frighten me. I am very foolish, and I know so little, that I had never dreamed... THAT."

Mercedes nodded her head comprehendingly.

"It is indeed to be frightened at," she said. "It is solemn; it is terrible; it is magnificent!"

CHAPTER IV

Saxon had been clear-eyed all her days, though her field of vision had been restricted. Clear-eyed, from her childhood days with the saloonkeeper Cady and Cady's good-natured but unmoral spouse, she had observed, and, later, generalized much upon sex. She knew the post-nuptial problem of retaining a husband's love, as few wives of any class knew it, just as she knew the pre-nuptial problem of selecting a husband, as few girls of the working class knew it.

She had of herself developed an eminently rational philosophy of love. Instinctively, and consciously, too, she had made toward delicacy, and shunned the perils of the habitual and commonplace. Thoroughly aware she was that as she cheapened herself so did she cheapen love. Never, in the weeks of their married life, had Billy found her dowdy, or harshly irritable, or lethargic. And she had deliberately permeated her house with her personal atmosphere of coolness, and freshness, and equableness. Nor had she been ignorant of such assets as surprise and charm. Her imagination had not been asleep, and she had been born with wisdom. In Billy she had won a prize, and she knew it. She appreciated his lover's ardor and was proud. His open-handed liberality, his desire for everything of the best, his own personal cleanliness and care of himself she recognized as far beyond the average. He was never coarse. He met delicacy with delicacy, though it was obvious to her that the initiative in all such matters lay with her and must lie with her always. He was largely unconscious of what he did and why. But she knew in all full clarity of judgment. And he was such a prize among men.

Despite her clear sight of her problem of keeping Billy a lover, and despite the considerable knowledge and experience arrayed before her mental vision, Mercedes Higgins had spread before her a vastly wider panorama. The old woman had verified her own conclusions, given her new ideas, clinched old ones, and even savagely emphasized the tragic importance of the whole problem. Much Saxon remembered of that mad preachment, much she guessed and felt, and much had been beyond her experience and understanding. But the metaphors of the veils and the flowers, and the rules of giving to abandonment with always more to abandon, she grasped thoroughly, and she was enabled to formulate a bigger and stronger love-philosophy. In the light of the revelation she re-examined the married lives of all she had ever known, and, with sharp definiteness as never before, she saw where and why so many of them had failed.

With renewed ardor Saxon devoted herself to her household, to her pretties, and to her charms. She marketed with a keener desire for the best, though never ignoring the need for economy. From the women's pages of the

Sunday supplements, and from the women's magazines in the free reading room two blocks away, she gleaned many ideas for the preservation of her looks. In a systematic way she exercised the various parts of her body, and a certain period of time each day she employed in facial exercises and massage for the purpose of retaining the roundness and freshness, and firmness and color. Billy did not know. These intimacies of the toilette were not for him. The results, only, were his. She drew books from the Carnegie Library and studied physiology and hygiene, and learned a myriad of things about herself and the ways of woman's health that she had never been taught by Sarah, the women of the orphan asylum, nor by Mrs. Cady.

After long debate she subscribed to a woman's magazine, the patterns and lessons of which she decided were the best suited to her taste and purse. The other woman's magazines she had access to in the free reading room, and more than one pattern of lace and embroidery she copied by means of tracing paper. Before the lingerie windows of the uptown shops she often stood and studied; nor was she above taking advantage, when small purchases were made, of looking over the goods at the hand-embroidered underwear counters. Once, she even considered taking up with hand-painted china, but gave over the idea when she learned its expensiveness.

She slowly replaced all her simple maiden underlinen with garments which, while still simple, were wrought with beautiful French embroidery, tucks, and drawnwork. She crocheted fine edgings on the inexpensive knitted underwear she wore in winter. She made little corset covers and chemises of fine but fairly inexpensive lawns, and, with simple flowered designs and perfect laundering, her nightgowns were always sweetly fresh and dainty. In some publication she ran across a brief printed note to the effect that French women were just beginning to wear fascinating beruffled caps at the breakfast table. It meant nothing to her that in her case she must first prepare the breakfast. Promptly appeared in the house a yard of dotted Swiss muslin, and Saxon was deep in experimenting on patterns for herself, and in sorting her bits of laces for suitable trimmings. The resultant dainty creation won Mercedes Higgins' enthusiastic approval.

Saxon made for herself simple house slips of pretty gingham, with neat low collars turned back from her fresh round throat. She crocheted yards of laces for her underwear, and made Battenberg in abundance for her table and for the bureau. A great achievement, that aroused Billy's applause, was an Afghan for the bed. She even ventured a rag carpet, which, the women's magazines informed her, had newly returned into fashion. As a matter of course she hemstitched the best table linen and bed linen they could afford.

As the happy months went by she was never idle. Nor was Billy forgotten. When the cold weather came on she knitted him wristlets, which he always religiously wore from the house and pocketed immediately thereafter. The two sweaters she made for him, however, received a better fate, as did the slippers which she insisted on his slipping into, on the evenings they remained at home.

The hard practical wisdom of Mercedes Higgins proved of immense help, for Saxon strove with a fervor almost religious to have everything of the best and at the same time to be saving. Here she faced the financial and economic problem of keeping house in a society where the cost of living rose faster than the wages of industry. And here the old woman taught her the science of marketing so thoroughly that she made a dollar of Billy's go half as far again as the wives of the neighborhood made the dollars of their men go.

Invariably, on Saturday night, Billy poured his total wages into her lap. He never asked for an accounting of what she did with it, though he continually reiterated that he had never fed so well in his life. And always, the wages still untouched in her lap, she had him take out what he estimated he would need for spending money for the week to come. Not only did she bid him take plenty but she insisted on his taking any amount extra that he might desire at any time through the week. And, further, she insisted he should not tell her what it was for.

"You've always had money in your pocket," she reminded him, "and there's no reason marriage should change that. If it did, I'd wish I'd never married you. Oh, I know about men when they get together. First one treats and then another, and it takes money. Now if you can't treat just as freely as the rest of them, why I know you so well that I know you'd stay away from them. And that wouldn't be right... to you, I mean. I want you to be together with men. It's good for a man."

And Billy buried her in his arms and swore she was the greatest little bit of woman that ever came down the pike.

"Why," he jubilated; "not only do I feed better, and live more comfortable, and hold up my end with the fellows; but I'm actually saving money—or you are for me. Here I am, with furniture being paid for regular every month, and a little woman I'm mad over, and on top of it money in the bank. How much is it now?"

"Sixty-two dollars," she told him. "Not so bad for a rainy day. You might get sick, or hurt, or something happen."

It was in mid-winter, when Billy, with quite a deal of obvious reluctance, broached a money matter to Saxon. His old friend, Billy Murphy, was laid up with la grippe, and one of his children, playing in the street, had been seriously injured by a passing wagon. Billy Murphy, still feeble after two weeks in bed, had asked Billy for the loan of fifty dollars.

"It's perfectly safe," Billy concluded to Saxon. "I've known him since we was kids at the Durant School together. He's straight as a die."

"That's got nothing to do with it," Saxon chided. "If you were single you'd have lent it to him immediately, wouldn't you?"

Billy nodded.

"Then it's no different because you're married. It's your money, Billy."

"Not by a damn sight," he cried. "It ain't mine. It's ourn. And I wouldn't think of lettin' anybody have it without seein' you first."

"I hope you didn't tell him that," she said with quick concern.

"Nope," Billy laughed. "I knew, if I did, you'd be madder'n a hatter. I just told him I'd try an' figure it out. After all, I was sure you'd stand for it if you had it."

"Oh, Billy," she murmured, her voice rich and low with love; "maybe you don't know it, but that's one of the sweetest things you've said since we got married."

The more Saxon saw of Mercedes Higgins the less did she understand her. That the old woman was a close-fisted miser, Saxon soon learned. And this trait she found hard to reconcile with her tales of squandering. On the other hand, Saxon was bewildered by Mercedes' extravagance in personal matters. Her underlinen, hand-made of course, was very costly. The table she set for Barry was good, but the table for herself was vastly better. Yet both tables were set on the same table. While Barry contented himself with solid round steak, Mercedes ate tenderloin. A huge, tough muttonchop on Barry's plate would be balanced by tiny French chops on Mercedes' plate. Tea was brewed in separate pots. So was coffee. While Barry gulped twenty-five cent tea from a large and heavy mug, Mercedes sipped three-dollar tea from a tiny cup of Belleek, rose-tinted, fragile as all egg-shell. In the same manner, his twenty-five cent coffee was diluted with milk, her eighty cent Turkish with cream.

"'Tis good enough for the old man," she told Saxon. "He knows no better, and it would be a wicked sin to waste it on him."

Little traffickings began between the two women. After Mercedes had freely taught Saxon the loose-wristed facility of playing accompaniments on the ukulele, she proposed an exchange. Her time was past, she said, for such frivolities, and she offered the instrument for the breakfast cap of which Saxon had made so good a success.

"It's worth a few dollars," Mercedes said. "It cost me twenty, though that was years ago. Yet it is well worth the value of the cap."

"But wouldn't the cap be frivolous, too?" Saxon queried, though herself well pleased with the bargain.

"'Tis not for my graying hair," Mercedes frankly disclaimed. "I shall sell it for the money. Much that I do, when the rheumatism is not maddening my fingers, I sell. La la, my dear, 'tis not old Barry's fifty a month that'll satisfy all my expensive tastes. 'Tis I that make up the difference. And old age needs money as never youth needs it. Some day you will learn for yourself."

"I am well satisfied with the trade," Saxon said. "And I shall make me another cap when I can lay aside enough for the material."

"Make several," Mercedes advised. "I'll sell them for you, keeping, of course, a small commission for my services. I can give you six dollars apiece for them. We will consult about them. The profit will more than provide material for your own."

CHAPTER V

Four eventful things happened in the course of the winter. Bert and Mary got married and rented a cottage in the neighborhood three blocks away. Billy's wages were cut, along with the wages of all the teamsters in Oakland. Billy took up shaving with a safety razor. And, finally, Saxon was proven a false prophet and Sarah a true one.

Saxon made up her mind, beyond any doubt, ere she confided the news to Billy. At first, while still suspecting, she had felt a frightened sinking of the heart and fear of the unknown and unexperienced. Then had come economic fear, as she contemplated the increased expense entailed. But by the time she had made surety doubly sure, all was swept away before a wave of passionate gladness. HERS AND BILLY'S! The phrase was continually in her mind, and each recurrent thought of it brought an actual physical pleasure-pang to her heart.

The night she told the news to Billy, he withheld his own news of the wage-cut, and joined with her in welcoming the little one.

"What'll we do? Go to the theater to celebrate?" he asked, relaxing the pressure of his embrace so that she might speak. "Or suppose we stay in, just you and me, and... and the three of us?"

"Stay in," was her verdict. "I just want you to hold me, and hold me, and hold me."

"That's what I wanted, too, only I wasn't sure, after bein' in the house all day, maybe you'd want to go out."

There was frost in the air, and Billy brought the Morris chair in by the kitchen stove. She lay cuddled in his arms, her head on his shoulder, his cheek against her hair.

"We didn't make no mistake in our lightning marriage with only a week's courtin'," he reflected aloud. "Why, Saxon, we've been courtin' ever since just the same. And now... my God, Saxon, it's too wonderful to be true. Think of it! Ourn! The three of us! The little rascal! I bet he's goin' to be a boy. An' won't I learn 'm to put up his fists an' take care of himself! An' swimmin' too. If he don't know how to swim by the time he's six..."

"And if HE'S a girl?"

"SHE'S goin' to be a boy," Billy retorted, joining in the playful misuse of pronouns.

And both laughed and kissed, and sighed with content. "I'm goin' to turn pincher, now," he announced, after quite an interval of meditation. "No more drinks with the boys. It's me for the water wagon. And I'm goin' to ease down on smokes. Huh! Don't see why I can't roll my own cigarettes. They're ten times cheaper'n tailor-mades. An' I can grow a beard. The amount of money the barbers get out of a fellow in a year would keep a baby."

"Just you let your beard grow, Mister Roberts, and I'll get a divorce," Saxon threatened. "You're just too handsome and strong with a smooth face. I love your face too much to have it covered up.—Oh, you dear! you dear! Billy, I never knew what happiness was until I came to live with you."

"Nor me neither."

"And it's always going to be so?"

"You can just bet," he assured her.

"I thought I was going to be happy married," she went on; "but I never dreamed it would be like this." She turned her head on his shoulder and kissed his cheek. "Billy, it isn't happiness. It's heaven."

And Billy resolutely kept undivulged the cut in wages. Not until two weeks later, when it went into effect, and he poured the diminished sum into her lap, did he break it to her. The next day, Bert and Mary, already a month married, had Sunday dinner with them, and the matter came up for discussion. Bert was particularly pessimistic, and muttered dark hints of an impending strike in the railroad shops.

"If you'd all shut your traps, it'd be all right," Mary criticized. "These union agitators get the railroad sore. They give me the cramp, the way they butt in an' stir up trouble. If I was boss I'd cut the wages of any man that listened to them."

"Yet you belonged to the laundry workers' union," Saxon rebuked gently.

"Because I had to or I wouldn't a-got work. An' much good it ever done me."

"But look at Billy," Bert argued. "The teamsters ain't ben sayin' a word, not a peep, an' everything lovely, and then, bang, right in the neck, a ten per cent cut. Oh, hell, what chance have we got? We lose. There's nothin' left for us in this country we've made and our fathers an' mothers before us. We're all shot to pieces. We can see our finish—we, the old stock, the children of the white people that broke away from England an' licked the tar outa her, that freed the slaves, an' fought the Indians, 'an made the West! Any gink with half an eye can see it comin'."

"But what are we going to do about it?" Saxon questioned anxiously.

"Fight. That's all. The country's in the hands of a gang of robbers. Look at the Southern Pacific. It runs California."

"Aw, rats, Bert," Billy interrupted. "You're talkin' through your lid. No railroad can ran the government of California."

"You're a bonehead," Bert sneered. "And some day, when it's too late, you an' all the other boneheads'll realize the fact. Rotten? I tell you it stinks. Why, there ain't a man who wants to go to state legislature but has to make a trip to San Francisco, an' go into the S. P. offices, an' take his hat off, an' humbly ask permission. Why, the governors of California has been railroad governors since before you and I was born. Huh! You can't tell me. We're finished. We're licked to a frazzle. But it'd do my heart good to help string up some of the dirty thieves before I passed out. D'ye know what we are?— we old white stock that fought in the wars, an' broke the land, an' made all this? I'll tell you. We're the last of the Mohegans."

"He scares me to death, he's so violent," Mary said with unconcealed hostility. "If he don't quit shootin' off his mouth he'll get fired from the shops. And then what'll we do? He don't consider me. But I can tell you one thing all right, all right. I'll not go back to the laundry." She held her right hand up and spoke with the solemnity of an oath. "Not so's you can see it. Never again for yours truly."

"Oh, I know what you're drivin' at," Bert said with asperity. "An' all I can tell you is, livin' or dead, in a job or out, no matter what happens to me, if you will lead that way, you will, an' there's nothin' else to it."

"I guess I kept straight before I met you," she came back with a toss of the head. "And I kept straight after I met you, which is going some if anybody should ask you."

Hot words were on Bert's tongue, but Saxon intervened and brought about peace. She was concerned over the outcome of their marriage. Both were highstrung, both were quick and irritable, and their continual clashes did not augur well for their future.

The safety razor was a great achievement for Saxon. Privily she conferred with a clerk she knew in Pierce's hardware store and made the purchase. On Sunday morning, after breakfast, when Billy was starting to go to the barber shop, she led him into the bedroom, whisked a towel aside, and revealed the razor box, shaving mug, soap, brush, and lather all ready. Billy recoiled, then came back to make curious investigation. He gazed pityingly at the safety razor.

"Huh! Call that a man's tool!"

"It'll do the work," she said. "It does it for thousands of men every day."

But Billy shook his head and backed away.

"You shave three times a week," she urged. "That's forty-five cents. Call it half a dollar, and there are fifty-two weeks in the year. Twenty-six dollars a year just for shaving. Come on, dear, and try it. Lots of men swear by it."

He shook his head mutinously, and the cloudy deeps of his eyes grew more cloudy. She loved that sullen handsomeness that made him look so boyish, and, laughing and kissing him, she forced him into a chair, got off his coat, and unbuttoned shirt and undershirt and turned them in.

Threatening him with, "If you open your mouth to kick I'll shove it in," she coated his face with lather.

"Wait a minute," she checked him, as he reached desperately for the razor. "I've been watching the barbers from the sidewalk. This is what they do after the lather is on."

And thereupon she proceeded to rub the lather in with her fingers.

"There," she said, when she had coated his face a second time. "You're ready to begin. Only remember, I'm not always going to do this for you. I'm just breaking you in, you see."

With great outward show of rebellion, half genuine, half facetious, he made several tentative scrapes with the razor. He winced violently, and violently exclaimed:

"Holy jumping Jehosaphat!"

He examined his face in the glass, and a streak of blood showed in the midst of the lather.

"Cut!—by a safety razor, by God! Sure, men swear by it. Can't blame 'em. Cut! By a safety!"

"But wait a second," Saxon pleaded. "They have to be regulated. The clerk told me. See those little screws. There…. That's it… turn them around."

Again Billy applied the blade to his face. After a couple of scrapes, he looked at himself closely in the mirror, grinned, and went on shaving. With swiftness and dexterity he scraped his face clean of lather. Saxon clapped her hands.

"Fine," Billy approved. "Great! Here. Give me your hand. See what a good job it made."

He started to rub her hand against his cheek. Saxon jerked away with a little cry of disappointment, then examined him closely.

"It hasn't shaved at all," she said.

"It's a fake, that's what it is. It cuts the hide, but not the hair. Me for the barber."

But Saxon was persistent.

"You haven't given it a fair trial yet. It was regulated too much. Let me try my hand at it. There, that's it, betwixt and between. Now, lather again and try it."

This time the unmistakable sand-papery sound of hair-severing could be heard.

"How is it?" she fluttered anxiously.

"It gets the—ouch!—hair," Billy grunted, frowning and making faces. "But it—gee!—say!—ouch!—pulls like Sam Hill."

"Stay with it," she encouraged. "Don't give up the ship, big Injun with a scalplock. Remember what Bert says and be the last of the Mohegans."

At the end of fifteen minutes he rinsed his face and dried it, sighing with relief.

"It's a shave, in a fashion, Saxon, but I can't say I'm stuck on it. It takes out the nerve. I'm as weak as a cat."

He groaned with sudden discovery of fresh misfortune.

"What's the matter now?" she asked.

"The back of my neck—how can I shave the back of my neck? I'll have to pay a barber to do it."

Saxon's consternation was tragic, but it only lasted a moment. She took the brush in her hand.

"Sit down, Billy."

"What?—you?" he demanded indignantly.

"Yes; me. If any barber is good enough to shave your neck, and then I am, too."

Billy moaned and groaned in the abjectness of humility and surrender, and let her have her way.

"There, and a good job," she informed him when she had finished. "As easy as falling off a log. And besides, it means twenty-six dollars a year. And you'll buy the crib, the baby buggy, the pinning blankets, and lots and lots of things with it. Now sit still a minute longer."

She rinsed and dried the back of his neck and dusted it with talcum powder.

"You're as sweet as a clean little baby, Billy Boy."

The unexpected and lingering impact of her lips on the back of his neck made him writhe with mingled feelings not all unpleasant.

Two days later, though vowing in the intervening time to have nothing further to do with the instrument of the devil, he permitted Saxon to assist him to a second shave. This time it went easier.

"It ain't so bad," he admitted. "I'm gettin' the hang of it. It's all in the regulating. You can shave as close as you want an' no more close than you want. Barbers can't do that. Every once an' awhile they get my face sore."

The third shave was an unqualified success, and the culminating bliss was reached when Saxon presented him with a bottle of witch hazel. After that he began active proselyting. He could not wait a visit from Bert, but carried the paraphernalia to the latter's house to demonstrate.

"We've ben boobs all these years, Bert, runnin' the chances of barber's itch an' everything. Look at this, eh? See her take hold. Smooth as silk. Just as easy.... There! Six minutes by the clock. Can you beat it? When I get my hand in, I can do it in three. It works in the dark. It works under water. You couldn't cut yourself if you tried. And it saves twenty-six dollars a year. Saxon figured it out, and she's a wonder, I tell you."

CHAPTER VI

The trafficking between Saxon and Mercedes increased. The latter commanded a ready market for all the fine work Saxon could supply, while Saxon was eager and happy in the work. The expected babe and the cut in Billy's wages had caused her to regard the economic phase of existence more seriously than ever. Too little money was being laid away in the bank, and her conscience pricked her as she considered how much she was laying out on the pretty necessaries for the household and herself. Also, for the first time in her life she was spending another's earnings. Since a young girl she had been used to spending her own, and now, thanks to Mercedes she was doing it again, and, out of her profits, assaying more expensive and delightful adventures in lingerie.

Mercedes suggested, and Saxon carried out and even bettered, the dainty things of thread and texture. She made ruffled chemises of sheer linen, with her own fine edgings and French embroidery on breast and shoulders; linen hand-made combination undersuits; and nightgowns, fairy and cobwebby, embroidered, trimmed with Irish lace. On Mercedes' instigation she executed an ambitious and wonderful breakfast cap for which the old woman returned her twelve dollars after deducting commission.

She was happy and busy every waking moment, nor was preparation for the little one neglected. The only ready made garments she bought were three fine little knit shirts. As for the rest, every bit was made by her own hands— featherstitched pinning blankets, a crocheted jacket and cap, knitted mittens, embroidered bonnets; slim little princess slips of sensible length; underskirts on absurd Lilliputian yokes; silk-embroidered white flannel petticoats; stockings and crocheted boots, seeming to burgeon before her eyes with wriggly pink toes and plump little calves; and last, but not least, many deliciously soft squares of bird's-eye linen. A little later, as a crowning masterpiece, she was guilty of a dress coat of white silk, embroidered. And into all the tiny garments, with every stitch, she sewed love. Yet this love, so unceasingly sewn, she knew when she came to consider and marvel, was more of Billy than of the nebulous, ungraspable new bit of life that eluded her fondest attempts at visioning.

"Huh," was Billy's comment, as he went over the mite's wardrobe and came back to center on the little knit shirts, "they look more like a real kid than the whole kit an' caboodle. Why, I can see him in them regular manshirts."

Saxon, with a sudden rush of happy, unshed tears, held one of the little shirts up to his lips. He kissed it solemnly, his eyes resting on Saxon's.

"That's some for the boy," he said, "but a whole lot for you."

But Saxon's money-earning was doomed to cease ignominiously and tragically. One day, to take advantage of a department store bargain sale, she crossed the bay to San Francisco. Passing along Sutter Street, her eye was attracted by a display in the small window of a small shop. At first she could not believe it; yet there, in the honored place of the window, was the wonderful breakfast cap for which she had received twelve dollars from Mercedes. It was marked twenty-eight dollars. Saxon went in and interviewed the shopkeeper, an emaciated, shrewd-eyed and middle-aged woman of foreign extraction.

"Oh, I don't want to buy anything," Saxon said. "I make nice things like you have here, and I wanted to know what you pay for them—for that breakfast cap in the window, for instance."

The woman darted a keen glance to Saxon's left hand, noted the innumerable tiny punctures in the ends of the first and second fingers, then appraised her clothing and her face.

"Can you do work like that?"

Saxon nodded.

"I paid twenty dollars to the woman that made that." Saxon repressed an almost spasmodic gasp, and thought coolly for a space. Mercedes had given her twelve. Then Mercedes had pocketed eight, while she, Saxon, had furnished the material and labor.

"Would you please show me other hand-made things -- nightgowns, chemises, and such things, and tell me the prices you pay?"

"Can you do such work?"

"Yes."

"And will you sell to me?"

"Certainly," Saxon answered. "That is why I am here."

"We add only a small amount when we sell," the woman went on; "you see, light and rent and such things, as well as a profit or else we could not be here."

"It's only fair," Saxon agreed.

Amongst the beautiful stuff Saxon went over, she found a nightgown and a combination undersuit of her own manufacture. For the former she had received eight dollars from Mercedes, it was marked eighteen, and the woman had paid fourteen; for the latter Saxon received six, it was marked fifteen, and the woman had paid eleven.

"Thank you," Saxon said, as she drew on her gloves. "I should like to bring you some of my work at those prices."

"And I shall be glad to buy it... if it is up to the mark." The woman looked at her severely. "Mind you, it must be as good as this. And if it is, I often get special orders, and I'll give you a chance at them."

Mercedes was unblushingly candid when Saxon reproached her.

"You told me you took only a commission," was Saxon's accusation.

"So I did; and so I have."

"But I did all the work and bought all the materials, yet you actually cleared more out of it than I did. You got the lion's share."

"And why shouldn't I, my dear? I was the middleman. It's the way of the world. 'Tis the middlemen that get the lion's share."

"It seems to me most unfair," Saxon reflected, more in sadness than anger.

"That is your quarrel with the world, not with me," Mercedes rejoined sharply, then immediately softened with one of her quick changes. "We mustn't quarrel, my dear. I like you so much. La la, it is nothing to you, who are young and strong with a man young and strong. Listen, I am an old woman. And old Barry can do little for me. He is on his last legs. His kidneys are 'most gone. Remember, 'tis I must bury him. And I do him honor, for beside me he'll have his last long sleep. A stupid, dull old man, heavy, an ox, 'tis true; but a good old fool with no trace of evil in him. The plot is bought and paid for—the final installment was made up, in part, out of my commissions from you. Then there are the funeral expenses. It must be done nicely. I have still much to save. And Barry may turn up his toes any day."

Saxon sniffed the air carefully, and knew the old woman had been drinking again.

"Come, my dear, let me show you." Leading Saxon to a large sea chest in the bedroom, Mercedes lifted the lid. A faint perfume, as of rose-petals, floated up. "Behold, my burial trousseau. Thus I shall wed the dust."

Saxon's amazement increased, as, article by article, the old woman displayed the airiest, the daintiest, the most delicious and most complete of bridal outfits. Mercedes held up an ivory fan.

"In Venice 'twas given me, my dear.—See, this comb, turtle shell; Bruce Anstey made it for me the week before he drank his last bottle and scattered his brave mad brains with a Colt's 44.—This scarf. La la, a Liberty scarf—"

"And all that will be buried with you," Saxon mused, "Oh, the extravagance of it!"

Mercedes laughed.

"Why not? I shall die as I have lived. It is my pleasure. I go to the dust as a bride. No cold and narrow bed for me. I would it were a coach, covered with the soft things of the East, and pillows, pillows, without end."

"It would buy you twenty funerals and twenty plots," Saxon protested, shocked by this blasphemy of conventional death. "It is downright wicked."

"'Twill be as I have lived," Mercedes said complacently. "And it's a fine bride old Barry'll have to come and lie beside him." She closed the lid and sighed. "Though I wish it were Bruce Anstey, or any of the pick of my young men to lie with me in the great dark and to crumble with me to the dust that is the real death."

She gazed at Saxon with eyes heated by alcohol and at the same time cool with the coolness of content.

"In the old days the great of earth were buried with their live slaves with them. I but take my flimsies, my dear."

"Then you aren't afraid of death?... in the least?"

Mercedes shook her head emphatically.

"Death is brave, and good, and kind. I do not fear death. 'Tis of men I am afraid when I am dead. So I prepare. They shall not have me when I am dead."

Saxon was puzzled.

"They would not want you then," she said.

"Many are wanted," was the answer. "Do you know what becomes of the aged poor who have no money for burial? They are not buried. Let me tell you. We stood before great doors. He was a queer man, a professor who ought to have been a pirate, a man who lectured in class rooms when he ought to have been storming walled cities or robbing banks. He was slender, like Don Juan. His hands were strong as steel. So was his spirit. And he was mad, a bit mad, as all my young men have been. 'Come, Mercedes,' he said; 'we will inspect our brethren and become humble, and glad that we are not as they—as yet not yet. And afterward, to-night, we will dine with a more devilish taste, and we will drink to them in golden wine that will be the more golden for having seen them. Come, Mercedes.'

"He thrust the great doors open, and by the hand led me in. It was a sad company. Twenty-four, that lay on marble slabs, or sat, half erect and propped, while many young men, bright of eye, bright little knives in their hands, glanced curiously at me from their work."

"They were dead?" Saxon interrupted to gasp.

"They were the pauper dead, my dear. 'Come, Mercedes,' said he. 'There is more to show you that will make us glad we are alive.' And he took me down, down to the vats. The salt vats, my dear. I was not afraid. But it was in my mind, then, as I looked, how it would be with me when I was dead. And there they were, so many lumps of pork. And the order came, 'A woman; an old woman.' And the man who worked there fished in the vats. The first was a man he drew to see. Again he fished and stirred. Again a man. He was impatient, and grumbled at his luck. And then, up through the brine, he drew a woman, and by the face of her she was old, and he was satisfied."

"It is not true!" Saxon cried out.

"I have seen, my dear, I know. And I tell you fear not the wrath of God when you are dead. Fear only the salt vats. And as I stood and looked, and as he who led me there looked at me and smiled and questioned and bedeviled me with those mad, black, tired-scholar's eyes of his, I knew that that was no way for my dear clay. Dear it is, my clay to me; dear it has been to others. La la, the salt vat is no place for my kissed lips and love-lavished body." Mercedes lifted the lid of the chest and gazed fondly at her burial pretties. "So I have made my bed. So I shall lie in it. Some old philosopher said we know we must die; we do not believe it. But the old do believe. I believe.

"My dear, remember the salt vats, and do not be angry with me because my commissions have been heavy. To escape the vats I would stop at nothing -- steal the widow's mite, the orphan's crust, and pennies from a dead man's eyes."

"Do you believe in God?" Saxon asked abruptly, holding herself together despite cold horror.

Mercedes dropped the lid and shrugged her shoulders.

"Who knows? I shall rest well."

"And punishment?" Saxon probed, remembering the unthinkable tale of the other's life.

"Impossible, my dear. As some old poet said, 'God's a good fellow.' Some time I shall talk to you about God. Never be afraid of him. Be afraid only of the salt vats and the things men may do with your pretty flesh after you are dead."

CHAPTER VII

Billy quarreled with good fortune. He suspected he was too prosperous on the wages he received. What with the accumulating savings account, the paying of the monthly furniture installment and the house rent, the spending money in pocket, and the good fare he was eating, he was puzzled as to how Saxon managed to pay for the goods used in her fancy work. Several times he had suggested his inability to see how she did it, and been baffled each time by Saxon's mysterious laugh.

"I can't see how you do it on the money," he was contending one evening.

He opened his mouth to speak further, then closed it and for five minutes thought with knitted brows.

"Say," he said, "what's become of that frilly breakfast cap you was workin' on so hard, I ain't never seen you wear it, and it was sure too big for the kid."

Saxon hesitated, with pursed lips and teasing eyes. With her, untruthfulness had always been a difficult matter. To Billy it was impossible. She could see the cloud-drift in his eyes deepening and his face hardening in the way she knew so well when he was vexed.

"Say, Saxon, you ain't... you ain't... sellin' your work?"

And thereat she related everything, not omitting Mercedes Higgins' part in the transaction, nor Mercedes Higgins' remarkable burial trousseau. But Billy was not to be led aside by the latter. In terms anything but uncertain he told Saxon that she was not to work for money.

"But I have so much spare time, Billy, dear," she pleaded.

He shook his head.

"Nothing doing. I won't listen to it. I married you, and I'll take care of you. Nobody can say Bill Roberts' wife has to work. And I don't want to think it myself. Besides, it ain't necessary."

"But Billy—" she began again.

"Nope. That's one thing I won't stand for, Saxon. Not that I don't like fancy work. I do. I like it like hell, every bit you make, but I like it on YOU. Go ahead and make all you want of it, for yourself, an' I'll put up for the goods. Why, I'm just whistlin' an' happy all day long, thinkin' of the boy an' seein' you at home here workin' away on all them nice things. Because I know how happy you are a-doin' it. But honest to God, Saxon, it'd all be spoiled if I knew you was doin' it to sell. You see, Bill Roberts' wife don't have to work. That's my brag—to myself, mind you. An' besides, it ain't right."

"You're a dear," she whispered, happy despite her disappointment.

"I want you to have all you want," he continued. "An' you're goin' to get it as long as I got two hands stickin' on the ends of my arms. I guess I know how good the things are you wear—good to me, I mean, too. I'm dry behind the ears, an' maybe I've learned a few things I oughtn't to before I knew you. But I know what I'm talkin' about, and I want to say that outside the clothes down underneath, an' the clothes down underneath the outside ones, I never saw a woman like you. Oh—"

He threw up his hands as if despairing of ability to express what he thought and felt, then essayed a further attempt.

"It's not a matter of bein' only clean, though that's a whole lot. Lots of women are clean. It ain't that. It's something more, an' different. It's... well, it's the look of it, so white, an' pretty, an' tasty. It gets on the imagination. It's something I can't get out of my thoughts of you. I want to tell you lots of men can't strip to advantage, an' lots of women, too. But you—well, you're a wonder, that's all, and you can't get too many of them nice things to suit me, and you can't get them too nice.

"For that matter, Saxon, you can just blow yourself. There's lots of easy money layin' around. I'm in great condition. Billy Murphy pulled down seventy-five round iron dollars only last week for puttin' away the Pride of North Beach. That's what ha paid us the fifty back out of."

But this time it was Saxon who rebelled.

"There's Carl Hansen," Billy argued. "The second Sharkey, the alfalfa sportin' writers are callin' him. An' he calls himself Champion of the United States Navy. Well, I got his number. He's just a big stiff. I've seen 'm fight, an' I can pass him the sleep medicine just as easy. The Secretary of the Sportin' Life Club offered to match me. An' a hundred iron dollars in it for the winner. And it'll all be yours to blow in any way you want. What d'ye say?"

"If I can't work for money, you can't fight," was Saxon's ultimatum, immediately withdrawn. "But you and I don't drive bargains. Even if you'd let me work for money, I wouldn't let you fight. I've never forgotten what you told me about how prizefighters lose their silk. Well, you're not going to lose yours. It's half my silk, you know. And if you won't fight, I won't work—there. And more, I'll never do anything you don't want me to, Billy."

"Same here," Billy agreed. "Though just the same I'd like most to death to have just one go at that squarehead Hansen." He smiled with pleasure at the thought. "Say, let's forget it all now, an' you sing me 'Harvest Days' on that dinky what-you-may-call-it."

When she had complied, accompanying herself on the ukulele, she suggested his weird "Cowboy's Lament." In some inexplicable way of love, she had come to like her husband's one song. Because he sang it, she liked its inanity and monotonousness; and most of all, it seemed to her, she loved his hopeless and adorable flatting of every note. She could even sing with him, flatting as accurately and deliciously as he. Nor did she undeceive him in his sublime faith.

"I guess Bert an' the rest have joshed me all the time," he said.

"You and I get along together with it fine," she equivocated; for in such matters she did not deem the untruth a wrong.

Spring was on when the strike came in the railroad shops. The Sunday before it was called, Saxon and Billy had dinner at Bert's house. Saxon's brother came, though he had found it impossible to bring Sarah, who refused to budge from her household rut. Bert was blackly pessimistic, and they found him singing with sardonic glee:

"Nobody loves a mil-yun-aire. Nobody likes his looks. Nobody'll share his slightest care, He classes with thugs and crooks. Thriftiness has become a crime, So spend everything you earn; We're living now in a funny time, When money is made to burn."

Mary went about the dinner preparation, flaunting unmistakable signals of rebellion; and Saxon, rolling up her sleeves and tying on an apron, washed the breakfast dishes. Bert fetched a pitcher of steaming beer from the corner saloon, and the three men smoked and talked about the coming strike.

"It oughta come years ago," was Bert's dictum. "It can't come any too quick now to suit me, but it's too late. We're beaten thumbs down. Here's where the last of the Mohegans gets theirs, in the neck, ker-whop!"

"Oh, I don't know," Tom, who had been smoking his pipe gravely, began to counsel. "Organized labor's gettin' stronger every day. Why, I can remember when there wasn't any unions in California. Look at us now—wages, an' hours, an' everything."

"You talk like an organizer," Bert sneered, "shovin' the bull con on the boneheads. But we know different. Organized wages won't buy as much now as unorganized wages used to buy. They've got us whipsawed. Look at Frisco, the labor leaders doin' dirtier politics than the old parties, pawin' an' squabblin' over graft, an' goin' to San Quentin, while—what are the Frisco carpenters doin'? Let me tell you one thing, Tom Brown, if you listen to all you hear you'll hear that every Frisco carpenter is union an' gettin' full union wages. Do you believe it? It's a damn lie. There ain't a carpenter that don't rebate his wages Saturday night to the contractor. An' that's your buildin' trades in San Francisco, while the leaders are makin' trips to Europe on the earnings of the tenderloin—when they ain't coughing it up to the lawyers to get out of wearin' stripes."

"That's all right," Tom concurred. "Nobody's denyin' it. The trouble is labor ain't quite got its eyes open. It ought to play politics, but the politics ought to be the right kind."

"Socialism, eh?" Bert caught him up with scorn. "Wouldn't they sell us out just as the Ruefs and Schmidts have?"

"Get men that are honest," Billy said. "That's the whole trouble. Not that I stand for socialism. I don't. All our folks was a long time in America, an' I for one won't stand for a lot of fat Germans an' greasy Russian Jews tellin' me how to run my country when they can't speak English yet."

"Your country!" Bert cried. "Why, you bonehead, you ain't got a country. That's a fairy story the grafters shove at you every time they want to rob you some more."

"But don't vote for the grafters," Billy contended. "If we selected honest men we'd get honest treatment."

"I wish you'd come to some of our meetings, Billy," Tom said wistfully. "If you would, you'd get your eyes open an' vote the socialist ticket next election."

"Not on your life," Billy declined. "When you catch me in a socialist meeting'll be when they can talk like white men."

Bert was humming:

"We're living now in a funny time, When money is made to burn."

Mary was too angry with her husband, because of the impending strike and his incendiary utterances, to hold conversation with Saxon, and the latter, bepuzzled, listened to the conflicting opinions of the men.

"Where are we at?" she asked them, with a merriness that concealed her anxiety at heart.

"We ain't at," Bert snarled. "We're gone."

"But meat and oil have gone up again," she chafed. "And Billy's wages have been cut, and the shop men's were cut last year. Something must be done."

"The only thing to do is fight like hell," Bert answered. "Fight, an' go down fightin'. That's all. We're licked anyhow, but we can have a last run for our money."

"That's no way to talk," Tom rebuked.

"The time for talkin' 's past, old cock. The time for fightin' 's come."

"A hell of a chance you'd have against regular troops and machine guns," Billy retorted.

"Oh, not that way. There's such things as greasy sticks that go up with a loud noise and leave holes. There's such things as emery powder—"

"Oh, ho!" Mary burst out upon him, arms akimbo. "So that's what it means. That's what the emery in your vest pocket meant."

Her husband ignored her. Tom smoked with a troubled air. Billy was hurt. It showed plainly in his face.

"You ain't ben doin' that, Bert?" he asked, his manner showing his expectancy of his friend's denial.

"Sure thing, if you want to know. I'd see'm all in hell if I could, before I go."

"He's a bloody-minded anarchist," Mary complained. "Men like him killed McKinley, and Garfield, an'—an' an' all the rest. He'll be hung. You'll see. Mark my words. I'm glad there's no children in sight, that's all."

"It's hot air," Billy comforted her.

"He's just teasing you," Saxon soothed. "He always was a josher."

But Mary shook her head.

"I know. I hear him talkin' in his sleep. He swears and curses something awful, an' grits his teeth. Listen to him now."

Bert, his handsome face bitter and devil-may-care, had tilted his chair back against the wall and was singing

"Nobody loves a mil-yun-aire, Nobody likes his looks, Nobody'll share his slightest care, He classes with thugs and crooks."

Tom was saying something about reasonableness and justice, and Bert ceased from singing to catch him up.

"Justice, eh? Another pipe-dream. I'll show you where the working class gets justice. You remember Forbes—J. Alliston Forbes—wrecked the Alta California Trust Company an' salted down two cold millions. I saw him yesterday, in a big hell-bent automobile. What'd he get? Eight years' sentence. How long did he serve? Less'n two years. Pardoned out on account of ill health. Ill hell! We'll be dead an' rotten before he kicks the bucket. Here. Look out this window. You see the back of that house with the broken porch rail. Mrs. Danaker lives there. She takes in washin'. Her old man was killed on the railroad. Nitsky on damages—contributory negligence, or fellow-servant-something-or-other flimflam. That's what the courts handed her.

Her boy, Archie, was sixteen. He was on the road, a regular road-kid. He blew into Fresno an' rolled a drunk. Do you want to know how much he got? Two dollars and eighty cents. Get that?—Two-eighty. And what did the alfalfa judge hand'm? Fifty years. He's served eight of it already in San Quentin. And he'll go on serving it till he croaks. Mrs. Danaker says he's bad with consumption—caught it inside, but she ain't got the pull to get'm pardoned. Archie the Kid steals two dollars an' eighty cents from a drunk and gets fifty years. J. Alliston Forbes sticks up the Alta Trust for two millions en' gets less'n two years. Who's country is this anyway? Yourn an' Archie the Kid's? Guess again. It's J. Alliston Forbes'—Oh:

"Nobody likes a mil-yun-aire, Nobody likes his looks, Nobody'll share his slightest care, He classes with thugs and crooks."

Mary, at the sink, where Saxon was just finishing the last dish, untied Saxon's apron and kissed her with the sympathy that women alone feel for each other under the shadow of maternity.

"Now you sit down, dear. You mustn't tire yourself, and it's a long way to go yet. I'll get your sewing for you, and you can listen to the men talk. But don't listen to Bert. He's crazy."

Saxon sewed and listened, and Bert's face grew bleak and bitter as he contemplated the baby clothes in her lap.

"There you go," he blurted out, "bringin' kids into the world when you ain't got any guarantee you can feed em."

"You must a-had a souse last night," Tom grinned.

Bert shook his head.

"Aw, what's the use of gettin' grouched?" Billy cheered. "It's a pretty good country."

"It WAS a pretty good country," Bert replied, "when we was all Mohegans. But not now. We're jiggerooed. We're hornswoggled. We're backed to a standstill. We're double-crossed to a fare-you-well. My folks fought for this country. So did yourn, all of you. We freed the niggers, killed the Indians, an' starved, an' froze, an' sweat, an' fought. This land looked good to us. We cleared it, an' broke it, an' made the roads, an' built the cities. And there was plenty for everybody. And we went on fightin' for it. I had two uncles killed at Gettysburg. All of us was mixed up in that war. Listen to Saxon talk any time what her folks went through to get out here an' get ranches, an' horses, an' cattle, an' everything. And they got 'em. All our folks' got 'em, Mary's, too—"

"And if they'd ben smart they'd a-held on to them," she interpolated.

"Sure thing," Bert continued. "That's the very point. We're the losers. We've ben robbed. We couldn't mark cards, deal from the bottom, an' ring in cold decks like the others. We're the white folks that failed. You see, times changed, and there was two kinds of us, the lions and the plugs. The plugs only worked, the lions only gobbled. They gobbled the farms, the mines, the factories, an' now they've gobbled the government. We're the white folks an' the children of white folks, that was too busy being good to be smart. We're the white folks that lost out. We're the ones that's ben skinned. D'ye get me?"

"You'd make a good soap-boxer," Tom commended, "if only you'd get the kinks straightened out in your reasoning."

"It sounds all right, Bert," Billy said, "only it ain't. Any man can get rich to-day—"

"Or be president of the United States," Bert snapped. "Sure thing—if he's got it in him. Just the same I ain't heard you makin' a noise like a millionaire or a president. Why? You ain't got it in you. You're a bonehead. A plug. That's why. Skiddoo for you. Skiddoo for all of us."

At the table, while they ate, Tom talked of the joys of farm-life he had known as a boy and as a young man, and confided that it was his dream to go and take up government land somewhere as his people had done before him. Unfortunately, as he explained, Sarah was set, so that the dream must remain a dream.

"It's all in the game," Billy sighed. "It's played to rules. Some one has to get knocked out, I suppose."

A little later, while Bert was off on a fresh diatribe, Billy became aware that he was making comparisons. This house was not like his house. Here was no satisfying atmosphere. Things seemed to run with a jar. He recollected that when they arrived the breakfast dishes had not yet been washed. With a man's general obliviousness of household affairs, he had not noted details; yet it had been borne in on him, all morning, in a myriad ways, that Mary was not the housekeeper Saxon was. He glanced proudly across at her, and felt the spur of an impulse to leave his seat, go around, and embrace her. She was a wife. He remembered her dainty undergarmenting, and on the instant, into his brain, leaped the image of her so appareled, only to be shattered by Bert.

"Hey, Bill, you seem to think I've got a grouch. Sure thing. I have. You ain't had my experiences. You've always done teamin' an' pulled down easy money prizefightin'. You ain't known hard times. You ain't ben through strikes. You ain't had to take care of an old mother an' swallow dirt on her account. It wasn't until after she died that I could rip loose an' take or leave as I felt like it.

"Take that time I tackled the Niles Electric an' see what a work-plug gets handed out to him. The Head Cheese sizes me up, pumps me a lot of questions, an' gives me an application blank. I make it out, payin' a dollar to a doctor they sent me to for a health certificate. Then I got to go to a picture garage an' get my mug taken for the Niles Electric rogues' gallery. And I cough up another dollar for the mug. The Head Squirt takes the blank, the health certificate, and the mug, an' fires more questions. DID I BELONG TO A LABOR UNION?—ME? Of course I told'm the truth I guess nit. I needed the job. The grocery wouldn't give me any more tick, and there was my mother.

"Huh, thinks I, here's where I'm a real carman. Back platform for me, where I can pick up the fancy skirts. Nitsky. Two dollars, please. Me—my two dollars. All for a pewter badge. Then there was the uniform—nineteen fifty, and get it anywhere else for fifteen. Only that was to be paid out of my first month. And then five dollars in change in my pocket, my own money. That was the rule.—I borrowed that five from Tom Donovan, the policeman. Then what? They worked me for two weeks without pay, breakin' me in."

"Did you pick up any fancy skirts?" Saxon queried teasingly.

Bert shook his head glumly.

"I only worked a month. Then we organized, and they busted our union higher'n a kite."

"And you boobs in the shops will be busted the same way if you go out on strike," Mary informed him.

"That's what I've ben tellin' you all along," Bert replied. "We ain't got a chance to win."

"Then why go out?" was Saxon's question.

He looked at her with lackluster eyes for a moment, then answered

"Why did my two uncles get killed at Gettysburg?"

CHAPTER VIII

Saxon went about her housework greatly troubled. She no longer devoted herself to the making of pretties. The materials cost money, and she did not dare. Bert's thrust had sunk home. It remained in her quivering consciousness like a shaft of steel that ever turned and rankled. She and Billy were responsible for this coming young life. Could they be sure, after all, that they could adequately feed and clothe it and prepare it for its way in the world? Where was the guaranty? She remembered, dimly, the blight of hard times in the past, and the plaints of fathers and mothers in those days returned to her with a new significance. Almost could she understand Sarah's chronic complaining.

Hard times were already in the neighborhood, where lived the families of the shopmen who had gone out on strike. Among the small storekeepers, Saxon, in the course of the daily marketing, could sense the air of despondency. Light and geniality seemed to have vanished. Gloom pervaded everywhere. The mothers of the children that played in the streets showed the gloom plainly in their faces. When they gossiped in the evenings, over front gates and on door stoops, their voices were subdued and less of laughter rang out.

Mary Donahue, who had taken three pints from the milkman, now took one pint. There were no more family trips to the moving picture shows. Scrap-meat was harder to get from the butcher. Nora Delaney, in the third house, no longer bought fresh fish for Friday. Salted codfish, not of the best quality, was now on her table. The sturdy children that ran out upon the street between meals with huge slices of bread and butter and sugar now came out with no sugar and with thinner slices spread more thinly with butter. The very custom was dying out, and some children already had desisted from piecing between meals.

Everywhere was manifest a pinching and scraping, a tightning and shortening down of expenditure. And everywhere was more irritation. Women became angered with one another, and with the children, more quickly than of yore; and Saxon knew that Bert and Mary bickered incessantly.

"If she'd only realize I've got troubles of my own," Bert complained to Saxon.

She looked at him closely, and felt fear for him in a vague, numb way. His black eyes seemed to burn with a continuous madness. The brown face was leaner, the skin drawn tightly across the cheekbones. A slight twist had come to the mouth, which seemed frozen into bitterness. The very carriage of his body and the way he wore his hat advertised a recklessness more intense than had been his in the past.

Sometimes, in the long afternoons, sitting by the window with idle hands, she caught herself reconstructing in her vision that folk-migration of her people across the plains and mountains and deserts to the sunset land by the Western sea. And often she found herself dreaming of the arcadian days of her people, when they had not lived in cities nor been vexed with labor unions and employers' associations. She would remember the old people's tales of self-sufficingness, when they shot or raised their own meat, grew their own vegetables, were their own blacksmiths and carpenters, made their own shoes—yes, and spun the cloth of the clothes they wore. And something of the wistfulness in Tom's face she could see as she recollected it when he talked of his dream of taking up government land.

A farmer's life must be fine, she thought. Why was it that people had to live in cities? Why had times changed? If there had been enough in the old days, why was there not enough now? Why was it necessary for men to quarrel and jangle, and strike and fight, all about the matter of getting work? Why wasn't there work for all?—Only that morning, and she shuddered with the recollection, she had seen two scabs, on their way to work, beaten up by the strikers, by men she knew by sight, and some by name, who lived in the neighhorhood. It had happened directly across the street. It had been cruel, terrible—a dozen men on two. The children had begun it by throwing rocks at the scabs and cursing them in ways children should not know. Policemen had run upon the scene with drawn revolvers, and the strikers had retreated into the houses and through the narrow alleys between the houses. One of the scabs, unconscious, had been carried away in an ambulance; the other, assisted by special railroad police, had been taken away to the shops. At him, Mary Donahue, standing on her front stoop, her child in her arms, had hurled such vile abuse that it had brought the blush of shame to Saxon's cheeks. On the stoop of the house on the other side, Saxon had noted Mercedes, in the height of the beating up, looking on with a queer smile. She had seemed very eager to witness, her nostrils dilated and swelling like the beat of pulses as she watched. It had struck Saxon at the time that the old woman was quite unalarmed and only curious to see.

To Mercedes, who was so wise in love, Saxon went for explanation of what was the matter with the world. But the old woman's wisdom in affairs industrial and economic was cryptic and unpalatable.

"La la, my dear, it is so simple. Most men are born stupid. They are the slaves. A few are born clever. They are the masters. God made men so, I suppose."

"Then how about God and that terrible beating across the street this morning?"

"I'm afraid he was not interested," Mercedes smiled. "I doubt he even knows that it happened."

"I was frightened to death," Saxon declared. "I was made sick by it. And yet you—I saw you—you looked on as cool as you please, as if it was a show."

"It was a show, my dear."

"Oh, how could you?"

"La la, I have seen men killed. It is nothing strange. All men die. The stupid ones die like oxen, they know not why. It is quite funny to see. They strike each other with fists and clubs, and break each other's heads. It is gross. They are like a lot of animals. They are like dogs wrangling over bones. Jobs are bones, you know. Now, if they fought for women, or ideas, or bars of gold, or fabulous diamonds, it would be splendid. But no; they are only hungry, and fight over scraps for their stomach."

"Oh, if I could only understand!" Saxon murmured, her hands tightly clasped in anguish of incomprehension and vital need to know.

"There is nothing to understand. It is clear as print. There have always been the stupid and the clever, the slave and the master, the peasant and the prince. There always will be."

"But why?"

"Why is a peasant a peasant, my dear? Because he is a peasant. Why is a flea a flea?"

Saxon tossed her head fretfully.

"Oh, but my dear, I have answered. The philosophies of the world can give no better answer. Why do you like your man for a husband rather than any other man? Because you like him that way, that is all. Why do you like? Because you like. Why does fire burn and frost bite? Why are there clever men and stupid men? masters and slaves? employers and workingmen? Why is black black? Answer that and you answer everything."

"But it is not right that men should go hungry and without work when they want to work if only they can get a square deal," Saxon protested.

"Oh, but it is right, just as it is right that stone won't burn like wood, that sea sand isn't sugar, that thorns prick, that water is wet, that smoke rises, that things fall down and not up."

But such doctrine of reality made no impression on Saxon. Frankly, she could not comprehend. It seemed like so much nonsense.

"Then we have no liberty and independence," she cried passionately. "One man is not as good as another. My child has not the right to live that a rich mother's child has."

"Certainly not," Mercedes answered.

"Yet all my people fought for these things," Saxon urged, remembering her school history and the sword of her father.

"Democracy—the dream of the stupid peoples. Oh, la la, my dear, democracy is a lie, an enchantment to keep the work brutes content, just as religion used to keep them content. When they groaned in their misery and toil, they were persuaded to keep on in their misery and toil by pretty tales of a land beyond the skies where they would live famously and fat while the clever ones roasted in everlasting fire. Ah, how the clever ones must have chuckled! And when that lie wore out, and democracy was dreamed, the clever ones saw to it that it should be in truth a dream, nothing but a dream. The world belongs to the great and clever."

"But you are of the working people," Saxon charged.

The old woman drew herself up, and almost was angry.

"I? Of the working people? My dear, because I had misfortune with moneys invested, because I am old and can no longer win the brave young men, because I have outlived the men of my youth and there is no one to go to, because I live here in the ghetto with Barry Higgins and prepare to die— why, my dear, I was born with the masters, and have trod all my days on the necks of the stupid. I have drunk rare wines and sat at feasts that would have supported this neighborhood for a lifetime. Dick Golden and I—it was Dickie's money, but I could have had it -- Dick Golden and I dropped four hundred thousand francs in a week's play at Monte Carlo. He was a Jew, but he was a spender. In India I have worn jewels that could have saved the lives of ten thousand families dying before my eyes."

"You saw them die?... and did nothing?" Saxon asked aghast.

"I kept my jewels—la la, and was robbed of them by a brute of a Russian officer within the year."

"And you let them die," Saxon reiterated.

"They were cheap spawn. They fester and multiply like maggots. They meant nothing—nothing, my dear, nothing. No more than your work people mean here, whose crowning stupidity is their continuing to beget more stupid spawn for the slavery of the masters."

So it was that while Saxon could get little glimmering of common sense from others, from the terrible old woman she got none at all. Nor could Saxon bring herself to believe much of what she considered Mercedes' romancing. As the weeks passed, the strike in the railroad shops grew bitter and deadly. Billy shook his head and confessed his inability to make head or tail of the troubles that were looming on the labor horizon.

"I don't get the hang of it," he told Saxon. "It's a mix-up. It's like a roughhouse with the lights out. Look at us teamsters. Here we are, the talk just starting of going out on sympathetic strike for the mill-workers. They've ben out a week, most of their places is filled, an' if us teamsters keep on haulin' the mill-work the strike's lost."

"Yet you didn't consider striking for yourselves when your wages were cut," Saxon said with a frown.

"Oh, we wasn't in position then. But now the Frisco teamsters and the whole Frisco Water Front Confederation is liable to back us up. Anyway, we're just talkin' about it, that's all. But if we do go out, we'll try to get back that ten per cent cut."

"It's rotten politics," he said another time. "Everybody's rotten. If we'd only wise up and agree to pick out honest men—"

"But if you, and Bert, and Tom can't agree, how do you expect all the rest to agree?" Saxon asked.

"It gets me," he admitted. "It's enough to give a guy the willies thinkin' about it. And yet it's plain as the nose on your face. Get honest men for politics, an' the whole thing's straightened out. Honest men'd make honest laws, an' then honest men'd get their dues. But Bert wants to smash things, an' Tom smokes his pipe and dreams pipe dreams about by an' by when everybody votes the way he thinks. But this by an' by ain't the point. We want things now. Tom says we can't get them now, an' Bert says we ain't never goin' to get them. What can a fellow do when everybody's of different minds? Look at the socialists themselves. They're always disagreeing, splittin' up, an' firin' each other out of the party. The whole thing's bughouse, that's what, an' I almost get dippy myself thinkin' about it. The point I can't get out of my mind is that we want things now."

He broke off abruptly and stared at Saxon.

"What is it?" he asked, his voice husky with anxiety. "You ain't sick... or... or anything?"

One hand she had pressed to her heart; but the startle and fright in her eyes was changing into a pleased intentness, while on her mouth was a little mysterious smile. She seemed oblivious to her husband, as if listening to some message from afar and not for his ears. Then wonder and joy transfused her face, and she looked at Billy, and her hand went out to his.

"It's life," she whispered. "I felt life. I am so glad, so glad."

The next evening when Billy came home from work, Saxon caused him to know and undertake more of the responsibilities of fatherhood.

"I've been thinking it over, Billy," she began, "and I'm such a healthy, strong woman that it won't have to be very expensive. There's Martha Skelton—she's a good midwife."

But Billy shook his head.

"Nothin' doin' in that line, Saxon. You're goin' to have Doc Hentley. He's Bill Murphy's doc, an' Bill swears by him. He's an old cuss, but he's a wooz."

"She confined Maggie Donahue," Saxon argued; "and look at her and her baby."

"Well, she won't confine you—not so as you can notice it."

"But the doctor will charge twenty dollars," Saxon pursued, "and make me get a nurse because I haven't any womenfolk to come in. But Martha Skelton would do everything, and it would be so much cheaper."

But Billy gathered her tenderly in his arms and laid down the law.

"Listen to me, little wife. The Roberts family ain't on the cheap. Never forget that. You've gotta have the baby. That's your business, an' it's enough for you. My business is to get the money an' take care of you. An' the best ain't none too good for you. Why, I wouldn't run the chance of the teeniest accident happenin' to you for a million dollars. It's you that counts. An' dollars is dirt. Maybe you think I like that kid some. I do. Why, I can't get him outa my head. I'm thinkin' about'm all day long. If I get fired, it'll be his fault. I'm clean dotty over him. But just the same, Saxon, honest to God, before I'd have anything happen to you, break your little finger, even, I'd see him dead an' buried first. That'll give you something of an idea what you mean to me.

"Why, Saxon, I had the idea that when folks got married they just settled down, and after a while their business was to get along with each other. Maybe it's the way it is with other people; but it ain't that way with you an' me. I love you more 'n more every day. Right now I love you more'n when I began talkin' to you five minutes ago. An' you won't have to get a nurse. Doc Hentley'll come every day, an' Mary'll come in an' do the housework, an' take care of you an' all that, just as you'll do for her if she ever needs it."

As the days and weeks passed, Saxon was possessed by a conscious feeling of proud motherhood in her swelling breasts. So essentially a normal woman was she, that motherhood was a satisfying and passionate happiness. It was true that she had her moments of apprehension, but they were so momentary and faint that they tended, if anything, to give zest to her happiness.

Only one thing troubled her, and that was the puzzling and perilous situation of labor which no one seemed to understand, her self least of all.

"They're always talking about how much more is made by machinery than by the old ways," she told her brother Tom. "Then, with all the machinery we've got now, why don't we get more?"

"Now you're talkin'," he answered. "It wouldn't take you long to understand socialism."

But Saxon had a mind to the immediate need of things.

"Tom, how long have you been a socialist?"

"Eight years."

"And you haven't got anything by it?"

"But we will... in time."

"At that rate you'll be dead first," she challenged.

Tom sighed.

"I'm afraid so. Things move so slow."

Again he sighed. She noted the weary, patient look in his face, the bent shoulders, the labor-gnarled hands, and it all seemed to symbolize the futility of his social creed.

CHAPTER IX

It began quietly, as the fateful unexpected so often begins. Children, of all ages and sizes, were playing in the street, and Saxon, by the open front window, was watching them and dreaming day dreams of her child soon to be. The sunshine mellowed peacefully down, and a light wind from the bay cooled the air and gave to it a tang of salt. One of the children pointed up Pine Street toward Seventh. All the children ceased playing, and stared and pointed. They formed into groups, the larger boys, of from ten to twelve, by themselves, the older girls anxiously clutching the small children by the hands or gathering them into their arms.

Saxon could not see the cause of all this, but she could guess when she saw the larger boys rush to the gutter, pick up stones, and sneak into the alleys between the houses. Smaller boys tried to imitate them. The girls, dragging the tots by the arms, banged gates and clattered up the front steps of the small houses. The doors slammed behind them, and the street was deserted, though here and there front shades were drawn aside so that anxious-faced women might peer forth. Saxon heard the uptown train puffing and snorting as it pulled out from Center Street. Then, from the direction of Seventh, came a hoarse, throaty manroar. Still, she could see nothing, and she remembered Mercedes Higgins' words "THEY ARE LIKE DOGS WRANGLING OVER BONES. JOBS ARE BONES, YOU KNOW."

The roar came closer, and Saxon, leaning out, saw a dozen scabs, conveyed by as many special police and Pinkertons, coming down the sidewalk on her side of the street. They came compactly, as if with discipline, while behind, disorderly, yelling confusedly, stooping to pick up rocks, were seventy-five or a hundred of the striking shopmen. Saxon discovered herself trembling with apprehension, knew that she must not, and controlled herself. She was helped in this by the conduct of Mercedes Higgins. The old woman came out of her front door, dragging a chair, on which she coolly seated herself on the tiny stoop at the top of the steps.

In the hands of the special police were clubs. The Pinkertons carried no visible weapons. The strikers, urging on from behind, seemed content with yelling their rage and threats, and it remained for the children to precipitate the conflict. From across the street, between the Olsen and the Isham houses, came a shower of stones. Most of these fell short, though one struck a scab on the head. The man was no more than twenty feet away from Saxon. He reeled toward her front picket fence, drawing a revolver. With one hand he brushed the blood from his eyes and with the other he discharged the revolver into the Isham house. A Pinkerton seized his arm to prevent a second shot, and dragged him along. At the same instant a wilder roar went up from the strikers, while a volley of stones came from between Saxon's house and Maggie Donahue's. The scabs and their protectors made a stand, drawing revolvers. From their hard, determined faces—fighting men by profession—Saxon could augur nothing but bloodshed and death. An elderly man, evidently the leader, lifted a soft felt hat and mopped the perspiration from the bald top of his head. He was a large man, very rotund of belly and helpless looking. His gray beard was stained with streaks of tobacco juice, and he was smoking a cigar. He was stoop-shouldered, and Saxon noted the dandruff on the collar of his coat.

One of the men pointed into the street, and several of his companions laughed. The cause of it was the little Olsen boy, barely four years old, escaped somehow from his mother and toddling toward his economic enemies. In his right he bore a rock so heavy that he could scarcely lift it. With this he feebly threatened them. His rosy little face was convulsed with rage, and he was screaming over and over "Dam scabs! Dam scabs! Dam scabs!" The laughter with which they greeted him only increased his fury. He toddled closer, and with a mighty exertion threw the rock. It fell a scant six feet beyond his hand.

This much Saxon saw, and also Mrs. Olsen rushing into the street for her child. A rattling of revolver-shots from the strikers drew Saxon's attention to the men beneath her. One of them cursed sharply and examined the biceps of his left arm, which hung limply by his side. Down the hand she saw the blood beginning to drip. She knew she ought not remain and watch, but the memory of her fighting forefathers was with her, while she possessed no more than normal human fear—if anything, less. She forgot her child in the eruption of battle that had broken upon her quiet street. And she forgot the strikers, and everything else, in amazement at what had happened to the round-bellied, cigar-smoking leader. In some strange way, she knew not how, his head had become wedged at the neck between the tops of the pickets of her fence. His body hung down outside, the knees not quite touching the ground. His hat had fallen off, and the sun was making an astounding high light on his bald spot. The cigar, too, was gone. She saw he was looking at her. One hand, between the pickets, seemed waving at her, and almost he seemed to wink at her jocosely, though she knew it to be the contortion of deadly pain.

Possibly a second, or, at most, two seconds, she gazed at this, when she was aroused by Bert's voice. He was running along the sidewalk, in front of her house, and behind him charged several more strikers, while he shouted: "Come on, you Mohegans! We got 'em nailed to the cross!"

In his left hand he carried a pick-handle, in his right a revolver, already empty, for he clicked the cylinder vainly around as he ran. With an abrupt stop, dropping the pick-handle, he whirled half about, facing Saxon's gate. He was sinking down, when he straightened himself to throw the revolver into the face of a scab who was jumping toward him. Then he began swaying, at the same time sagging at the knees and waist. Slowly, with infinite effort, he caught a gate picket in his right hand, and, still slowly, as if lowering himself, sank down, while past him leaped the crowd of strikers he had led.

It was battle without quarter—a massacre. The scabs and their protectors, surrounded, backed against Saxon's fence, fought like cornered rats, but could not withstand the rush of a hundred men. Clubs and pick-handles were swinging, revolvers were exploding, and cobblestones were flung with crushing effect at arm's distance. Saxon saw young Frank Davis, a friend of Bert's and a father of several months' standing, press the muzzle of his revolver against a scab's stomach and fire. There were curses and snarls of rage, wild cries of terror and pain. Mercedes was right. These things were not men. They were beasts, fighting over bones, destroying one another for bones.

JOBS ARE BONES; JOBS ARE BONES. The phrase was an incessant iteration in Saxon's brain. Much as she might have wished it, she was powerless now to withdraw from the window. It was as if she were paralyzed. Her brain no longer worked. She sat numb, staring, incapable of anything save seeing the rapid horror before her eyes that flashed along like a moving picture film gone mad. She saw Pinkertons, special police, and strikers go down. One scab, terribly wounded, on his knees and begging for mercy, was kicked in the face. As he sprawled backward another striker, standing over him, fired a revolver into his chest, quickly and deliberately, again and again, until the weapon was empty. Another scab, backed over the pickets by a hand clutching his throat, had his face pulped by a revolver butt. Again and again, continually, the revolver rose and fell, and Saxon knew the man who wielded it—Chester Johnson. She had met him at dances and danced with him in the days before she was married. He had always been kind and good natured. She remembered the Friday night, after a City Hall band concert, when he had taken her and two other girls to Tony's Tamale Grotto on Thirteenth street. And after that they had all gone to Pabst's Cafe and drunk a glass of beer before they went home. It was impossible that this could be the same Chester Johnson. And as she looked, she saw the round-bellied leader, still wedged by the neck between the pickets, draw a revolver with his free hand, and, squinting horribly sidewise, press the muzzle against Chester's side. She tried to scream a warning. She did scream, and Chester looked up and saw her. At that moment the revolver went off, and he collapsed prone upon the body of the scab. And the bodies of three men hung on her picket fence.

Anything could happen now. Quite without surprise, she saw the strikers leaping the fence, trampling her few little geraniums and pansies into the earth as they fled between Mercedes' house and hers. Up Pine street, from the railroad yards, was coming a rush of railroad police and Pinkertons, firing as they ran. While down Pine street, gongs clanging, horses at a gallop, came three patrol wagons packed with police. The strikers were in a trap. The only way out was between the houses and over the back yard fences. The jam in the narrow alley prevented them all from escaping. A dozen were cornered in the angle between the front of her house and the steps. And as they had done, so were they done by. No effort was made to arrest. They were clubbed down and shot down to the last man by the guardians of the peace who were infuriated by what had been wreaked on their brethren.

It was all over, and Saxon, moving as in a dream, clutching the banister tightly, came down the front steps. The round-bellied leader still leered at her and fluttered one hand, though two big policemen were just bending to extricate him. The gate was off its hinges, which seemed strange, for she had been watching all the time and had not seen it happen.

Bert's eyes were closed. His lips were blood-flecked, and there was a gurgling in his throat as if he were trying to say something. As she stooped above him, with her handkerchief brushing the blood from his cheek where some one had stepped on him, his eyes opened. The old defiant light was in them. He did not know her. The lips moved, and faintly, almost reminiscently, he murmured, "The last of the Mohegans, the last of the Mohegans." Then he groaned, and the eyelids drooped down again. He was not dead. She knew that, the chest still rose and fell, and the gurgling still continued in his throat.

She looked up. Mercedes stood beside her. The old woman's eyes were very bright, her withered cheeks flushed.

"Will you help me carry him into the house?" Saxon asked.

Mercedes nodded, turned to a sergeant of police, and made the request to him. The sergeant gave a swift glance at Bert, and his eyes were bitter and ferocious as he refused.

"To hell with'm. We'll care for our own."

"Maybe you and I can do it," Saxon said.

"Don't be a fool." Mercedes was beckoning to Mrs. Olsen across the street. "You go into the house, little mother that is to be. This is bad for you. We'll carry him in. Mrs. Olsen is coming, and we'll get Maggie Donahue."

Saxon led the way into the back bedroom which Billy had insisted on furnishing. As she opened the door, the carpet seemed to fly up into her face as with the force of a blow, for she remembered Bert had laid that carpet.

And as the women placed him on the bed she recalled that it was Bert and she, between them, who had set the bed up one Sunday morning.

And then she felt very queer, and was surprised to see Mercedes regarding her with questioning, searching eyes. After that her queerness came on very fast, and she descended into the hell of pain that is given to women alone to know. She was supported, half-carried, to the front bedroom. Many faces were about her—Mercedes, Mrs. Olsen, Maggie Donahue. It seemed she must ask Mrs. Olsen if she had saved little Emil from the street, but Mercedes cleared Mrs. Olsen out to look after Bert, and Maggie Donahue went to answer a knock at the front door. From the street came a loud hum of voices, punctuated by shouts and commands, and from time to time there was a clanging of the gongs of ambulances and patrol wagons. Then appeared the fat, comfortable face of Martha Shelton, and, later, Dr. Hentley came. Once, in a clear interval, through the thin wall Saxon heard the high opening notes of Mary's hysteria. And, another time, she heard Mary repeating over and over. "I'll never go back to the laundry. Never. Never."

CHAPTER X

Billy could never get over the shock, during that period, of Saxon's appearance. Morning after morning, and evening after evening when he came home from work, he would enter the room where she lay and fight a royal battle to hide his feelings and make a show of cheerfulness and geniality. She looked so small lying there so small and shrunken and weary, and yet so child-like in her smallness. Tenderly, as he sat beside her, he would take up her pale hand and stroke the slim, transparent arm, marveling at the smallness and delicacy of the bones.

One of her first questions, puzzling alike to Billy and Mary, was:

"Did they save little Emil Olsen?"

And when she told them how he had attacked, singlehanded, the whole twenty-four fighting men, Billy's face glowed with appreciation.

"The little cuss!" he said. "That's the kind of a kid to be proud of."

He halted awkwardly, and his very evident fear that he had hurt her touched Saxon. She put her hand out to his.

"Billy," she began; then waited till Mary left the room.

"I never asked before—not that it matters... now. But I waited for you to tell me. Was it...?"

He shook his head.

"No; it was a girl. A perfect little girl. Only... it was too soon."

She pressed his hand, and almost it was she that sympathized with him in his affliction.

"I never told you, Billy—you were so set on a boy; but I planned, just the same, if it was a girl, to call her Daisy. You remember, that was my mother's name."

He nodded his approbation.

"Say, Saxon, you know I did want a boy like the very dickens... well, I don't care now. I think I'm set just as hard on a girl, an', well, here's hopin' the next will be called... you wouldn't mind, would you?"

"What?"

"If we called it the same name, Daisy?"

"Oh, Billy! I was thinking the very same thing."

Then his face grew stern as he went on.

"Only there ain't goin' to be a next. I didn't know what havin' children was like before. You can't run any more risks like that."

"Hear the big, strong, afraid-man talk!" she jeered, with a wan smile. "You don't know anything about it. How can a man? I am a healthy, natural woman. Everything would have been all right this time if... if all that fighting hadn't happened. Where did they bury Bert?"

"You knew?"

"All the time. And where is Mercedes? She hasn't been in for two days."

"Old Barry's sick. She's with him."

He did not tell her that the old night watchman was dying, two thin walls and half a dozen feet away.

Saxon's lips were trembling, and she began to cry weakly, clinging to Billy's hand with both of hers.

"I—I can't help it," she sobbed. "I'll be all right in a minute.... Our little girl, Billy. Think of it! And I never saw her!"

She was still lying on her bed, when, one evening, Mary saw fit to break out in bitter thanksgiving that she had escaped, and was destined to escape, what Saxon had gone through.

"Aw, what are you talkin' about?" Billy demanded. "You'll get married some time again as sure as beans is beans."

"Not to the best man living," she proclaimed. "And there ain't no call for it. There's too many people in the world now, else why are there two or three men for every job? And, besides, havin' children is too terrible."

Saxon, with a look of patient wisdom in her face that became glorified as she spoke, made answer:

"I ought to know what it means. I've been through it, and I'm still in the thick of it, and I want to say to you right now, out of all the pain and the ache and the sorrow, that it is the most beautiful, wonderful thing in the world."

As Saxon's strength came back to her (and when Doctor Hentley had privily assured Billy that she was sound as a dollar), she herself took up the matter of the industrial tragedy that had taken place before her door. The militia had been called out immediately, Billy informed her, and was encamped then at the foot of Pine street on the waste ground next to the railroad yards. As for the strikers, fifteen of them were in jail. A house to house search had been made in the neighborhood by the police, and in this way nearly the whole fifteen, all wounded, had been captured. It would go hard with them,

Billy foreboded gloomily. The newspapers were demanding blood for blood, and all the ministers in Oakland had preached fierce sermons against the strikers. The railroad had filled every place, and it was well known that the striking shopmen not only would never get their old jobs back but were blacklisted in every railroad in the United States. Already they were beginning to scatter. A number had gone to Panama, and four were talking of going to Ecuador to work in the shops of the railroad that ran over the Andes to Quito.

With anxiety keenly concealed, she tried to feel out Billy's opinion on what had happened.

"That shows what Bert's violent methods come to," she said.

He shook his head slowly and gravely.

"They'll hang Chester Johnson, anyway," he answered indirectly. "You know him. You told me you used to dance with him. He was caught red-handed, lyin' on the body of a scab he beat to death. Old Jelly Belly's got three bullet holes in him, but he ain't goin' to die, and he's got Chester's number. They'll hang'm on Jelly Belly's evidence. It was all in the papers. Jelly Belly shot him, too, a-hangin' by the neck on our pickets."

Saxon shuddered. Jelly Belly must be the man with the bald spot and the tobacco-stained whiskers.

"Yes," she said. "I saw it all. It seemed he must have hung there for hours."

"It was all over, from first to last, in five minutes."

"It seemed ages and ages."

"I guess that's the way it seemed to Jelly Belly, stuck on the pickets," Billy smiled grimly. "But he's a hard one to kill. He's been shot an' cut up a dozen different times. But they say now he'll be crippled for life—have to go around on crutches, or in a wheel-chair. That'll stop him from doin' any more dirty work for the railroad. He was one of their top gun-fighters—always up to his ears in the thick of any fightin' that was goin' on. He never was leery of anything on two feet, I'll say that much for'm."

"Where does he live?" Saxon inquired.

"Up on Adeline, near Tenth—fine neighborhood an' fine two-storied house. He must pay thirty dollars a month rent. I guess the railroad paid him pretty well."

"Then he must be married?"

"Yep. I never seen his wife, but he's got one son, Jack, a passenger engineer. I used to know him. He was a nifty boxer, though he never went into the ring. An' he's got another son that's teacher in the high school. His name's Paul. We're about the same age. He was great at baseball. I knew him when we was kids. He pitched me out three times hand-runnin' once, when the Durant played the Cole School."

Saxon sat back in the Morris chair, resting and thinking. The problem was growing more complicated than ever. This elderly, round-bellied, and bald-headed gunfighter, too, had a wife and family. And there was Frank Davis, married barely a year and with a baby boy. Perhaps the scab he shot in the stomach had a wife and children. All seemed to be acquainted, members of a very large family, and yet, because of their particular families, they battered and killed each other. She had seen Chester Johnson kill a scab, and now they were going to hang Chester Johnson, who had married Kittie Brady out of the cannery, and she and Kittie Brady had worked together years before in the paper box factory.

Vainly Saxon waited for Billy to say something that would show he did not countenance the killing of the scabs.

"It was wrong," she ventured finally.

"They killed Bert," he countered. "An' a lot of others. An' Frank Davis. Did you know he was dead? Had his whole lower jaw shot away—died in the ambulance before they could get him to the receiving hospital. There was never so much killin' at one time in Oakland before."

"But it was their fault," she contended. "They began it. It was murder."

Billy did not reply, but she heard him mutter hoarsely. She knew he said "God damn them"; but when she asked, "What?" he made no answer. His eyes were deep with troubled clouds, while the mouth had hardened, and all his face was bleak.

To her it was a heart-stab. Was he, too, like the rest? Would he kill other men who had families, like Bert, and Frank Davis, and Chester Johnson had killed? Was he, too, a wild beast, a dog that would snarl over a bone?

She sighed. Life was a strange puzzle. Perhaps Mercedes Higgins was right in her cruel statement of the terms of existence.

"What of it," Billy laughed harshly, as if in answer to her unuttered questions. "It's dog eat dog, I guess, and it's always ben that way. Take that scrap outside there. They killed each other just like the North an' South did in the Civil War."

"But workingmen can't win that way, Billy. You say yourself that it spoiled their chance of winning."

"I suppose not," he admitted reluctantly. "But what other chance they've got to win I don't see. Look at 'us. We'll be up against it next."

"Not the teamsters?" she cried.

He nodded gloomily.

"The bosses are cuttin' loose all along the line for a high old time. Say they're goin' to beat us to our knees till we come crawlin' back a-beggin' for our jobs. They've bucked up real high an' mighty what of all that killin' the other day. Havin' the troops out is half the fight, along with havin' the preachers an' the papers an' the public behind 'em. They're shootin' off their mouths already about what they're goin' to do. They're sure gunning for trouble. First, they're goin' to hang Chester Johnson an' as many more of the fifteen as they can. They say that flat. The Tribune, an' the Enquirer an' the Times keep sayin' it over an over every day. They're all union-bustin' to beat the band. No more closed shop. To hell with organized labor. Why, the dirty little Intelligencer come out this morning an' said that every union official in Oakland ought to be run outa town or stretched up. Fine, eh? You bet it's fine.

"Look at us. It ain't a case any more of sympathetic strike for the mill-workers. We got our own troubles. They've fired our four best men—the ones that was always on the conference committees. Did it without cause. They're lookin' for trouble, as I told you, an' they'll get it, too, if they don't watch out. We got our tip from the Frisco Water Front Confederation. With them backin' us we'll go some."

"You mean you'll... strike?" Saxon asked.

He bent his head.

"But isn't that what they want you to do?—from the way they're acting?"

"What's the difference?" Billy shrugged his shoulders, then continued. "It's better to strike than to get fired. We beat 'em to it, that's all, an' we catch 'em before they're ready. Don't we know what they're doin'? They're collectin' gradin'-camp drivers an' mule-skinners all up an' down the state. They got forty of 'em, feedin' 'em in a hotel in Stockton right now, an' ready to rush 'em in on us an' hundreds more like 'em. So this Saturday's the last wages I'll likely bring home for some time."

Saxon closed her eyes and thought quietly for five minutes. It was not her way to take things excitedly. The coolness of poise that Billy so admired never deserted her in time of emergency. She realized that she herself was no more than a mote caught up in this tangled, nonunderstandable conflict of many motes.

"We'll have to draw from our savings to pay for this month's rent," she said brightly.

Billy's face fell.

"We ain't got as much in the bank as you think," he confessed. "Bert had to be buried, you know, an I coughed up what the others couldn't raise."

"How much was it?"

"Forty dollars. I was goin' to stand off the butcher an' the rest for a while. They knew I was good pay. But they put it to me straight. They'd been carryin' the shopmen right along an was up against it themselves. An' now with that strike smashed they're pretty much smashed themselves. So I took it all out of the bank. I knew you wouldn't mind. You don't, do you?"

She smiled bravely, and bravely overcame the sinking feeling at her heart.

"It was the only right thing to do, Billy. I would have done it if you were lying sick, and Bert would have done it for you an' me if it had been the other way around."

His face was glowing.

"Gee, Saxon, a fellow can always count on you. You're like my right hand. That's why I say no more babies. If I lose you I'm crippled for life."

"We've got to economize," she mused, nodding her appreciation. "How much is in bank?"

"Just about thirty dollars. You see, I had to pay Martha Skelton an' for the... a few other little things. An' the union took time by the neck and levied a four dollar emergency assessment on every member just to be ready if the strike was pulled off. But Doc Hentley can wait. He said as much. He's the goods, if anybody should ask you. How'd you like'm?"

"I liked him. But I don't know about doctors. He's the first I ever had— except when I was vaccinated once, and then the city did that."

"Looks like the street car men are goin' out, too. Dan Fallon's come to town. Came all the way from New York. Tried to sneak in on the quiet, but the fellows knew when he left New York, an' kept track of him all the way acrost. They have to. He's Johnny-on-the-Spot whenever street car men are licked into shape. He's won lots of street car strikes for the bosses. Keeps an army of strike breakers an' ships them all over the country on special trains wherever they're needed. Oakland's never seen labor troubles like she's got and is goin' to get. All hell's goin' to break loose from the looks of it."

"Watch out for yourself, then, Billy. I don't want to lose you either."

"Aw, that's all right. I can take care of myself. An' besides, it ain't as though we was licked. We got a good chance."

"But you'll lose if there is any killing."

"Yep; we gotta keep an eye out against that."

"No violence."

"No gun-fighting or dynamite," he assented. "But a heap of scabs'll get their heads broke. That has to be."

"But you won't do any of that, Billy."

"Not so as any slob can testify before a court to havin' seen me." Then, with a quick shift, he changed the subject. "Old Barry Higgins is dead. I didn't want to tell you till you was outa bed. Buried'm a week ago. An' the old woman's movin' to Frisco. She told me she'd be in to say good-bye. She stuck by you pretty well them first couple of days, an' she showed Martha Shelton a few that made her hair curl. She got Martha's goat from the jump."

CHAPTER XI

With Billy on strike and away doing picket duty, and with the departure of Mercedes and the death of Bert, Saxon was left much to herself in a loneliness that even in one as healthy-minded as she could not fail to produce morbidness. Mary, too, had left, having spoken vaguely of taking a job at housework in Piedmont.

Billy could help Saxon little in her trouble. He dimly sensed her suffering, without comprehending the scope and intensity of it. He was too man-practical, and, by his very sex, too remote from the intimate tragedy that was hers. He was an outsider at the best, a friendly onlooker who saw little. To her the baby had been quick and real. It was still quick and real. That was her trouble. By no deliberate effort of will could she fill the aching void of its absence. Its reality became, at times, an hallucination. Somewhere it still was, and she must find it. She would catch herself, on occasion, listening with strained ears for the cry she had never heard, yet which, in fancy, she had heard a thousand times in the happy months before the end. Twice she left her bed in her sleep and went searching—each time coming to herself beside her mother's chest of drawers in which were the tiny garments. To herself, at such moments, she would say, "I had a baby once." And she would say it, aloud, as she watched the children playing in the street.

One day, on the Eighth street cars, a young mother sat beside her, a crowing infant in her arms. And Saxon said to her:

"I had a baby once. It died."

The mother looked at her, startled, half-drew the baby tighter in her arms, jealously, or as if in fear; then she softened as she said:

"You poor thing."

"Yes," Saxon nodded. "It died."

Tears welled into her eyes, and the telling of her grief seemed to have brought relief. But all the day she suffered from an almost overwhelming desire to recite her sorrow to the world—to the paying teller at the bank, to the elderly floor-walker in Salinger's, to the blind woman, guided by a little boy, who played on the concertina—to every one save the policeman. The police were new and terrible creatures to her now. She had seen them kill the strikers as mercilessly as the strikers had killed the scabs. And, unlike the strikers, the police were professional killers. They were not fighting for jobs. They did it as a business. They could have taken prisoners that day, in the angle of her front steps and the house. But they had not. Unconsciously, whenever approaching one, she edged across the sidewalk so as to get as far as possible away from him. She did not reason it out, but deeper than consciousness was the feeling that they were typical of something inimical to her and hers.

At Eighth and Broadway, waiting for her car to return home, the policeman on the corner recognized her and greeted her. She turned white to the lips, and her heart fluttered painfully. It was only Ned Hermanmann, fatter, broader-faced, jollier looking than ever. He had sat across the aisle from her for three terms at school. He and she had been monitors together of the composition books for one term. The day the powder works blew up at Pinole, breaking every window in the school, he and she had not joined in the panic rush for out-of-doors. Both had remained in the room, and the irate principal had exhibited them, from room to room, to the cowardly classes, and then rewarded them with a month's holiday from school. And after that Ned Hermanmann had become a policeman, and married Lena Highland, and Saxon had heard they had five children.

But, in spite of all that, he was now a policeman, and Billy was now a striker. Might not Ned Hermanmann some day club and shoot Billy just as those other policemen clubbed and shot the strikers by her front steps?

"What's the matter, Saxon?" he asked. "Sick?"

She nodded and choked, unable to speak, and started to move toward her car which was coming to a stop.

"I'll help you," he offered.

She shrank away from his hand.

"No; I'm all right," she gasped hurriedly. "I'm not going to take it. I've forgotten something."

She turned away dizzily, up Broadway to Ninth. Two blocks along Ninth, she turned down Clay and back to Eighth street, where she waited for another car.

As the summer months dragged along, the industrial situation in Oakland grew steadily worse. Capital everywhere seemed to have selected this city for the battle with organized labor. So many men in Oakland were out on strike, or were locked out, or were unable to work because of the dependence of their trades on the other tied-up trades, that odd jobs at common labor were hard to obtain. Billy occasionally got a day's work to do, but did not earn enough to make both ends meet, despite the small strike wages received at first, and despite the rigid economy he and Saxon practiced.

The table she set had scarcely anything in common with that of their first married year. Not alone was every item of cheaper quality, but many items had disappeared. Meat, and the poorest, was very seldom on the table. Cow's milk had given place to condensed milk, and even the sparing use of the latter had ceased. A roll of butter, when they had it, lasted half a dozen times as long as formerly. Where Billy had been used to drinking three cups of coffee for breakfast, he now drank one. Saxon boiled this coffee an atrocious length of time, and she paid twenty cents a pound for it.

The blight of hard times was on all the neighborhood. The families not involved in one strike were touched by some other strike or by the cessation of work in some dependent trade. Many single young men who were lodgers had drifted away, thus increasing the house rent of the families which had sheltered them.

"Gott!" said the butcher to Saxon. "We working class all suffer together. My wife she cannot get her teeth fixed now. Pretty soon I go smash broke maybe."

Once, when Billy was preparing to pawn his watch, Saxon suggested his borrowing the money from Billy Murphy.

"I was plannin' that," Billy answered, "only I can't now. I didn't tell you what happened Tuesday night at the Sporting Life Club. You remember that squarehead Champion of the United States Navy? Bill was matched with him, an' it was sure easy money. Bill had 'm goin' south by the end of the sixth round, an' at the seventh went in to finish 'm. And then—just his luck, for his trade's idle now—he snaps his right forearm. Of course the squarehead comes back at 'm on the jump, an' it's good night for Bill. Gee! Us Mohegans are gettin' our bad luck handed to us in chunks these days."

"Don't!" Saxon cried, shuddering involuntarily.

"What?" Billy asked with open mouth of surprise.

"Don't say that word again. Bert was always saying it."

"Oh, Mohegans. All right, I won't. You ain't superstitious, are you?"

"No; but just the same there's too much truth in the word for me to like it. Sometimes it seems as though he was right. Times have changed. They've changed even since I was a little girl. We crossed the plains and opened up this country, and now we're losing even the chance to work for a living in it. And it's not my fault, it's not your fault. We've got to live well or bad just by luck, it seems. There's no other way to explain it."

"It beats me," Billy concurred. "Look at the way I worked last year. Never missed a day. I'd want to never miss a day this year, an' here I haven't done a tap for weeks an' weeks an' weeks. Say! Who runs this country anyway?"

Saxon had stopped the morning paper, but frequently Maggie Donahue's boy, who served a Tribune route, tossed an "extra" on her steps. From its editorials Saxon gleaned that organized labor was trying to run the country and that it was making a mess of it. It was all the fault of domineering labor—so ran the editorials, column by column, day by day; and Saxon was convinced, yet remained unconvinced. The social puzzle of living was too intricate.

The teamsters' strike, backed financially by the teamsters of San Francisco and by the allied unions of the San Francisco Water Front Confederation, promised to be long-drawn, whether or not it was successful. The Oakland harness-washers and stablemen, with few exceptions, had gone out with the teamsters. The teaming firms were not half-filling their contracts, but the employers' association was helping them. In fact, half the employers' associations of the Pacific Coast were helping the Oakland Employers' Association.

Saxon was behind a month's rent, which, when it is considered that rent was paid in advance, was equivalent to two months. Likewise, she was two months behind in the installments on the furniture. Yet she was not pressed very hard by Salinger's, the furniture dealers.

"We're givin' you all the rope we can," said their collector. "My orders is to make you dig up every cent I can and at the same time not to be too hard. Salinger's are trying to do the right thing, but they're up against it, too. You've no idea how many accounts like yours they're carrying along. Sooner or later they'll have to call a halt or get it in the neck themselves. And in the meantime just see if you can't scrape up five dollars by next week—just to cheer them along, you know."

One of the stablemen who had not gone out, Henderson by name, worked at Billy's stables. Despite the urging of the bosses to eat and sleep in the stable like the other men, Henderson had persisted in coming home each morning to his little house around the corner from Saxon's on Fifth street. Several times she had seen him swinging along defiantly, his dinner pail in his hand, while the neighborhood boys dogged his heels at a safe distance and informed him in yapping chorus that he was a scab and no good. But one evening, on his way to work, in a spirit of bravado he went into the Pile-Drivers' Home, the saloon at Seventh and Pine. There it was his mortal mischance to encounter Otto Frank, a striker who drove from the same stable. Not many minutes later an ambulance was hurrying Henderson to the receiving hospital with a fractured skull, while a patrol wagon was no less swiftly carrying Otto Frank to the city prison.

Maggie Donahue it was, eyes shining with gladness, who told Saxon of the happening.

"Served him right, too, the dirty scab," Maggie concluded.

"But his poor wife!" was Saxon's cry. "She's not strong. And then the children. She'll never be able to take care of them if her husband dies."

"An' serve her right, the damned slut!"

Saxon was both shocked and hurt by the Irishwoman's brutality. But Maggie was implacable.

"'Tis all she or any woman deserves that'll put up an' live with a scab. What about her children? Let'm starve, an' her man a-takin' the food out of other children's mouths."

Mrs. Olsen's attitude was different. Beyond passive sentimental pity for Henderson's wife and children, she gave them no thought, her chief concern being for Otto Frank and Otto Frank's wife and children—herself and Mrs. Frank being full sisters.

"If he dies, they will hang Otto," she said. "And then what will poor Hilda do? She has varicose veins in both legs, and she never can stand on her feet all day an' work for wages. And me, I cannot help. Ain't Carl out of work, too?"

Billy had still another point of view.

"It will give the strike a black eye, especially if Henderson croaks," he worried, when he came home. "They'll hang Frank on record time. Besides, we'll have to put up a defense, an' lawyers charge like Sam Hill. They'll eat a hole in our treasury you could drive every team in Oakland through. An' if Frank hadn't ben screwed up with whisky he'd never a-done it. He's the mildest, good-naturedest man sober you ever seen."

Twice that evening Billy left the house to find out if Henderson was dead yet. In the morning the papers gave little hope, and the evening papers published his death. Otto Frank lay in jail without bail. The Tribune demanded a quick trial and summary execution, calling on the prospective jury manfully to do its duty and dwelling at length on the moral effect that would be so produced upon the lawless working class. It went further, emphasizing the salutary effect machine guns would have on the mob that had taken the fair city of Oakland by the throat.

And all such occurrences struck at Saxon personally. Practically alone in the world, save for Billy, it was her life, and his, and their mutual love-life, that was menaced. From the moment he left the house to the moment of his return she knew no peace of mind. Rough work was afoot, of which he told her nothing, and she knew he was playing his part in it. On more than one occasion she noticed fresh-broken skin on his knuckles. At such times he was remarkably taciturn, and would sit in brooding silence or go almost immediately to bed. She was afraid to have this habit of reticence grow on him, and bravely she bid for his confidence. She climbed into his lap and inside his arms, one of her arms around his neck, and with the free hand she caressed his hair back from the forehead and smoothed out the moody brows.

"Now listen to me, Billy Boy," she began lightly. "You haven't been playing fair, and I won't have it. No!" She pressed his lips shut with her fingers. "I'm doing the talking now, and because you haven't been doing your share of the talking for some time. You remember we agreed at the start to always talk things over. I was the first to break this, when I sold my fancy work to Mrs. Higgins without speaking to you about it. And I was very sorry. I am still sorry. And I've never done it since. Now it's your turn. You're not talking things over with me. You are doing things you don't tell me about.

"Billy, you're dearer to me than anything else in the world. You know that. We're sharing each other's lives, only, just now, there's something you're not sharing. Every time your knuckles are sore, there's something you don't share. If you can't trust me, you can't trust anybody. And, besides, I love you so that no matter what you do I'll go on loving you just the same."

Billy gazed at her with fond incredulity.

"Don't be a pincher," she teased. "Remember, I stand for whatever you do."

"And you won't buck against me?" he queried.

"How can I? I'm not your boss, Billy. I wouldn't boss you for anything in the world. And if you'd let me boss you, I wouldn't love you half as much."

He digested this slowly, and finally nodded.

"An' you won't be mad?"

"With you? You've never seen me mad yet. Now come on and be generous and tell me how you hurt your knuckles. It's fresh to-day. Anybody can see that."

"All right. I'll tell you how it happened." He stopped and giggled with genuine boyish glee at some recollection. "It's like this. You won't be mad, now? We gotta do these sort of things to hold our own. Well, here's the show, a regular movin' picture except for file talkin'. Here's a big rube comin' along, hayseed stickin' out all over, hands like hams an' feet like Mississippi gunboats. He'd make half as much again as me in size an' he's young, too. Only he ain't lookin' for trouble, an' he's as innocent as... well, he's the innocentest scab that ever come down the pike an' bumped into a couple of pickets. Not a regular strike-breaker, you see, just a big rube that's read the bosses' ads an' come a-humpin' to town for the big wages.

"An' here's Bud Strothers an' me comin' along. We always go in pairs that way, an' sometimes bigger bunches. I flag the rube. 'Hello,' says I, 'lookin' for a job?' 'You bet,' says he. 'Can you drive?' 'Yep.' 'Four horses!' 'Show me to 'em,' says he. 'No josh, now,' says I; 'you're sure wantin' to drive?' 'That's what I come to town for,' he says. 'You're the man we're lookin' for,' says I. 'Come along, an' we'll have you busy in no time.'

"You see, Saxon, we can't pull it off there, because there's Tom Scanlon— you know, the red-headed cop only a couple of blocks away an' pipin' us off though not recognizin' us. So away we go, the three of us, Bud an' me leadin' that boob to take our jobs away from us I guess nit. We turn into the alley back of Campwell's grocery. Nobody in sight. Bud stops short, and the rube an' me stop.

"'I don't think he wants to drive,' Bud says, considerin'. An' the rube says quick, 'You betcher life I do.' 'You're dead sure you want that job?' I says. Yes, he's dead sure. Nothin's goin' to keep him away from that job. Why, that job's what he come to town for, an' we can't lead him to it too quick.

"'Well, my friend,' says I, 'it's my sad duty to inform you that you've made a mistake.' 'How's that?' he says. 'Go on,' I says; 'you're standin' on your foot.' And, honest to God, Saxon, that gink looks down at his feet to see. 'I don't understand,' says he. 'We're goin' to show you,' says I.

"An' then—Biff! Bang! Bingo! Swat! Zooie! Ker-slambango-blam! Fireworks, Fourth of July, Kingdom Come, blue lights, sky-rockets, an' hell fire—just like that. It don't take long when you're scientific an' trained to tandem work. Of course it's hard on the knuckles. But say, Saxon, if you'd seen that rube before an' after you'd thought he was a lightnin' change artist. Laugh? You'd a-busted."

Billy halted to give vent to his own mirth. Saxon forced herself to join with him, but down in her heart was horror. Mercedes was right. The stupid workers wrangled and snarled over jobs. The clever masters rode in automobiles and did not wrangle and snarl. They hired other stupid ones to do the wrangling and snarling for them. It was men like Bert and Frank Davis, like Chester Johnson and Otto Frank, like Jelly Belly and the Pinkertons, like Henderson and all the rest of the scabs, who were beaten up, shot, clubbed, or hanged. Ah, the clever ones were very clever. Nothing happened to them. They only rode in their automobiles.

"'You big stiffs,' the rube snivels as he crawls to his feet at the end," Billy was continuing. "'You think you still want that job?' I ask. He shakes his head. Then I read'm the riot act 'They's only one thing for you to do, old hoss, an' that's beat it. D'ye get me? Beat it. Back to the farm for YOU. An' if you come monkeyin' around town again, we'll be real mad at you. We was only foolin' this time. But next time we catch you your own mother won't know you when we get done with you.'

"An'—say!—you oughta seen'm beat it. I bet he's goin' yet. Ah' when he gets back to Milpitas, or Sleepy Hollow, or wherever he hangs out, an' tells how the boys does things in Oakland, it's dollars to doughnuts they won't be a rube in his district that'd come to town to drive if they offered ten dollars an hour."

"It was awful," Saxon said, then laughed well-simulated appreciation.

"But that was nothin'," Billy went on. "A bunch of the boys caught another one this morning. They didn't do a thing to him. My goodness gracious, no. In less'n two minutes he was the worst wreck they ever hauled to the receivin' hospital. The evenin' papers gave the score: nose broken, three bad scalp wounds, front teeth out, a broken collarbone, an' two broken ribs. Gee! He certainly got all that was comin' to him. But that's nothin'. D'ye want to know what the Frisco teamsters did in the big strike before the Earthquake? They took every scab they caught an' broke both his arms with a crowbar. That was so he couldn't drive, you see. Say, the hospitals was filled with 'em. An' the teamsters won that strike, too."

"But is it necessary, Billy, to be so terrible? I know they're scabs, and that they're taking the bread out of the strikers' children's mouths to put in their own children's mouths, and that it isn't fair and all that; but just the same is it necessary to be so... terrible?"

"Sure thing," Billy answered confidently. "We just gotta throw the fear of God into them—when we can do it without bein' caught."

"And if you're caught?"

"Then the union hires the lawyers to defend us, though that ain't much good now, for the judges are pretty hostyle, an' the papers keep hammerin' away at them to give stiffer an' stiffer sentences. Just the same, before this strike's over there'll be a whole lot of guys a-wishin' they'd never gone scabbin'."

Very cautiously, in the next half hour, Saxon tried to feel out her husband's attitude, to find if he doubted the rightness of the violence he and his brother teamsters committed. But Billy's ethical sanction was rock-bedded and profound. It never entered his head that he was not absolutely right. It was the game. Caught in its tangled meshes, he could see no other way to play it than the way all men played it. He did not stand for dynamite and murder, however. But then the unions did not stand for such. Quite naive was his explanation that dynamite and murder did not pay; that such actions always brought down the condemnation of the public and broke the strikes. But the healthy beating up of a scab, he contended—the "throwing of the fear of

God into a scab," as he expressed it—was the only right and proper thing to do.

"Our folks never had to do such things," Saxon said finally. "They never had strikes nor scabs in those times."

"You bet they didn't," Billy agreed. "Them was the good old days. I'd liked to a-lived then." He drew a long breath and sighed. "But them times will never come again."

"Would you have liked living in the country?" Saxon asked.

"Sure thing."

"There's lots of men living in the country now," she suggested.

"Just the same I notice them a-hikin' to town to get our jobs," was his reply.

CHAPTER XII

A gleam of light came, when Billy got a job driving a grading team for the contractors of the big bridge then building at Niles. Before he went he made certain that it was a union job. And a union job it was for two days, when the concrete workers threw down their tools. The contractors, evidently prepared for such happening, immediately filled the places of the concrete men with nonunion Italians. Whereupon the carpenters, structural ironworkers and teamsters walked out; and Billy, lacking train fare, spent the rest of the day in walking home.

"I couldn't work as a scab," he concluded his tale.

"No," Saxon said; "you couldn't work as a scab."

But she wondered why it was that when men wanted to work, and there was work to do, yet they were unable to work because their unions said no. Why were there unions? And, if unions had to be, why were not all workingmen in them? Then there would be no scabs, and Billy could work every day. Also, she wondered where she was to get a sack of flour, for she had long since ceased the extravagance of baker's bread. And so many other of the neighborhood women had done this, that the little Welsh baker had closed up shop and gone away, taking his wife and two little daughters with him. Look where she would, everybody was being hurt by the industrial strife.

One afternoon came a caller at her door, and that evening came Billy with dubious news. He had been approached that day. All he had to do, he told Saxon, was to say the word, and he could go into the stable as foreman at one hundred dollars a month.

The nearness of such a sum, the possibility of it, was almost stunning to Saxon, sitting at a supper which consisted of boiled potatoes, warmed-over beans, and a small dry onion which they were eating raw. There was neither bread, coffee, nor butter. The onion Billy had pulled from his pocket, having picked it up in the street. One hundred dollars a month! She moistened her lips and fought for control.

"What made them offer it to you?" she questioned.

"That's easy," was his answer. "They got a dozen reasons. The guy the boss has had exercisin' Prince and King is a dub. King has gone lame in the shoulders. Then they're guessin' pretty strong that I'm the party that's put a lot of their scabs outa commission. Macklin's ben their foreman for years an' years—why I was in knee pants when he was foreman. Well, he's sick an' all in. They gotta have somebody to take his place. Then, too, I've been with 'em a long time. An' on top of that, I'm the man for the job. They know I know horses from the ground up. Hell, it's all I'm good for, except sluggin'.""

- 167 -

"Think of it, Billy!" she breathed. "A hundred dollars a month! A hundred dollars a month!"

"An' throw the fellows down," he said.

It was not a question. Nor was it a statement. It was anything Saxon chose to make of it. They looked at each other. She waited for him to speak; but he continued merely to look. It came to her that she was facing one of the decisive moments of her life, and she gripped herself to face it in all coolness. Nor would Billy proffer her the slightest help. Whatever his own judgment might be, he masked it with an expressionless face. His eyes betrayed nothing. He looked and waited.

"You... you can't do that, Billy," she said finally. "You can't throw the fellows down."

His hand shot out to hers, and his face was a sudden, radiant dawn.

"Put her there!" he cried, their hands meeting and clasping. "You're the truest true blue wife a man ever had. If all the other fellows' wives was like you, we could win any strike we tackled."

"What would you have done if you weren't married, Billy?"

"Seen 'em in hell first."

"Than it doesn't make any difference being married. I've got to stand by you in everything you stand for. I'd be a nice wife if I didn't."

She remembered her caller of the afternoon, and knew the moment was too propitious to let pass.

"There was a man here this afternoon, Billy. He wanted a room. I told him I'd speak to you. He said he would pay six dollars a month for the back bedroom. That would pay half a month's installment on the furniture and buy a sack of flour, and we're all out of flour."

Billy's old hostility to the idea was instantly uppermost, and Saxon watched him anxiously.

"Some scab in the shops, I suppose?"

"No; he's firing on the freight run to San Jose. Harmon, he said his name was, James Harmon. They've just transferred him from the Truckee division. He'll sleep days mostly, he said; and that's why he wanted a quiet house without children in it."

In the end, with much misgiving, and only after Saxon had insistently pointed out how little work it entailed on her, Billy consented, though he continued to protest, as an afterthought:

"But I don't want you makin' beds for any man. It ain't right, Saxon. I oughta take care of you."

"And you would," she flashed back at him, "if you'd take the foremanship. Only you can't. It wouldn't be right. And if I'm to stand by you it's only fair to let me do what I can."

James Harmon proved even less a bother than Saxon had anticipated. For a fireman he was scrupulously clean, always washing up in the roundhouse before he came home. He used the key to the kitchen door, coming and going by the back steps. To Saxon he barely said how-do-you-do or good day; and, sleeping in the day time and working at night, he was in the house a week before Billy laid eyes on him.

Billy had taken to coming home later and later, and to going out after supper by himself. He did not offer to tell Saxon where he went. Nor did she ask. For that matter it required little shrewdness on her part to guess. The fumes of whisky were on his lips at such times. His slow, deliberate ways were even slower, even more deliberate. Liquor did not affect his legs. He walked as soberly as any man. There was no hesitancy, no faltering, in his muscular movements. The whisky went to his brain, making his eyes heavy-lidded and the cloudiness of them more cloudy. Not that he was flighty, nor quick, nor irritable. On the contrary, the liquor imparted to his mental processes a deep gravity and brooding solemnity. He talked little, but that little was ominous and oracular. At such times there was no appeal from his judgment, no discussion. He knew, as God knew. And when he chose to speak a harsh thought, it was ten-fold harsher than ordinarily, because it seemed to proceed out of such profundity of cogitation, because it was as prodigiously deliberate in its incubation as it was in its enunciation.

It was not a nice side he was showing to Saxon. It was, almost, as if a stranger had come to live with her. Despite herself, she found herself beginning to shrink from him. And little could she comfort herself with the thought that it was not his real self, for she remembered his gentleness and considerateness, all his finenesses of the past. Then he had made a continual effort to avoid trouble and fighting. Now he enjoyed it, exulted in it, went looking for it. All this showed in his face. No longer was he the smiling, pleasant-faced boy. He smiled infrequently now. His face was a man's face. The lips, the eyes, the lines were harsh as his thoughts were harsh.

He was rarely unkind to Saxon; but, on the other hand he was rarely kind. His attitude toward her was growing negative. He was disinterested. Despite the fight for the union she was enduring with him, putting up with him shoulder to shoulder, she occupied but little space in his mind. When he acted toward her gently, she could see that it was merely mechanical, just as she was well aware that the endearing terms he used, the endearing caresses he gave, were only habitual. The spontaneity and warmth had gone out. Often, when he was not in liquor, flashes of the old Billy came back, but even such flashes dwindled in frequency. He was growing preoccupied, moody. Hard times and the bitter stresses of industrial conflict strained him. Especially was this apparent in his sleep, when he suffered paroxysms of lawless dreams, groaning and muttering, clenching his fists, grinding his teeth, twisting with muscular tensions, his face writhing with passions and violences, his throat guttering with terrible curses that rasped and aborted on his lips. And Saxon, lying beside him, afraid of this visitor to her bed whom she did not know, remembered what Mary had told her of Bert. He, too, had cursed and clenched his fists, in his nights fought out the battles of his days.

One thing, however, Saxon saw clearly. By no deliberate act of Billy's was he becoming this other and unlovely Billy. Were there no strike, no snarling and wrangling over jobs, there would be only the old Billy she had loved in all absoluteness. This sleeping terror in him would have lain asleep. It was something that was being awakened in him, an image incarnate of outward conditions, as cruel, as ugly, as maleficent as were those outward conditions. But if the strike continued, then, she feared, with reason, would this other and grisly self of Billy strengthen to fuller and more forbidding stature. And this, she knew, would mean the wreck of their love-life. Such a Billy she could not love; in its nature such a Billy was not lovable nor capable of love. And then, at the thought of offspring, she shuddered. It was too terrible. And at such moments of contemplation, from her soul the inevitable plaint of the human went up: WHY? WHY? WHY?

Billy, too, had his unanswerable queries.

"Why won't the building trades come out?" he demanded wrathfuly of the obscurity that veiled the ways of living and the world. "But no; O'Brien won't stand for a strike, and he has the Building Trades Council under his thumb. But why don't they chuck him and come out anyway? We'd win hands down all along the line. But no, O'Brien's got their goat, an' him up to his dirty neck in politics an' graft! An' damn the Federation of Labor! If all the railroad boys had come out, wouldn't the shop men have won instead of bein' licked to a frazzle? Lord, I ain't had a smoke of decent tobacco or a cup of decent coffee in a coon's age. I've forgotten what a square meal tastes like. I weighed myself yesterday. Fifteen pounds lighter than when the strike begun. If it keeps on much more I can fight middleweight. An' this is what I get after payin' dues into the union for years and years. I can't get a square meal, an' my wife has to make other men's beds. It makes my tired ache. Some day I'll get real huffy an' chuck that lodger out."

"But it's not his fault, Billy," Saxon protested.

"Who said it was?" Billy snapped roughly. "Can't I kick in general if I want to? Just the same it makes me sick. What's the good of organized labor if it don't stand together? For two cents I'd chuck the whole thing up an' go over to the employers. Only I wouldn't, God damn them! If they think they can beat us down to our knees, let 'em go ahead an' try it, that's all. But it gets me just the same. The whole world's clean dippy. They ain't no sense in anything. What's the good of supportin' a union that can't win a strike? What's the good of knockin' the blocks off of scabs when they keep a-comin' thick as ever? The whole thing's bughouse, an' I guess I am, too."

Such an outburst on Billy's part was so unusual that it was the only time Saxon knew it to occur. Always he was sullen, and dogged, and unwhipped; while whisky only served to set the maggots of certitude crawling in his brain.

One night Billy did not get home till after twelve. Saxon's anxiety was increased by the fact that police fighting and head breaking had been reported to have occurred. When Billy came, his appearance verified the report. His coatsleeves were half torn off. The Windsor tie had disappeared from under his soft turned-down collar, and every button had been ripped off the front of the shirt. When he took his hat off, Saxon was frightened by a lump on his head the size of an apple.

"D'ye know who did that? That Dutch slob Hermanmann, with a riot club. An' I'll get'm for it some day, good an' plenty. An' there's another fellow I got staked out that'll be my meat when this strike's over an' things is settled down. Blanchard's his name, Roy Blanchard."

"Not of Blanchard, Perkins and Company?" Saxon asked, busy washing Billy's hurt and making her usual fight to keep him calm.

"Yep; except he's the son of the old man. What's he do, that ain't done a tap of work in all his life except to blow the old man's money? He goes strike-breakin'. Grandstand play, that's what I call it. Gets his name in the papers an makes all the skirts he runs with fluster up an' say: 'My! Some bear, that Roy Blanchard, some bear.' Some bear—the gazabo! He'll be bear-meat for me some day. I never itched so hard to lick a man in my life.

"And—oh, I guess I'll pass that Dutch cop up. He got his already. Somebody broke his head with a lump of coal the size of a water bucket. That was when the wagons was turnin' into Franklin, just off Eighth, by the old Galindo Hotel. They was hard fightin' there, an' some guy in the hotel lams that coal down from the second story window.

"They was fightin' every block of the way—bricks, cobblestones, an' police-clubs to beat the band. They don't dast call out the troops. An' they was afraid to shoot. Why, we tore holes through the police force, an' the ambulances and patrol wagons worked over-time. But say, we got the procession blocked at Fourteenth and Broadway, right under the nose of the City Hall, rushed the rear end, cut out the horses of five wagons, an' handed them college guys a few love-pats in passin'. All that saved 'em from hospital was the police reserves. Just the same we had 'em jammed an hour there. You oughta seen the street cars blocked, too—Broadway, Fourteenth, San Pablo, as far as you could see."

"But what did Blanchard do?" Saxon called him back.

"He led the procession, an' he drove my team. All the teams was from my stable. He rounded up a lot of them college fellows—fraternity guys, they're called—yaps that live off their fathers' money. They come to the stable in big tourin' cars an' drove out the wagons with half the police of Oakland to help them. Say, it was sure some day. The sky rained cobblestones. An' you oughta heard the clubs on our heads—rat-tat-tat-tat, rat-tat-tat-tat! An' say, the chief of police, in a police auto, sittin' up like God Almighty—just before we got to Peralta street they was a block an' the police chargin', an' an old woman, right from her front gate, lammed the chief of police full in the face with a dead cat. Phew! You could hear it. 'Arrest that woman!' he yells, with his handkerchief out. But the boys beat the cops to her an' got her away. Some day? I guess yes. The receivin' hospital went outa commission on the jump, an' the overflow was spilled into St. Mary's Hospital, an' Fabiola, an' I don't know where else. Eight of our men was pulled, an' a dozen of the Frisco teamsters that's come over to help. They're holy terrors, them Frisco teamsters. It seemed half the workingmen of Oakland was helpin' us, an' they must be an army of them in jail. Our lawyers'll have to take their cases, too.

"But take it from me, it's the last we'll see of Roy Blanchard an' yaps of his kidney buttin' into our affairs. I guess we showed 'em some football. You know that brick buildin' they're puttin' up on Bay street? That's where we loaded up first, an', say, you couldn't see the wagon-seats for bricks when they started from the stables. Blanchard drove the first wagon, an' he was knocked clean off the seat once, but he stayed with it."

"He must have been brave," Saxon commented.

"Brave?" Billy flared. "With the police, an' the army an' navy behind him? I suppose you'll be takin' their part next. Brave? A-takin' the food outa the mouths of our women an children. Didn't Curley Jones's little kid die last night? Mother's milk not nourishin', that's what it was, because she didn't have the right stuff to eat. An' I know, an' you know, a dozen old aunts, an' sister-in-laws, an' such, that's had to hike to the poorhouse because their folks couldn't take care of 'em in these times."

In the morning paper Saxon read the exciting account of the futile attempt to break the teamsters' strike. Roy Blanchard was hailed a hero and held up as a model of wealthy citizenship. And to save herself she could not help glowing with appreciation of his courage. There was something fine in his going out to face the snarling pack. A brigadier general of the regular army was quoted as lamenting the fact that the troops had not been called out to take the mob by the throat and shake law and order into it. "This is the time for a little healthful bloodletting," was the conclusion of his remarks, after deploring the pacific methods of the police. "For not until the mob has been thoroughly beaten and cowed will tranquil industrial conditions obtain."

That evening Saxon and Billy went up town. Returning home and finding nothing to eat, he had taken her on one arm, his overcoat on the other. The overcoat he had pawned at Uncle Sam's, and he and Saxon had eaten drearily at a Japanese restaurant which in some miraculous way managed to set a semi-satisfying meal for ten cents. After eating, they started on their way to spend an additional five cents each on a moving picture show.

At the Central Bank Building, two striking teamsters accosted Billy and took him away with them. Saxon waited on the corner, and when he returned, three quarters of an hour later, she knew he had been drinking.

Half a block on, passing the Forum Cafe, he stopped suddenly. A limousine stood at the curb, and into it a young man was helping several wonderfully gowned women. A chauffeur sat in the driver's sent. Billy touched the young man on the arm. He was as broad-shouldered as Billy and slightly taller. Blue-eyed, strong-featured, in Saxon's opinion he was undeniably handsome.

"Just a word, sport," Billy said, in a low, slow voice.

The young man glanced quickly at Billy and Saxon, and asked impatiently:

"Well, what is it?"

"You're Blanchard," Billy began. "I seen you yesterday lead out that bunch of teams."

"Didn't I do it all right?" Blanchard asked gaily, with a flash of glance to Saxon and back again.

"Sure. But that ain't what I want to talk about."

"Who are you?" the other demanded with sudden suspicion.

"A striker. It just happens you drove my team, that's all. No; don't move for a gun." (As Blanchard half reached toward his hip pocket.) "I ain't startin' anythin' here. But I just want to tell you something."

"Be quick, then."

Blanchard lifted one foot to step into the machine.

"Sure," Billy went on without any diminution of his exasperating slowness. "What I want to tell you is that I'm after you. Not now, when the strike's on, but some time later I'm goin' to get you an' give you the beatin' of your life."

Blanchard looked Billy over with new interest and measuring eyes that sparkled with appreciation.

"You are a husky yourself," he said. "But do you think you can do it?"

"Sure. You're my meat."

"All right, then, my friend. Look me up after the strike is settled, and I'll give you a chance at me."

"Remember," Billy added, "I got you staked out."

Blanchard nodded, smiled genially to both of them, raised his hat to Saxon, and stepped into the machine.

CHAPTER XIII

From now on, to Saxon, life seemed bereft of its last reason and rhyme. It had become senseless, nightmarish. Anything irrational was possible. There was nothing stable in the anarchic flux of affairs that swept her on she knew not to what catastrophic end. Had Billy been dependable, all would still have been well. With him to cling to she would have faced everything fearlessly. But he had been whirled away from her in the prevailing madness. So radical was the change in him that he seemed almost an intruder in the house. Spiritually he was such an intruder. Another man looked out of his eyes—a man whose thoughts were of violence and hatred; a man to whom there was no good in anything, and who had become an ardent protagonist of the evil that was rampant and universal. This man no longer condemned Bert, himself muttering vaguely of dynamite, and sabotage, and revolution.

Saxon strove to maintain that sweetness and coolness of flesh and spirit that Billy had praised in the old days. Once, only, she lost control. He had been in a particularly ugly mood, and a final harshness and unfairness cut her to the quick.

"Who are you speaking to?" she flamed out at him.

He was speechless and abashed, and could only stare at her face, which was white with anger.

"Don't you ever speak to me like that again, Billy," she commanded.

"Aw, can't you put up with a piece of bad temper?" he muttered, half apologetically, yet half defiantly. "God knows I got enough to make me cranky."

After he left the house she flung herself on the bed and cried heart-brokenly. For she, who knew so thoroughly the humility of love, was a proud woman. Only the proud can be truly humble, as only the strong may know the fullness of gentleness. But what was the use, she demanded, of being proud and game, when the only person in the world who mattered to her lost his own pride and gameness and fairness and gave her the worse share of their mutual trouble?

And now, as she had faced alone the deeper, organic hurt of the loss of her baby, she faced alone another, and, in a way, an even greater personal trouble. Perhaps she loved Billy none the less, but her love was changing into something less proud, less confident, less trusting; it was becoming shot through with pity—with the pity that is parent to contempt. Her own loyalty was threatening to weaken, and she shuddered and shrank from the contempt she could see creeping in.

She struggled to steel herself to face the situation. Forgiveness stole into her heart, and she knew relief until the thought came that in the truest, highest love forgiveness should have no place. And again she cried, and continued her battle. After all, one thing was incontestable: THIS BILLY WAS NOT THE BILLY SHE HAD LOVED. This Billy was another man, a sick man, and no more to be held responsible than a fever-patient in the ravings of delirium. She must be Billy's nurse, without pride, without contempt, with nothing to forgive. Besides, he was really bearing the brunt of the fight, was in the thick of it, dizzy with the striking of blows and the blows he received. If fault there was, it lay elsewhere, somewhere in the tangled scheme of things that made men snarl over jobs like dogs over bones.

So Saxon arose and buckled on her armor again for the hardest fight of all in the world's arena—the woman's fight. She ejected from her thought all doubting and distrust. She forgave nothing, for there was nothing requiring forgiveness. She pledged herself to an absoluteness of belief that her love and Billy's was unsullied, unperturbed—severe as it had always been, as it would be when it came back again after the world settled down once more to rational ways.

That night, when he came home, she proposed, as an emergency measure, that she should resume her needlework and help keep the pot boiling until the strike was over. But Billy would hear nothing of it.

"It's all right," he assured her repeatedly. "They ain't no call for you to work. I'm goin' to get some money before the week is out. An' I'll turn it over to you. An' Saturday night we'll go to the show—a real show, no movin' pictures. Harvey's nigger minstrels is comin' to town. We'll go Saturday night. I'll have the money before that, as sure as beans is beans."

Friday evening he did not come home to supper, which Saxon regretted, for Maggie Donahue had returned a pan of potatoes and two quarts of flour (borrowed the week before), and it was a hearty meal that awaited him. Saxon kept the stove going till nine o'clock, when, despite her reluctance, she went to bed. Her preference would have been to wait up, but she did not dare, knowing full well what the effect would be on him did he come home in liquor.

The clock had just struck one, when she heard the click of the gate. Slowly, heavily, ominously, she heard him come up the steps and fumble with his key at the door. He entered the bedroom, and she heard him sigh as he sat down. She remained quiet, for she had learned the hypersensitiveness induced by drink and was fastidiously careful not to hurt him even with the knowledge that she had lain awake for him. It was not easy. Her hands were clenched till the nails dented the palms, and her body was rigid in her passionate effort for control. Never had he come home as bad as this.

"Saxon," he called thickly. "Saxon."

She stirred and yawned.

"What is it?" she asked.

"Won't you strike a light? My fingers is all thumbs."

Without looking at him, she complied; but so violent was the nervous trembling of her hands that the glass chimney tinkled against the globe and the match went out.

"I ain't drunk, Saxon," he said in the darkness, a hint of amusement in his thick voice. "I've only had two or three jolts ... of that sort."

On her second attempt with the lamp she succeeded. When she turned to look at him she screamed with fright. Though she had heard his voice and knew him to be Billy, for the instant she did not recognize him. His face was a face she had never known. Swollen, bruised, discolored, every feature had been beaten out of all semblance of familiarity. One eye was entirely closed, the other showed through a narrow slit of blood-congested flesh. One ear seemed to have lost most of its skin. The whole face was a swollen pulp. His right jaw, in particular, was twice the size of the left. No wonder his speech had been thick, was her thought, as she regarded the fearfully cut and swollen lips that still bled. She was sickened by the sight, and her heart went out to him in a great wave of tenderness. She wanted to put her arms around him, and cuddle and soothe him; but her practical judgment bade otherwise.

"You poor, poor boy," she cried. "Tell me what you want me to do first. I don't know about such things."

"If you could help me get my clothes off," he suggested meekly and thickly. "I got 'em on before I stiffened up."

"And then hot water—that will be good," she said, as she began gently drawing his coat sleeve over a puffed and helpless hand.

"I told you they was all thumbs," he grimaced, holding up his hand and squinting at it with the fraction of sight remaining to him.

"You sit and wait," she said, "till I start the fire and get the hot water going. I won't be a minute. Then I'll finish getting your clothes off."

From the kitchen she could hear him mumbling to himself, and when she returned he was repeating over and over:

"We needed the money, Saxon. We needed the money."

Drunken he was not, she could see that, and from his babbling she knew he was partly delirious.

"He was a surprise box," he wandered on, while she proceeded to undress him; and bit by bit she was able to piece together what had happened. "He was an unknown from Chicago. They sprang him on me. The secretary of the Acme Club warned me I'd have my hands full. An' I'd a-won if I'd been in condition. But fifteen pounds off without trainin' ain't condition. Then I'd been drinkin' pretty regular, an' I didn't have my wind."

But Saxon, stripping his undershirt, no longer heard him. As with his face, she could not recognize his splendidly muscled back. The white sheath of silken skin was torn and bloody. The lacerations occurred oftenest in horizontal lines, though there were perpendicular lines as well.

"How did you get all that?" she asked.

"The ropes. I was up against 'em more times than I like to remember. Gee! He certainly gave me mine. But I fooled 'm. He couldn't put me out. I lasted the twenty rounds, an' I wanta tell you he's got some marks to remember me by. If he ain't got a couple of knuckles broke in the left hand I'm a geezer.— Here, feel my head here. Swollen, eh? Sure thing. He hit that more times than he's wishin' he had right now. But, oh, what a lacin'! What a lacin'! I never had anything like it before. The Chicago Terror, they call 'm. I take my hat off to 'm. He's some bear. But I could a-made 'm take the count if I'd ben in condition an' had my wind.—Oh! Ouch! Watch out! It's like a boil!"

Fumbling at his waistband, Saxon's hand had come in contact with a brightly inflamed surface larger than a soup plate.

"That's from the kidney blows," Billy explained. "He was a regular devil at it. 'Most every clench, like clock work, down he'd chop one on me. It got so sore I was wincin'... until I got groggy an' didn't know much of anything. It ain't a knockout blow, you know, but it's awful wearin' in a long fight. It takes the starch out of you."

When his knees were bared, Saxon could see the skin across the knee-caps was broken and gone.

"The skin ain't made to stand a heavy fellow like me on the knees," he volunteered. "An' the rosin in the canvas cuts like Sam Hill."

The tears were in Saxon's eyes, and she could have cried over the manhandled body of her beautiful sick boy.

As she carried his pants across the room to hang them up, a jingle of money came from them. He called her back, and from the pocket drew forth a handful of silver.

"We needed the money, we needed the money," he kept muttering, as he vainly tried to count the coins; and Saxon knew that his mind was wandering again.

It cut her to the heart, for she could not but remember the harsh thoughts that had threatened her loyalty during the week past. After all, Billy, the splendid physical man, was only a boy, her boy. And he had faced and endured all this terrible punishment for her, for the house and the furniture that were their house and furniture. He said so, now, when he scarcely knew what he said. He said "WE needed the money." She was not so absent from his thoughts as she had fancied. Here, down to the naked tie-ribs of his soul, when he was half unconscious, the thought of her persisted, was uppermost. We needed the money. WE!

The tears were trickling down her checks as she bent over him, and it seemed she had never loved him so much as now.

"Here; you count," he said, abandoning the effort and handing the money to her. "... How much do you make it?"

"Nineteen dollars and thirty-five cents."

"That's right... the loser's end... twenty dollars. I had some drinks, an' treated a couple of the boys, an' then there was carfare. If I'd a-won, I'd a-got a hundred. That's what I fought for. It'd a-put us on Easy street for a while. You take it an' keep it. It's better 'n nothin'."

In bed, he could not sleep because of his pain, and hour by hour she worked over him, renewing the hot compresses over his bruises, soothing the lacerations with witch hazel and cold cream and the tenderest of finger tips. And all the while, with broken intervals of groaning, he babbled on, living over the fight, seeking relief in telling her his trouble, voicing regret at loss of the money, and crying out the hurt to his pride. Far worse than the sum of his physical hurts was his hurt pride.

"He couldn't put me out, anyway. He had full swing at me in the times when I was too much in to get my hands up. The crowd was crazy. I showed 'em some stamina. They was times when he only rocked me, for I'd evaporated plenty of his steam for him in the openin' rounds. I don't know how many times he dropped me. Things was gettin' too dreamy....

"Sometimes, toward the end, I could see three of him in the ring at once, an' I wouldn't know which to hit an' which to duck....

"But I fooled 'm. When I couldn't see, or feel, an' when my knees was shakin an my head goin' like a merry-go-round, I'd fall safe into clenches just the same. I bet the referee's arms is tired from draggin' us apart....

"But what a lacin'! What a lacin'! Say, Saxon... where are you? Oh, there, eh? I guess I was dreamin'. But, say, let this be a lesson to you. I broke my word an' went fightin', an' see what I got. Look at me, an' take warnin' so you won't make the same mistake an' go to makin' an' sellin' fancy work again....

"But I fooled 'em—everybody. At the beginnin' the bettin' was even. By the sixth round the wise gazabos was offerin' two to one against me. I was licked from the first drop outa the box—anybody could see that; but he couldn't put me down for the count. By the tenth round they was offerin' even that I wouldn't last the round. At the eleventh they was offerin' I wouldn't last the fifteenth. An' I lasted the whole twenty. But some punishment, I want to tell you, some punishment.

"Why, they was four rounds I was in dreamland all the time... only I kept on my feet an' fought, or took the count to eight an' got up, an' stalled an' covered an' whanged away. I don't know what I done, except I must a-done like that, because I wasn't there. I don't know a thing from the thirteenth, when he sent me to the mat on my head, till the eighteenth.

"Where was I? Oh, yes. I opened my eyes, or one eye, because I had only one that would open. An' there I was, in my corner, with the towels goin' an' ammonia in my nose an' Bill Murphy with a chunk of ice at the back of my neck. An' there, across the ring, I could see the Chicago Terror, an' I had to do some thinkin' to remember I was fightin' him. It was like I'd been away somewhere an' just got back. 'What round's this comin'?' I ask Bill. 'The eighteenth,' says he. 'The hell,' I says. 'What's come of all the other rounds? The last I was fightin' in was the thirteenth.' 'You're a wonder,' says Bill. 'You've ben out four rounds, only nobody knows it except me. I've ben tryin' to get you to quit all the time.' Just then the gong sounds, an' I can see the Terror startin' for me. 'Quit,' says Bill, makin' a move to throw in the towel. 'Not on your life,' I says. 'Drop it, Bill.' But he went on wantin' me to quit. By that time the Terror had come across to my corner an' was standin' with his hands down, lookin' at me. The referee was lookin', too, an' the house was that quiet, lookin', you could hear a pin drop. An' my head was gettin' some clearer, but not much.

"'You can't win,' Bill says.

"'Watch me,' says I. An' with that I make a rush for the Terror, catchin' him unexpected. I'm that groggy I can't stand, but I just keep a-goin', wallopin' the Terror clear across the ring to his corner, where he slips an' falls, an' I fall on top of 'm. Say, that crowd goes crazy.

"Where was I?—My head's still goin' round I guess. It's buzzin' like a swarm of bees."

"You'd just fallen on top of him in his corner," Saxon prompted.

"Oh, yes. Well, no sooner are we on our feet—an' I can't stand—I rush 'm the same way back across to my corner an' fall on 'm. That was luck. We got up, an' I'd a-fallen, only I clenched an' held myself up by him. 'I got your goat,' I says to him. 'An' now I'm goin' to eat you up.'

"I hadn't his goat, but I was playin' to get a piece of it, an' I got it, rushin' 'm as soon as the referee drags us apart an' fetchin' 'm a lucky wallop in the stomach that steadied 'm an' made him almighty careful. Too almighty careful. He was afraid to chance a mix with me. He thought I had more fight left in me than I had. So you see I got that much of his goat anyway.

"An' he couldn't get me. He didn't get me. An' in the twentieth we stood in the middle of the ring an' exchanged wallops even. Of course, I'd made a fine showin' for a licked man, but he got the decision, which was right. But I fooled 'm. He couldn't get me. An' I fooled the gazabos that was bettin' he would on short order."

At last, as dawn came on, Billy slept. He groaned and moaned, his face twisting with pain, his body vainly moving and tossing in quest of easement.

So this was prizefighting, Saxon thought. It was much worse than she had dreamed. She had had no idea that such damage could be wrought with padded gloves. He must never fight again. Street rioting was preferable. She was wondering how much of his silk had been lost, when he mumbled and opened his eyes.

"What is it?" she asked, ere it came to her that his eyes were unseeing and that he was in delirium.

"Saxon!... Saxon!" he called.

"Yes, Billy. What is it?"

His hand fumbled over the bed where ordinarily it would have encountered her.

Again he called her, and she cried her presence loudly in his ear. He sighed with relief and muttered brokenly:

"I had to do it.... We needed the money."

His eyes closed, and he slept more soundly, though his muttering continued. She had heard of congestion of the brain, and was frightened. Then she remembered his telling her of the ice Billy Murphy had held against his head.

Throwing a shawl over her head, she ran to the Pile Drivers' Home on Seventh street. The barkeeper had just opened, and was sweeping out. From the refrigerator he gave her all the ice she wished to carry, breaking it into convenient pieces for her. Back in the house, she applied the ice to the base of Billy's brain, placed hot irons to his feet, and bathed his head with witch hazel made cold by resting on the ice.

He slept in the darkened room until late afternoon, when, to Saxon's dismay, he insisted on getting up.

"Gotta make a showin'," he explained. "They ain't goin' to have the laugh on me."

In torment he was helped by her to dress, and in torment he went forth from the house so that his world should have ocular evidence that the beating he had received did not keep him in bed.

It was another kind of pride, different from a woman's, and Saxon wondered if it were the less admirable for that.

CHAPTER XIV

In the days that followed Billy's swellings went down and the bruises passed away with surprising rapidity. The quick healing of the lacerations attested the healthiness of his blood. Only remained the black eyes, unduly conspicuous on a face as blond as his. The discoloration was stubborn, persisting half a month, in which time happened divers events of importance.

Otto Frank's trial had been expeditious. Found guilty by a jury notable for the business and professional men on it, the death sentence was passed upon him and he was removed to San Quentin for execution.

The case of Chester Johnson and the fourteen others had taken longer, but within the same week, it, too, was finished. Chester Johnson was sentenced to be hanged. Two got life; three, twenty years. Only two were acquitted. The remaining seven received terms of from two to ten years.

The effect on Saxon was to throw her into deep depression. Billy was made gloomy, but his fighting spirit was not subdued.

"Always some men killed in battle," he said. "That's to be expected. But the way of sentencin' 'em gets me. All found guilty was responsible for the killin'; or none was responsible. If all was, then they should get the same sentence. They oughta hang like Chester Johnson, or else he oughtn't to hang. I'd just like to know how the judge makes up his mind. It must be like markin' China lottery tickets. He plays hunches. He looks at a guy an' waits for a spot or a number to come into his head. How else could he give Johnny Black four years an' Cal Hutchins twenty years? He played the hunches as they came into his head, an' it might just as easy ben the other way around an' Cal Hutchins got four years an' Johnny Black twenty.

"I know both them boys. They hung out with the Tenth an' Kirkham gang mostly, though sometimes they ran with my gang. We used to go swimmin' after school down to Sandy Beach on the marsh, an' in the Transit slip where they said the water was sixty feet deep, only it wasn't. An' once, on a Thursday, we dug a lot of clams together, an' played hookey Friday to peddle them. An' we used to go out on the Rock Wall an' catch pogies an' rock cod. One day—the day of the eclipse—Cal caught a perch half as big as a door. I never seen such a fish. An' now he's got to wear the stripes for twenty years. Lucky he wasn't married. If he don't get the consumption he'll be an old man when he comes out. Cal's mother wouldn't let 'm go swimmin', an' whenever she suspected she always licked his hair with her tongue. If it tasted salty, he got a beltin'. But he was onto himself. Comin' home, he'd jump somebody's front fence an' hold his head under a faucet."

"I used to dance with Chester Johnson," Saxon said. "And I knew his wife, Kittie Brady, long and long ago. She had next place at the table to me in the paper-box factory. She's gone to San Francisco to her married sister's. She's going to have a baby, too. She was awfully pretty, and there was always a string of fellows after her."

The effect of the conviction and severe sentences was a bad one on the union men. Instead of being disheartening, it intensified the bitterness. Billy's repentance for having fought and the sweetness and affection which had flashed up in the days of Saxon's nursing of him were blotted out. At home, he scowled and brooded, while his talk took on the tone of Bert's in the last days ere that Mohegan died. Also, Billy stayed away from home longer hours, and was again steadily drinking.

Saxon well-nigh abandoned hope. Almost was she steeled to the inevitable tragedy which her morbid fancy painted in a thousand guises. Oftenest, it was of Billy being brought home on a stretcher. Sometimes it was a call to the telephone in the corner grocery and the curt information by a strange voice that her husband was lying in the receiving hospital or the morgue. And when the mysterious horse-poisoning cases occurred, and when the residence of one of the teaming magnates was half destroyed by dynamite, she saw Billy in prison, or wearing stripes, or mounting to the scaffold at San Quentin while at the same time she could see the little cottage on Pine street besieged by newspaper reporters and photographers.

Yet her lively imagination failed altogether to anticipate the real catastrophe. Harmon, the fireman lodger, passing through the kitchen on his way out to work, had paused to tell Saxon about the previous day's train-wreck in the Alviso marshes, and of how the engineer, imprisoned under the overturned engine and unhurt, being drowned by the rising tide, had begged to be shot. Billy came in at the end of the narrative, and from the somber light in his heavy-lidded eyes Saxon knew he had been drinking. He glowered at Harmon, and, without greeting to him or Saxon, leaned his shoulder against the wall.

Harmon felt the awkwardness of the situation, and did his best to appear oblivious.

"I was just telling your wife—" he began, but was savagely interrupted.

"I don't care what you was tellin' her. But I got something to tell you, Mister Man. My wife's made up your bed too many times to suit me."

"Billy!" Saxon cried, her face scarlet with resentment, and hurt, and shame.

Billy ignored her. Harmon was saying:

"I don't understand—"

"Well, I don't like your mug," Billy informed him. "You're standin' on your foot. Get off of it. Get out. Beat it. D'ye understand that?"

"I don't know what's got into him," Saxon gasped hurriedly to the fireman. "He's not himself. Oh, I am so ashamed, so ashamed."

Billy turned on her.

"You shut your mouth an' keep outa this."

"But, Billy," she remonstrated.

"An' get outa here. You go into the other room."

"Here, now," Harmon broke in. "This is a fine way to treat a fellow."

"I've given you too much rope as it is," was Billy's answer.

"I've paid my rent regularly, haven't I?"

"An' I oughta knock your block off for you. Don't see any reason I shouldn't, for that matter."

"If you do anything like that, Billy—" Saxon began.

"You here still? Well, if you won't go into the other room, I'll see that you do."

His hand clutched her arm. For one instant she resisted his strength; and in that instant, the flesh crushed under his fingers, she realized the fullness of his strength.

In the front room she could only lie back in the Morris chair sobbing, and listen to what occurred in the kitchen. "I'll stay to the end of the week," the fireman was saying. "I've paid in advance."

"Don't make no mistake," came Billy's voice, so slow that it was almost a drawl, yet quivering with rage. "You can't get out too quick if you wanta stay healthy—you an' your traps with you. I'm likely to start something any moment."

"Oh, I know you're a slugger—" the fireman's voice began.

Then came the unmistakable impact of a blow; the crash of glass; a scuffle on the back porch; and, finally, the heavy bumps of a body down the steps. She heard Billy reenter the kitchen, move about, and knew he was sweeping up the broken glass of the kitchen door. Then he washed himself at the sink, whistling while he dried his face and hands, and walked into the front room. She did not look at him. She was too sick and sad. He paused irresolutely, seeming to make up his mind.

"I'm goin' up town," he stated. "They's a meeting of the union. If I don't come back it'll be because that geezer's sworn out a warrant."

He opened the front door and paused. She knew he was looking at her. Then the door closed and she heard him go down the steps.

Saxon was stunned. She did not think. She did not know what to think. The whole thing was incomprehensible, incredible. She lay back in the chair, her eyes closed, her mind almost a blank, crushed by a leaden feeling that the end had come to everything.

The voices of children playing in the street aroused her. Night had fallen. She groped her way to a lamp and lighted it. In the kitchen she stared, lips trembling, at the pitiful, half prepared meal. The fire had gone out. The water had boiled away from the potatoes. When she lifted the lid, a burnt smell arose. Methodically she scraped and cleaned the pot, put things in order, and peeled and sliced the potatoes for next day's frying. And just as methodically she went to bed. Her lack of nervousness, her placidity, was abnormal, so abnormal that she closed her eyes and was almost immediately asleep. Nor did she awaken till the sunshine was streaming into the room.

It was the first night she and Billy had slept apart. She was amazed that she had not lain awake worrying about him. She lay with eyes wide open, scarcely thinking, until pain in her arm attracted her attention. It was where Billy had gripped her. On examination she found the bruised flesh fearfully black and blue. She was astonished, not by the spiritual fact that such bruise had been administered by the one she loved most in the world, but by the sheer physical fact that an instant's pressure had inflicted so much damage. The strength of a man was a terrible thing. Quite impersonally, she found herself wondering if Charley Long were as strong as Billy.

It was not until she dressed and built the fire that she began to think about more immediate things. Billy had not returned. Then he was arrested. What was she to do?—leave him in jail, go away, and start life afresh? Of course it was impossible to go on living with a man who had behaved as he had. But then, came another thought, WAS it impossible? After all, he was her husband. FOR BETTER OR WORSE—the phrase reiterated itself, a monotonous accompaniment to her thoughts, at the back of her consciousness. To leave him was to surrender. She carried the matter before the tribunal of her mother's memory. No; Daisy would never have surrendered. Daisy was a fighter. Then she, Saxon, must fight. Besides—and she acknowledged it—readily, though in a cold, dead way—besides, Billy was better than most husbands. Better than any other husband she had heard of, she concluded, as she remembered many of his earlier nicenesses and finenesses, and especially his eternal chant: NOTHING IS TOO GOOD FOR US. THE ROBERTSES AIN'T ON THE CHEAP.

At eleven o'clock she had a caller. It was Bud Strothers, Billy's mate on strike duty. Billy, he told her, had refused bail, refused a lawyer, had asked to be tried by the Court, had pleaded guilty, and had received a sentence of sixty dollars or thirty days. Also, he had refused to let the boys pay his fine.

"He's clean looney," Strothers summed up. "Won't listen to reason. Says he'll serve the time out. He's been tankin' up too regular, I guess. His wheels are buzzin'. Here, he give me this note for you. Any time you want anything send for me. The boys'll all stand by Bill's wife. You belong to us, you know. How are you off for money?"

Proudly she disclaimed any need for money, and not until her visitor departed did she read Billy's note:

Dear Saxon—Bud Strothers is going to give you this. Don't worry about me. I am going to take my medicine. I deserve it—you know that. I guess I am gone bughouse. Just the same, I am sorry for what I done. Don't come to see me. I don't want you to. If you need money, the union will give you some. The business agent is all right. I will be out in a month. Now, Saxon, you know I love you, and just say to yourself that you forgive me this time, and you won't never have to do it again.

Billy.

Bud Strothers was followed by Maggie Donahue, and Mrs. Olsen, who paid neighborly calls of cheer and were tactful in their offers of help and in studiously avoiding more reference than was necessary to Billy's predicament.

In the afternoon James Harmon arrived. He limped slightly, and Saxon divined that he was doing his best to minimize that evidence of hurt. She tried to apologize to him, but he would not listen.

"I don't blame you, Mrs. Roberts," he said. "I know it wasn't your doing. But your husband wasn't just himself, I guess. He was fightin' mad on general principles, and it was just my luck to get in the way, that was all."

"But just the same—"

The fireman shook his head.

"I know all about it. I used to punish the drink myself, and I done some funny things in them days. And I'm sorry I swore that warrant out and testified. But I was hot in the collar. I'm cooled down now, an' I'm sorry I done it."

"You're awfully good and kind," she said, and then began hesitantly on what was bothering her. "You... you can't stay now, with him... away, you know."

"Yes; that wouldn't do, would it? I'll tell you: I'll pack up right now, and skin out, and then, before six o'clock, I'll send a wagon for my things. Here's the key to the kitchen door."

Much as he demurred, she compelled him to receive back the unexpired portion of his rent. He shook her hand heartily at leaving, and tried to get her to promise to call upon him for a loan any time she might be in need.

"It's all right," he assured her. "I'm married, and got two boys. One of them's got his lungs touched, and she's with 'em down in Arizona campin' out. The railroad helped with passes."

And as he went down the steps she wondered that so kind a man should be in so madly cruel a world.

The Donahue boy threw in a spare evening paper, and Saxon found half a column devoted to Billy. It was not nice. The fact that he had stood up in the police court with his eyes blacked from some other fray was noted. He was described as a bully, a hoodlum, a rough-neck, a professional slugger whose presence in the ranks was a disgrace to organized labor. The assault he had pleaded guilty of was atrocious and unprovoked, and if he were a fair sample of a striking teamster, the only wise thing for Oakland to do was to break up the union and drive every member from the city. And, finally, the paper complained at the mildness of the sentence. It should have been six months at least. The judge was quoted as expressing regret that he had been unable to impose a six months' sentence, this inability being due to the condition of the jails, already crowded beyond capacity by the many cases of assault committed in the course of the various strikes.

That night, in bed, Saxon experienced her first loneliness. Her brain seemed in a whirl, and her sleep was broken by vain gropings for the form of Billy she imagined at her side. At last, she lighted the lamp and lay staring at the ceiling, wide-eyed, conning over and over the details of the disaster that had overwhelmed her. She could forgive, and she could not forgive. The blow to her love-life had been too savage, too brutal. Her pride was too lacerated to permit her wholly to return in memory to the other Billy whom she loved. Wine in, wit out, she repeated to herself; but the phrase could not absolve the man who had slept by her side, and to whom she had consecrated herself. She wept in the loneliness of the all-too-spacious bed, strove to forget Billy's incomprehensible cruelty, even pillowed her cheek with numb fondness against the bruise of her arm; but still resentment burned within her, a steady flame of protest against Billy and all that Billy had done. Her throat was parched, a dull ache never ceased in her breast, and she was oppressed by a feeling of goneness. WHY, WHY?—And from the puzzle of the world came no solution.

In the morning she received a visit from Sarah—the second in all the period of her marriage; and she could easily guess her sister-in-law's ghoulish errand. No exertion was required for the assertion of all of Saxon's pride. She refused to be in the slightest on the defensive. There was nothing to defend, nothing to explain. Everything was all right, and it was nobody's business anyway. This attitude but served to vex Sarah.

"I warned you, and you can't say I didn't," her diatribe ran. "I always knew he was no good, a jailbird, a hoodlum, a slugger. My heart sunk into my boots when I heard you was runnin' with a prizefighter. I told you so at the time. But no; you wouldn't listen, you with your highfalutin' notions an' more pairs of shoes than any decent woman should have. You knew better'n me. An' I said then, to Tom, I said, 'It's all up with Saxon now.' Them was my very words. Them that touches pitch is defiled. If you'd only a-married Charley Long! Then the family wouldn't a-ben disgraced. An' this is only the beginnin', mark me, only the beginnin'. Where it'll end, God knows. He'll kill somebody yet, that plug-ugly of yourn, an' be hanged for it. You wait an' see, that's all, an' then you'll remember my words. As you make your bed, so you will lay in it"

"Best bed I ever had," Saxon commented.

"So you can say, so you can say," Sarah snorted.

"I wouldn't trade it for a queen's bed," Saxon added.

"A jailbird's bed," Sarah rejoined witheringly.

"Oh, it's the style," Saxon retorted airily. "Everybody's getting a taste of jail. Wasn't Tom arrested at some street meeting of the socialists? Everybody goes to jail these days."

The barb had struck home.

"But Tom was acquitted," Sarah hastened to proclaim.

"Just the same he lay in jail all night without bail."

This was unanswerable, and Sarah executed her favorite tactic of attack in flank.

"A nice come-down for you, I must say, that was raised straight an' right, a-cuttin' up didoes with a lodger."

"Who says so?" Saxon blazed with an indignation quickly mastered.

"Oh, a blind man can read between the lines. A lodger, a young married woman with no self respect, an' a prizefighter for a husband—what else would they fight about?"

"Just like any family quarrel, wasn't it?" Saxon smiled placidly.

Sarah was shocked into momentary speechlessness.

"And I want you to understand it," Saxon continued. "It makes a woman proud to have men fight over her. I am proud. Do you hear? I am proud. I want you to tell them so. I want you to tell all your neighbors. Tell everybody. I am no cow. Men like me. Men fight for me. Men go to jail for me. What is a woman in the world for, if it isn't to have men like her? Now, go, Sarah; go at once, and tell everybody what you've read between the lines. Tell them Billy is a jailbird and that I am a bad woman whom all men desire. Shout it out, and good luck to you. And get out of my house. And never put your feet in it again. You are too decent a woman to come here. You might lose your reputation. And think of your children. Now get out. Go."

Not until Sarah had taken an amazed and horrified departure did Saxon fling herself on the bed in a convulsion of tears. She had been ashamed, before, merely of Billy's inhospitality, and surliness, and unfairness. But she could see, now, the light in which others looked on the affair. It had not entered Saxon's head. She was confident that it had not entered Billy's. She knew his attitude from the first. Always he had opposed taking a lodger because of his proud faith that his wife should not work. Only hard times had compelled his consent, and, now that she looked back, almost had she inveigled him into consenting.

But all this did not alter the viewpoint the neighborhood must hold, that every one who had ever known her must hold. And for this, too, Billy was responsible. It was more terrible than all the other things he had been guilty of put together. She could never look any one in the face again. Maggie Donahue and Mrs. Olsen had been very kind, but of what must they have been thinking all the time they talked with her? And what must they have said to each other? What was everybody saying?—over front gates and back fences,—the men standing on the corners or talking in saloons?

Later, exhausted by her grief, when the tears no longer fell, she grew more impersonal, and dwelt on the disasters that had befallen so many women since the strike troubles began—Otto Frank's wife, Henderson's widow, pretty Kittie Brady, Mary, all the womenfolk of the other workmen who were now wearing the stripes in San Quentin. Her world was crashing about her ears. No one was exempt. Not only had she not escaped, but hers was the worst disgrace of all. Desperately she tried to hug the delusion that she was asleep, that it was all a nightmare, and that soon the alarm would go off and she would get up and cook Billy's breakfast so that he could go to work.

She did not leave the bed that day. Nor did she sleep. Her brain whirled on and on, now dwelling at insistent length upon her misfortunes, now pursuing the most fantastic ramifications of what she considered her disgrace, and, again, going back to her childhood and wandering through endless trivial detail. She worked at all the tasks she had ever done, performing, in fancy, the myriads of mechanical movements peculiar to each occupation—shaping and pasting in the paper box factory, ironing in the laundry, weaving in the jute mill, peeling fruit in the cannery and countless boxes of scalded tomatoes. She attended all her dances and all her picnics over again; went through her school days, recalling the face and name and seat of every schoolmate; endured the gray bleakness of the years in the orphan asylum; revisioned every memory of her mother, every tale; and relived all her life with Billy. But ever—and here the torment lay—she was drawn back from these far-wanderings to her present trouble, with its parch in the throat, its ache in the breast, and its gnawing, vacant goneness.

CHAPTER XV

All that night Saxon lay, unsleeping, without taking off her clothes, and when she arose in the morning and washed her face and dressed her hair she was aware of a strange numbness, of a feeling of constriction about her head as if it were bound by a heavy band of iron. It seemed like a dull pressure upon her brain. It was the beginning of an illness that she did not know as illness. All she knew was that she felt queer. It was not fever. It was not cold. Her bodily health was as it should be, and, when she thought about it, she put her condition down to nerves—nerves, according to her ideas and the ideas of her class, being unconnected with disease.

She had a strange feeling of loss of self, of being a stranger to herself, and the world in which she moved seemed a vague and shrouded world. It lacked sharpness of definition. Its customary vividness was gone. She had lapses of memory, and was continually finding herself doing unplanned things. Thus, to her astonishment, she came to in the back yard hanging up the week's wash. She had no recollection of having done it, yet it had been done precisely as it should have been done. She had boiled the sheets and pillow-slips and the table linen. Billy's woolens had been washed in warm water only, with the home-made soap, the recipe of which Mercedes had given her. On investigation, she found she had eaten a mutton chop for breakfast. This meant that she had been to the butcher shop, yet she had no memory of having gone. Curiously, she went into the bedroom. The bed was made up and everything in order.

At twilight she came upon herself in the front room, seated by the window, crying in an ecstasy of joy. At first she did not know what this joy was; then it came to her that it was because she had lost her baby. "A blessing, a blessing," she was chanting aloud, wringing her hands, but with joy, she knew it was with joy that she wrung her hands.

The days came and went. She had little notion of time. Sometimes, centuries agone, it seemed to her it was since Billy had gone to jail. At other times it was no more than the night before. But through it all two ideas persisted: she must not go to see Billy in jail; it was a blessing she had lost her baby.

Once, Bud Strothers came to see her. She sat in the front room and talked with him, noting with fascination that there were fringes to the heels of his trousers. Another day, the business agent of the union called. She told him, as she had told Bud Strothers, that everything was all right, that she needed nothing, that she could get along comfortably until Billy came out.

A fear began to haunt her. WHEN HE CAME OUT. No; it must not be. There must not be another baby. It might LIVE. No, no, a thousand times no. It must not be. She would run away first. She would never see Billy again. Anything but that. Anything but that.

This fear persisted. In her nightmare-ridden sleep it became an accomplished fact, so that she would awake, trembling, in a cold sweat, crying out. Her sleep had become wretched. Sometimes she was convinced that she did not sleep at all, and she knew that she had insomnia, and remembered that it was of insomnia her mother had died.

She came to herself one day, sitting in Doctor Hentley's office. He was looking at her in a puzzled way.

"Got plenty to eat?" he was asking.

She nodded.

"Any serious trouble?"

She shook her head.

"Everything's all right, doctor... except..."

"Yes, yes," he encouraged.

And then she knew why she had come. Simply, explicitly, she told him. He shook his head slowly.

"It can't be done, little woman," he said

"Oh, but it can!" she cried. "I know it can."

"I don't mean that," he answered. "I mean I can't tell you. I dare not. It is against the law. There is a doctor in Leavenworth prison right now for that."

In vain she pleaded with him. He instanced his own wife and children whose existence forbade his imperiling.

"Besides, there is no likelihood now," he told her.

"But there will be, there is sure to be," she urged.

But he could only shake his head sadly.

"Why do you want to know?" he questioned finally.

Saxon poured her heart out to him. She told of her first year of happiness with Billy, of the hard times caused by the labor troubles, of the change in Billy so that there was no love-life left, of her own deep horror. Not if it died, she concluded. She could go through that again. But if it should live. Billy would soon be out of jail, and then the danger would begin. It was only a few words. She would never tell any one. Wild horses could not drag it out of her.

But Doctor Hentley continued to shake his head. "I can't tell you, little woman. It's a shame, but I can't take the risk. My hands are tied. Our laws are all wrong. I have to consider those who are dear to me."

It was when she got up to go that he faltered. "Come here," he said. "Sit closer."

He prepared to whisper in her ear, then, with a sudden excess of caution, crossed the room swiftly, opened the door, and looked out. When he sat down again he drew his chair so close to hers that the arms touched, and when he whispered his beard tickled her ear.

"No, no," he shut her off when she tried to voice her gratitude. "I have told you nothing. You were here to consult me about your general health. You are run down, out of condition—"

As he talked he moved her toward the door. When he opened it, a patient for the dentist in the adjoining office was standing in the hall. Doctor Hentley lifted his voice.

"What you need is that tonic I prescribed. Remember that. And don't pamper your appetite when it comes back. Eat strong, nourishing food, and beefsteak, plenty of beefsteak. And don't cook it to a cinder. Good day."

At times the silent cottage became unendurable, and Saxon would throw a shawl about her head and walk out the Oakland Mole, or cross the railroad yards and the marshes to Sandy Beach where Billy had said he used to swim. Also, by going out the Transit slip, by climbing down the piles on a precarious ladder of iron spikes, and by crossing a boom of logs, she won access to the Rock Wall that extended far out into the bay and that served as a barrier between the mudflats and the tide-scoured channel of Oakland Estuary. Here the fresh sea breezes blew and Oakland sank down to a smudge of smoke behind her, while across the bay she could see the smudge that represented San Francisco. Ocean steamships passed up and down the estuary, and lofty-masted ships, towed by red-stacked tugs.

She gazed at the sailors on the ships, wondered on what far voyages and to what far lands they went, wondered what freedoms were theirs. Or were they girt in by as remorseless and cruel a world as the dwellers in Oakland were? Were they as unfair, as unjust, as brutal, in their dealings with their fellows as were the city dwellers? It did not seem so, and sometimes she wished herself on board, out-bound, going anywhere, she cared not where, so long as it was away from the world to which she had given her best and which had trampled her in return.

She did not know always when she left the house, nor where her feet took her. Once, she came to herself in a strange part of Oakland. The street was wide and lined with rows of shade trees. Velvet lawns, broken only by cement sidewalks, ran down to the gutters. The houses stood apart and were large. In her vocabulary they were mansions. What had shocked her to consciousness of herself was a young man in the driver's seat of a touring car standing at the curb. He was looking at her curiously and she recognized him as Roy Blanchard, whom, in front of the Forum, Billy had threatened to whip. Beside the car, bareheaded, stood another young man. He, too, she remembered. He it was, at the Sunday picnic where she first met Billy, who had thrust his cane between the legs of the flying foot-racer and precipitated the free-for-all fight. Like Blanchard, he was looking at her curiously, and she became aware that she had been talking to herself. The babble of her lips still beat in her ears. She blushed, a rising tide of shame heating her face, and quickened her pace. Blanchard sprang out of the car and came to her with lifted hat. "Is anything the matter?" he asked.

She shook her head, and, though she had stopped, she evinced her desire to go on.

"I know you," he said, studying her face. "You were with the striker who promised me a licking."

"He is my husband," she said.

"Oh! Good for him." He regarded her pleasantly and frankly. "But about yourself? Isn't there anything I can do for you? Something IS the matter."

"No, I'm all right," she answered. "I have been sick," she lied; for she never dreamed of connecting her queerness with sickness.

"You look tired," he pressed her. "I can take you in the machine and run you anywhere you want. It won't be any trouble. I've plenty of time."

Saxon shook her head.

"If... if you would tell me where I can catch the Eighth street cars. I don't often come to this part of town."

He told her where to find an electric car and what transfers to make, and she was surprised at the distance she had wandered.

"Thank you," she said. "And good bye."

"Sure I can't do anything now?"

"Sure."

"Well, good bye," he smiled good humoredly. "And tell that husband of yours to keep in good condition. I'm likely to make him need it all when he tangles up with me."

"Oh, but you can't fight with him," she warned. "You mustn't. You haven't got a show."

"Good for you," he admired. "That's the way for a woman to stand up for her man. Now the average woman would be so afraid he was going to get licked—"

"But I'm not afraid... for him. It's for you. He's a terrible fighter. You wouldn't have any chance. It would be like... like..."

"Like taking candy from a baby?" Blanchard finished for her.

"Yes," she nodded. "That's just what he would call it. And whenever he tells you you are standing on your foot watch out for him. Now I must go. Good bye, and thank you again."

She went on down the sidewalk, his cheery good bye ringing in her ears. He was kind—she admitted it honestly; yet he was one of the clever ones, one of the masters, who, according to Billy, were responsible for all the cruelty to labor, for the hardships of the women, for the punishment of the labor men who were wearing stripes in San Quentin or were in the death cells awaiting the scaffold. Yet he was kind, sweet natured, clean, good. She could read his character in his face. But how could this be, if he were responsible for so much evil? She shook her head wearily. There was no explanation, no understanding of this world which destroyed little babes and bruised women's breasts.

As for her having strayed into that neighborhood of fine residences, she was unsurprised. It was in line with her queerness. She did so many things without knowing that she did them. But she must be careful. It was better to wander on the marshes and the Rock Wall.

Especially she liked the Rock Wall. There was a freedom about it, a wide spaciousness that she found herself instinctively trying to breathe, holding her arms out to embrace and make part of herself. It was a more natural world, a more rational world. She could understand it—understand the green crabs with white-bleached claws that scuttled before her and which she could see pasturing on green-weeded rocks when the tide was low. Here, hopelessly man-made as the great wall was, nothing seemed artificial. There were no men here, no laws nor conflicts of men. The tide flowed and ebbed; the sun rose and set; regularly each afternoon the brave west wind came romping in through the Golden Gate, darkening the water, cresting tiny wavelets, making the sailboats fly. Everything ran with frictionless order. Everything was free. Firewood lay about for the taking. No man sold it by the sack. Small boys fished with poles from the rocks, with no one to drive them away for trespass, catching fish as Billy had caught fish, as Cal Hutchins had caught fish. Billy had told her of the great perch Cal Hutchins caught on the day of the eclipse, when he had little dreamed the heart of his manhood would be spent in convict's garb.

And here was food, food that was free. She watched the small boys on a day when she had eaten nothing, and emulated them, gathering mussels from the rocks at low water, cooking them by placing them among the coals of a fire she built on top of the wall. They tasted particularly good. She learned to knock the small oysters from the rocks, and once she found a string of fresh-caught fish some small boy had forgotten to take home with him.

Here drifted evidences of man's sinister handiwork—from a distance, from the cities. One flood tide she found the water covered with muskmelons. They bobbed and bumped along up the estuary in countless thousands. Where they stranded against the rocks she was able to get them. But each and every melon—and she patiently tried scores of them—had been spoiled by a sharp gash that let in the salt water. She could not understand. She asked an old Portuguese woman gathering driftwood.

"They do it, the people who have too much," the old woman explained, straightening her labor-stiffened back with such an effort that almost Saxon could hear it creak. The old woman's black eyes flashed angrily, and her wrinkled lips, drawn tightly across toothless gums, wry with bitterness. "The people that have too much. It is to keep up the price. They throw them overboard in San Francisco."

"But why don't they give them away to the poor people?" Saxon asked.

"They must keep up the price."

"But the poor people cannot buy them anyway," Saxon objected. "It would not hurt the price."

The old woman shrugged her shoulders.

"I do not know. It is their way. They chop each melon so that the poor people cannot fish them out and eat anyway. They do the same with the oranges, with the apples. Ah, the fishermen! There is a trust. When the boats catch too much fish, the trust throws them overboard from Fisherman Wharf, boat-loads, and boat-loads, and boatloads of the beautiful fish. And the beautiful good fish sink and are gone. And no one gets them. Yet they are dead and only good to eat. Fish are very good to eat."

And Saxon could not understand a world that did such things—a world in which some men possessed so much food that they threw it away, paying men for their labor of spoiling it before they threw it away; and in the same world so many people who did not have enough food, whose babies died because their mothers' milk was not nourishing, whose young men fought and killed one another for the chance to work, whose old men and women went to the poorhouse because there was no food for them in the little shacks they wept at leaving. She wondered if all the world were that way, and remembered Mercedes' tales. Yes; all the world was that way. Had not Mercedes seen ten thousand families starve to death in that far away India, when, as she had said, her own jewels that she wore would have fed and saved them all? It was the poorhouse and the salt vats for the stupid, jewels and automobiles for the clever ones.

She was one of the stupid. She must be. The evidence all pointed that way. Yet Saxon refused to accept it. She was not stupid. Her mother had not been stupid, nor had the pioneer stock before her. Still it must be so. Here she sat, nothing to eat at home, her love-husband changed to a brute beast and lying in jail, her arms and heart empty of the babe that would have been there if only the stupid ones had not made a shambles of her front yard in their wrangling over jobs.

She sat there, racking her brain, the smudge of Oakland at her back, staring across the bay at the smudge of San Francisco. Yet the sun was good; the wind was good, as was the keen salt air in her nostrils; the blue sky, flecked with clouds, was good. All the natural world was right, and sensible, and beneficent. It was the man-world that was wrong, and mad, and horrible. Why were the stupid stupid? Was it a law of God? No; it could not be. God had made the wind, and air, and sun. The man-world was made by man, and a rotten job it was. Yet, and she remembered it well, the teaching in the orphan asylum, God had made everything. Her mother, too, had believed this, had believed in this God. Things could not be different. It was ordained.

For a time Saxon sat crushed, helpless. Then smoldered protest, revolt. Vainly she asked why God had it in for her. What had she done to deserve such fate? She briefly reviewed her life in quest of deadly sins committed, and found them not. She had obeyed her mother; obeyed Cady, the saloon-keeper, and Cady's wife; obeyed the matron and the other women in the orphan asylum; obeyed Tom when she came to live in his house, and never run in the streets because he didn't wish her to. At school she had always been honorably promoted, and never had her deportment report varied from one hundred per cent. She had worked from the day she left school to the day of her marriage. She had been a good worker, too. The little Jew who ran the paper box factory had almost wept when she quit. It was the same at the cannery. She was among the high-line weavers when the jute mills closed down. And she had kept straight. It was not as if she had been ugly or unattractive. She had known her temptations and encountered her dangers. The fellows had been crazy about her. They had run after her, fought over her, in a way to turn most girls' heads. But she had kept straight. And then had come Billy, her reward. She had devoted herself to him, to his house, to all that would nourish his love; and now she and Billy were sinking down into this senseless vortex of misery and heartbreak of the man-made world.

No, God was not responsible. She could have made a better world herself—a finer, squarer world. This being so, then there was no God. God could not make a botch. The matron had been wrong, her mother had been wrong. Then there was no immortality, and Bert, wild and crazy Bert, falling at her front gate with his foolish death-cry, was right. One was a long time dead.

Looking thus at life, shorn of its superrational sanctions, Saxon floundered into the morass of pessimism. There was no justification for right conduct in the universe, no square deal for her who had earned reward, for the millions who worked like animals, died like animals, and were a long time and forever dead. Like the hosts of more learned thinkers before her, she concluded that the universe was unmoral and without concern for men.

And now she sat crushed in greater helplessness than when she had included God in the scheme of injustice. As long as God was, there was always chance for a miracle, for some supernatural intervention, some rewarding with ineffable bliss. With God missing, the world was a trap. Life was a trap. She was like a linnet, caught by small boys and imprisoned in a cage. That was because the linnet was stupid. But she rebelled. She fluttered and beat her soul against the hard face of things as did the linnet against the bars of wire. She was not stupid. She did not belong in the trap. She would fight her way out of the trap. There must be such a way out. When canal boys and rail-splitters, the lowliest of the stupid lowly, as she had read in her school history, could find their way out and become presidents of the nation and rule over even the clever ones in their automobiles, then could she find her way out and win to the tiny reward she craved—Billy, a little love, a little happiness. She would not mind that the universe was unmoral, that there was no God, no immortality. She was willing to go into the black grave and remain in its blackness forever, to go into the salt vats and let the young men cut her dead flesh to sausage-meat, if—if only she could get her small meed of happiness first.

How she would work for that happiness! How she would appreciate it, make the most of each least particle of it! But how was she to do it. Where was the path? She could not vision it. Her eyes showed her only the smudge of San Francisco, the smudge of Oakland, where men were breaking heads and killing one another, where babies were dying, born and unborn, and where women were weeping with bruised breasts.

CHAPTER XVI

Her vague, unreal existence continued. It seemed in some previous life-time that Billy had gone away, that another life-time would have to come before he returned. She still suffered from insomnia. Long nights passed in succession, during which she never closed her eyes. At other times she slept through long stupors, waking stunned and numbed, scarcely able to open her heavy eyes, to move her weary limbs. The pressure of the iron band on her head never relaxed. She was poorly nourished. Nor had she a cent of money. She often went a whole day without eating. Once, seventy-two hours elapsed without food passing her lips. She dug clams in the marsh, knocked the tiny oysters from the rocks, and gathered mussels.

And yet, when Bud Strothers came to see how she was getting along, she convinced him that all was well. One evening after work, Tom came, and forced two dollars upon her. He was terribly worried. He would like to help more, but Sarah was expecting another baby. There had been slack times in his trade because of the strikes in the other trades. He did not know what the country was coming to. And it was all so simple. All they had to do was see things in his way and vote the way he voted. Then everybody would get a square deal. Christ was a Socialist, he told her.

"Christ died two thousand years ago," Saxon said.

"Well?" Tom queried, not catching her implication.

"Think," she said, "think of all the men and women who died in those two thousand years, and socialism has not come yet. And in two thousand years more it may be as far away as ever. Tom, your socialism never did you any good. It is a dream."

"It wouldn't be if—" he began with a flash of resentment.

"If they believed as you do. Only they don't. You don't succeed in making them."

"But we are increasing every year," he argued.

"Two thousand years is an awfully long time," she said quietly.

Her brother's tired face saddened as he noted. Then he sighed:

"Well, Saxon, if it's a dream, it is a good dream."

"I don't want to dream," was her reply. "I want things real. I want them now."

And before her fancy passed the countless generations of the stupid lowly, the Billys and Saxons, the Berts and Marys, the Toms and Sarahs. And to what end? The salt vats and the grave. Mercedes was a hard and wicked woman, but Mercedes was right. The stupid must always be under the heels of the clever ones. Only she, Saxon, daughter of Daisy who had written wonderful poems and of a soldier-father on a roan war-horse, daughter of the strong generations who had won half a world from wild nature and the savage Indian—no, she was not stupid. It was as if she suffered false imprisonment. There was some mistake. She would find the way out.

With the two dollars she bought a sack of flour and half a sack of potatoes. This relieved the monotony of her clams and mussels. Like the Italian and Portuguese women, she gathered driftwood and carried it home, though always she did it with shamed pride, timing her arrival so that it would be after dark. One day, on the mud-flat side of the Rock Wall, an Italian fishing boat hauled up on the sand dredged from the channel. From the top of the wall Saxon watched the men grouped about the charcoal brazier, eating crusty Italian bread and a stew of meat and vegetables, washed down with long draughts of thin red wine. She envied them their freedom that advertised itself in the heartiness of their meal, in the tones of their chatter and laughter, in the very boat itself that was not tied always to one place and that carried them wherever they willed. Afterward, they dragged a seine across the mud-flats and up on the sand, selecting for themselves only the larger kinds of fish. Many thousands of small fish, like sardines, they left dying on the sand when they sailed away. Saxon got a sackful of the fish, and was compelled to make two trips in order to carry them home, where she salted them down in a wooden washtub.

Her lapses of consciousness continued. The strangest thing she did while in such condition was on Sandy Beach. There she discovered herself, one windy afternoon, lying in a hole she had dug, with sacks for blankets. She had even roofed the hole in rough fashion by means of drift wood and marsh grass. On top of the grass she had piled sand.

Another time she came to herself walking across the marshes, a bundle of driftwood, tied with bale-rope, on her shoulder. Charley Long was walking beside her. She could see his face in the starlight. She wondered dully how long he had been talking, what he had said. Then she was curious to hear what he was saying. She was not afraid, despite his strength, his wicked nature, and the loneliness and darkness of the marsh.

"It's a shame for a girl like you to have to do this," he was saying, apparently in repetition of what he had already urged. "Come on an' say the word, Saxon. Come on an' say the word."

Saxon stopped and quietly faced him.

"Listen, Charley Long. Billy's only doing thirty days, and his time is almost up. When he gets out your life won't be worth a pinch of salt if I tell him you've been bothering me. Now listen. If you go right now away from here, and stay away, I won't tell him. That's all I've got to say."

The big blacksmith stood in scowling indecision, his face pathetic in its fierce yearning, his hands making unconscious, clutching contractions.

"Why, you little, small thing," he said desperately, "I could break you in one hand. I could—why, I could do anything I wanted. I don't want to hurt you, Saxon. You know that. Just say the word—"

"I've said the only word I'm going to say."

"God!" he muttered in involuntary admiration. "You ain't afraid. You ain't afraid."

They faced each other for long silent minutes.

"Why ain't you afraid?" he demanded at last, after peering into the surrounding darkness as if searching for her hidden allies.

"Because I married a man," Saxon said briefly. "And now you'd better go."

When he had gone she shifted the load of wood to her other shoulder and started on, in her breast a quiet thrill of pride in Billy. Though behind prison bars, still she leaned against his strength. The mere naming of him was sufficient to drive away a brute like Charley Long.

On the day that Otto Frank was hanged she remained indoors. The evening papers published the account. There had been no reprieve. In Sacramento was a railroad Governor who might reprieve or even pardon bank-wreckers and grafters, but who dared not lift his finger for a workingman. All this was the talk of the neighborhood. It had been Billy's talk. It had been Bert's talk.

The next day Saxon started out the Rock Wall, and the specter of Otto Frank walked by her side. And with him was a dimmer, mistier specter that she recognized as Billy. Was he, too, destined to tread his way to Otto Frank's dark end? Surely so, if the blood and strike continued. He was a fighter. He felt he was right in fighting. It was easy to kill a man. Even if he did not intend it, some time, when he was slugging a scab, the scab would fracture his skull on a stone curbing or a cement sidewalk. And then Billy would hang. That was why Otto Frank hanged. He had not intended to kill Henderson. It was only by accident that Henderson's skull was fractured. Yet Otto Frank had been hanged for it just the same.

She wrung her hands and wept loudly as she stumbled among the windy rocks. The hours passed, and she was lost to herself and her grief. When she came to she found herself on the far end of the wall where it jutted into the bay between the Oakland and Alameda Moles. But she could see no wall. It was the time of the full moon, and the unusual high tide covered the rocks. She was knee deep in the water, and about her knees swam scores of big rock rats, squeaking and fighting, scrambling to climb upon her out of the flood. She screamed with fright and horror, and kicked at them. Some dived and swam away under water; others circled about her warily at a distance; and one big fellow laid his teeth into her shoe. Him she stepped on and crushed with her free foot. By this time, though still trembling, she was able coolly to consider the situation. She waded to a stout stick of driftwood a few feet away, and with this quickly cleared a space about herself.

A grinning small boy, in a small, bright-painted and half-decked skiff, sailed close in to the wall and let go his sheet to spill the wind. "Want to get aboard?" he called.

"Yes," she answered. "There are thousands of big rats here. I'm afraid of them."

He nodded, ran close in, spilled the wind from his sail, the boat's way carrying it gently to her.

"Shove out its bow," he commanded. "That's right. I don't want to break my centerboard.... An' then jump aboard in the stern—quick!—alongside of me."

She obeyed, stepping in lightly beside him. He held the tiller up with his elbow, pulled in on the sheet, and as the sail filled the boat sprang away over the rippling water.

"You know boats," the boy said approvingly.

He was a slender, almost frail lad, of twelve or thirteen years, though healthy enough, with sunburned freckled face and large gray eyes that were clear and wistful.

Despite his possession of the pretty boat, Saxon was quick to sense that he was one of them, a child of the people.

"First boat I was ever in, except ferryboats," Saxon laughed.

He looked at her keenly. "Well, you take to it like a duck to water is all I can say about it. Where d'ye want me to land you?"

"Anywhere."

He opened his mouth to speak, gave her another long look, considered for a space, then asked suddenly: "Got plenty of time?"

She nodded.

"All day?"

Again she nodded.

"Say—I'll tell you, I'm goin' out on this ebb to Goat Island for rockcod, an' I'll come in on the flood this evening. I got plenty of lines an' bait. Want to come along? We can both fish. And what you catch you can have."

Saxon hesitated. The freedom and motion of the small boat appealed to her. Like the ships she had envied, it was outbound.

"Maybe you'll drown me," she parleyed.

The boy threw back his head with pride.

"I guess I've been sailin' many a long day by myself, an' I ain't drowned yet."

"All right," she consented. "Though remember, I don't know anything about boats."

"Aw, that's all right.—Now I'm goin' to go about. When I say 'Hard a-lee!' like that, you duck your head so the boom don't hit you, an' shift over to the other side."

He executed the maneuver, Saxon obeyed, and found herself sitting beside him on the opposite side of the boat, while the boat itself, on the other tack, was heading toward Long Wharf where the coal bunkers were. She was aglow with admiration, the more so because the mechanics of boat-sailing was to her a complex and mysterious thing.

"Where did you learn it all?" she inquired.

"Taught myself, just naturally taught myself. I liked it, you see, an' what a fellow likes he's likeliest to do. This is my second boat. My first didn't have a centerboard. I bought it for two dollars an' learned a lot, though it never stopped leaking. What d 'ye think I paid for this one? It's worth twenty-five dollars right now. What d 'ye think I paid for it?"

"I give up," Saxon said. "How much?"

"Six dollars. Think of it! A boat like this! Of course I done a lot of work, an' the sail cost two dollars, the oars one forty, an' the paint one seventy-five. But just the same eleven dollars and fifteen cents is a real bargain. It took me a long time saving for it, though. I carry papers morning and evening— there's a boy taking my route for me this afternoon—I give 'm ten cents, an' all the extras he sells is his; and I'd a-got the boat sooner only I had to pay for my shorthand lessons. My mother wants me to become a court reporter. They get sometimes as much as twenty dollars a day. Gee! But I don't want it. It's a shame to waste the money on the lessons."

"What do you want?" she asked, partly from idleness, and yet with genuine curiosity; for she felt drawn to this boy in knee pants who was so confident and at the same time so wistful.

"What do I want?" he repeated after her.

Turning his head slowly, he followed the sky-line, pausing especially when his eyes rested landward on the brown Contra Costa hills, and seaward, past Alcatraz, on the Golden Gate. The wistfulness in his eyes was overwhelming and went to her heart.

"That," he said, sweeping the circle of the world with a wave of his arm.

"That?" she queried.

He looked at her, perplexed in that he had not made his meaning clear.

"Don't you ever feel that way?" he asked, bidding for sympathy with his dream. "Don't you sometimes feel you'd die if you didn't know what's beyond them hills an' what's beyond the other hills behind them hills? An' the Golden Gate! There's the Pacific Ocean beyond, and China, an' Japan, an' India, an'... an' all the coral islands. You can go anywhere out through the Golden Gate—to Australia, to Africa, to the seal islands, to the North Pole, to Cape Horn. Why, all them places are just waitin' for me to come an' see 'em. I've lived in Oakland all my life, but I'm not going to live in Oakland the rest of my life, not by a long shot. I'm goin' to get away... away...."

Again, as words failed to express the vastness of his desire, the wave of his arm swept the circle of the world.

Saxon thrilled with him. She too, save for her earlier childhood, had lived in Oakland all her life. And it had been a good place in which to live... until now. And now, in all its nightmare horror, it was a place to get away from, as with her people the East had been a place to get away from. And why not? The world tugged at her, and she felt in touch with the lad's desire. Now that she thought of it, her race had never been given to staying long in one place. Always it had been on the move. She remembered back to her mother's tales, and to the wood engraving in her scrapbook where her half-clad forebears, sword in hand, leaped from their lean beaked boats to do battle on the blood-drenched sands of England.

"Did you ever hear about the Anglo-Saxons?" she asked the boy.

"You bet!" His eyes glistened, and he looked at her with new interest. "I'm an Anglo-Saxon, every inch of me. Look at the color of my eyes, my skin. I'm awful white where I ain't sunburned. An' my hair was yellow when I was a baby. My mother says it'll be dark brown by the time I'm grown up, worse luck. Just the same, I'm Anglo-Saxon. I am of a fighting race. We ain't afraid of nothin'. This bay—think I'm afraid of it!" He looked out over the water with flashing eye of scorn. "Why, I've crossed it when it was howlin' an' when the scow schooner sailors said I lied an' that I didn't. Huh! They were only squareheads. Why, we licked their kind thousands of years ago. We lick everything we go up against. We've wandered all over the world, licking the world. On the sea, on the land, it's all the same. Look at Ivory Nelson, look at Davy Crockett, look at Paul Jones, look at Clive, an' Kitchener, an' Fremont, an' Kit Carson, an' all of 'em."

Saxon nodded, while he continued, her own eyes shining, and it came to her what a glory it would be to be the mother of a man-child like this. Her body ached with the fancied quickening of unborn life. A good stock, a good stock, she thought to herself. Then she thought of herself and Billy, healthy shoots of that same stock, yet condemned to childlessness because of the trap of the manmade world and the curse of being herded with the stupid ones.

She came back to the boy.

"My father was a soldier in the Civil War," he was telling her, "a scout an' a spy. The rebels were going to hang him twice for a spy. At the battle of Wilson's Creek he ran half a mile with his captain wounded on his back. He's got a bullet in his leg right now, just above the knee. It's been there all these years. He let me feel it once. He was a buffalo hunter and a trapper before the war. He was sheriff of his county when he was twenty years old. An' after the war, when he was marshal of Silver City, he cleaned out the bad men an' gun-fighters. He's been in almost every state in the Union. He could wrestle any man at the railings in his day, an' he was bully of the raftsmen of the Susquehanna when he was only a youngster. His father killed a man in a standup fight with a blow of his fist when he was sixty years old. An' when he was seventy-four, his second wife had twins, an' he died when he was plowing in the field with oxen when he was ninety-nine years old. He just unyoked the oxen, an' sat down under a tree, an' died there sitting up. An' my father's just like him. He's pretty old now, but he ain't afraid of nothing. He's a regular Anglo-Saxon, you see. He's a special policeman, an' he didn't do a thing to the strikers in some of the fightin'. He had his face all cut up with a rock, but he broke his club short off over some hoodlum's head."

He paused breathlessly and looked at her.

"Gee!" he said. "I'd hate to a-ben that hoodlum."

"My name is Saxon," she said.

"Your name?"

"My first name."

"Gee!" he cried. "You're lucky. Now if mine had been only Erling—you know, Erling the Bold—or Wolf, or Swen, or Jarl!"

"What is it?" she asked.

"Only John," he admitted sadly. "But I don't let 'em call me John. Everybody's got to call me Jack. I've scrapped with a dozen fellows that tried to call me John, or Johnnie—wouldn't that make you sick?—Johnnie!"

They were now off the coal bunkers of Long Wharf, and the boy put the skiff about, heading toward San Francisco. They were well out in the open bay. The west wind had strengthened and was whitecapping the strong ebb tide. The boat drove merrily along. When splashes of spray flew aboard, wetting them, Saxon laughed, and the boy surveyed her with approval. They passed a ferryboat, and the passengers on the upper deck crowded to one side to watch them. In the swell of the steamer's wake, the skiff shipped quarter-full of water. Saxon picked up an empty can and looked at the boy.

"That's right," he said. "Go ahead an' bale out." And, when she had finished: "We'll fetch Goat Island next tack. Right there off the Torpedo Station is where we fish, in fifty feet of water an' the tide runnin' to beat the band. You're wringing wet, ain't you? Gee! You're like your name. You're a Saxon, all right. Are you married?"

Saxon nodded, and the boy frowned.

"What'd you want to do that for? Now you can't wander over the world like I'm going to. You're tied down. You're anchored for keeps."

"It's pretty good to be married, though," she smiled.

"Sure, everybody gets married. But that's no reason to be in a rush about it. Why couldn't you wait a while, like me. I'm goin' to get married, too, but not until I'm an old man an' have been everywheres."

Under the lee of Goat Island, Saxon obediently sitting still, he took in the sail, and, when the boat had drifted to a position to suit him, he dropped a tiny anchor. He got out the fish lines and showed Saxon how to bait her hooks with salted minnows. Then they dropped the lines to bottom, where they vibrated in the swift tide, and waited for bites.

"They'll bite pretty soon," he encouraged. "I've never failed but twice to catch a mess here. What d'ye say we eat while we're waiting?"

Vainly she protested she was not hungry. He shared his lunch with her with a boy's rigid equity, even to the half of a hard-boiled egg and the half of a big red apple.

Still the rockcod did not bite. From under the stern-sheets he drew out a cloth-bound book.

"Free Library," he vouchsafed, as he began to read, with one hand holding the place while with the other he waited for the tug on the fishline that would announce rockcod.

Saxon read the title. It was "Afloat in the Forest."

"Listen to this," he said after a few minutes, and he read several pages descriptive of a great flooded tropical forest being navigated by boys on a raft.

"Think of that!" he concluded. "That's the Amazon river in flood time in South America. And the world's full of places like that—everywhere, most likely, except Oakland. Oakland's just a place to start from, I guess. Now that's adventure, I want to tell you. Just think of the luck of them boys! All the same, some day I'm going to go over the Andes to the headwaters of the Amazon, all through the rubber country, an' canoe down the Amazon thousands of miles to its mouth where it's that wide you can't see one bank from the other an' where you can scoop up perfectly fresh water out of the ocean a hundred miles from land."

But Saxon was not listening. One pregnant sentence had caught her fancy. Oakland just a place to start from. She had never viewed the city in that light. She had accepted it as a place to live in, as an end in itself. But a place to start from! Why not! Why not like any railroad station or ferry depot! Certainly, as things were going, Oakland was not a place to stop in. The boy was right. It was a place to start from. But to go where? Here she was halted, and she was driven from the train of thought by a strong pull and a series of jerks on the line. She began to haul in, hand under hand, rapidly and deftly, the boy encouraging her, until hooks, sinker, and a big gasping rockcod tumbled into the bottom of the boat. The fish was free of the hook, and she baited afresh and dropped the line over. The boy marked his place and closed the book.

"They'll be biting soon as fast as we can haul 'em in," he said.

But the rush of fish did not come immediately.

"Did you ever read Captain Mayne Reid?" he asked. "Or Captain Marryatt? Or Ballantyne?"

She shook her head.

"And you an Anglo-Saxon!" he cried derisively. "Why, there's stacks of 'em in the Free Library. I have two cards, my mother's an' mine, an' I draw 'em out all the time, after school, before I have to carry my papers. I stick the books inside my shirt, in front, under the suspenders. That holds 'em. One time, deliverin' papers at Second an' Market—there's an awful tough gang of kids hang out there—I got into a fight with the leader. He hauled off to knock my wind out, an' he landed square on a book. You ought to seen his face. An' then I landed on him. An' then his whole gang was goin' to jump on me, only a couple of iron-molders stepped in an' saw fair play. I gave 'em the books to hold."

"Who won?" Saxon asked.

"Nobody," the boy confessed reluctantly. "I think I was lickin' him, but the molders called it a draw because the policeman on the beat stopped us when we'd only ben fightin' half an hour. But you ought to seen the crowd. I bet there was five hundred—"

He broke off abruptly and began hauling in his line. Saxon, too, was hauling in. And in the next couple of hours they caught twenty pounds of fish between them.

That night, long after dark, the little, half-decked skiff sailed up the Oakland Estuary. The wind was fair but light, and the boat moved slowly, towing a long pile which the boy had picked up adrift and announced as worth three dollars anywhere for the wood that was in it. The tide flooded smoothly under the full moon, and Saxon recognized the points they passed—the Transit slip, Sandy Beach, the shipyards, the nail works, Market street wharf. The boy took the skiff in to a dilapidated boat-wharf at the foot of Castro street, where the scow schooners, laden with sand and gravel, lay hauled to the shore in a long row. He insisted upon an equal division of the fish, because Saxon had helped catch them, though he explained at length the ethics of flotsam to show her that the pile was wholly his.

At Seventh and Poplar they separated, Saxon walking on alone to Pine street with her load of fish. Tired though she was from the long day, she had a strange feeling of well-being, and, after cleaning the fish, she fell asleep wondering, when good times came again, if she could persuade Billy to get a boat and go out with her on Sundays as she had gone out that day.

CHAPTER XVII

She slept all night, without stirring, without dreaming, and awoke naturally and, for the first time in weeks, refreshed. She felt her old self, as if some depressing weight had been lifted, or a shadow had been swept away from between her and the sun. Her head was clear. The seeming iron band that had pressed it so hard was gone. She was cheerful. She even caught herself humming aloud as she divided the fish into messes for Mrs. Olsen, Maggie Donahue, and herself. She enjoyed her gossip with each of them, and, returning home, plunged joyfully into the task of putting the neglected house in order. She sang as she worked, and ever as she sang the magic words of the boy danced and sparkled among the notes: OAKLAND IS JUST A PLACE TO START FROM.

Everything was clear as print. Her and Billy's problem was as simple as an arithmetic problem at school: to carpet a room so many feet long, so many feet wide, to paper a room so many feet high, so many feet around. She had been sick in her head, she had had strange lapses, she had been irresponsible. Very well. All this had been because of her troubles—troubles in which she had had no hand in the making. Billy's case was hers precisely. He had behaved strangely because he had been irresponsible. And all their troubles were the troubles of the trap. Oakland was the trap. Oakland was a good place to start from.

She reviewed the events of her married life. The strikes and the hard times had caused everything. If it had not been for the strike of the shopmen and the fight in her front yard, she would not have lost her baby. If Billy had not been made desperate by the idleness and the hopeless fight of the teamsters, he would not have taken to drinking. If they had not been hard up, they would not have taken a lodger, and Billy would not be in jail.

Her mind was made up. The city was no place for her and Billy, no place for love nor for babies. The way out was simple. They would leave Oakland. It was the stupid that remained and bowed their heads to fate. But she and Billy were not stupid. They would not bow their heads. They would go forth and face fate.—Where, she did not know. But that would come. The world was large. Beyond the encircling hills, out through the Golden Gate, somewhere they would find what they desired. The boy had been wrong in one thing. She was not tied to Oakland, even if she was married. The world was free to her and Billy as it had been free to the wandering generations before them. It was only the stupid who had been left behind everywhere in the race's wandering. The strong had gone on. Well, she and Billy were strong. They would go on, over the brown Contra Costa hills or out through the Golden Gate.

The day before Billy's release Saxon completed her meager preparations to receive him. She was without money, and, except for her resolve not to offend Billy in that way again, she would have borrowed ferry fare from Maggie Donahue and journeyed to San Francisco to sell some of her personal pretties. As it was, with bread and potatoes and salted sardines in the house, she went out at the afternoon low tide and dug clams for a chowder. Also, she gathered a load of driftwood, and it was nine in the evening when she emerged from the marsh, on her shoulder a bundle of wood and a short-handled spade, in her free hand the pail of clams. She sought the darker side of the street at the corner and hurried across the zone of electric light to avoid detection by the neighbors. But a woman came toward her, looked sharply and stopped in front of her. It was Mary.

"My God, Saxon!" she exclaimed. "Is it as bad as this?"

Saxon looked at her old friend curiously, with a swift glance that sketched all the tragedy. Mary was thinner, though there was more color in her cheeks— color of which Saxon had her doubts. Mary's bright eyes were handsomer, larger—too large, too feverish bright, too restless. She was well dressed— too well dressed; and she was suffering from nerves. She turned her head apprehensively to glance into the darkness behind her.

"My God!" Saxon breathed. "And you..." She shut her lips, then began anew. "Come along to the house," she said.

"If you're ashamed to be seen with me—" Mary blurted, with one of her old quick angers.

"No, no," Saxon disclaimed. "It's the driftwood and the clams. I don't want the neighbors to know. Come along."

"No; I can't, Saxon. I'd like to, but I can't. I've got to catch the next train to Frisco. I've ben waitin' around. I knocked at your back door. But the house was dark. Billy's still in, ain't he?"

"Yes, he gets out to-morrow."

"I read about it in the papers," Mary went on hurriedly, looking behind her. "I was in Stockton when it happened." She turned upon Saxon almost savagely. "You don't blame me, do you? I just couldn't go back to work after bein' married. I was sick of work. Played out, I guess, an' no good anyway. But if you only knew how I hated the laundry even before I got married. It's a dirty world. You don't dream. Saxon, honest to God, you could never guess a hundredth part of its dirtiness. Oh, I wish I was dead, I wish I was dead an' out of it all. Listen—no, I can't now. There's the down train puffin' at Adeline. I'll have to run for it. Can I come—"

"Aw, get a move on, can't you?" a man's voice interrupted.

Behind her the speaker had partly emerged from the darkness. No workingman, Saxon could see that—lower in the world scale, despite his good clothes, than any workingman.

"I'm comin', if you'll only wait a second," Mary placated.

And by her answer and its accents Saxon knew that Mary was afraid of this man who prowled on the rim of light.

Mary turned to her.

"I got to beat it; good bye," she said, fumbling in the palm of her glove.

She caught Saxon's free hand, and Saxon felt a small hot coin pressed into it. She tried to resist, to force it back.

"No, no," Mary pleaded. "For old times. You can do as much for me some day. I'll see you again. Good bye."

Suddenly, sobbing, she threw her arms around Saxon's waist, crushing the feathers of her hat against the load of wood as she pressed her face against Saxon's breast. Then she tore herself away to arm's length, passionate, quivering, and stood gazing at Saxon.

"Aw, get a hustle, get a hustle," came from the darkness the peremptory voice of the man.

"Oh, Saxon!" Mary sobbed; and was gone.

In the house, the lamp lighted, Saxon looked at the coin. It was a five-dollar piece—to her, a fortune. Then she thought of Mary, and of the man of whom she was afraid. Saxon registered another black mark against Oakland. Mary was one more destroyed. They lived only five years, on the average, Saxon had heard somewhere. She looked at the coin and tossed it into the kitchen sink. When she cleaned the clams, she heard the coin tinkle down the vent pipe.

It was the thought of Billy, next morning, that led Saxon to go under the sink, unscrew the cap to the catchtrap, and rescue the five-dollar piece. Prisoners were not well fed, she had been told; and the thought of placing clams and dry bread before Billy, after thirty days of prison fare, was too appalling for her to contemplate. She knew how he liked to spread his butter on thick, how he liked thick, rare steak fried on a dry hot pan, and how he liked coffee that was coffee and plenty of it.

Not until after nine o'clock did Billy arrive, and she was dressed in her prettiest house gingham to meet him. She peeped on him as he came slowly up the front steps, and she would have run out to him except for a group of neighborhood children who were staring from across the street. The door opened before him as his hand reached for the knob, and, inside, he closed it by backing against it, for his arms were filled with Saxon. No, he had not had breakfast, nor did he want any now that he had her. He had only stopped for a shave. He had stood the barber off, and he had walked all the way from the City Hall because of lack of the nickel carfare. But he'd like a bath most mighty well, and a change of clothes. She mustn't come near him until he was clean.

When all this was accomplished, he sat in the kitchen and watched her cook, noting the driftwood she put in the stove and asking about it. While she moved about, she told how she had gathered the wood, how she had managed to live and not be beholden to the union, and by the time they were seated at the table she was telling him about her meeting with Mary the night before. She did not mention the five dollars.

Billy stopped chewing the first mouthful of steak. His expression frightened her. He spat the meat out on his plate.

"You got the money to buy the meat from her," he accused slowly. "You had no money, no more tick with the butcher, yet here's meat. Am I right?"

Saxon could only bend her head.

The terrifying, ageless look had come into his face, the bleak and passionless glaze into his eyes, which she had first seen on the day at Weasel Park when he had fought with the three Irishmen.

"What else did you buy?" he demanded—not roughly, not angrily, but with the fearful coldness of a rage that words could not express.

To her surprise, she had grown calm. What did it matter? It was merely what one must expect, living in Oakland—something to be left behind when Oakland was a thing behind, a place started from.

"The coffee," she answered. "And the butter."

He emptied his plate of meat and her plate into the frying pan, likewise the roll of butter and the slice on the table, and on top he poured the contents of the coffee canister. All this he carried into the back yard and dumped in the garbage can. The coffee pot he emptied into the sink. "How much of the money you got left?" he next wanted to know.

Saxon had already gone to her purse and taken it out.

"Three dollars and eighty cents," she counted, handing it to him. "I paid forty-five cents for the steak."

He ran his eye over the money, counted it, and went to the front door. She heard the door open and close, and knew that the silver had been flung into the street. When he came back to the kitchen, Saxon was already serving him fried potatoes on a clean plate.

"Nothin's too good for the Robertses," he said; "but, by God, that sort of truck is too high for my stomach. It's so high it stinks."

He glanced at the fried potatoes, the fresh slice of dry bread, and the glass of water she was placing by his plate.

"It's all right," she smiled, as he hesitated. "There's nothing left that's tainted."

He shot a swift glance at her face, as if for sarcasm, then sighed and sat down. Almost immediately he was up again and holding out his arms to her.

"I'm goin' to eat in a minute, but I want to talk to you first," he said, sitting down and holding her closely. "Besides, that water ain't like coffee. Gettin' cold won't spoil it none. Now, listen. You're the only one I got in this world. You wasn't afraid of me an' what I just done, an' I'm glad of that. Now we'll forget all about Mary. I got charity enough. I'm just as sorry for her as you. I'd do anything for her. I'd wash her feet for her like Christ did. I'd let her eat at my table, an' sleep under my roof. But all that ain't no reason I should touch anything she's earned. Now forget her. It's you an' me, Saxon, only you an' me an' to hell with the rest of the world. Nothing else counts. You won't never have to be afraid of me again. Whisky an' I don't mix very well, so I'm goin' to cut whisky out. I've been clean off my nut, an' I ain't treated you altogether right. But that's all past. It won't never happen again. I'm goin' to start out fresh.

"Now take this thing. I oughtn't to acted so hasty. But I did. I oughta talked it over. But I didn't. My damned temper got the best of me, an' you know I got one. If a fellow can keep his temper in boxin', why he can keep it in bein' married, too. Only this got me too sudden-like. It's something I can't stomach, that I never could stomach. An' you wouldn't want me to any more'n I'd want you to stomach something you just couldn't."

She sat up straight on his knees and looked at him, afire with an idea.

"You mean that, Billy?"

"Sure I do."

"Then I'll tell you something I can't stomach any more. I'll die if I have to."

"Well?" he questioned, after a searching pause.

"It's up to you," she said.

"Then fire away."

"You don't know what you're letting yourself in for," she warned. "Maybe you'd better back out before it's too late."

He shook his head stubbornly.

"What you don't want to stomach you ain't goin' to stomach. Let her go."

"First," she commenced, "no more slugging of scabs."

His mouth opened, but he checked the involuntary protest.

"And, second, no more Oakland."

"I don't get that last."

"No more Oakland. No more living in Oakland. I'll die if I have to. It's pull up stakes and get out."

He digested this slowly.

"Where?" he asked finally.

"Anywhere. Everywhere. Smoke a cigarette and think it over."

He shook his head and studied her.

"You mean that?" he asked at length.

"I do. I want to chuck Oakland just as hard as you wanted to chuck the beefsteak, the coffee, and the butter."

She could see him brace himself. She could feel him brace his very body ere he answered.

"All right then, if that's what you want. We'll quit Oakland. We'll quit it cold. God damn it, anyway, it never done nothin' for me, an' I guess I'm husky enough to scratch for us both anywheres. An' now that's settled, just tell me what you got it in for Oakland for."

And she told him all she had thought out, marshaled all the facts in her indictment of Oakland, omitting nothing, not even her last visit to Doctor Hentley's office nor Billy's drinking. He but drew her closer and proclaimed his resolves anew. The time passed. The fried potatoes grew cold, and the stove went out.

When a pause came, Billy stood up, still holding her. He glanced at the fried potatoes.

"Stone cold," he said, then turned to her. "Come on. Put on your prettiest. We're goin' up town for something to eat an' to celebrate. I guess we got a celebration comin', seein' as we're going to pull up stakes an' pull our freight from the old burg. An' we won't have to walk. I can borrow a dime from the barber, an' I got enough junk to hock for a blowout."

His junk proved to be several gold medals won in his amateur days at boxing tournaments. Once up town and in the pawnshop, Uncle Sam seemed thoroughly versed in the value of the medals, and Billy jingled a handful of silver in his pocket as they walked out.

He was as hilarious as a boy, and she joined in his good spirits. When he stopped at a corner cigar store to buy a sack of Bull Durham, he changed his mind and bought Imperials.

"Oh, I'm a regular devil," he laughed. "Nothing's too good to-day—not even tailor-made smokes. An' no chop houses nor Jap joints for you an' me. It's Barnum's."

They strolled to the restaurant at Seventh and Broadway where they had had their wedding supper.

"Let's make believe we're not married," Saxon suggested.

"Sure," he agreed, "—an' take a private room so as the waiter'll have to knock on the door each time he comes in."

Saxon demurred at that.

"It will be too expensive, Billy. You'll have to tip him for the knocking. We'll take the regular dining room."

"Order anything you want," Billy said largely, when they were seated. "Here's family porterhouse, a dollar an' a half. What d'ye say?"

"And hash-browned," she abetted, "and coffee extra special, and some oysters first—I want to compare them with the rock oysters."

Billy nodded, and looked up from the bill of fare.

"Here's mussels bordelay. Try an order of them, too, an' see if they beat your Rock Wall ones."

"Why not?" Saxon cried, her eyes dancing. "The world is ours. We're just travelers through this town."

"Yep, that's the stuff," Billy muttered absently. He was looking at the theater column. He lifted his eyes from the paper. "Matinee at Bell's. We can get reserved seats for a quarter.—Doggone the luck anyway!"

His exclamation was so aggrieved and violent that it brought alarm into her eyes.

"If I'd only thought," he regretted, "we could a-gone to the Forum for grub. That's the swell joint where fellows like Roy Blanchard hangs out, blowin' the money we sweat for them."

They bought reserved tickets at Bell's Theater; but it was too early for the performance, and they went down Broadway and into the Electric Theater to while away the time on a moving picture show. A cowboy film was run off, and a French comic; then came a rural drama situated somewhere in the Middle West. It began with a farm yard scene. The sun blazed down on a corner of a barn and on a rail fence where the ground lay in the mottled shade of large trees overhead. There were chickens, ducks, and turkeys, scratching, waddling, moving about. A big sow, followed by a roly-poly litter of seven little ones, marched majestically through the chickens, rooting them out of the way. The hens, in turn, took it out on the little porkers, pecking them when they strayed too far from their mother. And over the top rail a horse looked drowsily on, ever and anon, at mathematically precise intervals, switching a lazy tail that flashed high lights in the sunshine.

"It's a warm day and there are flies—can't you just feel it?" Saxon whispered.

"Sure. An' that horse's tail! It's the most natural ever. Gee! I bet he knows the trick of clampin' it down over the reins. I wouldn't wonder if his name was Iron Tail."

A dog ran upon the scene. The mother pig turned tail and with short ludicrous jumps, followed by her progeny and pursued by the dog, fled out of the film. A young girl came on, a sunbonnet hanging down her back, her apron caught up in front and filled with grain which she threw to the fluttering fowls. Pigeons flew down from the top of the film and joined in the scrambling feast. The dog returned, wading scarcely noticed among the feathered creatures, to wag his tail and laugh up at the girl. And, behind, the horse nodded over the rail and switched on. A young man entered, his errand immediately known to an audience educated in moving pictures. But Saxon had no eyes for the love-making, the pleading forcefulness, the shy reluctance, of man and maid. Ever her gaze wandered back to the chickens, to the mottled shade under the trees, to the warm wall of the barn, to the sleepy horse with its ever recurrent whisk of tail.

She drew closer to Billy, and her hand, passed around his arm, sought his hand.

"Oh, Billy," she sighed. "I'd just die of happiness in a place like that." And, when the film was ended. "We got lots of time for Bell's. Let's stay and see that one over again."

They sat through a repetition of the performance, and when the farm yard scene appeared, the longer Saxon looked at it the more it affected her. And this time she took in further details. She saw fields beyond, rolling hills in the background, and a cloud-flecked sky. She identified some of the chickens, especially an obstreperous old hen who resented the thrust of the sow's muzzle, particularly pecked at the little pigs, and laid about her with a vengeance when the grain fell. Saxon looked back across the fields to the hills and sky, breathing the spaciousness of it, the freedom, the content. Tears welled into her eyes and she wept silently, happily.

"I know a trick that'd fix that old horse if he ever clamped his tail down on me," Billy whispered.

"Now I know where we're going when we leave Oakland," she informed him.

"Where?"

"There."

He looked at her, and followed her gaze to the screen. "Oh," he said, and cogitated. "An' why shouldn't we?" he added.

"Oh, Billy, will you?"

Her lips trembled in her eagerness, and her whisper broke and was almost inaudible "Sure," he said. It was his day of royal largess.

"What you want is yourn, an' I'll scratch my fingers off for it. An' I've always had a hankerin' for the country myself. Say! I've known horses like that to sell for half the price, an' I can sure cure 'em of the habit."

CHAPTER XVIII

It was early evening when they got off the car at Seventh and Pine on their way home from Bell's Theater. Billy and Saxon did their little marketing together, then separated at the corner, Saxon to go on to the house and prepare supper, Billy to go and see the boys—the teamsters who had fought on in the strike during his month of retirement.

"Take care of yourself, Billy," she called, as he started off.

"Sure," he answered, turning his face to her over his shoulder.

Her heart leaped at the smile. It was his old, unsullied love-smile which she wanted always to see on his face—for which, armed with her own wisdom and the wisdom of Mercedes, she would wage the utmost woman's war to possess. A thought of this flashed brightly through her brain, and it was with a proud little smile that she remembered all her pretty equipment stored at home in the bureau and the chest of drawers.

Three-quarters of an hour later, supper ready, all but the putting on of the lamb chops at the sound of his step, Saxon waited. She heard the gate click, but instead of his step she heard a curious and confused scraping of many steps. She flew to open the door. Billy stood there, but a different Billy from the one she had parted from so short a time before. A small boy, beside him, held his hat. His face had been fresh-washed, or, rather, drenched, for his shirt and shoulders were wet. His pale hair lay damp and plastered against his forehead, and was darkened by oozing blood. Both arms hung limply by his side. But his face was composed, and he even grinned.

"It's all right," he reassured Saxon. "The joke's on me. Somewhat damaged but still in the ring." He stepped gingerly across the threshold. "—Come on in, you fellows. We're all mutts together."

He was followed in by the boy with his hat, by Bud Strothers and another teamster she knew, and by two strangers. The latter were big, hard-featured, sheepish-faced men, who stared at Saxon as if afraid of her.

"It's all right, Saxon," Billy began, but was interrupted by Bud.

"First thing is to get him on the bed an' cut his clothes off him. Both arms is broke, and here are the ginks that done it."

He indicated the two strangers, who shuffled their feet with embarrassment and looked more sheepish than ever.

Billy sat down on the bed, and while Saxon held the lamp, Bud and the strangers proceeded to cut coat, shirt, and undershirt from him.

"He wouldn't go to the receivin' hospital," Bud said to Saxon.

"Not on your life," Billy concurred. "I had 'em send for Doc Hentley. He'll be here any minute. Them two arms is all I got. They've done pretty well by me, an' I gotta do the same by them.—No medical students a-learnin' their trade on me."

"But how did it happen?" Saxon demanded, looking from Billy to the two strangers, puzzled by the amity that so evidently existed among them all.

"Oh, they're all right," Billy dashed in. "They done it through mistake. They're Frisco teamsters, an' they come over to help us—a lot of 'em."

The two teamsters seemed to cheer up at this, and nodded their heads.

"Yes, missus," one of them rumbled hoarsely. "It's all a mistake, an'... well, the joke's on us."

"The drinks, anyway," Billy grinned.

Not only was Saxon not excited, but she was scarcely perturbed. What had happened was only to be expected.

It was in line with all that Oakland had already done to her and hers, and, besides, Billy was not dangerously hurt. Broken arms and a sore head would heal. She brought chairs and seated everybody.

"Now tell me what happened," she begged. "I'm all at sea, what of you two burleys breaking my husband's arms, then seeing him home and holding a love-fest with him."

"An' you got a right," Bud Strothers assured her. "You see, it happened this way—"

"You shut up, Bud," Billy broke it. "You didn't see anything of it."

Saxon looked to the San Francisco teamsters.

"We'd come over to lend a hand, seein' as the Oakland boys was gettin' some the short end of it," one spoke up, "an' we've sure learned some scabs there's better trades than drivin' team. Well, me an' Jackson here was nosin' around to see what we can see, when your husband comes moseyin' along. When he—"

"Hold on," Jackson interrupted. "Get it straight as you go along. We reckon we know the boys by sight. But your husband we ain't never seen around, him bein'..."

"As you might say, put away for a while," the first teamster took up the tale. "So, when we sees what we thinks is a scab dodgin' away from us an' takin' the shortcut through the alley—"

"The alley back of Campbell's grocery," Billy elucidated.

"Yep, back of the grocery," the first teamster went on; "why, we're sure he's one of them squarehead scabs, hired through Murray an' Ready, makin' a sneak to get into the stables over the back fences."

"We caught one there, Billy an' me," Bud interpolated.

"So we don't waste any time," Jackson said, addressing himself to Saxon. "We've done it before, an' we know how to do 'em up brown an' tie 'em with baby ribbon. So we catch your husband right in the alley."

"I was lookin' for Bud," said Billy. "The boys told me I'd find him somewhere around the other end of the alley. An' the first thing I know, Jackson, here, asks me for a match."

"An' right there's where I get in my fine work," resumed the first teamster.

"What?" asked Saxon.

"That." The man pointed to the wound in Billy's scalp. "I laid 'm out. He went down like a steer, an' got up on his knees dippy, a-gabblin' about somebody standin' on their foot. He didn't know where he was at, you see, clean groggy. An' then we done it."

The man paused, the tale told.

"Broke both his arms with the crowbar," Bud supplemented.

"That's when I come to myself, when the bones broke," Billy corroborated. "An' there was the two of 'em givin' me the ha-ha. 'That'll last you some time,' Jackson was sayin'. An' Anson says, 'I'd like to see you drive horses with them arms.' An' then Jackson says, 'let's give 'm something for luck.' An' with that he fetched me a wallop on the jaw—"

"No," corrected Anson. "That wallop was mine."

"Well, it sent me into dreamland over again," Billy sighed. "An' when I come to, here was Bud an' Anson an' Jackson dousin' me at a water trough. An' then we dodged a reporter an' all come home together."

Bud Strothers held up his fist and indicated freshly abraded skin.

"The reporter-guy just insisted on samplin' it," he said. Then, to Billy: "That's why I cut around Ninth an' caught up with you down on Sixth."

A few minutes later Doctor Hentley arrived, and drove the men from the rooms. They waited till he had finished, to assure themselves of Billy's well being, and then departed. In the kitchen Doctor Hentley washed his hands and gave Saxon final instructions. As he dried himself he sniffed the air and looked toward the stove where a pot was simmering.

"Clams," he said. "Where did you buy them?"

"I didn't buy them," replied Saxon. "I dug them myself."

"Not in the marsh?" he asked with quickened interest.

"Yes."

"Throw them away. Throw them out. They're death and corruption. Typhoid—I've got three cases now, all traced to the clams and the marsh."

When he had gone, Saxon obeyed. Still another mark against Oakland, she reflected—Oakland, the man-trap, that poisoned those it could not starve.

"If it wouldn't drive a man to drink," Billy groaned, when Saxon returned to him. "Did you ever dream such luck? Look at all my fights in the ring, an' never a broken bone, an' here, snap, snap, just like that, two arms smashed."

"Oh, it might be worse," Saxon smiled cheerfully.

"I'd like to know how.

It might have been your neck."

"An' a good job. I tell you, Saxon, you gotta show me anything worse."

"I can," she said confidently.

"Well?"

"Well, wouldn't it be worse if you intended staying on in Oakland where it might happen again?"

"I can see myself becomin' a farmer an' plowin' with a pair of pipe-stems like these," he persisted.

"Doctor Hentley says they'll be stronger at the break than ever before. And you know yourself that's true of clean-broken bones. Now you close your eyes and go to sleep. You're all done up, and you need to keep your brain quiet and stop thinking."

He closed his eyes obediently. She slipped a cool hand under the nape of his neck and let it rest.

"That feels good," he murmured. "You're so cool, Saxon. Your hand, and you, all of you. Bein' with you is like comin' out into the cool night after dancin' in a hot room."

After several minutes of quiet, he began to giggle.

"What is it?" she asked.

"Oh, nothin'. I was just thinkin'—thinking of them mutts doin' me up—me, that's done up more scabs than I can remember."

Next morning Billy awoke with his blues dissipated. From the kitchen Saxon heard him painfully wrestling strange vocal acrobatics.

"I got a new song you never heard," he told her when she came in with a cup of coffee. "I only remember the chorus though. It's the old man talkin' to some hobo of a hired man that wants to marry his daughter. Mamie, that Billy Murphy used to run with before he got married, used to sing it. It's a kind of a sobby song. It used to always give Mamie the weeps. Here's the way the chorus goes—an' remember, it's the old man spielin'.""

And with great solemnity and excruciating flatting, Billy sang:

"O treat my daughter kind-i-ly; An' say you'll do no harm, An' when I die I'll will to you My little house an' farm—My horse, my plow, my sheep, my cow, An' all them little chickens in the ga-a-rden.

"It's them little chickens in the garden that gets me," he explained. "That's how I remembered it—from the chickens in the movin' pictures yesterday. An' some day we'll have little chickens in the garden, won't we, old girl?"

"And a daughter, too," Saxon amplified.

"An' I'll be the old geezer sayin' them same words to the hired man," Billy carried the fancy along. "It don't take long to raise a daughter if you ain't in a hurry."

Saxon took her long-neglected ukulele from its case and strummed it into tune.

"And I've a song you never heard, Billy. Tom's always singing it. He's crazy about taking up government land and going farming, only Sarah won't think of it. He sings it something like this:

"We'll have a little farm, A pig, a horse, a cow, And you will drive the wagon, And I will drive the plow."

"Only in this case I guess it's me that'll do the plowin'," Billy approved. "Say, Saxon, sing 'Harvest Days.' That's a farmer's song, too."

After that she feared the coffee was growing cold and compelled Billy to take it. In the helplessness of two broken arms, he had to be fed like a baby, and as she fed him they talked.

"I'll tell you one thing," Billy said, between mouthfuls. "Once we get settled down in the country you'll have that horse you've been wishin' for all your life. An' it'll be all your own, to ride, drive, sell, or do anything you want with."

And, again, he ruminated: "One thing that'll come handy in the country is that I know horses; that's a big start. I can always get a job at that—if it ain't at union wages. An' the other things about farmin' I can learn fast enough.—Say, d'ye remember that day you first told me about wantin' a horse to ride all your life?"

Saxon remembered, and it was only by a severe struggle that she was able to keep the tears from welling into her eyes. She seemed bursting with happiness, and she was remembering many things—all the warm promise of life with Billy that had been hers in the days before hard times. And now the promise was renewed again. Since its fulfillment had not come to them, they were going away to fulfill it for themselves and make the moving pictures come true.

Impelled by a half-feigned fear, she stole away into the kitchen bedroom where Bert had died, to study her face in the bureau mirror. No, she decided; she was little changed. She was still equipped for the battlefield of love. Beautiful she was not. She knew that. But had not Mercedes said that the great women of history who had won men had not been beautiful? And yet, Saxon insisted, as she gazed at her reflection, she was anything but unlovely. She studied her wide gray eyes that were so very gray, that were always alive with light and vivacities, where, in the surface and depths, always swam thoughts unuttered, thoughts that sank down and dissolved to give place to other thoughts. The brows were excellent—she realized that. Slenderly penciled, a little darker than her light brown hair, they just fitted her irregular nose that was feminine but not weak, that if anything was piquant and that picturesquely might be declared impudent.

She could see that her face was slightly thin, that the red of her lips was not quite so red, and that she had lost some of her quick coloring. But all that would come back again. Her mouth was not of the rosebud type she saw in the magazines. She paid particular attention to it. A pleasant mouth it was, a mouth to be joyous with, a mouth for laughter and to make laughter in others. She deliberately experimented with it, smiled till the corners dented deeper. And she knew that when she smiled her smile was provocative of smiles. She laughed with her eyes alone—a trick of hers. She threw back her head and laughed with eyes and mouth together, between her spread lips showing the even rows of strong white teeth.

And she remembered Billy's praise of her teeth, the night at Germanic Hall after he had told Charley Long he was standing on his foot. "Not big, and not little dinky baby's teeth either," Billy had said, "... just right, and they fit you." Also, he had said that to look at them made him hungry, and that they were good enough to eat.

She recollected all the compliments he had ever paid her. Beyond all treasures, these were treasures to her—the love phrases, praises, and admirations. He had said her skin was cool—soft as velvet, too, and smooth as silk. She rolled up her sleeve to the shoulder, brushed her cheek with the white skin for a test, with deep scrutiny examined the fineness of its texture. And he had told her that she was sweet; that he hadn't known what it meant when they said a girl was sweet, not until he had known her. And he had told her that her voice was cool, that it gave him the feeling her hand did when it rested on his forehead. Her voice went all through him, he had said, cool and fine, like a wind of coolness. And he had likened it to the first of the sea breeze setting in the afternoon after a scorching hot morning. And, also, when she talked low, that it was round and sweet, like the 'cello in the Macdonough Theater orchestra.

He had called her his Tonic Kid. He had called her a thoroughbred, clean-cut and spirited, all fine nerves and delicate and sensitive. He had liked the way she carried her clothes. She carried them like a dream, had been his way of putting it. They were part of her, just as much as the cool of her voice and skin and the scent of her hair.

And her figure! She got upon a chair and tilted the mirror so that she could see herself from hips to feet. She drew her skirt back and up. The slender ankle was just as slender. The calf had lost none of its delicately mature swell. She studied her hips, her waist, her bosom, her neck, the poise of her head, and sighed contentedly. Billy must be right, and he had said that she was built like a French woman, and that in the matter of lines and form she could give Annette Kellerman cards and spades.

He had said so many things, now that she recalled them all at one time. Her lips! The Sunday he proposed he had said: "I like to watch your lips talking. It's funny, but every move they make looks like a tickly kiss." And afterward, that same day: "You looked good to me from the first moment I spotted you." He had praised her housekeeping. He had said he fed better, lived more comfortably, held up his end with the fellows, and saved money. And she remembered that day when he had crushed her in his arms and declared she was the greatest little bit of a woman that had ever come down the pike.

She ran her eyes over all herself in the mirror again, gathered herself together into a whole, compact and good to look upon—delicious, she knew. Yes, she would do. Magnificent as Billy was in his man way, in her own way she was a match for him. Yes, she had done well by Billy. She deserved much— all he could give her, the best he could give her. But she made no blunder of egotism. Frankly valuing herself, she as frankly valued him. When he was himself, his real self, not harassed by trouble, not pinched by the trap, not maddened by drink, her man-boy and lover, he was well worth all she gave him or could give him.

Saxon gave herself a farewell look. No. She was not dead, any more than was Billy's love dead, than was her love dead. All that was needed was the proper soil, and their love would grow and blossom. And they were turning their backs upon Oakland to go and seek that proper soil.

"Oh, Billy!" she called through the partition, still standing on the chair, one hand tipping the mirror forward and back, so that she was able to run her eyes from the reflection of her ankles and calves to her face, warm with color and roguishly alive.

"Yes?" she heard him answer.

"I'm loving myself," she called back.

"What's the game?" came his puzzled query. "What are you so stuck on yourself for!"

"Because you love me," she answered. "I love every bit of me, Billy, because... because... well, because you love every bit of me."

CHAPTER XIX

Between feeding and caring for Billy, doing the housework, making plans, and selling her store of pretty needlework, the days flew happily for Saxon. Billy's consent to sell her pretties had been hard to get, but at last she succeeded in coaxing it out of him.

"It's only the ones I haven't used," she urged; "and I can always make more when we get settled somewhere."

What she did not sell, along with the household linen and hers and Billy's spare clothing, she arranged to store with Tom.

"Go ahead," Billy said. "This is your picnic. What you say goes. You're Robinson Crusoe an' I'm your man Friday. Make up your mind yet which way you're goin' to travel?"

Saxon shook her head.

"Or how?"

She held up one foot and then the other, encased in stout walking shoes which she had begun that morning to break in about the house. "Shank's mare, eh?"

"It's the way our people came into the West," she said proudly.

"It'll be regular trampin', though," he argued. "An' I never heard of a woman tramp."

"Then here's one. Why, Billy, there's no shame in tramping. My mother tramped most of the way across the Plains. And 'most everybody else's mother tramped across in those days. I don't care what people will think. I guess our race has been on the tramp since the beginning of creation, just like we'll be, looking for a piece of land that looked good to settle down on."

After a few days, when his scalp was sufficiently healed and the bone-knitting was nicely in process, Billy was able to be up and about. He was still quite helpless, however, with both his arms in splints.

Doctor Hentley not only agreed, but himself suggested, that his bill should wait against better times for settlement. Of government land, in response to Saxon's eager questioning, he knew nothing, except that he had a hazy idea that the days of government land were over.

Tom, on the contrary, was confident that there was plenty of government land. He talked of Honey Lake, of Shasta County, and of Humboldt.

"But you can't tackle it at this time of year, with winter comin' on," he advised Saxon. "The thing for you to do is head south for warmer weather—

say along the coast. It don't snow down there. I tell you what you do. Go down by San Jose and Salinas an' come out on the coast at Monterey. South of that you'll find government land mixed up with forest reserves and Mexican rancheros. It's pretty wild, without any roads to speak of. All they do is handle cattle. But there's some fine redwood canyons, with good patches of farming ground that run right down to the ocean. I was talkin' last year with a fellow that's been all through there. An' I'd a-gone, like you an' Billy, only Sarah wouldn't hear of it. There's gold down there, too. Quite a bunch is in there prospectin', an' two or three good mines have opened. But that's farther along and in a ways from the coast. You might take a look."

Saxon shook her head. "We're not looking for gold but for chickens and a place to grow vegetables. Our folks had all the chance for gold in the early days, and what have they got to show for it?"

"I guess you're right," Tom conceded. "They always played too big a game, an' missed the thousand little chances right under their nose. Look at your pa. I've heard him tell of selling three Market street lots in San Francisco for fifty dollars each. They're worth five hundred thousand right now. An' look at Uncle Will. He had ranches till the cows come home. Satisfied? No. He wanted to be a cattle king, a regular Miller and Lux. An' when he died he was a night watchman in Los Angeles at forty dollars a month. There's a spirit of the times, an' the spirit of the times has changed. It's all big business now, an' we're the small potatoes. Why, I've heard our folks talk of livin' in the Western Reserve. That was all around what's Ohio now. Anybody could get a farm them days. All they had to do was yoke their oxen an' go after it, an' the Pacific Ocean thousands of miles to the west, an' all them thousands of miles an' millions of farms just waitin' to be took up. A hundred an' sixty acres? Shucks. In the early days in Oregon they talked six hundred an' forty acres. That was the spirit of them times—free land, an' plenty of it. But when we reached the Pacific Ocean them times was ended. Big business begun; an' big business means big business men; an' every big business man means thousands of little men without any business at all except to work for the big ones. They're the losers, don't you see? An' if they don't like it they can lump it, but it won't do them no good. They can't yoke up their oxen an' pull on. There's no place to pull on. China's over there, an' in between's a mighty lot of salt water that's no good for farmin' purposes."

"That's all clear enough," Saxon commented.

"Yes," her brother went on. "We can all see it after it's happened, when it's too late."

"But the big men were smarter," Saxon remarked.

"They were luckier," Tom contended. "Some won, but most lost, an' just as good men lost. It was almost like a lot of boys scramblin' on the sidewalk for a handful of small change. Not that some didn't have far-seein'. But just take your pa, for example. He come of good Down East stock that's got business instinct an' can add to what it's got. Now suppose your pa had developed a weak heart, or got kidney disease, or caught rheumatism, so he couldn't go gallivantin' an' rainbow chasin', an' fightin' an' explorin' all over the West. Why, most likely he'd a settled down in San Francisco—he'd a-had to—an' held onto them three Market street lots, an' bought more lots, of course, an' gone into steamboat companies, an' stock gamblin', an' railroad buildin', an' Comstock-tunnelin'.

"Why, he'd a-become big business himself. I know 'm. He was the most energetic man I ever saw, think quick as a wink, as cool as an icicle an' as wild as a Comanche. Why, he'd a-cut a swath through the free an' easy big business gamblers an' pirates of them days; just as he cut a swath through the hearts of the ladies when he went gallopin' past on that big horse of his, sword clatterin', spurs jinglin', his long hair flyin', straight as an Indian, clean-built an' graceful as a blue-eyed prince out of a fairy book an' a Mexican caballero all rolled into one; just as he cut a swath through the Johnny Rebs in Civil War days, chargin' with his men all the way through an' back again, an' yellin' like a wild Indian for more. Cady, that helped raise you, told me about that. Cady rode with your pa.

"Why, if your pa'd only got laid up in San Francisco, he would a-ben one of the big men of the West. An' in that case, right now, you'd be a rich young woman, travelin' in Europe, with a mansion on Nob Hill along with the Floods and Crockers, an' holdin' majority stock most likely in the Fairmount Hotel an' a few little concerns like it. An' why ain't you? Because your pa wasn't smart? No. His mind was like a steel trap. It's because he was filled to burstin' an' spillin' over with the spirit of the times; because he was full of fire an' vinegar an' couldn't set down in one place. That's all the difference between you an' the young women right now in the Flood and Crocker families. Your father didn't catch rheumatism at the right time, that's all."

Saxon sighed, then smiled.

"Just the same, I've got them beaten," she said. "The Miss Floods and Miss Crockers can't marry prize-fighters, and I did."

Tom looked at her, taken aback for the moment, with admiration, slowly at first, growing in his face.

"Well, all I got to say," he enunciated solemnly, "is that Billy's so lucky he don't know how lucky he is."

Not until Doctor Hentley gave the word did the splints come off Billy's arms, and Saxon insisted upon an additional two weeks' delay so that no risk would be run. These two weeks would complete another month's rent, and the landlord had agreed to wait payment for the last two months until Billy was on his feet again.

Salinger's awaited the day set by Saxon for taking back their furniture. Also, they had returned to Billy seventy-five dollars.

"The rest you've paid will be rent," the collector told Saxon. "And the furniture's second hand now, too. The deal will be a loss to Salinger's' and they didn't have to do it, either; you know that. So just remember they've been pretty square with you, and if you start over again don't forget them."

Out of this sum, and out of what was realized from Saxon's pretties, they were able to pay all their small bills and yet have a few dollars remaining in pocket.

"I hate owin' things worse 'n poison," Billy said to Saxon. "An' now we don't owe a soul in this world except the landlord an' Doc Hentley."

"And neither of them can afford to wait longer than they have to," she said.

"And they won't," Billy answered quietly.

She smiled her approval, for she shared with Billy his horror of debt, just as both shared it with that early tide of pioneers with a Puritan ethic, which had settled the West.

Saxon timed her opportunity when Billy was out of the house to pack the chest of drawers which had crossed the Atlantic by sailing ship and the Plains by ox team. She kissed the bullet hole in it, made in the fight at Little Meadow, as she kissed her father's sword, the while she visioned him, as she always did, astride his roan warhorse. With the old religious awe, she pored over her mother's poems in the scrap-book, and clasped her mother's red satin Spanish girdle about her in a farewell embrace. She unpacked the scrap-book in order to gaze a last time at the wood engraving of the Vikings, sword in hand, leaping upon the English sands. Again she identified Billy as one of the Vikings, and pondered for a space on the strange wanderings of the seed from which she sprang. Always had her race been land-hungry, and she took delight in believing she had bred true; for had not she, despite her life passed in a city, found this same land-hunger in her? And was she not going forth to satisfy that hunger, just as her people of old time had done, as her father and mother before her? She remembered her mother's tale of how the promised land looked to them as their battered wagons and weary oxen dropped down through the early winter snows of the Sierras to the vast and flowering sun-land of California: In fancy, herself a child of nine, she looked down from the snowy heights as her mother must have looked down. She recalled and repeated aloud one of her mother's stanzas:

"'Sweet as a wind-lute's airy strains Your gentle muse has learned to sing And California's boundless plains Prolong the soft notes echoing.'"

She sighed happily and dried her eyes. Perhaps the hard times were past. Perhaps they had constituted HER Plains, and she and Billy had won safely across and were even then climbing the Sierras ere they dropped down into the pleasant valley land.

Salinger's wagon was at the house, taking out the furniture, the morning they left. The landlord, standing at the gate, received the keys, shook hands with them, and wished them luck. "You're goin' at it right," he congratulated them. "Sure an' wasn't it under me roll of blankets I tramped into Oakland meself forty year ago! Buy land, like me, when it's cheap. It'll keep you from the poorhouse in your old age. There's plenty of new towns springin' up. Get in on the ground floor. The work of your hands'll keep you in food an' under a roof, an' the land 'll make you well to do. An' you know me address. When you can spare send me along that small bit of rent. An' good luck. An' don't mind what people think. 'Tis them that looks that finds."

Curious neighbors peeped from behind the blinds as Billy and Saxon strode up the street, while the children gazed at them in gaping astonishment. On Billy's back, inside a painted canvas tarpaulin, was slung the roll of bedding. Inside the roll were changes of underclothing and odds and ends of necessaries. Outside, from the lashings, depended a frying pan and cooking pail. In his hand he carried the coffee pot. Saxon carried a small telescope basket protected by black oilcloth, and across her back was the tiny ukulele case.

"We must look like holy frights," Billy grumbled, shrinking from every gaze that was bent upon him.

"It'd be all right, if we were going camping," Saxon consoled. "Only we're not."

"But they don't know that," she continued. "It's only you know that, and what you think they're thinking isn't what they're thinking at all. Most probably they think we're going camping. And the best of it is we are going camping. We are! We are!"

At this Billy cheered up, though he muttered his firm intention to knock the block off of any guy that got fresh. He stole a glance at Saxon. Her cheeks were red, her eyes glowing.

"Say," he said suddenly. "I seen an opera once, where fellows wandered over the country with guitars slung on their backs just like you with that strummy-strum. You made me think of them. They was always singin' songs."

"That's what I brought it along for," Saxon answered.

"And when we go down country roads we'll sing as we go along, and we'll sing by the campfires, too. We're going camping, that's all. Taking a vacation and seeing the country. So why shouldn't we have a good time? Why, we don't even know where we're going to sleep to-night, or any night. Think of the fun!"

"It's a sporting proposition all right, all right," Billy considered. "But, just the same, let's turn off an' go around the block. There's some fellows I know, standin' up there on the next corner, an' I don't want to knock THEIR blocks off."

BOOK III

CHAPTER I

The car ran as far as Hayward's, but at Saxon's suggestion they got off at San Leandro.

"It doesn't matter where we start walking," she said, "for start to walk somewhere we must. And as we're looking for land and finding out about land, the quicker we begin to investigate the better. Besides, we want to know all about all kinds of land, close to the big cities as well as back in the mountains."

"Gee!—this must be the Porchugeeze headquarters," was Billy's reiterated comment, as they walked through San Leandro.

"It looks as though they'd crowd our kind out," Saxon adjudged.

"Some tall crowdin', I guess," Billy grumbled. "It looks like the free-born American ain't got no room left in his own land."

"Then it's his own fault," Saxon said, with vague asperity, resenting conditions she was just beginning to grasp.

"Oh, I don't know about that. I reckon the American could do what the Porchugeeze do if he wanted to. Only he don't want to, thank God. He ain't much given to livin' like a pig offen leavin's."

"Not in the country, maybe," Saxon controverted. "But I've seen an awful lot of Americans living like pigs in the cities."

Billy grunted unwilling assent. "I guess they quit the farms an' go to the city for something better, an' get it in the neck."

"Look at all the children!" Saxon cried. "School's letting out. And nearly all are Portuguese, Billy, NOT Porchugeeze. Mercedes taught me the right way."

"They never wore glad rags like them in the old country," Billy sneered. "They had to come over here to get decent clothes and decent grub. They're as fat as butterballs."

Saxon nodded affirmation, and a great light seemed suddenly to kindle in her understanding.

"That's the very point, Billy. They're doing it—doing it farming, too. Strikes don't bother THEM."

"You don't call that dinky gardening farming," he objected, pointing to a piece of land barely the size of an acre, which they were passing.

"Oh, your ideas are still big," she laughed. "You're like Uncle Will, who owned thousands of acres and wanted to own a million, and who wound up as night watchman. That's what was the trouble with all us Americans. Everything large scale. Anything less than one hundred and sixty acres was small scale."

"Just the same," Billy held stubbornly, "large scale's a whole lot better'n small scale like all these dinky gardens."

Saxon sighed. "I don't know which is the dinkier," she observed finally, "— owning a few little acres and the team you're driving, or not owning any acres and driving a team somebody else owns for wages."

Billy winced.

"Go on, Robinson Crusoe," he growled good naturedly. "Rub it in good an' plenty. An' the worst of it is it's correct. A hell of a free-born American I've been, adrivin' other folkses' teams for a livin', a-strikin' and a-sluggin' scabs, an' not bein' able to keep up with the installments for a few sticks of furniture. Just the same I was sorry for one thing. I hated worse 'n Sam Hill to see that Morris chair go back—you liked it so. We did a lot of honeymoonin' in that chair."

They were well out of San Leandro, walking through a region of tiny holdings—"farmlets," Billy called them; and Saxon got out her ukulele to cheer him with a song.

First, it was "Treat my daughter kind-i-ly," and then she swung into old-fashioned darky camp-meeting hymns, beginning with:

"Oh! de Judgmen' Day am rollin' roun', Rollin', yes, a-rollin', I hear the trumpets' awful soun', Rollin', yes, a-rollin'."

A big touring car, dashing past, threw a dusty pause in her singing, and Saxon delivered herself of her latest wisdom.

"Now, Billy, remember we're not going to take up with the first piece of land we see. We've got to go into this with our eyes open—"

"An' they ain't open yet," he agreed.

"And we've got to get them open. 'Tis them that looks that finds.' There's lots of time to learn things. We don't care if it takes months and months. We're footloose. A good start is better than a dozen bad ones. We've got to talk and find out. We'll talk with everybody we meet. Ask questions. Ask everybody. It's the only way to find out."

"I ain't much of a hand at askin' questions," Billy demurred.

"Then I'll ask," she cried. "We've got to win out at this game, and the way is to know. Look at all these Portuguese. Where are all the Americans? They owned the land first, after the Mexicans. What made the Americans clear out? How do the Portuguese make it go? Don't you see? We've got to ask millions of questions."

She strummed a few chords, and then her clear sweet voice rang out gaily:

"I's g'wine back to Dixie, I's g'wine back to Dixie, I's g'wine where de orange blossoms grow, For I hear de chillun callin', I see de sad tears fallin'—My heart's turned back to Dixie, An' I mus'go."

She broke off to exclaim: "Oh! What a lovely place! See that arbor—just covered with grapes!"

Again and again she was attracted by the small places they passed. Now it was: "Look at the flowers!" or: "My! those vegetables!" or: "See! They've got a cow!"

Men—Americans—driving along in buggies or runabouts looked at Saxon and Billy curiously. This Saxon could brook far easier than could Billy, who would mutter and grumble deep in his throat.

Beside the road they came upon a lineman eating his lunch.

"Stop and talk," Saxon whispered.

"Aw, what's the good? He's a lineman. What'd he know about farmin'?"

"You never can tell. He's our kind. Go ahead, Billy. You just speak to him. He isn't working now anyway, and he'll be more likely to talk. See that tree in there, just inside the gate, and the way the branches are grown together. It's a curiosity. Ask him about it. That's a good way to get started."

Billy stopped, when they were alongside.

"How do you do," he said gruffly.

The lineman, a young fellow, paused in the cracking of a hard-boiled egg to stare up at the couple.

"How do you do," he said.

Billy swung his pack from his shoulders to the ground, and Saxon rested her telescope basket.

"Peddlin'?" the young man asked, too discreet to put his question directly to Saxon, yet dividing it between her and Billy, and cocking his eye at the covered basket.

"No," she spoke up quickly. "We're looking for land. Do you know of any around here?"

Again he desisted from the egg, studying them with sharp eyes as if to fathom their financial status.

"Do you know what land sells for around here?" he asked.

"No," Saxon answered. "Do you?"

"I guess I ought to. I was born here. And land like this all around you runs at from two to three hundred to four an' five hundred dollars an acre."

"Whew!" Billy whistled. "I guess we don't want none of it."

"But what makes it that high? Town lots?" Saxon wanted to know.

"Nope. The Porchugeeze make it that high, I guess."

"I thought it was pretty good land that fetched a hundred an acre," Billy said.

"Oh, them times is past. They used to give away land once, an' if you was good, throw in all the cattle runnin' on it."

"How about government land around here?" was Billy'a next query.

"Ain't none, an' never was. This was old Mexican grants. My grandfather bought sixteen hundred of the best acres around here for fifteen hundred dollars—five hundred down an' the balance in five years without interest. But that was in the early days. He come West in '48, tryin' to find a country without chills an' fever."

"He found it all right," said Billy.

"You bet he did. An' if him an' father 'd held onto the land it'd been better than a gold mine, an' I wouldn't be workin' for a livin'. What's your business?"

"Teamster."

"Ben in the strike in Oakland?"

"Sure thing. I've teamed there most of my life."

Here the two men wandered off into a discussion of union affairs and the strike situation; but Saxon refused to be balked, and brought back the talk to the land.

"How was it the Portuguese ran up the price of land?" she asked.

The young fellow broke away from union matters with an effort, and for a moment regarded her with lack luster eyes, until the question sank into his consciousness.

"Because they worked the land overtime. Because they worked mornin', noon, an' night, all hands, women an' kids. Because they could get more out of twenty acres than we could out of a hundred an' sixty. Look at old Silva— Antonio Silva. I've known him ever since I was a shaver. He didn't have the price of a square meal when he hit this section and begun leasin' land from my folks. Look at him now—worth two hundred an' fifty thousan' cold, an' I bet he's got credit for a million, an' there's no tellin' what the rest of his family owns."

"And he made all that out of your folks' land?" Saxon demanded.

The young man nodded his head with evident reluctance.

"Then why didn't your folks do it?" she pursued.

The lineman shrugged his shoulders.

"Search me," he said.

"But the money was in the land," she persisted.

"Blamed if it was," came the retort, tinged slightly with color. "We never saw it stickin' out so as you could notice it. The money was in the hands of the Porchugeeze, I guess. They knew a few more 'n we did, that's all."

Saxon showed such dissatisfaction with his explanation that he was stung to action. He got up wrathfully. "Come on, an' I'll show you," he said. "I'll show you why I'm workin' for wages when I might a-ben a millionaire if my folks hadn't been mutts. That's what we old Americans are, Mutts, with a capital M."

He led them inside the gate, to the fruit tree that had first attracted Saxon's attention. From the main crotch diverged the four main branches of the tree. Two feet above the crotch the branches were connected, each to the ones on both sides, by braces of living wood.

"You think it growed that way, eh? Well, it did. But it was old Silva that made it just the same—caught two sprouts, when the tree was young, an' twisted 'em together. Pretty slick, eh? You bet. That tree'll never blow down. It's a natural, springy brace, an' beats iron braces stiff. Look along all the rows. Every tree's that way. See? An' that's just one trick of the Porchugeeze. They got a million like it.

"Figure it out for yourself. They don't need props when the crop's heavy. Why, when we had a heavy crop, we used to use five props to a tree. Now take ten acres of trees. That'd be some several thousan' props. Which cost money, an' labor to put in an' take out every year. These here natural braces don't have to have a thing done. They're Johnny-on-the-spot all the time. Why, the Porchugeeze has got us skinned a mile. Come on, I'll show you."

Billy, with city notions of trespass, betrayed perturbation at the freedom they were making of the little farm.

"Oh, it's all right, as long as you don't step on nothin'," the lineman reassured him. "Besides, my grandfather used to own this. They know me. Forty years ago old Silva come from the Azores. Went sheep-herdin' in the mountains for a couple of years, then blew in to San Leandro. These five acres was the first land he leased. That was the beginnin'. Then he began leasin' by the hundreds of acres, an' by the hundred-an'-sixties. An' his sisters an' his uncles an' his aunts begun pourin' in from the Azores—they're all related there, you know; an' pretty soon San Leandro was a regular Porchugeeze settlement.

"An' old Silva wound up by buyin' these five acres from grandfather. Pretty soon—an' father by that time was in the hole to the neck—he was buyin' father's land by the hundred-an'-sixties. An' all the rest of his relations was doin' the same thing. Father was always gettin' rich quick, an' he wound up by dyin' in debt. But old Silva never overlooked a bet, no matter how dinky. An' all the rest are just like him. You see outside the fence there, clear to the wheel-tracks in the road—horse-beans. We'd a-scorned to do a picayune thing like that. Not Silva. Why he's got a town house in San Leandro now. An' he rides around in a four-thousan'-dollar tourin' car. An' just the same his front door yard grows onions clear to the sidewalk. He clears three hundred a year on that patch alone. I know ten acres of land he bought last year,—a thousan' an acre they asked'm, an' he never batted an eye. He knew it was worth it, that's all. He knew he could make it pay. Back in the hills, there, he's got a ranch of five hundred an' eighty acres, bought it dirt cheap, too; an' I want to tell you I could travel around in a different tourin' car every day in the week just outa the profits he makes on that ranch from the horses all the way from heavy draughts to fancy steppers.

"But how?—how?—how did he get it all?" Saxon clamored.

"By bein' wise to farmin'. Why, the whole blame family works. They ain't ashamed to roll up their sleeves an' dig—sons an' daughters an' daughter-in-laws, old man, old woman, an' the babies. They have a sayin' that a kid four years old that can't pasture one cow on the county road an' keep it fat ain't worth his salt. Why, the Silvas, the whole tribe of 'em, works a hundred acres in peas, eighty in tomatoes, thirty in asparagus, ten in pie-plant, forty in cucumbers, an'—oh, stacks of other things."

"But how do they do it?" Saxon continued to demand. "We've never been ashamed to work. We've worked hard all our lives. I can out-work any Portuguese woman ever born. And I've done it, too, in the jute mills. There were lots of Portuguese girls working at the looms all around me, and I could out-weave them, every day, and I did, too. It isn't a case of work. What is it?"

The lineman looked at her in a troubled way.

"Many's the time I've asked myself that same question. 'We're better'n these cheap emigrants,' I'd say to myself. 'We was here first, an' owned the land. I can lick any Dago that ever hatched in the Azores. I got a better education. Then how in thunder do they put it all over us, get our land, an' start accounts in the banks?' An' the only answer I know is that we ain't got the sabe. We don't use our head-pieces right. Something's wrong with us. Anyway, we wasn't wised up to farming. We played at it. Show you? That's what I brung you in for—the way old Silva an' all his tribe farms. Look at this place. Some cousin of his, just out from the Azores, is makin' a start on it, an' payin' good rent to Silva. Pretty soon he'll be up to snuff an' buyin' land for himself from some perishin' American farmer.

"Look at that—though you ought to see it in summer. Not an inch wasted. Where we got one thin crop, they get four fat crops. An' look at the way they crowd it—currants between the tree rows, beans between the currant rows, a row of beans close on each side of the trees, an' rows of beans along the ends of the tree rows. Why, Silva wouldn't sell these five acres for five hundred an acre cash down. He gave grandfather fifty an acre for it on long time, an' here am I, workin' for the telephone company an' putting' in a telephone for old Silva's cousin from the Azores that can't speak American yet. Horse-beans along the road—say, when Silva swung that trick he made more outa fattenin' hogs with 'em than grandfather made with all his farmin'. Grandfather stuck up his nose at horse-beans. He died with it stuck up, an' with more mortgages on the land he had left than you could shake a stick at. Plantin' tomatoes wrapped up in wrappin' paper—ever heard of that? Father snorted when he first seen the Porchugeeze doin' it. An' he went on snortin'. Just the same they got bumper crops, an' father's house-patch of tomatoes was eaten by the black beetles. We ain't got the sabe, or the knack, or something or other. Just look at this piece of ground—four crops a year, an' every inch of soil workin' over time. Why, back in town there, there's single acres that earns more than fifty of ours in the old days. The Porchugeeze is natural-born farmers, that's all, an' we don't know nothin' about farmin' an' never did."

Saxon talked with the lineman, following him about, till one o'clock, when he looked at his watch, said good bye, and returned to his task of putting in a telephone for the latest immigrant from the Azores.

When in town, Saxon carried her oilcloth-wrapped telescope in her hand; but it was so arranged with loops, that, once on the road, she could thrust her arms through the loops and carry it on her back. When she did this, the tiny ukulele case was shifted so that it hung under her left arm.

A mile on from the lineman, they stopped where a small creek, fringed with brush, crossed the county road. Billy was for the cold lunch, which was the last meal Saxon had prepared in the Pine street cottage; but she was determined upon building a fire and boiling coffee. Not that she desired it for herself, but that she was impressed with the idea that everything at the starting of their strange wandering must be as comfortable as possible for Billy's sake. Bent on inspiring him with enthusiasm equal to her own, she declined to dampen what sparks he had caught by anything so uncheerful as a cold meal.

"Now one thing we want to get out of our heads right at the start, Billy, is that we're in a hurry. We're not in a hurry, and we don't care whether school keeps or not. We're out to have a good time, a regular adventure like you read about in books.—My! I wish that boy that took me fishing to Goat Island could see me now. Oakland was just a place to start from, he said. And, well, we've started, haven't we? And right here's where we stop and boil coffee. You get the fire going, Billy, and I'll get the water and the things ready to spread out."

"Say," Billy remarked, while they waited for the water to boil, "d'ye know what this reminds me of?"

Saxon was certain she did know, but she shook her head. She wanted to hear him say it.

"Why, the second Sunday I knew you, when we drove out to Moraga Valley behind Prince and King. You spread the lunch that day."

"Only it was a more scrumptious lunch," she added, with a happy smile.

"But I wonder why we didn't have coffee that day," he went on.

"Perhaps it would have been too much like housekeeping," she laughed; "kind of what Mary would call indelicate—"

"Or raw," Billy interpolated. "She was always springin' that word."

"And yet look what became of her."

"That's the way with all of them," Billy growled somberly. "I've always noticed it's the fastidious, la-de-da ones that turn out the rottenest. They're like some horses I know, a-shyin' at the things they're the least afraid of."

Saxon was silent, oppressed by a sadness, vague and remote, which the mention of Bert's widow had served to bring on.

"I know something else that happened that day which you'd never guess," Billy reminisced. "I bet you couldn't.

"I wonder," Saxon murmured, and guessed it with her eyes.

Billy's eyes answered, and quite spontaneously he reached over, caught her hand, and pressed it caressingly to his cheek.

"It's little, but oh my," he said, addressing the imprisoned hand. Then he gazed at Saxon, and she warmed with his words. "We're beginnin' courtin' all over again, ain't we?"

Both ate heartily, and Billy was guilty of three cups of coffee.

"Say, this country air gives some appetite," he mumbled, as he sank his teeth into his fifth bread-and-meat sandwich. "I could eat a horse, an' drown his head off in coffee afterward."

Saxon's mind had reverted to all the young lineman had told her, and she completed a sort of general resume of the information. "My!" she exclaimed, "but we've learned a lot!"

"An' we've sure learned one thing," Billy said. "An' that is that this is no place for us, with land a thousan' an acre an' only twenty dollars in our pockets."

"Oh, we're not going to stop here," she hastened to say.

"But just the same it's the Portuguese that gave it its price, and they make things go on it—send their children to school... and have them; and, as you said yourself, they're as fat as butterballs."

"An' I take my hat off to them," Billy responded.

"But all the same, I'd sooner have forty acres at a hundred an acre than four at a thousan' an acre. Somehow, you know, I'd be scared stiff on four acres— scared of fallin' off, you know."

She was in full sympathy with him. In her heart of hearts the forty acres tugged much the harder. In her way, allowing for the difference of a generation, her desire for spaciousness was as strong as her Uncle Will's.

"Well, we're not going to stop here," she assured Billy. "We're going in, not for forty acres, but for a hundred and sixty acres free from the government."

"An' I guess the government owes it to us for what our fathers an' mothers done. I tell you, Saxon, when a woman walks across the plains like your mother done, an' a man an' wife gets massacred by the Indians like my grandfather an' mother done, the government does owe them something."

"Well, it's up to us to collect."

"An' we'll collect all right, all right, somewhere down in them redwood mountains south of Monterey."

CHAPTER II

It was a good afternoon's tramp to Niles, passing through the town of Haywards; yet Saxon and Billy found time to diverge from the main county road and take the parallel roads through acres of intense cultivation where the land was farmed to the wheel-tracks. Saxon looked with amazement at these small, brown-skinned immigrants who came to the soil with nothing and yet made the soil pay for itself to the tune of two hundred, of five hundred, and of a thousand dollars an acre.

On every hand was activity. Women and children were in the fields as well as men. The land was turned endlessly over and over. They seemed never to let it rest. And it rewarded them. It must reward them, or their children would not be able to go to school, nor would so many of them be able to drive by in rattletrap, second-hand buggies or in stout light wagons.

"Look at their faces," Saxon said. "They are happy and contented. They haven't faces like the people in our neighborhood after the strikes began."

"Oh, sure, they got a good thing," Billy agreed. "You can see it stickin' out all over them. But they needn't get chesty with ME, I can tell you that much—just because they've jiggerooed us out of our land an' everything."

"But they're not showing any signs of chestiness," Saxon demurred.

"No, they're not, come to think of it. All the same, they ain't so wise. I bet I could tell 'em a few about horses."

It was sunset when they entered the little town of Niles. Billy, who had been silent for the last half mile, hesitantly ventured a suggestion.

"Say... I could put up for a room in the hotel just as well as not. What d 'ye think?"

But Saxon shook her head emphatically.

"How long do you think our twenty dollars will last at that rate? Besides, the only way to begin is to begin at the beginning. We didn't plan sleeping in hotels."

"All right," he gave in. "I'm game. I was just thinkin' about you."

"Then you'd better think I'm game, too," she flashed forgivingly. "And now we'll have to see about getting things for supper."

They bought a round steak, potatoes, onions, and a dozen eating apples, then went out from the town to the fringe of trees and brush that advertised a creek. Beside the trees, on a sand bank, they pitched camp. Plenty of dry wood lay about, and Billy whistled genially while he gathered and chopped.

Saxon, keen to follow his every mood, was cheered by the atrocious discord on his lips. She smiled to herself as she spread the blankets, with the tarpaulin underneath, for a table, having first removed all twigs from the sand. She had much to learn in the matter of cooking over a camp-fire, and made fair progress, discovering, first of all, that control of the fire meant far more than the size of it. When the coffee was boiled, she settled the grounds with a part-cup of cold water and placed the pot on the edge of the coals where it would keep hot and yet not boil. She fried potato dollars and onions in the same pan, but separately, and set them on top of the coffee pot in the tin plate she was to eat from, covering it with Billy's inverted plate. On the dry hot pan, in the way that delighted Billy, she fried the steak. This completed, and while Billy poured the coffee, she served the steak, putting the dollars and onions back into the frying pan for a moment to make them piping hot again.

"What more d'ye want than this?" Billy challenged with deep-toned satisfaction, in the pause after his final cup of coffee, while he rolled a cigarette. He lay on his side, full length, resting on his elbow. The fire was burning brightly, and Saxon's color was heightened by the flickering flames. "Now our folks, when they was on the move, had to be afraid for Indians, and wild animals and all sorts of things; an' here we are, as safe as bugs in a rug. Take this sand. What better bed could you ask? Soft as feathers. Say— you look good to me, heap little squaw. I bet you don't look an inch over sixteen right now, Mrs. Babe-in-the-Woods."

"Don't I?" she glowed, with a flirt of the head sideward and a white flash of teeth. "If you weren't smoking a cigarette I'd ask you if your mother knew you're out, Mr. Babe-in-the-Sandbank."

"Say," he began, with transparently feigned seriousness. "I want to ask you something, if you don't mind. Now, of course, I don't want to hurt your feelin's or nothin', but just the same there's something important I'd like to know."

"Well, what is it?" she inquired, after a fruitless wait.

"Well, it's just this, Saxon. I like you like anything an' all that, but here's night come on, an' we're a thousand miles from anywhere, and—well, what I wanta know is: are we really an' truly married, you an' me?"

"Really and truly," she assured him. "Why?"

"Oh, nothing; but I'd kind a-forgotten, an' I was gettin' embarrassed, you know, because if we wasn't, seein' the way I was brought up, this'd be no place—"

"That will do you," she said severely. "And this is just the time and place for you to get in the firewood for morning while I wash up the dishes and put the kitchen in order."

He started to obey, but paused to throw his arm about her and draw her close. Neither spoke, but when he went his way Saxon's breast was fluttering and a song of thanksgiving breathed on her lips.

The night had come on, dim with the light of faint stars. But these had disappeared behind clouds that seemed to have arisen from nowhere. It was the beginning of California Indian summer. The air was warm, with just the first hint of evening chill, and there was no wind.

"I've a feeling as if we've just started to live," Saxon said, when Billy, his firewood collected, joined her on the blankets before the fire. "I've learned more to-day than ten years in Oakland." She drew a long breath and braced her shoulders. "Farming's a bigger subject than I thought."

Billy said nothing. With steady eyes he was staring into the fire, and she knew he was turning something over in his mind.

"What is it," she asked, when she saw he had reached a conclusion, at the same time resting her hand on the back of his.

"Just been framin' up that ranch of ourn," he answered. "It's all well enough, these dinky farmlets. They'll do for foreigners. But we Americans just gotta have room. I want to be able to look at a hilltop an' know it's my land, and know it's my land down the other side an' up the next hilltop, an' know that over beyond that, down alongside some creek, my mares are most likely grazin', an' their little colts grazin' with 'em or kickin' up their heels. You know, there's money in raisin' horses—especially the big workhorses that run to eighteen hundred an' two thousand pounds. They're payin' for 'em, in the cities, every day in the year, seven an' eight hundred a pair, matched geldings, four years old. Good pasture an' plenty of it, in this kind of a climate, is all they need, along with some sort of shelter an' a little hay in long spells of bad weather. I never thought of it before, but let me tell you that this ranch proposition is beginnin' to look good to ME."

Saxon was all excitement. Here was new information on the cherished subject, and, best of all, Billy was the authority. Still better, he was taking an interest himself.

"There'll be room for that and for everything on a quarter section," she encouraged.

"Sure thing. Around the house we'll have vegetables an' fruit and chickens an' everything, just like the Porchugeeze, an' plenty of room beside to walk around an' range the horses."

"But won't the colts cost money, Billy?"

"Not much. The cobblestones eat horses up fast. That's where I'll get my brood mares, from the ones knocked out by the city. I know THAT end of it. They sell 'em at auction, an' they're good for years an' years, only no good on the cobbles any more."

There ensued a long pause. In the dying fire both were busy visioning the farm to be.

"It's pretty still, ain't it?" Billy said, rousing himself at last. He gazed about him. "An' black as a stack of black cats." He shivered, buttoned his coat, and tossed several sticks on the fire. "Just the same, it's the best kind of a climate in the world. Many's the time, when I was a little kid, I've heard my father brag about California's bein' a blanket climate. He went East, once, an' staid a summer an' a winter, an' got all he wanted. Never again for him."

"My mother said there never was such a land for climate. How wonderful it must have seemed to them after crossing the deserts and mountains. They called it the land of milk and honey. The ground was so rich that all they needed to do was scratch it, Cady used to say."

"And wild game everywhere," Billy contributed. "Mr. Roberts, the one that adopted my father, he drove cattle from the San Joaquin to the Columbia river. He had forty men helpin' him, an' all they took along was powder an' salt. They lived off the game they shot."

"The hills were full of deer, and my mother saw whole herds of elk around Santa Rosa. Some time we'll go there, Billy. I've always wanted to."

"And when my father was a young man, somewhere up north of Sacramento, in a creek called Cache Slough, the tules was full of grizzlies. He used to go in an' shoot 'em. An' when they caught 'em in the open, he an' the Mexicans used to ride up an' rope them—catch them with lariats, you know. He said a horse that wasn't afraid of grizzlies fetched ten times as much as any other horse. An' panthers!—all the old folks called 'em painters an' catamounts an' varmints. Yes, we'll go to Santa Rosa some time. Maybe we won't like that land down the coast, an' have to keep on hikin'."

By this time the fire had died down, and Saxon had finished brushing and braiding her hair. Their bed-going preliminaries were simple, and in a few minutes they were side by side under the blankets. Saxon closed her eyes, but could not sleep. On the contrary, she had never been more wide awake. She had never slept out of doors in her life, and by no exertion of will could she overcome the strangeness of it. In addition, she was stiffened from the long trudge, and the sand, to her surprise, was anything but soft. An hour passed. She tried to believe that Billy was asleep, but felt certain he was not. The sharp crackle of a dying ember startled her. She was confident that Billy had moved slightly.

"Billy," she whispered, "are you awake?"

"Yep," came his low answer, "—an' thinkin' this sand is harder'n a cement floor. It's one on me, all right. But who'd a-thought it?"

Both shifted their postures slightly, but vain was the attempt to escape from the dull, aching contact of the sand.

An abrupt, metallic, whirring noise of some nearby cricket gave Saxon another startle. She endured the sound for some minutes, until Billy broke forth.

"Say, that gets my goat whatever it is."

"Do you think it's a rattlesnake?" she asked, maintaining a calmness she did not feel.

"Just what I've been thinkin'."

"I saw two, in the window of Bowman's Drug Store. An' you know, Billy, they've got a hollow fang, and when they stick it into you the poison runs down the hollow."

"Br-r-r-r," Billy shivered, in fear that was not altogether mockery. "Certain death, everybody says, unless you're a Bosco. Remember him?"

"He eats 'em alive! He eats 'em alive! Bosco! Bosco!" Saxon responded, mimicking the cry of a side-show barker. "Just the same, all Bosco's rattlers had the poison-sacs cut outa them. They must a-had. Gee! It's funny I can't get asleep. I wish that damned thing'd close its trap. I wonder if it is a rattlesnake."

"No; it can't be," Saxon decided. "All the rattlesnakes are killed off long ago."

"Then where did Bosco get his?" Billy demanded with unimpeachable logic. "An' why don't you get to sleep?"

"Because it's all new, I guess," was her reply. "You see, I never camped out in my life."

"Neither did I. An' until now I always thought it was a lark." He changed his position on the maddening sand and sighed heavily. "But we'll get used to it in time, I guess. What other folks can do, we can, an' a mighty lot of 'em has camped out. It's all right. Here we are, free an' independent, no rent to pay, our own bosses—"

He stopped abruptly. From somewhere in the brush came an intermittent rustling. When they tried to locate it, it mysteriously ceased, and when the first hint of drowsiness stole upon them the rustling as mysteriously recommenced.

"It sounds like something creeping up on us," Saxon suggested, snuggling closer to Billy.

"Well, it ain't a wild Indian, at all events," was the best he could offer in the way of comfort. He yawned deliberately. "Aw, shucks! What's there to be scared of? Think of what all the pioneers went through."

Several minutes later his shoulders began to shake, and Saxon knew he was giggling.

"I was just thinkin' of a yarn my father used to tell about," he explained. "It was about old Susan Kleghorn, one of the Oregon pioneer women. Wall-Eyed Susan, they used to call her; but she could shoot to beat the band. Once, on the Plains, the wagon train she was in, was attacked by Indians. They got all the wagons in a circle, an' all hands an' the oxen inside, an' drove the Indians off, killin' a lot of 'em. They was too strong that way, so what'd the Indians do, to draw 'em out into the open, but take two white girls, captured from some other train, an' begin to torture 'em. They done it just out of gunshot, but so everybody could see. The idea was that the white men couldn't stand it, an' would rush out, an' then the Indians'd have 'em where they wanted 'em.

"The white men couldn't do a thing. If they rushed out to save the girls, they'd be finished, an' then the Indians'd rush the train. It meant death to everybody. But what does old Susan do, but get out an old, long-barreled Kentucky rifle. She rams down about three times the regular load of powder, takes aim at a big buck that's pretty busy at the torturin', an' bangs away. It knocked her clean over backward, an' her shoulder was lame all the rest of the way to Oregon, but she dropped the big Indian deado. He never knew what struck 'm.

"But that wasn't the yarn I wanted to tell. It seems old Susan liked John Barleycorn. She'd souse herself to the ears every chance she got. An' her sons an' daughters an' the old man had to be mighty careful not to leave any around where she could get hands on it."

"On what?" asked Saxon.

"On John Barleycorn.—Oh, you ain't on to that. It's the old fashioned name for whisky. Well, one day all the folks was goin' away—that was over somewhere at a place called Bodega, where they'd settled after comin' down from Oregon. An' old Susan claimed her rheumatics was hurtin' her an' so she couldn't go. But the family was on. There was a two-gallon demijohn of whisky in the house. They said all right, but before they left they sent one of the grandsons to climb a big tree in the barnyard, where he tied the demijohn sixty feet from the ground. Just the same, when they come home that night they found Susan on the kitchen floor dead to the world."

"And she'd climbed the tree after all," Saxon hazarded, when Billy had shown no inclination of going on.

"Not on your life," he laughed jubilantly. "All she'd done was to put a washtub on the ground square under the demijohn. Then she got out her old rifle an' shot the demijohn to smithereens, an' all she had to do was lap the whisky outa the tub."

Again Saxon was drowsing, when the rustling sound was heard, this time closer. To her excited apprehension there was something stealthy about it, and she imagined a beast of prey creeping upon them. "Billy," she whispered.

"Yes, I'm a-listenin' to it," came his wide awake answer.

"Mightn't that be a panther, or maybe... a wildcat?"

"It can't be. All the varmints was killed off long ago. This is peaceable farmin' country."

A vagrant breeze sighed through the trees and made Saxon shiver. The mysterious cricket-noise ceased with suspicious abruptness. Then, from the rustling noise, ensued a dull but heavy thump that caused both Saxon and Billy to sit up in the blankets. There were no further sounds, and they lay down again, though the very silence now seemed ominous.

"Huh," Billy muttered with relief. "As though I don't know what it was. It was a rabbit. I've heard tame ones bang their hind feet down on the floor that way."

In vain Saxon tried to win sleep. The sand grew harder with the passage of time. Her flesh and her bones ached from contact with it. And, though her reason flouted any possibility of wild dangers, her fancy went on picturing them with unflagging zeal.

A new sound commenced. It was neither a rustling nor a rattling, and it tokened some large body passing through the brush. Sometimes twigs crackled and broke, and, once, they heard bush-branches press aside and spring back into place.

"If that other thing was a panther, this is an elephant," was Billy's uncheering opinion. "It's got weight. Listen to that. An' it's comin' nearer."

There were frequent stoppages, then the sounds would begin again, always louder, always closer. Billy sat up in the blankets once more, passing one arm around Saxon, who had also sat up.

"I ain't slept a wink," he complained. "—There it goes again. I wish I could see."

"It makes a noise big enough for a grizzly," Saxon chattered, partly from nervousness, partly from the chill of the night.

"It ain't no grasshopper, that's sure."

Billy started to leave the blankets, but Saxon caught his arm.

"What are you going to do?"

"Oh, I ain't scairt none," he answered. "But, honest to God, this is gettin' on my nerves. If I don't find what that thing is, it'll give me the willies. I'm just goin' to reconnoiter. I won't go close."

So intensely dark was the night, that the moment Billy crawled beyond the reach of her hand he was lost to sight. She sat and waited. The sound had ceased, though she could follow Billy's progress by the cracking of dry twigs and limbs. After a few moments he returned and crawled under the blankets.

"I scared it away, I guess. It's got better ears, an' when it heard me comin' it skinned out most likely. I did my dangdest, too, not to make a sound.—O Lord, there it goes again."

They sat up. Saxon nudged Billy.

"There," she warned, in the faintest of whispers. "I can hear it breathing. It almost made a snort."

A dead branch cracked loudly, and so near at hand, that both of them jumped shamelessly.

"I ain't goin' to stand any more of its foolin'," Billy declared wrathfully. "It'll be on top of us if I don't."

"What are you going to do?" she queried anxiously.

"Yell the top of my head off. I'll get a fall outa whatever it is."

He drew a deep breath and emitted a wild yell.

The result far exceeded any expectation he could have entertained, and Saxon's heart leaped up in sheer panic. On the instant the darkness erupted into terrible sound and movement. There were trashings of underbrush and lunges and plunges of heavy bodies in different directions. Fortunately for their ease of mind, all these sounds receded and died away.

"An' what d'ye think of that?" Billy broke the silence.

"Gee! all the fight fans used to say I was scairt of nothin'. Just the same I'm glad they ain't seein' me to-night."

He groaned. "I've got all I want of that blamed sand. I'm goin' to get up and start the fire."

This was easy. Under the ashes were live embers which quickly ignited the wood he threw on. A few stars were peeping out in the misty zenith. He looked up at them, deliberated, and started to move away.

"Where are you going now?" Saxon called.

"Oh, I've got an idea," he replied noncommittally, and walked boldly away beyond the circle of the firelight.

Saxon sat with the blankets drawn closely under her chin, and admired his courage. He had not even taken the hatchet, and he was going in the direction in which the disturbance had died away.

Ten minutes later he came back chuckling.

"The sons-of-guns, they got my goat all right. I'll be scairt of my own shadow next.—What was they? Huh! You couldn't guess in a thousand years. A bunch of half-grown calves, an' they was worse scairt than us."

He smoked a cigarette by the fire, then rejoined Saxon under the blankets.

"A hell of a farmer I'll make," he chafed, "when a lot of little calves can scare the stuffin' outa me. I bet your father or mine wouldn't a-batted an eye. The stock has gone to seed, that's what it has."

"No, it hasn't," Saxon defended. "The stock is all right. We're just as able as our folks ever were, and we're healthier on top of it. We've been brought up different, that's all. We've lived in cities all our lives. We know the city sounds and thugs, but we don't know the country ones. Our training has been unnatural, that's the whole thing in a nutshell. Now we're going in for natural training. Give us a little time, and we'll sleep as sound out of doors as ever your father or mine did."

"But not on sand," Billy groaned.

"We won't try. That's one thing, for good and all, we've learned the very first time. And now hush up and go to sleep."

Their fears had vanished, but the sand, receiving now their undivided attention, multiplied its unyieldingness. Billy dozed off first, and roosters were crowing somewhere in the distance when Saxon's eyes closed. But they could not escape the sand, and their sleep was fitful.

At the first gray of dawn, Billy crawled out and built a roaring fire. Saxon drew up to it shiveringly. They were hollow-eyed and weary. Saxon began to laugh. Billy joined sulkily, then brightened up as his eyes chanced upon the coffee pot, which he immediately put on to boil.

CHAPTER III

It is forty miles from Oakland to San Jose, and Saxon and Billy accomplished it in three easy days. No more obliging and angrily garrulous linemen were encountered, and few were the opportunities for conversation with chance wayfarers. Numbers of tramps, carrying rolls of blankets, were met, traveling both north and south on the county road; and from talks with them Saxon quickly learned that they knew little or nothing about farming. They were mostly old men, feeble or besotted, and all they knew was work—where jobs might be good, where jobs had been good; but the places they mentioned were always a long way off. One thing she did glean from them, and that was that the district she and Billy were passing through was "small-farmer" country in which labor was rarely hired, and that when it was it generally was Portuguese.

The farmers themselves were unfriendly. They drove by Billy and Saxon, often with empty wagons, but never invited them to ride. When chance offered and Saxon did ask questions, they looked her over curiously, or suspiciously, and gave ambiguous and facetious answers.

"They ain't Americans, damn them," Billy fretted. "Why, in the old days everybody was friendly to everybody."

But Saxon remembered her last talk with her brother.

"It's the spirit of the times, Billy. The spirit has changed. Besides, these people are too near. Wait till we get farther away from the cities, then we'll find them more friendly."

"A measly lot these ones are," he sneered.

"Maybe they've a right to be," she laughed. "For all you know, more than one of the scabs you've slugged were sons of theirs."

"If I could only hope so," Billy said fervently. "But I don't care if I owned ten thousand acres, any man hikin' with his blankets might be just as good a man as me, an' maybe better, for all I'd know. I'd give 'm the benefit of the doubt, anyway."

Billy asked for work, at first, indiscriminately, later, only at the larger farms. The unvarying reply was that there was no work. A few said there would be plowing after the first rains. Here and there, in a small way, dry plowing was going on. But in the main the farmers were waiting.

"But do you know how to plow?" Saxon asked Billy.

"No; but I guess it ain't much of a trick to turn. Besides, next man I see plowing I'm goin' to get a lesson from."

In the mid-afternoon of the second day his opportunity came. He climbed on top of the fence of a small field and watched an old man plow round and round it.

"Aw, shucks, just as easy as easy," Billy commented scornfully. "If an old codger like that can handle one plow, I can handle two."

"Go on and try it," Saxon urged.

"What's the good?"

"Cold feet," she jeered, but with a smiling face. "All you have to do is ask him. All he can do is say no. And what if he does? You faced the Chicago Terror twenty rounds without flinching."

"Aw, but it's different," he demurred, then dropped to the ground inside the fence. "Two to one the old geezer turns me down."

"No, he won't. Just tell him you want to learn, and ask him if he'll let you drive around a few times. Tell him it won't cost him anything."

"Huh! If he gets chesty I'll take his blamed plow away from him."

From the top of the fence, but too far away to hear, Saxon watched the colloquy. After several minutes, the lines were transferred to Billy's neck, the handles to his hands. Then the team started, and the old man, delivering a rapid fire of instructions, walked alongside of Billy. When a few turns had been made, the farmer crossed the plowed strip to Saxon, and joined her on the rail.

"He's plowed before, a little mite, ain't he?"

Saxon shook her head.

"Never in his life. But he knows how to drive horses."

"He showed he wasn't all greenhorn, an' he learns pretty quick." Here the farmer chuckled and cut himself a chew from a plug of tobacco. "I reckon he won't tire me out a-settin' here."

The unplowed area grew smaller and smaller, but Billy evinced no intention of quitting, and his audience on the fence was deep in conversation. Saxon's questions flew fast and furious, and she was not long in concluding that the old man bore a striking resemblance to the description the lineman had given of his father.

Billy persisted till the field was finished, and the old man invited him and Saxon to stop for the night. There was a disused outbuilding where they would find a small cook stove, he said, and also he would give them fresh milk. Further, if Saxon wanted to test HER desire for farming, she could try her hand on the cow.

The milking lesson did not prove as successful as Billy's plowing; but when he had mocked sufficiently, Saxon challenged him to try, and he failed as grievously as she. Saxon had eyes and questions for everything, and it did not take her long to realize that she was looking upon the other side of the farming shield. Farm and farmer were old-fashioned. There was no intensive cultivation. There was too much land too little farmed. Everything was slipshod. House and barn and outbuildings were fast falling into ruin. The front yard was weed-grown. There was no vegetable garden. The small orchard was old, sickly, and neglected. The trees were twisted, spindling, and overgrown with a gray moss. The sons and daughters were away in the cities, Saxon found out. One daughter had married a doctor, the other was a teacher in the state normal school; one son was a locomotive engineer, the second was an architect, and the third was a police court reporter in San Francisco. On occasion, the father said, they helped out the old folks.

"What do you think?" Saxon asked Billy as he smoked his after-supper cigarette.

His shoulders went up in a comprehensive shrug.

"Huh! That's easy. The old geezer's like his orchard—covered with moss. It's plain as the nose on your face, after San Leandro, that he don't know the first thing. An' them horses. It'd be a charity to him, an' a savin' of money for him, to take 'em out an' shoot 'em both. You bet you don't see the Porchugeeze with horses like them. An' it ain't a case of bein' proud, or puttin' on side, to have good horses. It's brass tacks an' business. It pays. That's the game. Old horses eat more 'n young ones to keep in condition an' they can't do the same amount of work. But you bet it costs just as much to shoe them. An' his is scrub on top of it. Every minute he has them horses he's losin' money. You oughta see the way they work an' figure horses in the city."

They slept soundly, and, after an early breakfast, prepared to start.

"I'd like to give you a couple of days' work," the old man regretted, at parting, "but I can't see it. The ranch just about keeps me and the old woman, now that the children are gone. An' then it don't always. Seems times have been bad for a long spell now. Ain't never been the same since Grover Cleveland."

Early in the afternoon, on the outskirts of San Jose, Saxon called a halt.

"I'm going right in there and talk," she declared, "unless they set the dogs on me. That's the prettiest place yet, isn't it?"

Billy, who was always visioning hills and spacious ranges for his horses, mumbled unenthusiastic assent.

"And the vegetables! Look at them! And the flowers growing along the borders! That beats tomato plants in wrapping paper."

"Don't see the sense of it," Billy objected. "Where's the money come in from flowers that take up the ground that good vegetables might be growin' on?"

"And that's what I'm going to find out." She pointed to a woman, stooped to the ground and working with a trowel; in front of the tiny bungalow. "I don't know what she's like, but at the worst she can only be mean. See! She's looking at us now. Drop your load alongside of mine, and come on in."

Billy slung the blankets from his shoulder to the ground, but elected to wait. As Saxon went up the narrow, flower-bordered walk, she noted two men at work among the vegetables—one an old Chinese, the other old and of some dark-eyed foreign breed. Here were neatness, efficiency, and intensive cultivation with a vengeance—even her untrained eye could see that. The woman stood up and turned from her flowers, and Saxon saw that she was middle-aged, slender, and simply but nicely dressed. She wore glasses, and Saxon's reading of her face was that it was kind but nervous looking.

"I don't want anything to-day," she said, before Saxon could speak, administering the rebuff with a pleasant smile.

Saxon groaned inwardly over the black-covered telescope basket. Evidently the woman had seen her put it down.

"We're not peddling," she explained quickly.

"Oh, I am sorry for the mistake."

This time the woman's smile was even pleasanter, and she waited for Saxon to state her errand.

Nothing loath, Saxon took it at a plunge.

"We're looking for land. We want to be farmers, you know, and before we get the land we want to find out what kind of land we want. And seeing your pretty place has just filled me up with questions. You see, we don't know anything about farming. We've lived in the city all our life, and now we've given it up and are going to live in the country and be happy."

She paused. The woman's face seemed to grow quizzical, though the pleasantness did not abate.

"But how do you know you will be happy in the country?" she asked.

"I don't know. All I do know is that poor people can't be happy in the city where they have labor troubles all the time. If they can't be happy in the country, then there's no happiness anywhere, and that doesn't seem fair, does it?"

"It is sound reasoning, my dear, as far as it goes. But you must remember that there are many poor people in the country and many unhappy people."

"You look neither poor nor unhappy," Saxon challenged.

"You ARE a dear."

Saxon saw the pleased flush in the other's face, which lingered as she went on.

"But still, I may be peculiarly qualified to live and succeed in the country. As you say yourself, you've spent your life in the city. You don't know the first thing about the country. It might even break your heart."

Saxon's mind went back to the terrible months in the Pine street cottage.

"I know already that the city will break my heart. Maybe the country will, too, but just the same it's my only chance, don't you see. It's that or nothing. Besides, our folks before us were all of the country. It seems the more natural way. And better, here I am, which proves that 'way down inside I must want the country, must, as you call it, be peculiarly qualified for the country, or else I wouldn't be here."

The other nodded approval, and looked at her with growing interest.

"That young man—" she began.

"Is my husband. He was a teamster until the big strike came. My name is Roberts, Saxon Roberts, and my husband is William Roberts."

"And I am Mrs. Mortimer," the other said, with a bow of acknowledgment. "I am a widow. And now, if you will ask your husband in, I shall try to answer some of your many questions. Tell him to put the bundles inside the gate.. .. And now what are all the questions you are filled with?"

"Oh, all kinds. How does it pay? How did you manage it all? How much did the land cost? Did you build that beautiful house? How much do you pay the men? How did you learn all the different kinds of things, and which grew best and which paid best? What is the best way to sell them? How do you sell them?" Saxon paused and laughed. "Oh, I haven't begun yet. Why do you have flowers on the borders everywhere? I looked over the Portuguese farms around San Leandro, but they never mixed flowers and vegetables."

Mrs. Mortimer held up her hand. "Let me answer the last first. It is the key to almost everything."

But Billy arrived, and the explanation was deferred until after his introduction.

"The flowers caught your eyes, didn't they, my dear?" Mrs. Mortimer resumed. "And brought you in through my gate and right up to me. And that's the very reason they were planted with the vegetables—to catch eyes. You can't imagine how many eyes they have caught, nor how many owners of eyes they have lured inside my gate. This is a good road, and is a very popular short country drive for townsfolk. Oh, no; I've never had any luck with automobiles. They can't see anything for dust. But I began when nearly everybody still used carriages. The townswomen would drive by. My flowers, and then my place, would catch their eyes. They would tell their drivers to stop. And—well, somehow, I managed to be in the front within speaking distance. Usually I succeeded in inviting them in to see my flowers... and vegetables, of course. Everything was sweet, clean, pretty. It all appealed. And—" Mrs. Mortimer shrugged her shoulders. "It is well known that the stomach sees through the eyes. The thought of vegetables growing among flowers pleased their fancy. They wanted my vegetables. They must have them. And they did, at double the market price, which they were only too glad to pay. You see, I became the fashion, or a fad, in a small way. Nobody lost. The vegetables were certainly good, as good as any on the market and often fresher. And, besides, my customers killed two birds with one stone; for they were pleased with themselves for philanthropic reasons. Not only did they obtain the finest and freshest possible vegetables, but at the same time they were happy with the knowledge that they were helping a deserving widow-woman. Yes, and it gave a certain tone to their establishments to be able to say they bought Mrs. Mortimer's vegetables. But that's too big a side to go into. In short, my little place became a show place—anywhere to go, for a drive or anything, you know, when time has to be killed. And it became noised about who I was, and who my husband had been, what I had been. Some of the townsladies I had known personally in the old days. They actually worked for my success. And then, too, I used to serve tea. My patrons became my guests for the time being. I still serve it, when they drive out to show me off to their friends. So you see, the flowers are one of the ways I succeeded."

Saxon was glowing with appreciation, but Mrs. Mortimer, glancing at Billy, noted not entire approval. His blue eyes were clouded.

"Well, out with it," she encouraged. "What are you thinking?"

To Saxon's surprise, he answered directly, and to her double surprise, his criticism was of a nature which had never entered her head.

"It's just a trick," Billy expounded. "That's what I was gettin' at—"

"But a paying trick," Mrs. Mortimer interrupted, her eyes dancing and vivacious behind the glasses.

"Yes, and no," Billy said stubbornly, speaking in his slow, deliberate fashion. "If every farmer was to mix flowers an' vegetables, then every farmer would get double the market price, an' then there wouldn't be any double market price. Everything'd be as it was before."

"You are opposing a theory to a fact," Mrs. Mortimer stated. "The fact is that all the farmers do not do it. The fact is that I do receive double the price. You can't get away from that."

Billy was unconvinced, though unable to reply.

"Just the same," he muttered, with a slow shake of the head, "I don't get the hang of it. There's something wrong so far as we're concerned—my wife an' me, I mean. Maybe I'll get hold of it after a while."

"And in the meantime, we'll look around," Mrs. Mortimer invited. "I want to show you everything, and tell you how I make it go. Afterward, we'll sit down, and I'll tell you about the beginning. You see—" she bent her gaze on Saxon—"I want you thoroughly to understand that you can succeed in the country if you go about it right. I didn't know a thing about it when I began, and I didn't have a fine big man like yours. I was all alone. But I'll tell you about that."

For the next hour, among vegetables, berry-bushes and fruit trees, Saxon stored her brain with a huge mass of information to be digested at her leisure. Billy, too, was interested, but he left the talking to Saxon, himself rarely asking a question. At the rear of the bungalow, where everything was as clean and orderly as the front, they were shown through the chicken yard. Here, in different runs, were kept several hundred small and snow-white hens.

"White Leghorns," said Mrs. Mortimer. "You have no idea what they netted me this year. I never keep a hen a moment past the prime of her laying period—"

"Just what I was tellin' you, Saxon, about horses," Billy broke in.

"And by the simplest method of hatching them at the right time, which not one farmer in ten thousand ever dreams of doing, I have them laying in the winter when most hens stop laying and when eggs are highest. Another thing: I have my special customers. They pay me ten cents a dozen more than the market price, because my specialty is one-day eggs."

Here she chanced to glance at Billy, and guessed that he was still wrestling with his problem.

"Same old thing?" she queried.

He nodded. "Same old thing. If every farmer delivered day-old eggs, there wouldn't be no ten cents higher 'n the top price. They'd be no better off than they was before."

"But the eggs would be one-day eggs, all the eggs would be one-day eggs, you mustn't forget that," Mrs. Mortimer pointed out.

"But that don't butter no toast for my wife an' me," he objected. "An' that's what I've been tryin' to get the hang of, an' now I got it. You talk about theory an' fact. Ten cents higher than top price is a theory to Saxon an' me. The fact is, we ain't got no eggs, no chickens, an' no land for the chickens to run an' lay eggs on."

Their hostess nodded sympathetically.

"An' there's something else about this outfit of yourn that I don't get the hang of," he pursued. "I can't just put my finger on it, but it's there all right."

They were shown over the cattery, the piggery, the milkers, and the kennelry, as Mrs. Mortimer called her live stock departments. None was large. All were moneymakers, she assured them, and rattled off her profits glibly. She took their breaths away by the prices given and received for pedigreed Persians, pedigreed Ohio Improved Chesters, pedigreed Scotch collies, and pedigreed Jerseys. For the milk of the last she also had a special private market, receiving five cents more a quart than was fetched by the best dairy milk. Billy was quick to point out the difference between the look of her orchard and the look of the orchard they had inspected the previous afternoon, and Mrs. Mortimer showed him scores of other differences, many of which he was compelled to accept on faith.

Then she told them of another industry, her home-made jams and jellies, always contracted for in advance, and at prices dizzyingly beyond the regular market. They sat in comfortable rattan chairs on the veranda, while she told the story of how she had drummed up the jam and jelly trade, dealing only with the one best restaurant and one best club in San Jose. To the proprietor and the steward she had gone with her samples, in long discussions beaten down their opposition, overcome their reluctance, and persuaded the proprietor, in particular, to make a "special" of her wares, to boom them quietly with his patrons, and, above all, to charge stiffly for dishes and courses in which they appeared.

Throughout the recital Billy's eyes were moody with dissatisfaction. Mrs. Mortimer saw, and waited.

"And now, begin at the beginning," Saxon begged.

But Mrs. Mortimer refused unless they agreed to stop for supper. Saxon frowned Billy's reluctance away, and accepted for both of them.

"Well, then," Mrs. Mortimer took up her tale, "in the beginning I was a greenhorn, city born and bred. All I knew of the country was that it was a place to go for vacations, and I always went to springs and mountain and seaside resorts. I had lived among books almost all my life. I was head librarian of the Doncaster Library for years. Then I married Mr. Mortimer. He was a book man, a professor in San Miguel University. He had a long sickness, and when he died there was nothing left. Even his life insurance was eaten into before I could be free of creditors. As for myself, I was worn out, on the verge of nervous prostration, fit for nothing. I had five thousand dollars left, however, and, without going into the details, I decided to go farming. I found this place, in a delightful climate, close to San Jose—the end of the electric line is only a quarter of a mile on—and I bought it. I paid two thousand cash, and gave a mortgage for two thousand. It cost two hundred an acre, you see."

"Twenty acres!" Saxon cried.

"Wasn't that pretty small?" Billy ventured.

"Too large, oceans too large. I leased ten acres of it the first thing. And it's still leased after all this time. Even the ten I'd retained was much too large for a long, long time. It's only now that I'm beginning to feel a tiny mite crowded."

"And ten acres has supported you an' two hired men?" Billy demanded, amazed.

Mrs. Mortimer clapped her hands delightedly.

"Listen. I had been a librarian. I knew my way among books. First of all I'd read everything written on the subject, and subscribed to some of the best farm magazines and papers. And you ask if my ten acres have supported me and two hired men. Let me tell you. I have four hired men. The ten acres certainly must support them, as it supports Hannah—she's a Swedish widow who runs the house and who is a perfect Trojan during the jam and jelly season—and Hannah's daughter, who goes to school and lends a hand, and my nephew whom I have taken to raise and educate. Also, the ten acres have come pretty close to paying for the whole twenty, as well as for this house, and all the outbuildings, and all the pedigreed stock."

Saxon remembered what the young lineman had said about the Portuguese.

"The ten acres didn't do a bit of it," she cried. "It was your head that did it all, and you know it."

"And that's the point, my dear. It shows the right kind of person can succeed in the country. Remember, the soil is generous. But it must be treated generously, and that is something the old style American farmer can't get

- 262 -

into his head. So it IS head that counts. Even when his starving acres have convinced him of the need for fertilizing, he can't see the difference between cheap fertilizer and good fertilizer."

"And that's something I want to know about," Saxon exclaimed. "And I'll tell you all I know, but, first, you must be very tired. I noticed you were limping. Let me take you in—never mind your bundles; I'll send Chang for them."

To Saxon, with her innate love of beauty and charm in all personal things, the interior of the bungalow was a revelation. Never before had she been inside a middle class home, and what she saw not only far exceeded anything she had imagined, but was vastly different from her imaginings. Mrs. Mortimer noted her sparkling glances which took in everything, and went out of her way to show Saxon around, doing it under the guise of gleeful boastings, stating the costs of the different materials, explaining how she had done things with her own hands, such as staining the doors, weathering the bookcases, and putting together the big Mission Morris chair. Billy stepped gingerly behind, and though it never entered his mind to ape to the manner born, he succeeded in escaping conspicuous awkwardness, even at the table where he and Saxon had the unique experience of being waited on in a private house by a servant.

"If you'd only come along next year," Mrs. Mortimer mourned; "then I should have had the spare room I had planned—"

"That's all right," Billy spoke up; "thank you just the same. But we'll catch the electric cars into San Jose an' get a room."

Mrs. Mortimer was still disturbed at her inability to put them up for the night, and Saxon changed the conversation by pleading to be told more.

"You remember, I told you I'd paid only two thousand down on the land," Mrs. Mortimer complied. "That left me three thousand to experiment with. Of course, all my friends and relatives prophesied failure. And, of course, I made my mistakes, plenty of them, but I was saved from still more by the thorough study I had made and continued to make." She indicated shelves of farm books and files of farm magazines that lined the walls. "And I continued to study. I was resolved to be up to date, and I sent for all the experiment station reports. I went almost entirely on the basis that whatever the old type farmer did was wrong, and, do you know, in doing that I was not so far wrong myself. It's almost unthinkable, the stupidity of the old-fashioned farmers. Oh, I consulted with them, talked things over with them, challenged their stereotyped ways, demanded demonstration of their dogmatic and prejudiced beliefs, and quite succeeded in convincing the last of them that I was a fool and doomed to come to grief."

"But you didn't! You didn't!"

Mrs. Mortimer smiled gratefully.

"Sometimes, even now, I'm amazed that I didn't. But I came of a hard-headed stock which had been away from the soil long enough to gain a new perspective. When a thing satisfied my judgment, I did it forthwith and downright, no matter how extravagant it seemed. Take the old orchard. Worthless! Worse than worthless! Old Calkins nearly died of heart disease when he saw the devastation I had wreaked upon it. And look at it now. There was an old rattletrap ruin where the bungalow now stands. I put up with it, but I immediately pulled down the cow barn, the pigsties, the chicken houses, everything—made a clean sweep. They shook their heads and groaned when they saw such wanton waste by a widow struggling to make a living. But worse was to come. They were paralyzed when I told them the price of the three beautiful O.I.C.'s—pigs, you know, Chesters—which I bought, sixty dollars for the three, and only just weaned. Then I hustled the nondescript chickens to market, replacing them with the White Leghorns. The two scrub cows that came with the place I sold to the butcher for thirty dollars each, paying two hundred and fifty for two blue-blooded Jersey heifers... and coined money on the exchange, while Calkins and the rest went right on with their scrubs that couldn't give enough milk to pay for their board."

Billy nodded approval.

"Remember what I told you about horses," he reiterated to Saxon; and, assisted by his hostess, he gave a very creditable disquisition on horseflesh and its management from a business point of view.

When he went out to smoke Mrs. Mortimer led Saxon into talking about herself and Billy, and betrayed not the slightest shock when she learned of his prizefighting and scab-slugging proclivities.

"He's a splendid young man, and good," she assured Saxon. "His face shows that. And, best of all, he loves you and is proud of you. You can't imagine how I have enjoyed watching the way he looks at you, especially when you are talking. He respects your judgment. Why, he must, for here he is with you on this pilgrimage which is wholly your idea." Mrs. Mortimer sighed. "You are very fortunate, dear child, very fortunate. And you don't yet know what a man's brain is. Wait till he is quite fired with enthusiasm for your project. You will be astounded by the way he takes hold. You will have to exert yourself to keep up with him. In the meantime, you must lead. Remember, he is city bred. It will be a struggle to wean him from the only life he's known."

"Oh, but he's disgusted with the city, too—" Saxon began.

"But not as you are. Love is not the whole of man, as it is of woman. The city hurt you more than it hurt him. It was you who lost the dear little babe. His interest, his connection, was no more than casual and incidental compared with the depth and vividness of yours."

Mrs. Mortimer turned her head to Billy, who was just entering.

"Have you got the hang of what was bothering you?" she asked.

"Pretty close to it," he answered, taking the indicated big Morris chair. "It's this—"

"One moment," Mrs. Mortimer checked him. "That is a beautiful, big, strong chair, and so are you, at any rate big and strong, and your little wife is very weary—no, no; sit down, it's your strength she needs. Yes, I insist. Open your arms."

And to him she led Saxon, and into his arms placed her. "Now, sir—and you look delicious, the pair of you—register your objections to my way of earning a living."

"It ain't your way," Billy repudiated quickly. "Your way's all right. It's great. What I'm trying to get at is that your way don't fit us. We couldn't make a go of it your way. Why you had pull—well-to-do acquaintances, people that knew you'd been a librarian an' your husband a professor. An' you had...." Here he floundered a moment, seeking definiteness for the idea he still vaguely grasped. "Well, you had a way we couldn't have. You were educated, an'... an'—I don't know, I guess you knew society ways an' business ways we couldn't know."

"But, my dear boy, you could learn what was necessary," she contended.

Billy shook his head.

"No. You don't quite get me. Let's take it this way. Just suppose it's me, with jam an' jelly, a-wadin' into that swell restaurant like you did to talk with the top guy. Why, I'd be outa place the moment I stepped into his office. Worse'n that, I'd feel outa place. That'd make me have a chip on my shoulder an' lookin' for trouble, which is a poor way to do business. Then, too, I'd be thinkin' he was thinkin' I was a whole lot of a husky to be peddlin' jam. What'd happen, I'd be chesty at the drop of the hat. I'd be thinkin' he was thinkin' I was standin' on my foot, an' I'd beat him to it in tellin' him he was standin' on HIS foot. Don't you see? It's because I was raised that way. It'd be take it or leave it with me, an' no jam sold."

"What you say is true," Mrs. Mortimer took up brightly. "But there is your wife. Just look at her. She'd make an impression on any business man. He'd be only too willing to listen to her."

Billy stiffened, a forbidding expression springing into his eyes.

"What have I done now?" their hostess laughed.

"I ain't got around yet to tradin' on my wife's looks," he rumbled gruffly.

"Right you are. The only trouble is that you, both of you, are fifty years behind the times. You're old American. How you ever got here in the thick of modern conditions is a miracle. You're Rip Van Winkles. Who ever heard, in these degenerate times, of a young man and woman of the city putting their blankets on their backs and starting out in search of land? Why, it's the old Argonaut spirit. You're as like as peas in a pod to those who yoked their oxen and held west to the lands beyond the sunset. I'll wager your fathers and mothers, or grandfathers and grandmothers, were that very stock."

Saxon's eyes were glistening, and Billy's were friendly once more. Both nodded their heads.

"I'm of the old stock myself," Mrs. Mortimer went on proudly. "My grandmother was one of the survivors of the Donner Party. My grandfather, Jason Whitney, came around the Horn and took part in the raising of the Bear Flag at Sonoma. He was at Monterey when John Marshall discovered gold in Sutter's mill-race. One of the streets in San Francisco is named after him."

"I know it," Billy put in. "Whitney Street. It's near Russian Hill. Saxon's mother walked across the Plains."

"And Billy's grandfather and grandmother were massacred by the Indians," Saxon contributed. "His father was a little baby boy, and lived with the Indians, until captured by the whites. He didn't even know his name and was adopted by a Mr. Roberts."

"Why, you two dear children, we're almost like relatives," Mrs. Mortimer beamed. "It's a breath of old times, alas! all forgotten in these fly-away days. I am especially interested, because I've catalogued and read everything covering those times. You—" she indicated Billy, "you are historical, or at least your father is. I remember about him. The whole thing is in Bancroft's History. It was the Modoc Indians. There were eighteen wagons. Your father was the only survivor, a mere baby at the time, with no knowledge of what happened. He was adopted by the leader of the whites."

"That's right," said Billy. "It was the Modocs. His train must have ben bound for Oregon. It was all wiped out. I wonder if you know anything about Saxon's mother. She used to write poetry in the early days."

"Was any of it printed?"

"Yes," Saxon answered. "In the old San Jose papers."

"And do you know any of it?"

"Yes, there's one beginning:

"'Sweet as the wind-lute's airy strains Your gentle muse has learned to sing, And California's boundless plains Prolong the soft notes echoing.'"

"It sounds familiar," Mrs. Mortimer said, pondering.

"And there was another I remember that began:

"'I've stolen away from the crowd in the groves, Where the nude statues stand, and the leaves point and shiver,'—

"And it run on like that. I don't understand it all. It was written to my father—"

"A love poem!" Mrs. Mortimer broke in. "I remember it. Wait a minute.... Da-da-dah, da-da-dah, da-da-dah, da-da—STANDS—

"'In the spray of a fountain, whose seed-amethysts Tremble lightly a moment on bosom and hands, Then drip in their basin from bosom and wrists.'

"I've never forgotten the drip of the seed-amethysts, though I don't remember your mother's name."

"It was Daisy—" Saxon began.

"No; Dayelle," Mrs. Mortimer corrected with quickening recollection.

"Oh, but nobody called her that."

"But she signed it that way. What is the rest?"

"Daisy Wiley Brown."

Mrs. Mortimer went to the bookshelves and quickly returned with a large, soberly-bound volume.

"It's 'The Story of the Files,'" she explained. "Among other things, all the good fugitive verse was gathered here from the old newspaper files." Her eyes running down the index suddenly stopped. "I was right. Dayelle Wiley Brown. There it is. Ten of her poems, too: 'The Viking's Quest'; 'Days of Gold'; 'Constancy'; 'The Caballero'; 'Graves at Little Meadow'—"

"We fought off the Indians there," Saxon interrupted in her excitement. "And mother, who was only a little girl, went out and got water for the wounded. And the Indians wouldn't shoot at her. Everybody said it was a miracle." She sprang out of Billy's arms, reaching for the book and crying: "Oh, let me see it! Let me see it! It's all new to me. I don't know these poems. Can I copy them? I'll learn them by heart. Just to think, my mother's!"

Mrs. Mortimer's glasses required repolishing; and for half an hour she and Billy remained silent while Saxon devoured her mother's lines. At the end, staring at the book which she had closed on her finger, she could only repeat in wondering awe:

"And I never knew, I never knew."

But during that half hour Mrs. Mortimer's mind had not been idle. A little later, she broached her plan. She believed in intensive dairying as well as intensive farming, and intended, as soon as the lease expired, to establish a Jersey dairy on the other ten acres. This, like everything she had done, would be model, and it meant that she would require more help. Billy and Saxon were just the two. By next summer she could have them installed in the cottage she intended building. In the meantime she could arrange, one way and another, to get work for Billy through the winter. She would guarantee this work, and she knew a small house they could rent just at the end of the car-line. Under her supervision Billy could take charge from the very beginning of the building. In this way they would be earning money, preparing themselves for independent farming life, and have opportunity to look about them.

But her persuasions were in vain. In the end Saxon succinctly epitomized their point of view.

"We can't stop at the first place, even if it is as beautiful and kind as yours and as nice as this valley is. We don't even know what we want. We've got to go farther, and see all kinds of places and all kinds of ways, in order to find out. We're not in a hurry to make up our minds. We want to make, oh, so very sure! And besides...." She hesitated. "Besides, we don't like altogether flat land. Billy wants some hills in his. And so do I."

When they were ready to leave Mrs. Mortimer offered to present Saxon with "The Story of the Files"; but Saxon shook her head and got some money from Billy.

"It says it costs two dollars," she said. "Will you buy me one, and keep it till we get settled? Then I'll write, and you can send it to me."

"Oh, you Americans," Mrs. Mortimer chided, accepting the money. "But you must promise to write from time to time before you're settled."

She saw them to the county road.

"You are brave young things," she said at parting. "I only wish I were going with you, my pack upon my back. You're perfectly glorious, the pair of you. If ever I can do anything for you, just let me know. You're bound to succeed, and I want a hand in it myself. Let me know how that government land turns out, though I warn you I haven't much faith in its feasibility. It's sure to be too far away from markets."

She shook hands with Billy. Saxon she caught into her arms and kissed.

"Be brave," she said, with low earnestness, in Saxon's ear. "You'll win. You are starting with the right ideas. And you were right not to accept my proposition. But remember, it, or better, will always be open to you. You're young yet, both of you. Don't be in a hurry. Any time you stop anywhere for a while, let me know, and I'll mail you heaps of agricultural reports and farm publications. Good-bye. Heaps and heaps and heaps of luck."

CHAPTER IV

Billy sat motionless on the edge of the bed in their little room in San Jose that night, a musing expression in his eyes.

"Well," he remarked at last, with a long-drawn breath, "all I've got to say is there's some pretty nice people in this world after all. Take Mrs. Mortimer. Now she's the real goods—regular old American."

"A fine, educated lady," Saxon agreed, "and not a bit ashamed to work at farming herself. And she made it go, too."

"On twenty acres—no, ten; and paid for 'em, an' all improvements, an' supported herself, four hired men, a Swede woman an' daughter, an' her own nephew. It gets me. Ten acres! Why, my father never talked less'n one hundred an' sixty acres. Even your brother Tom still talks in quarter sections.—An' she was only a woman, too. We was lucky in meetin' her."

"Wasn't it an adventure!" Saxon cried. "That's what comes of traveling. You never know what's going to happen next. It jumped right out at us, just when we were tired and wondering how much farther to San Jose. We weren't expecting it at all. And she didn't treat us as if we were tramping. And that house—so clean and beautiful. You could eat off the floor. I never dreamed of anything so sweet and lovely as the inside of that house."

"It smelt good," Billy supplied.

"That's the very thing. It's what the women's pages call atmosphere. I didn't know what they meant before. That house has beautiful, sweet atmosphere—"

"Like all your nice underthings," said Billy.

"And that's the next step after keeping your body sweet and clean and beautiful. It's to have your house sweet and clean and beautiful."

"But it can't be a rented one, Saxon. You've got to own it. Landlords don't build houses like that. Just the same, one thing stuck out plain: that house was not expensive. It wasn't the cost. It was the way. The wood was ordinary wood you can buy in any lumber yard. Why, our house on Pine street was made out of the same kind of wood. But the way it was made was different. I can't explain, but you can see what I'm drivin' at."

Saxon, revisioning the little bungalow they had just left, repeated absently: "That's it—the way."

The next morning they were early afoot, seeking through the suburbs of San Jose the road to San Juan and Monterey. Saxon's limp had increased. Beginning with a burst blister, her heel was skinning rapidly. Billy remembered his father's talks about care of the feet, and stopped at a butcher shop to buy five cents' worth of mutton tallow.

"That's the stuff," he told Saxon. "Clean foot-gear and the feet well greased. We'll put some on as soon as we're clear of town. An' we might as well go easy for a couple of days. Now, if I could get a little work so as you could rest up several days it'd be just the thing. I 'll keep my eye peeled."

Almost on the outskirts of town he left Saxon on the county road and went up a long driveway to what appeared a large farm. He came back beaming.

"It's all hunkydory," he called as he approached. "We'll just go down to that clump of trees by the creek an' pitch camp. I start work in the mornin', two dollars a day an' board myself. It'd been a dollar an' a half if he furnished the board. I told 'm I liked the other way best, an' that I had my camp with me. The weather's fine, an' we can make out a few days till your foot's in shape. Come on. We'll pitch a regular, decent camp."

"How did you get the job," Saxon asked, as they cast about, determining their camp-site.

"Wait till we get fixed an' I'll tell you all about it. It was a dream, a cinch."

Not until the bed was spread, the fire built, and a pot of beans boiling did Billy throw down the last armful of wood and begin.

"In the first place, Benson's no old-fashioned geezer. You wouldn't think he was a farmer to look at 'm. He's up to date, sharp as tacks, talks an' acts like a business man. I could see that, just by lookin' at his place, before I seen HIM. He took about fifteen seconds to size me up.

"'Can you plow?' says he.

"'Sure thing,' I told 'm.

"'Know horses?'

"'I was hatched in a box-stall,' says I.

"An' just then—you remember that four-horse load of machinery that come in after me?—just then it drove up.

"'How about four horses?' he asks, casual-like.

"'Right to home. I can drive 'm to a plow, a sewin' machine, or a merry-go-round.'

"'Jump up an' take them lines, then,' he says, quick an' sharp, not wastin' seconds. 'See that shed. Go 'round the barn to the right an' back in for unloadin'.'

"An' right here I wanta tell you it was some nifty drivin' he was askin'. I could see by the tracks the wagons'd all ben goin' around the barn to the left. What he was askin' was too close work for comfort—a double turn, like an S, between a corner of a paddock an' around the corner of the barn to the last swing. An', to eat into the little room there was, there was piles of manure just thrown outa the barn an' not hauled away yet. But I wasn't lettin' on nothin'. The driver gave me the lines, an' I could see he was grinnin', sure I'd make a mess of it. I bet he couldn't a-done it himself. I never let on, an away we went, me not even knowin' the horses—but, say, if you'd seen me throw them leaders clean to the top of the manure till the nigh horse was scrapin' the side of the barn to make it, an' the off hind hub was cuttin' the corner post of the paddock to miss by six inches. It was the only way. An' them horses was sure beauts. The leaders slacked back an' darn near sat down on their singletrees when I threw the back into the wheelers an' slammed on the brake an' stopped on the very precise spot.

"'You'll do,' Benson says. 'That was good work.'

"'Aw, shucks,' I says, indifferent as hell. 'Gimme something real hard.'

"He smiles an' understands.

"'You done that well,' he says. 'An' I'm particular about who handles my horses. The road ain't no place for you. You must be a good man gone wrong. Just the same you can plow with my horses, startin' in to-morrow mornin'.'

"Which shows how wise he wasn't. I hadn't showed I could plow."

When Saxon had served the beans, and Billy the coffee, she stood still a moment and surveyed the spread meal on the blankets—the canister of sugar, the condensed milk tin, the sliced corned beef, the lettuce salad and sliced tomatoes, the slices of fresh French bread, and the steaming plates of beans and mugs of coffee.

"What a difference from last night!" Saxon exclaimed, clapping her hands. "It's like an adventure out of a book. Oh, that boy I went fishing with! Think of that beautiful table and that beautiful house last night, and then look at this. Why, we could have lived a thousand years on end in Oakland and never met a woman like Mrs. Mortimer nor dreamed a house like hers existed. And, Billy, just to think, we've only just started."

Billy worked for three days, and while insisting that he was doing very well, he freely admitted that there was more in plowing than he had thought. Saxon experienced quiet satisfaction when she learned he was enjoying it.

"I never thought I'd like plowin'—much," he observed. "But it's fine. It's good for the leg-muscles, too. They don't get exercise enough in teamin'. If ever I trained for another fight, you bet I'd take a whack at plowin'. An', you know, the ground has a regular good smell to it, a-turnin' over an' turnin' over. Gosh, it's good enough to eat, that smell. An' it just goes on, turnin' up an' over, fresh an' thick an' good, all day long. An' the horses are Joe-dandies. They know their business as well as a man. That's one thing, Benson ain't got a scrub horse on the place."

The last day Billy worked, the sky clouded over, the air grew damp, a strong wind began to blow from the southeast, and all the signs were present of the first winter rain. Billy came back in the evening with a small roll of old canvas he had borrowed, which he proceeded to arrange over their bed on a framework so as to shed rain. Several times he complained about the little finger of his left hand. It had been bothering him all day he told Saxon, for several days slightly, in fact, and it was as tender as a boil—most likely a splinter, but he had been unable to locate it.

He went ahead with storm preparations, elevating the bed on old boards which he lugged from a disused barn falling to decay on the opposite bank of the creek. Upon the boards he heaped dry leaves for a mattress. He concluded by reinforcing the canvas with additional guys of odd pieces of rope and bailing-wire.

When the first splashes of rain arrived Saxon was delighted. Billy betrayed little interest. His finger was hurting too much, he said. Neither he nor Saxon could make anything of it, and both scoffed at the idea of a felon.

"It might be a run-around," Saxon hazarded.

"What's that?"

"I don't know. I remember Mrs. Cady had one once, but I was too small. It was the little finger, too. She poulticed it, I think. And I remember she dressed it with some kind of salve. It got awful bad, and finished by her losing the nail. After that it got well quick, and a new nail grew out. Suppose I make a hot bread poultice for yours."

Billy declined, being of the opinion that it would be better in the morning. Saxon was troubled, and as she dozed off she knew that he was lying restlessly wide awake. A few minutes afterward, roused by a heavy blast of wind and rain on the canvas, she heard Billy softly groaning. She raised herself on her elbow and with her free hand, in the way she knew, manipulating his forehead and the surfaces around his eyes, soothed him off to sleep.

Again she slept. And again she was aroused, this time not by the storm, but by Billy. She could not see, but by feeling she ascertained his strange position.

He was outside the blankets and on his knees, his forehead resting on the boards, his shoulders writhing with suppressed anguish.

"She's pulsin' to beat the band," he said, when she spoke. "It's worsen a thousand toothaches. But it ain't nothin'... if only the canvas don't blow down. Think what our folks had to stand," he gritted out between groans. "Why, my father was out in the mountains, an' the man with 'm got mauled by a grizzly—clean clawed to the bones all over. An' they was outa grub an' had to travel. Two times outa three, when my father put 'm on the horse, he'd faint away. Had to be tied on. An' that lasted five weeks, an' HE pulled through. Then there was Jack Quigley. He blowed off his whole right hand with the burstin' of his shotgun, an' the huntin' dog pup he had with 'm ate up three of the fingers. An' he was all alone in the marsh, an'—"

But Saxon heard no more of the adventures of Jack Quigley. A terrific blast of wind parted several of the guys, collapsed the framework, and for a moment buried them under the canvas. The next moment canvas, framework, and trailing guys were whisked away into the darkness, and Saxon and Billy were deluged with rain.

"Only one thing to do," he yelled in her ear. "—Gather up the things an' get into that old barn."

They accomplished this in the drenching darkness, making two trips across the stepping stones of the shallow creek and soaking themselves to the knees. The old barn leaked like a sieve, but they managed to find a dry space on which to spread their anything but dry bedding. Billy's pain was heart-rending to Saxon. An hour was required to subdue him to a doze, and only by continuously stroking his forehead could she keep him asleep. Shivering and miserable, she accepted a night of wakefulness gladly with the knowledge that she kept him from knowing the worst of his pain.

At the time when she had decided it must be past midnight, there was an interruption. From the open doorway came a flash of electric light, like a tiny searchlight, which quested about the barn and came to rest on her and Billy. From the source of light a harsh voice said:

"Ah! ha! I've got you! Come out of that!"

Billy sat up, his eyes dazzled by the light. The voice behind the light was approaching and reiterating its demand that they come out of that.

"What's up?" Billy asked.

"Me," was the answer; "an' wide awake, you bet."

The voice was now beside them, scarcely a yard away, yet they could see nothing on account of the light, which was intermittent, frequently going out for an instant as the operator's thumb tired on the switch.

"Come on, get a move on," the voice went on. "Roll up your blankets an' trot along. I want you."

"Who in hell are you?" Billy demanded.

"I'm the constable. Come on."

"Well, what do you want?"

"You, of course, the pair of you."

"What for?"

"Vagrancy. Now hustle. I ain't goin' to loaf here all night."

"Aw, chase yourself," Billy advised. "I ain't a vag. I'm a workingman."

"Maybe you are an' maybe you ain't," said the constable; "but you can tell all that to Judge Neusbaumer in the mornin'."

"Why you... you stinkin', dirty cur, you think you're goin' to pull me," Billy began. "Turn the light on yourself. I want to see what kind of an ugly mug you got. Pull me, eh? Pull me? For two cents I'd get up there an' beat you to a jelly, you—"

"No, no, Billy," Saxon pleaded. "Don't make trouble. It would mean jail."

"That's right," the constable approved, "listen to your woman."

"She's my wife, an' see you speak of her as such," Billy warned. "Now get out, if you know what's good for yourself."

"I've seen your kind before," the constable retorted. "An' I've got my little persuader with me. Take a squint."

The shaft of light shifted, and out of the darkness, illuminated with ghastly brilliance, they saw thrust a hand holding a revolver. This hand seemed a thing apart, self-existent, with no corporeal attachment, and it appeared and disappeared like an apparition as the thumb-pressure wavered on the switch. One moment they were staring at the hand and revolver, the next moment at impenetrable darkness, and the next moment again at the hand and revolver.

"Now, I guess you'll come," the constable gloated.

"You got another guess comin'," Billy began.

But at that moment the light went out. They heard a quick movement on the officer's part and the thud of the light-stick on the ground. Both Billy and the constable fumbled for it, but Billy found it and flashed it on the other. They saw a gray-bearded man clad in streaming oilskins. He was an old man, and reminded Saxon of the sort she had been used to see in Grand Army processions on Decoration Day.

"Give me that stick," he bullied.

Billy sneered a refusal.

"Then I'll put a hole through you, by criminy."

He leveled the revolver directly at Billy, whose thumb on the switch did not waver, and they could see the gleaming bullet-tips in the chambers of the cylinder.

"Why, you whiskery old skunk, you ain't got the grit to shoot sour apples," was Billy's answer. "I know your kind—brave as lions when it comes to pullin' miserable, broken-spirited bindle stiffs, but as leery as a yellow dog when you face a man. Pull that trigger! Why, you pusillanimous piece of dirt, you'd run with your tail between your legs if I said boo!"

Suiting action to the word, Billy let out an explosive "BOO!" and Saxon giggled involuntarily at the startle it caused in the constable.

"I'll give you a last chance," the latter grated through his teeth. "Turn over that light-stick an' come along peaceable, or I'll lay you out."

Saxon was frightened for Billy's sake, and yet only half frightened. She had a faith that the man dared not fire, and she felt the old familiar thrills of admiration for Billy's courage. She could not see his face, but she knew in all certitude that it was bleak and passionless in the terrifying way she had seen it when he fought the three Irishmen.

"You ain't the first man I killed," the constable threatened. "I'm an old soldier, an' I ain't squeamish over blood—"

"And you ought to be ashamed of yourself," Saxon broke in, "trying to shame and disgrace peaceable people who've done no wrong."

"You've done wrong sleepin' here," was his vindication. "This ain't your property. It's agin the law. An' folks that go agin the law go to jail, as the two of you'll go. I've sent many a tramp up for thirty days for sleepin' in this very shack. Why, it's a regular trap for 'em. I got a good glimpse of your faces an' could see you was tough characters." He turned on Billy. "I've fooled enough with you. Are you goin' to give in an' come peaceable?"

"I'm goin' to tell you a couple of things, old hoss," Billy answered. "Number one: you ain't goin' to pull us. Number two: we're goin' to sleep the night out here."

"Gimme that light-stick," the constable demanded peremptorily.

"G'wan, Whiskers. You're standin' on your foot. Beat it. Pull your freight. As for your torch you'll find it outside in the mud."

Billy shifted the light until it illuminated the doorway, and then threw the stick as he would pitch a baseball. They were now in total darkness, and they could hear the intruder gritting his teeth in rage.

"Now start your shootin' an' see what'll happen to you," Billy advised menacingly.

Saxon felt for Billy's hand and squeezed it proudly. The constable grumbled some threat.

"What's that?" Billy demanded sharply. "Ain't you gone yet? Now listen to me, Whiskers. I've put up with all your shenanigan I'm goin' to. Now get out or I'll throw you out. An' if you come monkeyin' around here again you'll get yours. Now get!"

So great was the roar of the storm that they could hear nothing. Billy rolled a cigarette. When he lighted it, they saw the barn was empty. Billy chuckled.

"Say, I was so mad I clean forgot my run-around. It's only just beginnin' to tune up again."

Saxon made him lie down and receive her soothing ministrations.

"There is no use moving till morning," she said. "Then, just as soon as it's light, we'll catch a car into San Jose, rent a room, get a hot breakfast, and go to a drug store for the proper stuff for poulticing or whatever treatment's needed."

"But Benson," Billy demurred.

"I'll telephone him from town. It will only cost five cents. I saw he had a wire. And you couldn't plow on account of the rain, even if your finger was well. Besides, we'll both be mending together. My heel will be all right by the time it clears up and we can start traveling."

CHAPTER V

Early on Monday morning, three days later, Saxon and Billy took an electric car to the end of the line, and started a second time for San Juan. Puddles were standing in the road, but the sun shone from a blue sky, and everywhere, on the ground, was a faint hint of budding green. At Benson's Saxon waited while Billy went in to get his six dollars for the three days' plowing.

"Kicked like a steer because I was quittin'," he told her when he came back. "He wouldn't listen at first. Said he'd put me to drivin' in a few days, an' that there wasn't enough good four-horse men to let one go easily."

"And what did you say?"

"Oh, I just told 'm I had to be movin' along. An' when he tried to argue I told 'm my wife was with me, an' she was blamed anxious to get along."

"But so are you, Billy."

"Sure, Pete; but just the same I wasn't as keen as you. Doggone it, I was gettin' to like that plowin'. I'll never be scairt to ask for a job at it again. I've got to where I savvy the burro, an' you bet I can plow against most of 'm right now."

An hour afterward, with a good three miles to their credit, they edged to the side of the road at the sound of an automobile behind them. But the machine did not pass. Benson was alone in it, and he came to a stop alongside.

"Where are you bound?" he inquired of Billy, with a quick, measuring glance at Saxon.

"Monterey—if you're goin' that far," Billy answered with a chuckle.

"I can give you a lift as far as Watsonville. It would take you several days on shank's mare with those loads. Climb in." He addressed Saxon directly. "Do you want to ride in front?"

Saxon glanced to Billy.

"Go on," he approved. "It's fine in front.—This is my wife, Mr. Benson— Mrs. Roberts."

"Oh, ho, so you're the one that took your husband away from me," Benson accused good humoredly, as he tucked the robe around her.

Saxon shouldered the responsibility and became absorbed in watching him start the car.

"I'd be a mighty poor farmer if I owned no more land than you'd plowed before you came to me," Benson, with a twinkling eye, jerked over his shoulder to Billy.

"I'd never had my hands on a plow but once before," Billy confessed. "But a fellow has to learn some time."

"At two dollars a day?"

"If he can get some alfalfa artist to put up for it," Billy met him complacently.

Benson laughed heartily.

"You're a quick learner," he complimented. "I could see that you and plows weren't on speaking acquaintance. But you took hold right. There isn't one man in ten I could hire off the county road that could do as well as you were doing on the third day. But your big asset is that you know horses. It was half a joke when I told you to take the lines that morning. You're a trained horseman and a born horseman as well."

"He's very gentle with horses," Saxon said.

"But there's more than that to it," Benson took her up. "Your husband's got the WAY with him. It's hard to explain. But that's what it is—the WAY. It's an instinct almost. Kindness is necessary. But GRIP is more so. Your husband grips his horses. Take the test I gave him with the four-horse load. It was too complicated and severe. Kindness couldn't have done it. It took grip. I could see it the moment he started. There wasn't any doubt in his mind. There wasn't any doubt in the horses. They got the feel of him. They just knew the thing was going to be done and that it was up to them to do it. They didn't have any fear, but just the same they knew the boss was in the seat. When he took hold of those lines, he took hold of the horses. He gripped them, don't you see. He picked them up and put them where he wanted them, swung them up and down and right and left, made them pull, and slack, and back—and they knew everything was going to come out right. Oh, horses may be stupid, but they're not altogether fools. They know when the proper horseman has hold of them, though how they know it so quickly is beyond me."

Benson paused, half vexed at his volubility, and gazed keenly at Saxon to see if she had followed him. What he saw in her face and eyes satisfied him, and he added, with a short laugh:

"Horseflesh is a hobby of mine. Don't think otherwise because I am running a stink engine. I'd rather be streaking along here behind a pair of fast-steppers. But I'd lose time on them, and, worse than that, I'd be too anxious about them all the time. As for this thing, why, it has no nerves, no delicate joints nor tendons; it's a case of let her rip."

The miles flew past and Saxon was soon deep in talk with her host. Here again, she discerned immediately, was a type of the new farmer. The knowledge she had picked up enabled her to talk to advantage, and when Benson talked she was amazed that she could understand so much. In response to his direct querying, she told him her and Billy's plans, sketching the Oakland life vaguely, and dwelling on their future intentions.

Almost as in a dream, when they passed the nurseries at Morgan Hill, she learned they had come twenty miles, and realized that it was a longer stretch than they had planned to walk that day. And still the machine hummed on, eating up the distance as ever it flashed into view.

"I wondered what so good a man as your husband was doing on the road," Benson told her.

"Yes," she smiled. "He said you said he must be a good man gone wrong."

"But you see, I didn't know about YOU. Now I understand. Though I must say it's extraordinary in these days for a young couple like you to pack your blankets in search of land. And, before I forget it, I want to tell you one thing." He turned to Billy. "I am just telling your wife that there's an all-the-year job waiting for you on my ranch. And there's a tight little cottage of three rooms the two of you can housekeep in. Don't forget."

Among other things Saxon discovered that Benson had gone through the College of Agriculture at the University of California—a branch of learning she had not known existed. He gave her small hope in her search for government land.

"The only government land left," he informed her, "is what is not good enough to take up for one reason or another. If it's good land down there where you're going, then the market is inaccessible. I know no railroads tap in there."

"Wait till we strike Pajaro Valley," he said, when they had passed Gilroy and were booming on toward Sargent's. "I'll show you what can be done with the soil—and not by cow-college graduates but by uneducated foreigners that the high and mighty American has always sneered at. I'll show you. It's one of the most wonderful demonstrations in the state."

At Sargent's he left them in the machine a few minutes while he transacted business.

"Whew! It beats hikin'," Billy said. "The day's young yet and when he drops us we'll be fresh for a few miles on our own. Just the same, when we get settled an' well off, I guess I'll stick by horses. They'll always be good enough for me."

"A machine's only good to get somewhere in a hurry," Saxon agreed. "Of course, if we got very, very rich—"

"Say, Saxon," Billy broke in, suddenly struck with an idea. "I've learned one thing. I ain't afraid any more of not gettin' work in the country. I was at first, but I didn't tell you. Just the same I was dead leery when we pulled out on the San Leandro pike. An' here, already, is two places open—Mrs. Mortimer's an' Benson's; an' steady jobs, too. Yep, a man can get work in the country."

"Ah," Saxon amended, with a proud little smile, "you haven't said it right. Any GOOD man can get work in the country. The big farmers don't hire men out of charity."

"Sure; they ain't in it for their health," he grinned.

"And they jump at you. That's because you are a good man. They can see it with half an eye. Why, Billy, take all the working tramps we've met on the road already. There wasn't one to compare with you. I looked them over. They're all weak—weak in their bodies, weak in their heads, weak both ways."

"Yep, they are a pretty measly bunch," Billy admitted modestly.

"It's the wrong time of the year to see Pajaro Valley," Benson said, when he again sat beside Saxon and Sargent's was a thing of the past. "Just the same, it's worth seeing any time. Think of it—twelve thousand acres of apples! Do you know what they call Pajaro Valley now? New Dalmatia. We're being squeezed out. We Yankees thought we were smart. Well, the Dalmatians came along and showed they were smarter. They were miserable immigrants—poorer than Job's turkey. First, they worked at day's labor in the fruit harvest. Next they began, in a small way, buying the apples on the trees. The more money they made the bigger became their deals. Pretty soon they were renting the orchards on long leases. And now, they are beginning to buy the land. It won't be long before they own the whole valley, and the last American will be gone.

"Oh, our smart Yankees! Why, those first ragged Slavs in their first little deals with us only made something like two and three thousand per cent. profits. And now they're satisfied to make a hundred per cent. It's a calamity if their profits sink to twenty-five or fifty per cent."

"It's like San Leandro," Saxon said. "The original owners of the land are about all gone already. It's intensive cultivation." She liked that phrase. "It isn't a case of having a lot of acres, but of how much they can get out of one acre."

"Yes, and more than that," Benson answered, nodding his head emphatically. "Lots of them, like Luke Scurich, are in it on a large scale. Several of them are worth a quarter of a million already. I know ten of them who will average one hundred and fifty thousand each. They have a WAY with apples. It's almost a gift. They KNOW trees in much the same way your husband knows horses. Each tree is just as much an individual to them as a horse is to me. They know each tree, its whole history, everything that ever happened to it, its every idiosyncrasy. They have their fingers on its pulse. They can tell if it's feeling as well to-day as it felt yesterday. And if it isn't, they know why and proceed to remedy matters for it. They can look at a tree in bloom and tell how many boxes of apples it will pack, and not only that—they'll know what the quality and grades of those apples are going to be. Why, they know each individual apple, and they pick it tenderly, with love, never hurting it, and pack it and ship it tenderly and with love, and when it arrives at market, it isn't bruised nor rotten, and it fetches top price.

"Yes, it's more than intensive. These Adriatic Slavs are long-headed in business. Not only can they grow apples, but they can sell apples. No market? What does it matter? Make a market. That's their way, while our kind let the crops rot knee-deep under the trees. Look at Peter Mengol. Every year he goes to England, and he takes a hundred carloads of yellow Newton pippins with him. Why, those Dalmatians are showing Pajaro apples on the South African market right now, and coining money out of it hand over fist."

"What do they do with all the money?" Saxon queried.

"Buy the Americans of Pajaro Valley out, of course, as they are already doing."

"And then?" she questioned.

Benson looked at her quickly.

"Then they'll start buying the Americans out of some other valley. And the Americans will spend the money and by the second generation start rotting in the cities, as you and your husband would have rotted if you hadn't got out."

Saxon could not repress a shudder.—As Mary had rotted, she thought; as Bert and all the rest had rotted; as Tom and all the rest were rotting.

"Oh, it's a great country," Benson was continuing. "But we're not a great people. Kipling is right. We're crowded out and sitting on the stoop. And the worst of it is there's no reason we shouldn't know better. We're teaching it in all our agricultural colleges, experiment stations, and demonstration trains. But the people won't take hold, and the immigrant, who has learned in a hard school, beats them out. Why, after I graduated, and before my father died—

he was of the old school and laughed at what he called my theories—I traveled for a couple of years. I wanted to see how the old countries farmed. Oh, I saw.

"We'll soon enter the valley. You bet I saw. First thing, in Japan, the terraced hillsides. Take a hill so steep you couldn't drive a horse up it. No bother to them. They terraced it—a stone wall, and good masonry, six feet high, a level terrace six feet wide; up and up, walls and terraces, the same thing all the way, straight into the air, walls upon walls, terraces upon terraces, until I've seen ten-foot walls built to make three-foot terraces, and twenty-foot walls for four or five feet of soil they could grow things on. And that soil, packed up the mountainsides in baskets on their backs!

"Same thing everywhere I went, in Greece, in Ireland, in Dalmatia—I went there, too. They went around and gathered every bit of soil they could find, gleaned it and even stole it by the shovelful or handful, and carried it up the mountains on their backs and built farms—BUILT them, MADE them, on the naked rock. Why, in France, I've seen hill peasants mining their stream-beds for soil as our fathers mined the streams of California for gold. Only our gold's gone, and the peasants' soil remains, turning over and over, doing something, growing something, all the time. Now, I guess I'll hush."

"My God!" Billy muttered in awe-stricken tones. "Our folks never done that. No wonder they lost out."

"There's the valley now," Benson said. "Look at those trees! Look at those hillsides! That's New Dalmatia. Look at it! An apple paradise! Look at that soil! Look at the way it's worked!"

It was not a large valley that Saxon saw. But everywhere, across the flat-lands and up the low rolling hills, the industry of the Dalmatians was evident. As she looked she listened to Benson.

"Do you know what the old settlers did with this beautiful soil? Planted the flats in grain and pastured cattle on the hills. And now twelve thousand acres of it are in apples. It's a regular show place for the Eastern guests at Del Monte, who run out here in their machines to see the trees in bloom or fruit. Take Matteo Lettunich—he's one of the originals. Entered through Castle Garden and became a dish-washer. When he laid eyes on this valley he knew it was his Klondike. To-day he leases seven hundred acres and owns a hundred and thirty of his own—the finest orchard in the valley, and he packs from forty to fifty thousand boxes of export apples from it every year. And he won't let a soul but a Dalmatian pick a single apple of all those apples. One day, in a banter, I asked him what he'd sell his hundred and thirty acres for. He answered seriously. He told me what it had netted him, year by year, and struck an average. He told me to calculate the principal from that at six per cent. I did. It came to over three thousand dollars an acre.''

"What are all the Chinks doin' in the Valley?" Billy asked. "Growin' apples, too?"

Benson shook his head.

"But that's another point where we Americans lose out. There isn't anything wasted in this valley, not a core nor a paring; and it isn't the Americans who do the saving. There are fifty-seven apple-evaporating furnaces, to say nothing of the apple canneries and cider and vinegar factories. And Mr. John Chinaman owns them. They ship fifteen thousand barrels of cider and vinegar each year."

"It was our folks that made this country," Billy reflected. "Fought for it, opened it up, did everything—"

"But develop it," Benson caught him up. "We did our best to destroy it, as we destroyed the soil of New England." He waved his hand, indicating some place beyond the hills. "Salinas lies over that way. If you went through there you'd think you were in Japan. And more than one fat little fruit valley in California has been taken over by the Japanese. Their method is somewhat different from the Dalmatians'. First they drift in fruit picking at day's wages. They give better satisfaction than the American fruit-pickers, too, and the Yankee grower is glad to get them. Next, as they get stronger, they form in Japanese unions and proceed to run the American labor out. Still the fruit-growers are satisfied. The next step is when the Japs won't pick. The American labor is gone. The fruit-grower is helpless. The crop perishes. Then in step the Jap labor bosses. They're the masters already. They contract for the crop. The fruit-growers are at their mercy, you see. Pretty soon the Japs are running the valley. The fruit-growers have become absentee landlords and are busy learning higher standards of living in the cities or making trips to Europe. Remains only one more step. The Japs buy them out. They've got to sell, for the Japs control the labor market and could bankrupt them at will."

"But if this goes on, what is left for us?" asked Saxon.

"What is happening. Those of us who haven't anything rot in the cities. Those of us who have land, sell it and go to the cities. Some become larger capitalists; some go into the professions; the rest spend the money and start rotting when it's gone, and if it lasts their life-time their children do the rotting for them."

Their long ride was soon over, and at parting Benson reminded Billy of the steady job that awaited him any time he gave the word.

"I guess we'll take a peep at that government land first," Billy answered. "Don't know what we'll settle down to, but there's one thing sure we won't tackle."

"What's that?"

"Start in apple-growin' at three thousan' dollars an acre."

Billy and Saxon, their packs upon the backs, trudged along a hundred yards. He was the first to break silence.

"An' I tell you another thing, Saxon. We'll never be goin' around smellin' out an' swipin' bits of soil an' carryin' it up a hill in a basket. The United States is big yet. I don't care what Benson or any of 'em says, the United States ain't played out. There's millions of acres untouched an' waitin', an' it's up to us to find 'em."

"And I'll tell you one thing," Saxon said. "We're getting an education. Tom was raised on a ranch, yet he doesn't know right now as much about farming conditions as we do. And I'll tell you another thing. The more I think of it, the more it seems we are going to be disappointed about that government land."

"Ain't no use believin' what everybody tells you," he protested.

"Oh, it isn't that. It's what I think. I leave it to you. If this land around here is worth three thousand an acre, why is it that government land, if it's any good, is waiting there, only a short way off, to be taken for the asking."

Billy pondered this for a quarter of a mile, but could come to no conclusion. At last he cleared his throat and remarked:

"Well, we can wait till we see it first, can't we?"

"All right," Saxon agreed. "We'll wait till we see it."

CHAPTER VI

They had taken the direct county road across the hills from Monterey, instead of the Seventeen Mile Drive around by the coast, so that Carmel Bay came upon them without any fore-glimmerings of its beauty. Dropping down through the pungent pines, they passed woods-embowered cottages, quaint and rustic, of artists and writers, and went on across wind-blown rolling sandhills held to place by sturdy lupine and nodding with pale California poppies. Saxon screamed in sudden wonder of delight, then caught her breath and gazed at the amazing peacock-blue of a breaker, shot through with golden sunlight, overfalling in a mile-long sweep and thundering into white ruin of foam on a crescent beach of sand scarcely less white.

How long they stood and watched the stately procession of breakers, rising from out the deep and wind-capped sea to froth and thunder at their feet, Saxon did not know. She was recalled to herself when Billy, laughing, tried to remove the telescope basket from her shoulders.

"You kind of look as though you was goin' to stop a while," he said. "So we might as well get comfortable."

"I never dreamed it, I never dreamed it," she repeated, with passionately clasped hands. "I... I thought the surf at the Cliff House was wonderful, but it gave no idea of this.—Oh! Look! LOOK! Did you ever see such an unspeakable color? And the sunlight flashing right through it! Oh! Oh! Oh!"

At last she was able to take her eyes from the surf and gaze at the sea-horizon of deepest peacock-blue and piled with cloud-masses, at the curve of the beach south to the jagged point of rocks, and at the rugged blue mountains seen across soft low hills, landward, up Carmel Valley.

"Might as well sit down an' take it easy," Billy indulged her. "This is too good to want to run away from all at once."

Saxon assented, but began immediately to unlace her shoes.

"You ain't a-goin' to?" Billy asked in surprised delight, then began unlacing his own.

But before they were ready to run barefooted on the perilous fringe of cream-wet sand where land and ocean met, a new and wonderful thing attracted their attention. Down from the dark pines and across the sandhills ran a man, naked save for narrow trunks. He was smooth and rosy-skinned, cherubic-faced, with a thatch of curly yellow hair, but his body was hugely thewed as a Hercules'.

"Gee!—must be Sandow," Billy muttered low to Saxon.

But she was thinking of the engraving in her mother's scrapbook and of the Vikings on the wet sands of England.

The runner passed them a dozen feet away, crossed the wet sand, never pausing, till the froth wash was to his knees while above him, ten feet at least, upreared a wall of overtopping water. Huge and powerful as his body had seemed, it was now white and fragile in the face of that imminent, great-handed buffet of the sea. Saxon gasped with anxiety, and she stole a look at Billy to note that he was tense with watching.

But the stranger sprang to meet the blow, and, just when it seemed he must be crushed, he dived into the face of the breaker and disappeared. The mighty mass of water fell in thunder on the beach, but beyond appeared a yellow head, one arm out-reaching, and a portion of a shoulder. Only a few strokes was he able to make ere he was compelled to dive through another breaker. This was the battle—to win seaward against the sweep of the shoreward hastening sea. Each time he dived and was lost to view Saxon caught her breath and clenched her hands. Sometimes, after the passage of a breaker, they could not find him, and when they did he would be scores of feet away, flung there like a chip by a smoke-bearded breaker. Often it seemed he must fail and be thrown upon the beach, but at the end of half an hour he was beyond the outer edge of the surf and swimming strong, no longer diving, but topping the waves. Soon he was so far away that only at intervals could they find the speck of him. That, too, vanished, and Saxon and Billy looked at each other, she with amazement at the swimmer's valor, Billy with blue eyes flashing.

"Some swimmer, that boy, some swimmer," he praised. "Nothing chicken-hearted about him.—Say, I only know tank-swimmin', an' bay-swimmin', but now I'm goin' to learn ocean-swimmin'. If I could do that I'd be so proud you couldn't come within forty feet of me. Why, Saxon, honest to God, I'd sooner do what he done than own a thousan' farms. Oh, I can swim, too, I'm tellin' you, like a fish—I swum, one Sunday, from the Narrow Gauge Pier to Sessions' Basin, an' that's miles—but I never seen anything like that guy in the swimmin' line. An' I'm not goin' to leave this beach until he comes back.—All by his lonely out there in a mountain sea, think of it! He's got his nerve all right, all right."

Saxon and Billy ran barefooted up and down the beach, pursuing each other with brandished snakes of seaweed and playing like children for an hour. It was not until they were putting on their shoes that they sighted the yellow head bearing shoreward. Billy was at the edge of the surf to meet him, emerging, not white-skinned as he had entered, but red from the pounding he had received at the hands of the sea.

"You're a wonder, and I just got to hand it to you," Billy greeted him in outspoken admiration.

"It was a big surf to-day," the young man replied, with a nod of acknowledgment.

"It don't happen that you are a fighter I never heard of?" Billy queried, striving to get some inkling of the identity of the physical prodigy.

The other laughed and shook his head, and Billy could not guess that he was an ex-captain of a 'Varsity Eleven, and incidentally the father of a family and the author of many books. He looked Billy over with an eye trained in measuring freshmen aspirants for the gridiron.

"You're some body of a man," he appreciated. "You'd strip with the best of them. Am I right in guessing that you know your way about in the ring?"

Billy nodded. "My name's Roberts."

The swimmer scowled with a futile effort at recollection.

"Bill—Bill Roberts," Billy supplemented.

"Oh, ho!—Not BIG Bill Roberts? Why, I saw you fight, before the earthquake, in the Mechanic's Pavilion. It was a preliminary to Eddie Hanlon and some other fellow. You're a two-handed fighter, I remember that, with an awful wallop, but slow. Yes, I remember, you were slow that night, but you got your man." He put out a wet hand. "My name's Hazard—Jim Hazard."

"An' if you're the football coach that was, a couple of years ago, I've read about you in the papers. Am I right?"

They shook hands heartily, and Saxon was introduced. She felt very small beside the two young giants, and very proud, withal, that she belonged to the race that gave them birth. She could only listen to them talk.

"I'd like to put on the gloves with you every day for half an hour," Hazard said. "You could teach me a lot. Are you going to stay around here?"

"No. We're goin' on down the coast, lookin' for land. Just the same, I could teach you a few, and there's one thing you could teach me—surf swimmin'."

"I'll swap lessons with you any time," Hazard offered. He turned to Saxon. "Why don't you stop in Carmel for a while? It isn't so bad."

"It's beautiful," she acknowledged, with a grateful smile, "but—" She turned and pointed to their packs on the edge of the lupine. "We're on the tramp, and lookin' for government land."

"If you're looking down past the Sur for it, it will keep," he laughed. "Well, I've got to run along and get some clothes on. If you come back this way, look me up. Anybody will tell you where I live. So long."

And, as he had first arrived, he departed, crossing the sandhills on the run.

Billy followed him with admiring eyes.

"Some boy, some boy," he murmured. "Why, Saxon, he's famous. If I've seen his face in the papers once, I've seen it a thousand times. An' he ain't a bit stuck on himself. Just man to man. Say!—I'm beginnin' to have faith in the old stock again."

They turned their backs on the beach and in the tiny main street bought meat, vegetables, and half a dozen eggs. Billy had to drag Saxon away from the window of a fascinating shop where were iridescent pearls of abalone, set and unset.

"Abalones grow here, all along the coast," Billy assured her; "an' I'll get you all you want. Low tide's the time."

"My father had a set of cuff-buttons made of abalone shell," she said. "They were set in pure, soft gold. I haven't thought about them for years, and I wonder who has them now."

They turned south. Everywhere from among the pines peeped the quaint pretty houses of the artist folk, and they were not prepared, where the road dipped to Carmel River, for the building that met their eyes.

"I know what it is," Saxon almost whispered. "It's an old Spanish Mission. It's the Carmel Mission, of course. That's the way the Spaniards came up from Mexico, building missions as they came and converting the Indians."

"Until we chased them out, Spaniards an' Indians, whole kit an' caboodle," Billy observed with calm satisfaction.

"Just the same, it's wonderful," Saxon mused, gazing at the big, half-ruined adobe structure. "There is the Mission Dolores, in San Francisco, but it's smaller than this and not as old."

Hidden from the sea by low hillocks, forsaken by human being and human habitation, the church of sun-baked clay and straw and chalk-rock stood hushed and breathless in the midst of the adobe ruins which once had housed its worshiping thousands. The spirit of the place descended upon Saxon and Billy, and they walked softly, speaking in whispers, almost afraid to go in through the open ports. There was neither priest nor worshiper, yet they found all the evidences of use, by a congregation which Billy judged must be small from the number of the benches. Later they climbed the earthquake-racked belfry, noting the hand-hewn timbers; and in the gallery, discovering the pure quality of their voices, Saxon, trembling at her own temerity, softly sang the opening bars of "Jesus Lover of My Soul." Delighted with the result, she leaned over the railing, gradually increasing her voice to its full strength as she sang:

"Jesus, Lover of my soul, Let me to Thy bosom fly, While the nearer waters roll, While the tempest still is nigh. Hide me, O my Saviour, hide, Till the storm of life is past; Safe into the haven guide And receive my soul at last."

Billy leaned against the ancient wall and loved her with his eyes, and, when she had finished, he murmured, almost in a whisper:

"That was beautiful—just beautiful. An' you ought to a-seen your face when you sang. It was as beautiful as your voice. Ain't it funny?—I never think of religion except when I think of you."

They camped in the willow bottom, cooked dinner, and spent the afternoon on the point of low rocks north of the mouth of the river. They had not intended to spend the afternoon, but found themselves too fascinated to turn away from the breakers bursting upon the rocks and from the many kinds of colorful sea life -- starfish, crabs, mussels, sea anemones, and, once, in a rock-pool, a small devilfish that chilled their blood when it cast the hooded net of its body around the small crabs they tossed to it. As the tide grew lower, they gathered a mess of mussels—huge fellows, five and six inches long and bearded like patriarchs. Then, while Billy wandered in a vain search for abalones, Saxon lay and dabbled in the crystal-clear water of a rock-pool, dipping up handfuls of glistening jewels—ground bits of shell and pebble of flashing rose and blue and green and violet. Billy came back and lay beside her, lazying in the sea-cool sunshine, and together they watched the sun sink into the horizon where the ocean was deepest peacock-blue.

She reached out her hand to Billy's and sighed with sheer repletion of content. It seemed she had never lived such a wonderful day. It was as if all old dreams were coming true. Such beauty of the world she had never guessed in her fondest imagining. Billy pressed her hand tenderly.

"What was you thinkin' of?" he asked, as they arose finally to go.

"Oh, I don't know, Billy. Perhaps that it was better, one day like this, than ten thousand years in Oakland."

CHAPTER VII

They left Carmel River and Carmel Valley behind, and with a rising sun went south across the hills between the mountains and the sea. The road was badly washed and gullied and showed little sign of travel.

"It peters out altogether farther down," Billy said. "From there on it's only horse trails. But I don't see much signs of timber, an' this soil's none so good. It's only used for pasture—no farmin' to speak of."

The hills were bare and grassy. Only the canyons were wooded, while the higher and more distant hills were furry with chaparral. Once they saw a coyote slide into the brush, and once Billy wished for a gun when a large wildcat stared at them malignantly and declined to run until routed by a clod of earth that burst about its ears like shrapnel.

Several miles along Saxon complained of thirst. Where the road dipped nearly at sea level to cross a small gulch Billy looked for water. The bed of the gulch was damp with hill-drip, and he left her to rest while he sought a spring.

"Say," he hailed a few minutes afterward. "Come on down. You just gotta see this. It'll 'most take your breath away."

Saxon followed the faint path that led steeply down through the thicket. Midway along, where a barbed wire fence was strung high across the mouth of the gulch and weighted down with big rocks, she caught her first glimpse of the tiny beach. Only from the sea could one guess its existence, so completely was it tucked away on three precipitous sides by the land, and screened by the thicket. Furthermore, the beach was the head of a narrow rock cove, a quarter of a mile long, up which pent way the sea roared and was subdued at the last to a gentle pulse of surf. Beyond the mouth many detached rocks, meeting the full force of the breakers, spouted foam and spray high in the air. The knees of these rocks, seen between the surges, were black with mussels. On their tops sprawled huge sea-lions tawny-wet and roaring in the sun, while overhead, uttering shrill cries, darted and wheeled a multitude of sea birds.

The last of the descent, from the barbed wire fence, was a sliding fall of a dozen feet, and Saxon arrived on the soft dry sand in a sitting posture.

"Oh, I tell you it's just great," Billy bubbled. "Look at it for a camping spot. In among the trees there is the prettiest spring you ever saw. An' look at all the good firewood, an'..." He gazed about and seaward with eyes that saw what no rush of words could compass. "... An', an' everything. We could live here. Look at the mussels out there. An' I bet you we could catch fish. What d'ye say we stop a few days?—It's vacation anyway—an' I could go back to Carmel for hooks an' lines."

Saxon, keenly appraising his glowing face, realized that he was indeed being won from the city.

"An' there ain't no wind here," he was recommending. "Not a breath. An' look how wild it is. Just as if we was a thousand miles from anywhere."

The wind, which had been fresh and raw across the bare hills, gained no entrance to the cove; and the beach was warm and balmy, the air sweetly pungent with the thicket odors. Here and there, in the midst of the thicket, severe small oak trees and other small trees of which Saxon did not know the names. Her enthusiasm now vied with Billy's, and, hand in hand, they started to explore.

"Here's where we can play real Robinson Crusoe," Billy cried, as they crossed the hard sand from highwater mark to the edge of the water. "Come on, Robinson. Let's stop over. Of course, I'm your Man Friday, an' what you say goes."

"But what shall we do with Man Saturday!" She pointed in mock consternation to a fresh footprint in the sand. "He may be a savage cannibal, you know."

"No chance. It's not a bare foot but a tennis shoe."

"But a savage could get a tennis shoe from a drowned or eaten sailor, couldn't he?" she contended.

"But sailors don't wear tennis shoes," was Billy's prompt refutation.

"You know too much for Man Friday," she chided; "but, just the same; if you'll fetch the packs we'll make camp. Besides, it mightn't have been a sailor that was eaten. It might have been a passenger."

By the end of an hour a snug camp was completed. The blankets were spread, a supply of firewood was chopped from the seasoned driftwood, and over a fire the coffee pot had begun to sing. Saxon called to Billy, who was improvising a table from a wave-washed plank. She pointed seaward. On the far point of rocks, naked except for swimming trunks, stood a man. He was gazing toward them, and they could see his long mop of dark hair blown by the wind. As he started to climb the rocks landward Billy called Saxon's attention to the fact that the stranger wore tennis shoes. In a few minutes he dropped down from the rock to the beach and walked up to them.

"Gosh!" Billy whispered to Saxon. "He's lean enough, but look at his muscles. Everybody down here seems to go in for physical culture."

As the newcomer approached, Saxon glimpsed sufficient of his face to be reminded of the old pioneers and of a certain type of face seen frequently among the old soldiers: Young though he was—not more than thirty, she decided—this man had the same long and narrow face, with the high cheekbones, high and slender forehead, and nose high, lean, and almost beaked. The lips were thin and sensitive; but the eyes were different from any she had ever seen in pioneer or veteran or any man. They were so dark a gray that they seemed brown, and there were a farness and alertness of vision in them as of bright questing through profounds of space. In a misty way Saxon felt that she had seen him before.

"Hello," he greeted. "You ought to be comfortable here." He threw down a partly filled sack. "Mussels. All I could get. The tide's not low enough yet."

Saxon heard Billy muffle an ejaculation, and saw painted on his face the extremest astonishment.

"Well, honest to God, it does me proud to meet you," he blurted out. "Shake hands. I always said if I laid eyes on you I'd shake.—Say!"

But Billy's feelings mastered him, and, beginning with a choking giggle, he roared into helpless mirth.

The stranger looked at him curiously across their clasped hands, and glanced inquiringly to Saxon.

"You gotta excuse me," Billy gurgled, pumping the other's hand up and down. "But I just gotta laugh. Why, honest to God, I've woke up nights an' laughed an' gone to sleep again. Don't you recognize 'm, Saxon? He's the same identical dude -- say, friend, you're some punkins at a hundred yards dash, ain't you?"

And then, in a sudden rush, Saxon placed him. He it was who had stood with Roy Blanchard alongside the automobile on the day she had wandered, sick and unwitting, into strange neighborhoods. Nor had that day been the first time she had seen him.

"Remember the Bricklayers' Picnic at Weasel Park?" Billy was asking. "An' the foot race? Why, I'd know that nose of yours anywhere among a million. You was the guy that stuck your cane between Timothy McManus's legs an' started the grandest roughhouse Weasel Park or any other park ever seen."

The visitor now commenced to laugh. He stood on one leg as he laughed harder, then stood on the other leg. Finally he sat down on a log of driftwood.

"And you were there," he managed to gasp to Billy at last. "You saw it. You saw it." He turned to Saxon. "—And you?"

She nodded.

"Say," Billy began again, as their laughter eased down, "what I wanta know is what'd you wanta do it for. Say, what'd you wanta do it for? I've been askin' that to myself ever since."

"So have I," was the answer.

"You didn't know Timothy McManus, did you?"

"No; I'd never seen him before, and I've never seen him since."

"But what'd you wanta do it for?" Billy persisted.

The young man laughed, then controlled himself.

"To save my life, I don't know. I have one friend, a most intelligent chap that writes sober, scientific books, and he's always aching to throw an egg into an electric fan to see what will happen. Perhaps that's the way it was with me, except that there was no aching. When I saw those legs flying past, I merely stuck my stick in between. I didn't know I was going to do it. I just did it. Timothy McManus was no more surprised than I was."

"Did they catch you?" Billy asked.

"Do I look as if they did? I was never so scared in my life. Timothy McManus himself couldn't have caught me that day. But what happened afterward? I heard they had a fearful roughhouse, but I couldn't stop to see."

It was not until a quarter of an hour had passed, during which Billy described the fight, that introductions took place. Mark Hall was their visitor's name, and he lived in a bungalow among the Carmel pines.

"But how did you ever find your way to Bierce's Cove?" he was curious to know. "Nobody ever dreams of it from the road."

"So that's its name?" Saxon said.

"It's the name we gave it. One of our crowd camped here one summer, and we named it after him. I'll take a cup of that coffee, if you don't mind."— This to Saxon. "And then I'll show your husband around. We're pretty proud of this cove. Nobody ever comes here but ourselves."

"You didn't get all that muscle from bein' chased by McManus," Billy observed over the coffee.

"Massage under tension," was the cryptic reply.

"Yes," Billy said, pondering vacantly. "Do you eat it with a spoon?"

Hall laughed.

"I'll show you. Take any muscle you want, tense it, then manipulate it with your fingers, so, and so."

"An' that done all that?" Billy asked skeptically.

"All that!" the other scorned proudly. "For one muscle you see, there's five tucked away but under command. Touch your finger to any part of me and see."

Billy complied, touching the right breast.

"You know something about anatomy, picking a muscleless spot," scolded Hall.

Billy grinned triumphantly, then, to his amazement, saw a muscle grow up under his finger. He prodded it, and found it hard and honest.

"Massage under tension!" Hall exulted. "Go on—anywhere you want."

And anywhere and everywhere Billy touched, muscles large and small rose up, quivered, and sank down, till the whole body was a ripple of willed quick.

"Never saw anything like it," Billy marveled at the end; "an' I've seen some few good men stripped in my time. Why, you're all living silk."

"Massage under tension did it, my friend. The doctors gave me up. My friends called me the sick rat, and the mangy poet, and all that. Then I quit the city, came down to Carmel, and went in for the open air—and massage under tension."

"Jim Hazard didn't get his muscles that way," Billy challenged.

"Certainly not, the lucky skunk; he was born with them. Mine's made. That's the difference. I'm a work of art. He's a cave bear. Come along. I'll show you around now. You'd better get your clothes off. Keep on only your shoes and pants, unless you've got a pair of trunks."

"My mother was a poet," Saxon said, while Billy was getting himself ready in the thicket. She had noted Hall's reference to himself.

He seemed incurious, and she ventured further.

"Some of it was printed."

"What was her name?" he asked idly.

"Dayelle Wiley Brown. She wrote: 'The Viking's Quest'; 'Days of Gold'; 'Constancy'; 'The Caballero'; 'Graves at Little Meadow'; and a lot more. Ten of them are in 'The Story of the Files.'"

"I've the book at home," he remarked, for the first time showing real interest. "She was a pioneer, of course—before my time. I'll look her up when I get back to the house. My people were pioneers. They came by Panama, in the Fifties, from Long Island. My father was a doctor, but he went into business in San Francisco and robbed his fellow men out of enough to keep me and the rest of a large family going ever since.—Say, where are you and your husband bound?"

When Saxon had told him of their attempt to get away from Oakland and of their quest for land, he sympathized with the first and shook his head over the second.

"It's beautiful down beyond the Sur," he told her. "I've been all over those redwood canyons, and the place is alive with game. The government land is there, too. But you'd be foolish to settle. It's too remote. And it isn't good farming land, except in patches in the canyons. I know a Mexican there who is wild to sell his five hundred acres for fifteen hundred dollars. Three dollars an acre! And what does that mean? That it isn't worth more. That it isn't worth so much; because he can find no takers. Land, you know, is worth what they buy and sell it for."

Billy, emerging from the thicket, only in shoes and in pants rolled to the knees, put an end to the conversation; and Saxon watched the two men, physically so dissimilar, climb the rocks and start out the south side of the cove. At first her eyes followed them lazily, but soon she grew interested and worried. Hall was leading Billy up what seemed a perpendicular wall in order to gain the backbone of the rock. Billy went slowly, displaying extreme caution; but twice she saw him slip, the weather-eaten stone crumbling away in his hand and rattling beneath him into the cove. When Hall reached the top, a hundred feet above the sea, she saw him stand upright and sway easily on the knife-edge which she knew fell away as abruptly on the other side. Billy, once on top, contented himself with crouching on hands and knees. The leader went on, upright, walking as easily as on a level floor. Billy abandoned the hands and knees position, but crouched closely and often helped himself with his hands.

The knife-edge backbone was deeply serrated, and into one of the notches both men disappeared. Saxon could not keep down her anxiety, and climbed out on the north side of the cove, which was less rugged and far less difficult to travel. Even so, the unaccustomed height, the crumbling surface, and the fierce buffets of the wind tried her nerve. Soon she was opposite the men. They had leaped a narrow chasm and were scaling another tooth. Already Billy was going more nimbly, but his leader often paused and waited for him. The way grew severer, and several times the clefts they essayed extended down to the ocean level and spouted spray from the growling breakers that burst through. At other times, standing erect, they would fall forward across deep and narrow clefts until their palms met the opposing side; then, clinging with their fingers, their bodies would be drawn across and up.

Near the end, Hall and Billy went out of sight over the south side of the backbone, and when Saxon saw them again they were rounding the extreme point of rock and coming back on the cove side. Here the way seemed barred. A wide fissure, with hopelessly vertical sides, yawned skywards from a foam-white vortex where the mad waters shot their level a dozen feet upward and dropped it as abruptly to the black depths of battered rock and writhing weed.

Clinging precariously, the men descended their side till the spray was flying about them. Here they paused. Saxon could see Hall pointing down across the fissure and imagined he was showing some curious thing to Billy. She was not prepared for what followed. The surf-level sucked and sank away, and across and down Hall jumped to a narrow foothold where the wash had roared yards deep the moment before. Without pause, as the returning sea rushed up, he was around the sharp corner and clawing upward hand and foot to escape being caught. Billy was now left alone. He could not even see Hall, much less be further advised by him, and so tensely did Saxon watch, that the pain in her finger-tips, crushed to the rock by which she held, warned her to relax. Billy waited his chance, twice made tentative preparations to leap and sank back, then leaped across and down to the momentarily exposed foothold, doubled the corner, and as he clawed up to join Hall was washed to the waist but not torn away.

Saxon did not breathe easily till they rejoined her at the fire. One glance at Billy told her that he was exceedingly disgusted with himself.

"You'll do, for a beginner," Hall cried, slapping him jovially on the bare shoulder. "That climb is a stunt of mine. Many's the brave lad that's started with me and broken down before we were half way out. I've had a dozen balk at that big jump. Only the athletes make it."

"I ain't ashamed of admittin' I was scairt," Billy growled. "You're a regular goat, an' you sure got my goat half a dozen times. But I'm mad now. It's mostly trainin', an' I'm goin' to camp right here an' train till I can challenge you to a race out an' around an' back to the beach."

"Done," said Hall, putting out his hand in ratification. "And some time, when we get together in San Francisco, I'll lead you up against Bierce—the one this cove is named after. His favorite stunt, when he isn't collecting rattlesnakes, is to wait for a forty-mile-an-hour breeze, and then get up and walk on the parapet of a skyscraper—on the lee side, mind you, so that if he blows off there's nothing to fetch him up but the street. He sprang that on me once."

"Did you do it?" Billy asked eagerly.

"I wouldn't have if I hadn't been on. I'd been practicing it secretly for a week. And I got twenty dollars out of him on the bet."

The tide was now low enough for mussel gathering and Saxon accompanied the men out the north wall. Hall had several sacks to fill. A rig was coming for him in the afternoon, he explained, to cart the mussels back to Carmel. When the sacks were full they ventured further among the rock crevices and were rewarded with three abalones, among the shells of which Saxon found one coveted blister-pearl. Hall initiated them into the mysteries of pounding and preparing the abalone meat for cooking.

By this time it seemed to Saxon that they had known him a long time. It reminded her of the old times when Bert had been with them, singing his songs or ranting about the last of the Mohicans.

"Now, listen; I'm going to teach you something," Hall commanded, a large round rock poised in his hand above the abalone meat. "You must never, never pound abalone without singing this song. Nor must you sing this song at any other time. It would be the rankest sacrilege. Abalone is the food of the gods. Its preparation is a religious function. Now listen, and follow, and remember that it is a very solemn occasion."

The stone came down with a thump on the white meat, and thereafter arose and fell in a sort of tom-tom accompaniment to the poet's song:

"Oh! some folks boast of quail on toast, Because they think it's tony; But I'm content to owe my rent And live on abalone.

"Oh! Mission Point's a friendly joint Where every crab's a crony, And true and kind you'll ever find The clinging abalone.

"He wanders free beside the sea Where 'er the coast is stony; He flaps his wings and madly sings—The plaintive abalone.

"Some stick to biz, some flirt with Liz Down on the sands of Coney; But we, by hell, stay in Carmel, And whang the abalone."

He paused with his mouth open and stone upraised. There was a rattle of wheels and a voice calling from above where the sacks of mussels had been carried. He brought the stone down with a final thump and stood up.

"There's a thousand more verses like those," he said. "Sorry I hadn't time to teach you them." He held out his hand, palm downward. "And now, children, bless you, you are now members of the clan of Abalone Eaters, and I solemnly enjoin you, never, no matter what the circumstances, pound abalone meat without chanting the sacred words I have revealed unto you."

"But we can't remember the words from only one hearing," Saxon expostulatcd.

"That shall be attended to. Next Sunday the Tribe of Abalone Eaters will descend upon you here in Bierce's Cove, and you will be able to see the rites, the writers and writeresses, down even to the Iron Man with the basilisk eyes, vulgarly known as the King of the Sacerdotal Lizards."

"Will Jim Hazard come?" Billy called, as Hall disappeared into the thicket.

"He will certainly come. Is he not the Cave-Bear Pot-Walloper and Gridironer, the most fearsome, and, next to me, the most exalted, of all the Abalone Eaters?"

Saxon and Billy could only look at each other till they heard the wheels rattle away.

"Well, I'll be doggoned," Billy let out. "He's some boy, that. Nothing stuck up about him. Just like Jim Hazard, comes along and makes himself at home, you're as good as he is an' he's as good as you, an' we're all friends together, just like that, right off the bat."

"He's old stock, too," Saxon said. "He told me while you were undressing. His folks came by Panama before the railroad was built, and from what he said I guess he's got plenty of money."

"He sure don't act like it."

"And isn't he full of fun!" Saxon cried.

"A regular josher. An' HIM!—a POET!"

"Oh, I don't know, Billy. I've heard that plenty of poets are odd."

"That's right, come to think of it. There's Joaquin Miller, lives out in the hills back of Fruitvale. He's certainly odd. It's right near his place where I proposed to you. Just the same I thought poets wore whiskers and eyeglasses, an' never tripped up foot-racers at Sunday picnics, nor run around with as few clothes on as the law allows, gatherin' mussels an' climbin' like goats."

That night, under the blankets, Saxon lay awake, looking at the stars, pleasuring in the balmy thicket-scents, and listening to the dull rumble of the outer surf and the whispering ripples on the sheltered beach a few feet away. Billy stirred, and she knew he was not yet asleep.

"Glad you left Oakland, Billy?" she snuggled.

"Huh!" came his answer. "Is a clam happy?"

CHAPTER VIII

Every half tide Billy raced out the south wall over the dangerous course he and Hall had traveled, and each trial found him doing it in faster time.

"Wait till Sunday," he said to Saxon. "I'll give that poet a run for his money. Why, they ain't a place that bothers me now. I've got the head confidence. I run where I went on hands an' knees. I figured it out this way: Suppose you had a foot to fall on each side, an' it was soft hay. They'd be nothing to stop you. You wouldn't fall. You'd go like a streak. Then it's just the same if it's a mile down on each side. That ain't your concern. Your concern is to stay on top and go like a streak. An', d'ye know, Saxon, when I went at it that way it never bothered me at all. Wait till he comes with his crowd Sunday. I'm ready for him."

"I wonder what the crowd will be like," Saxon speculated.

"Like him, of course. Birds of a feather flock together. They won't be stuck up, any of them, you'll see."

Hall had sent out fish-lines and a swimming suit by a Mexican cowboy bound south to his ranch, and from the latter they learned much of the government land and how to get it. The week flew by; each day Saxon sighed a farewell of happiness to the sun; each morning they greeted its return with laughter of joy in that another happy day had begun. They made no plans, but fished, gathered mussels and abalones, and climbed among the rocks as the moment moved them. The abalone meat they pounded religiously to a verse of doggerel improvised by Saxon. Billy prospered. Saxon had never seen him at so keen a pitch of health. As for herself, she scarcely needed the little hand-mirror to know that never, since she was a young girl, had there been such color in her cheeks, such spontaneity of vivacity.

"It's the first time in my life I ever had real play," Billy said. "An' you an' me never played at all all the time we was married. This beats bein' any kind of a millionaire."

"No seven o'clock whistle," Saxon exulted. "I'd lie abed in the mornings on purpose, only everything is too good not to be up. And now you just play at chopping some firewood and catching a nice big perch, Man Friday, if you expect to get any dinner."

Billy got up, hatchet in hand, from where he had been lying prone, digging holes in the sand with his bare toes.

"But it ain't goin' to last," he said, with a deep sigh of regret. "The rains'll come any time now. The good weather's hangin' on something wonderful."

On Saturday morning, returning from his run out the south wall, he missed Saxon. After helloing for her without result, he climbed to the road. Half a mile away, he saw her astride an unsaddled, unbridled horse that moved unwillingly, at a slow walk, across the pasture.

"Lucky for you it was an old mare that had been used to ridin'—see them saddle marks," he grumbled, when she at last drew to a halt beside him and allowed him to help her down.

"Oh, Billy," she sparkled, "I was never on a horse before. It was glorious! I felt so helpless, too, and so brave."

"I'm proud of you, just the same," he said, in more grumbling tones than before. "'Tain't every married woman'd tackle a strange horse that way, especially if she'd never ben on one. An' I ain't forgot that you're goin' to have a saddle animal all to yourself some day—a regular Joe dandy."

The Abalone Eaters, in two rigs and on a number of horses, descended in force on Bierce's Cove. There were half a score of men and almost as many women. All were young, between the ages of twenty-five and forty, and all seemed good friends. Most of them were married. They arrived in a roar of good spirits, tripping one another down the slippery trail and engulfing Saxon and Billy in a comradeship as artless and warm as the sunshine itself. Saxon was appropriated by the girls—she could not realize them women; and they made much of her, praising her camping and traveling equipment and insisting on hearing some of her tale. They were experienced campers themselves, as she quickly discovered when she saw the pots and pans and clothes-boilers for the mussels which they had brought.

In the meantime Billy and the men had undressed and scattered out after mussels and abalones. The girls lighted on Saxon's ukulele and nothing would do but she must play and sing. Several of them had been to Honolulu, and knew the instrument, confirming Mercedes' definition of ukulele as "jumping flea." Also, they knew Hawaiian songs she had learned from Mercedes, and soon, to her accompaniment, all were singing: "Aloha Oe," "Honolulu Tomboy," and "Sweet Lei Lehua." Saxon was genuinely shocked when some of them, even the more matronly, danced hulas on the sand.

When the men returned, burdened with sacks of shellfish, Mark Hall, as high priest, commanded the due and solemn rite of the tribe. At a wave of his hand, the many poised stones came down in unison on the white meat, and all voices were uplifted in the Hymn to the Abalone. Old verses all sang, occasionally some one sang a fresh verse alone, whereupon it was repeated in chorus. Billy betrayed Saxon by begging her in an undertone to sing the verse she had made, and her pretty voice was timidly raised in:

"We sit around and gaily pound, And bear no acrimony Because our ob—ject is a gob Of sizzling abalone."

"Great!" cried the poet, who had winced at ob—ject. "She speaks the language of the tribe! Come on, children—now!"

And all chanted Saxon's lines. Then Jim Hazard had a new verse, and one of the girls, and the Iron Man with the basilisk eyes of greenish-gray, whom Saxon recognized from Hall's description. To her it seemed he had the face of a priest.

"Oh! some like ham and some like lamb And some like macaroni; But bring me in a pail of gin And a tub of abalone.

"Oh! some drink rain and some champagne Or brandy by the pony; But I will try a little rye With a dash of abalone.

"Some live on hope and some on dope And some on alimony. But our tom-cat, he lives on fat And tender abalone."

A black-haired, black-eyed man with the roguish face of a satyr, who, Saxon learned, was an artist who sold his paintings at five hundred apiece, brought on himself universal execration and acclamation by singing:

"The more we take, the more they make In deep sea matrimony; Race suicide cannot betide The fertile abalone."

And so it went, verses new and old, verses without end, all in glorification of the succulent shellfish of Carmel. Saxon's enjoyment was keen, almost ecstatic, and she had difficulty in convincing herself of the reality of it all. It seemed like some fairy tale or book story come true. Again, it seemed more like a stage, and these the actors, she and Billy having blundered into the scene in some incomprehensible way. Much of wit she sensed which she did not understand. Much she did understand. And she was aware that brains were playing as she had never seen brains play before. The puritan streak in her training was astonished and shocked by some of the broadness; but she refused to sit in judgment. They SEEMED good, these light-hearted young people; they certainly were not rough or gross as were many of the crowds she had been with on Sunday picnics. None of the men got drunk, although there were cocktails in vacuum bottles and red wine in a huge demijohn.

What impressed Saxon most was their excessive jollity, their childlike joy, and the childlike things they did. This effect was heightened by the fact that they were novelists and painters, poets and critics, sculptors and musicians. One man, with a refined and delicate face—a dramatic critic on a great San Francisco daily, she was told—introduced a feat which all the men tried and failed at most ludicrously. On the beach, at regular intervals, planks were placed as obstacles. Then the dramatic critic, on all fours, galloped along the sand for all the world like a horse, and for all the world like a horse taking hurdles he jumped the planks to the end of the course.

Quoits had been brought along, and for a while these were pitched with zest. Then jumping was started, and game slid into game. Billy took part in everything, but did not win first place as often as he had expected. An English writer beat him a dozen feet at tossing the caber. Jim Hazard beat him in putting the heavy "rock." Mark Hall out-jumped him standing and running. But at the standing high back-jump Billy did come first. Despite the handicap of his weight, this victory was due to his splendid back and abdominal lifting muscles. Immediately after this, however, he was brought to grief by Mark Hall's sister, a strapping young amazon in cross-saddle riding costume, who three times tumbled him ignominiously heels over head in a bout of Indian wrestling.

"You're easy," jeered the Iron Man, whose name they had learned was Pete Bideaux. "I can put you down myself, catch-as-catch-can."

Billy accepted the challenge, and found in all truth that the other was rightly nicknamed. In the training camps Billy had sparred and clinched with giant champions like Jim Jeffries and Jack Johnson, and met the weight of their strength, but never had he encountered strength like this of the Iron Man. Do what he could, Billy was powerless, and twice his shoulders were ground into the sand in defeat.

"You'll get a chance back at him," Hazard whispered to Billy, off at one side. "I've brought the gloves along. Of course, you had no chance with him at his own game. He's wrestled in the music halls in London with Hackenschmidt. Now you keep quiet, and we'll lead up to it in a casual sort of way. He doesn't know about you."

Soon, the Englishman who had tossed the caber was sparring with the dramatic critic, Hazard and Hall boxed in fantastic burlesque, then, gloves in hand, looked for the next appropriately matched couple. The choice of Bideaux and Billy was obvious.

"He's liable to get nasty if he's hurt," Hazard warned Billy, as he tied on the gloves for him. "He's old American French, and he's got a devil of a temper. But just keep your head and tap him—whatever you do, keep tapping him."

"Easy sparring now"; "No roughhouse, Bideaux"; "Just light tapping, you know," were admonitions variously addressed to the Iron Man.

"Hold on a second," he said to Billy, dropping his hands. "When I get rapped I do get a bit hot. But don't mind me. I can't help it, you know. It's only for the moment, and I don't mean it."

Saxon felt very nervous, visions of Billy's bloody fights and all the scabs he had slugged rising in her brain; but she had never seen her husband box, and but few seconds were required to put her at ease. The Iron Man had no chance. Billy was too completely the master, guarding every blow, himself continually and almost at will tapping the other's face and body. There was no weight in Billy's blows, only a light and snappy tingle; but their incessant iteration told on the Iron Man's temper. In vain the onlookers warned him to go easy. His face purpled with anger, and his blows became savage. But Billy went on, tap, tap, tap, calmly, gently, imperturbably. The Iron Man lost control, and rushed and plunged, delivering great swings and upper-cuts of man-killing quality. Billy ducked, side-stepped, blocked, stalled, and escaped all damage. In the clinches, which were unavoidable, he locked the Iron Man's arms, and in the clinches the Iron Man invariably laughed and apologized, only to lose his head with the first tap the instant they separated and be more infuriated than ever.

And when it was over and Billy's identity had been divulged, the Iron Man accepted the joke on himself with the best of humor. It had been a splendid exhibition on Billy's part. His mastery of the sport, coupled with his self-control, had most favorably impressed the crowd, and Saxon, very proud of her man boy, could not but see the admiration all had for him.

Nor did she prove in any way a social failure. When the tired and sweating players lay down in the dry sand to cool off, she was persuaded into accompanying their nonsense songs with the ukulele. Nor was it long, catching their spirit, ere she was singing to them and teaching them quaint songs of early days which she had herself learned as a little girl from Cady— Cady, the saloonkeeper, pioneer, and ex-cavalryman, who had been a bull-whacker on the Salt Intake Trail in the days before the railroad.

One song which became an immediate favorite was:

"Oh! times on Bitter Creek, they never can be beat, Root hog or die is on every wagon sheet; The sand within your throat, the dust within your eye, Bend your back and stand it—root hog or die."

After the dozen verses of "Root Hog or Die," Mark Hall claimed to be especially infatuated with:

"Obadier, he dreampt a dream, Dreampt he was drivin' a ten-mule team, But when he woke he heaved a sigh, The lead-mule kicked e-o-wt the swing-mule's eye."

It was Mark Hall who brought up the matter of Billy's challenge to race out the south wall of the cove, though he referred to the test as lying somewhere in the future. Billy surprised him by saying he was ready at any time. Forthwith the crowd clamored for the race. Hall offered to bet on himself, but there were no takers. He offered two to one to Jim Hazard, who shook his head and said he would accept three to one as a sporting proposition. Billy heard and gritted his teeth.

"I'll take you for five dollars," he said to Hall, "but not at those odds. I'll back myself even."

"It isn't your money I want; it's Hazard's," Hall demurred. "Though I'll give either of you three to one."

"Even or nothing," Billy held out obstinately.

Hall finally closed both bets—even with Billy, and three to one with Hazard.

The path along the knife-edge was so narrow that it was impossible for runners to pass each other, so it was arranged to time the men, Hall to go first and Billy to follow after an interval of half a minute.

Hall toed the mark and at the word was off with the form of a sprinter. Saxon's heart sank. She knew Billy had never crossed the stretch of sand at that speed. Billy darted forward thirty seconds later, and reached the foot of the rock when Hall was half way up. When both were on top and racing from notch to notch, the Iron Man announced that they had scaled the wall in the same time to a second.

"My money still looks good," Hazard remarked, "though I hope neither of them breaks a neck. I wouldn't take that run that way for all the gold that would fill the cove."

"But you'll take bigger chances swimming in a storm on Carmel Beach," his wife chided.

"Oh, I don't know," he retorted. "You haven't so far to fall when swimming."

Billy and Hall had disappeared and were making the circle around the end. Those on the beach were certain that the poet had gained in the dizzy spurts of flight along the knife-edge. Even Hazard admitted it.

"What price for my money now?" he cried excitedly, dancing up and down.

Hall had reappeared, the great jump accomplished, and was running shoreward. But there was no gap. Billy was on his heels, and on his heels he stayed, in to shore, down the wall, and to the mark on the beach. Billy had won by half a minute.

"Only by the watch," he panted. "Hall was over half a minute ahead of me out to the end. I'm not slower than I thought, but he's faster. He's a wooz of a sprinter. He could beat me ten times outa ten, except for accident. He was hung up at the jump by a big sea. That's where I caught 'm. I jumped right after 'm on the same sea, then he set the pace home, and all I had to do was take it."

"That's all right," said Hall. "You did better than beat me. That's the first time in the history of Bierce's Cove that two men made that jump on the same sea. And all the risk was yours, coming last."

"It was a fluke," Billy insisted.

And at that point Saxon settled the dispute of modesty and raised a general laugh by rippling chords on the ukulele and parodying an old hymn in negro minstrel fashion:

"De Lawd move in er mischievous way His blunders to perform."

In the afternoon Jim Hazard and Hall dived into the breakers and swam to the outlying rocks, routing the protesting sea-lions and taking possession of their surf-battered stronghold. Billy followed the swimmers with his eyes, yearning after them so undisguisedly that Mrs. Hazard said to him:

"Why don't you stop in Carmel this winter? Jim will teach you all he knows about the surf. And he's wild to box with you. He works long hours at his desk, and he really needs exercise."

Not until sunset did the merry crowd carry their pots and pans and trove of mussels up to the road and depart. Saxon and Billy watched them disappear, on horses and behind horses, over the top of the first hill, and then descended hand in hand through the thicket to the camp. Billy threw himself on the sand and stretched out.

"I don't know when I've been so tired," he yawned. "An' there's one thing sure: I never had such a day. It's worth livin' twenty years for an' then some."

He reached out his hand to Saxon, who lay beside him.

"And, oh, I was so proud of you, Billy," she said. "I never saw you box before. I didn't know it was like that. The Iron Man was at your mercy all the time, and you kept it from being violent or terrible. Everybody could look on and enjoy—and they did, too."

"Huh, I want to say you was goin' some yourself. They just took to you. Why, honest to God, Saxon, in the singin' you was the whole show, along with the ukulele. All the women liked you, too, an' that's what counts."

It was their first social triumph, and the taste of it was sweet:

"Mr. Hall said he'd looked up the 'Story of the Files,'" Saxon recounted. "And he said mother was a true poet. He said it was astonishing the fine stock that had crossed the Plains. He told me a lot about those times and the people I didn't know. And he's read all about the fight at Little Meadow. He says he's got it in a book at home, and if we come back to Carmel he'll show it to me."

"He wants us to come back all right. D'ye know what he said to me, Saxon? He gave me a letter to some guy that's down on the government land—some poet that's holdin' down a quarter of a section—so we'll be able to stop there, which'll come in handy if the big rains catch us. An'—Oh! that's what I was drivin' at. He said he had a little shack he lived in while the house was buildin'. The Iron Man's livin' in it now, but he's goin' away to some Catholic college to study to be a priest, an' Hall said the shack'd be ours as long as we wanted to use it. An' he said I could do what the Iron Man was doin' to make a livin'. Hall was kind of bashful when he was offerin' me work. Said it'd be only odd jobs, but that we'd make out. I could help'm plant potatoes, he said; an' he got half savage when he said I couldn't chop wood. That was his job, he said; an' you could see he was actually jealous over it."

"And Mrs. Hall said just about the same to me, Billy. Carmel wouldn't be so bad to pass the rainy season in. And then, too, you could go swimming with Mr. Hazard."

"Seems as if we could settle down wherever we've a mind to," Billy assented. "Carmel's the third place now that's offered. Well, after this, no man need be afraid of makin' a go in the country."

"No good man," Saxon corrected.

"I guess you're right." Billy thought for a moment. "Just the same a dub, too, has a better chance in the country than in the city."

"Who'd have ever thought that such fine people existed?" Saxon pondered. "It's just wonderful, when you come to think of it."

"It's only what you'd expect from a rich poet that'd trip up a foot-racer at an Irish picnic," Billy exposited.

"The only crowd such a guy'd run with would be like himself, or he'd make a crowd that was. I wouldn't wonder that he'd make this crowd. Say, he's got some sister, if anybody'd ride up on a sea-lion an' ask you. She's got that Indian wrestlin' down pat, an' she's built for it. An' say, ain't his wife a beaut?"

A little longer they lay in the warm sand. It was Billy who broke the silence, and what he said seemed to proceed out of profound meditation.

"Say, Saxon, d'ye know I don't care if I never see movie pictures again."

CHAPTER IX

Saxon and Billy were gone weeks on the trip south, but in the end they came back to Carmel. They had stopped with Hafler, the poet in the Marble House, which he had built with his own hands. This queer dwelling was all in one room, built almost entirely of white marble. Hafler cooked, as over a campfire, in the huge marble fireplace, which he used in all ways as a kitchen. There were divers shelves of books, and the massive furniture he had made from redwood, as he had made the shakes for the roof. A blanket, stretched across a corner, gave Saxon privacy. The poet was on the verge of departing for San Francisco and New York, but remained a day over with them to explain the country and run over the government land with Billy. Saxon had wanted to go along that morning, but Hafler scornfully rejected her, telling her that her legs were too short. That night, when the men returned, Billy was played out to exhaustion. He frankly acknowledged that Hafler had walked him into the ground, and that his tongue had been hanging out from the first hour. Hafler estimated that they had covered fifty-five miles.

"But such miles!" Billy enlarged. "Half the time up or down, an' 'most all the time without trails. An' such a pace. He was dead right about your short legs, Saxon. You wouldn't a-lasted the first mile. An' such country! We ain't seen anything like it yet."

Hafler left the next day to catch the train at Monterey. He gave them the freedom of the Marble House, and told them to stay the whole winter if they wanted. Billy elected to loaf around and rest up that day. He was stiff and sore. Moreover, he was stunned by the exhibition of walking prowess on the part of the poet.

"Everybody can do something top-notch down in this country," he marveled. "Now take that Hafler. He's a bigger man than me, an' a heavier. An' weight's against walkin', too. But not with him. He's done eighty miles inside twenty-four hours, he told me, an' once a hundred an' seventy in three days. Why, he made a show outa me. I felt ashamed as a little kid."

"Remember, Billy," Saxon soothed him, "every man to his own game. And down here you're a top-notcher at your own game. There isn't one you're not the master of with the gloves."

"I guess that's right," he conceded. "But just the same it goes against the grain to be walked off my legs by a poet—by a poet, mind you."

They spent days in going over the government land, and in the end reluctantly decided against taking it up. The redwood canyons and great cliffs of the Santa Lucia Mountains fascinated Saxon; but she remembered what Hafler had told her of the summer fogs which hid the sun sometimes for a week or two at a time, and which lingered for months. Then, too, there was no access to market. It was many miles to where the nearest wagon road began, at Post's, and from there on, past Point Sur to Carmel, it was a weary and perilous way. Billy, with his teamster judgment, admitted that for heavy hauling it was anything but a picnic. There was the quarry of perfect marble on Hafler's quarter section. He had said that it would be worth a fortune if near a railroad; but, as it was, he'd make them a present of it if they wanted it.

Billy visioned the grassy slopes pastured with his horses and cattle, and found it hard to turn his back; but he listened with a willing ear to Saxon's argument in favor of a farm-home like the one they had seen in the moving pictures in Oakland. Yes, he agreed, what they wanted was an all-around farm, and an all-around farm they would have if they hiked forty years to find it.

"But it must have redwoods on it," Saxon hastened to stipulate. "I've fallen in love with them. And we can get along without fog. And there must be good wagon-roads, and a railroad not more than a thousand miles away."

Heavy winter rains held them prisoners for two weeks in the Marble House. Saxon browsed among Hafler's books, though most of them were depressingly beyond her, while Billy hunted with Hafler's guns. But he was a poor shot and a worse hunter. His only success was with rabbits, which he managed to kill on occasions when they stood still. With the rifle he got nothing, although he fired at half a dozen different deer, and, once, at a huge cat-creature with a long tail which he was certain was a mountain lion. Despite the way he grumbled at himself, Saxon could see the keen joy he was taking. This belated arousal of the hunting instinct seemed to make almost another man of him. He was out early and late, compassing prodigious climbs and tramps—once reaching as far as the gold mines Tom had spoken of, and being away two days.

"Talk about pluggin' away at a job in the city, an' goin' to movie' pictures and Sunday picnics for amusement!" he would burst out. "I can't see what was eatin' me that I ever put up with such truck. Here's where I oughta ben all the time, or some place like it."

He was filled with this new mode of life, and was continually recalling old hunting tales of his father and telling them to Saxon.

"Say, I don't get stiffened any more after an all-day tramp," he exulted. "I'm broke in. An' some day, if I meet up with that Hafler, I'll challenge'm to a tramp that'll break his heart."

"Foolish boy, always wanting to play everybody's game and beat them at it," Saxon laughed delightedly.

"Aw, I guess you're right," he growled. "Hafler can always out-walk me. He's made that way. But some day, just the same, if I ever see 'm again, I'll invite 'm to put on the gloves.. .. though I won't be mean enough to make 'm as sore as he made me."

After they left Post's on the way back to Carmel, the condition of the road proved the wisdom of their rejection of the government land. They passed a rancher's wagon overturned, a second wagon with a broken axle, and the stage a hundred yards down the mountainside, where it had fallen, passengers, horses, road, and all.

"I guess they just about quit tryin' to use this road in the winter," Billy said. "It's horse-killin' an' man-killin', an' I can just see 'm freightin' that marble out over it I don't think."

Settling down at Carmel was an easy matter. The Iron Man had already departed to his Catholic college, and the "shack" turned out to be a three-roomed house comfortably furnished for housekeeping. Hall put Billy to work on the potato patch—a matter of three acres which the poet farmed erratically to the huge delight of his crowd. He planted at all seasons, and it was accepted by the community that what did not rot in the ground was evenly divided between the gophers and trespassing cows. A plow was borrowed, a team of horses hired, and Billy took hold. Also he built a fence around the patch, and after that was set to staining the shingled roof of the bungalow. Hall climbed to the ridge-pole to repeat his warning that Billy must keep away from his wood-pile. One morning Hall came over and watched Billy chopping wood for Saxon. The poet looked on covetously as long as he could restrain himself.

"It's plain you don't know how to use an axe," he sneered. "Here, let me show you."

He worked away for an hour, all the while delivering an exposition on the art of chopping wood.

"Here," Billy expostulated at last, taking hold of the axe. "I'll have to chop a cord of yours now in order to make this up to you."

Hall surrendered the axe reluctantly.

"Don't let me catch you around my wood-pile, that's all," he threatened. "My wood-pile is my castle, and you've got to understand that."

From a financial standpoint, Saxon and Billy were putting aside much money. They paid no rent, their simple living was cheap, and Billy had all the work he cared to accept. The various members of the crowd seemed in a conspiracy to keep him busy. It was all odd jobs, but he preferred it so, for it enabled him to suit his time to Jim Hazard's. Each day they boxed and took a long swim through the surf. When Hazard finished his morning's writing, he would whoop through the pines to Billy, who dropped whatever work he was doing. After the swim, they would take a fresh shower at Hazard's house, rub each other down in training camp style, and be ready for the noon meal. In the afternoon Hazard returned to his desk, and Billy to his outdoor work, although, still later, they often met for a few miles' run over the hills. Training was a matter of habit to both men. Hazard, when he had finished with seven years of football, knowing the dire death that awaits the big-muscled athlete who ceases training abruptly, had been compelled to keep it up. Not only was it a necessity, but he had grown to like it. Billy also liked it, for he took great delight in the silk of his body.

Often, in the early morning, gun in hand, he was off with Mark Hall, who taught him to shoot and hunt. Hall had dragged a shotgun around from the days when he wore knee pants, and his keen observing eyes and knowledge of the habits of wild life were a revelation to Billy. This part of the country was too settled for large game, but Billy kept Saxon supplied with squirrels and quail, cottontails and jackrabbits, snipe and wild ducks. And they learned to eat roasted mallard and canvasback in the California style of sixteen minutes in a hot oven. As he became expert with shotgun and rifle, he began to regret the deer and the mountain lion he had missed down below the Sur; and to the requirements of the farm he and Saxon sought he added plenty of game.

But it was not all play in Carmel. That portion of the community which Saxon and Billy came to know, "the crowd," was hard-working. Some worked regularly, in the morning or late at night. Others worked spasmodically, like the wild Irish playwright, who would shut himself up for a week at a time, then emerge, pale and drawn, to play like a madman against the time of his next retirement. The pale and youthful father of a family, with the face of Shelley, who wrote vaudeville turns for a living and blank verse tragedies and sonnet cycles for the despair of managers and publishers, hid himself in a concrete cell with three-foot walls, so piped, that, by turning a lever, the whole structure spouted water upon the impending intruder. But in the main, they respected each other's work-time. They drifted into one another's houses as the spirit prompted, but if they found a man at work they went their way. This obtained to all except Mark Hall, who did not have to work for a living; and he climbed trees to get away from popularity and compose in peace.

The crowd was unique in its democracy and solidarity. It had little intercourse with the sober and conventional part of Carmel. This section constituted the aristocracy of art and letters, and was sneered at as bourgeois. In return, it looked askance at the crowd with its rampant bohemianism. The taboo extended to Billy and Saxon. Billy took up the attitude of the clan and sought no work from the other camp. Nor was work offered him.

Hall kept open house. The big living room, with its huge fireplace, divans, shelves and tables of books and magazines, was the center of things. Here, Billy and Saxon were expected to be, and in truth found themselves to be, as much at home as anybody. Here, when wordy discussions on all subjects under the sun were not being waged, Billy played at cut-throat Pedro, horrible fives, bridge, and pinochle. Saxon, a favorite of the young women, sewed with them, teaching them pretties and being taught in fair measure in return.

It was Billy, before they had been in Carmel a week, who said shyly to Saxon:

"Say, you can't guess how I'm missin' all your nice things. What's the matter with writin' Tom to express 'm down? When we start trampin' again, we'll express 'm back."

Saxon wrote the letter, and all that day her heart was singing. Her man was still her lover. And there were in his eyes all the old lights which had been blotted out during the nightmare period of the strike.

"Some pretty nifty skirts around here, but you've got 'em all beat, or I'm no judge," he told her. And again: "Oh, I love you to death anyway. But if them things ain't shipped down there'll be a funeral."

Hall and his wife owned a pair of saddle horses which were kept at the livery stable, and here Billy naturally gravitated. The stable operated the stage and carried the mails between Carmel and Monterey. Also, it rented out carriages and mountain wagons that seated nine persons. With carriages and wagons a driver was furnished. The stable often found itself short a driver, and Billy was quickly called upon. He became an extra man at the stable. He received three dollars a day at such times, and drove many parties around the Seventeen Mile Drive, up Carmel Valley, and down the coast to the various points and beaches.

"But they're a pretty uppish sort, most of 'em," he said to Saxon, referring to the persons he drove. "Always MISTER Roberts this, an' MISTER Roberts that—all kinds of ceremony so as to make me not forget they consider themselves better 'n me. You see, I ain't exactly a servant, an' yet I ain't good enough for them. I'm the driver—something half way between a hired man and a chauffeur. Huh! When they eat they give me my lunch off to one side, or afterward. No family party like with Hall an' HIS kind. An' that crowd to-day, why, they just naturally didn't have no lunch for me at all. After this, always, you make me up my own lunch. I won't be be holdin' to 'em for nothin', the damned geezers. An' you'd a-died to seen one of 'em try to give me a tip. I didn't say nothin'. I just looked at 'm like I didn't see 'm, an' turned away casual-like after a moment, leavin' him as embarrassed as hell."

Nevertheless, Billy enjoyed the driving, never more so than when he held the reins, not of four plodding workhorses, but of four fast driving animals, his foot on the powerful brake, and swung around curves and along dizzy cliff-rims to a frightened chorus of women passengers. And when it came to horse judgment and treatment of sick and injured horses even the owner of the stable yielded place to Billy.

"I could get a regular job there any time," he boasted quietly to Saxon. "Why, the country's just sproutin' with jobs for any so-so sort of a fellow. I bet anything, right now, if I said to the boss that I'd take sixty dollars an' work regular, he'd jump for me. He's hinted as much.—And, say! Are you onta the fact that yours truly has learnt a new trade. Well he has. He could take a job stage-drivin' anywheres. They drive six on some of the stages up in Lake County. If we ever get there, I'll get thick with some driver, just to get the reins of six in my hands. An' I'll have you on the box beside me. Some goin' that! Some goin'!"

Billy took little interest in the many discussions waged in Hall's big living room. "Wind-chewin'," was his term for it. To him it was so much good time wasted that might be employed at a game of Pedro, or going swimming, or wrestling in the sand. Saxon, on the contrary, delighted in the logomachy, though little enough she understood of it, following mainly by feeling, and once in a while catching a high light.

But what she could never comprehend was the pessimism that so often cropped up. The wild Irish playwright had terrible spells of depression. Shelley, who wrote vaudeville turns in the concrete cell, was a chronic pessimist. St. John, a young magazine writer, was an anarchic disciple of Nietzsche. Masson, a painter, held to a doctrine of eternal recurrence that was petrifying. And Hall, usually so merry, could outfoot them all when he once got started on the cosmic pathos of religion and the gibbering anthropomorphisms of those who loved not to die. At such times Saxon was oppressed by these sad children of art. It was inconceivable that they, of all people, should be so forlorn.

One night Hall turned suddenly upon Billy, who had been following dimly and who only comprehended that to them everything in life was rotten and wrong.

"Here, you pagan, you, you stolid and flesh-fettered ox, you monstrosity of over-weening and perennial health and joy, what do you think of it?" Hall demanded.

"Oh, I've had my troubles," Billy answered, speaking in his wonted slow way. "I've had my hard times, an' fought a losin' strike, an' soaked my watch, an' ben unable to pay my rent or buy grub, an' slugged scabs, an' ben slugged, and ben thrown into jail for makin' a fool of myself. If I get you, I'd be a whole lot better to be a swell hog fattenin' for market an' nothin' worryin', than to be a guy sick to his stomach from not savvyin' how the world is made or from wonderin' what's the good of anything."

"That's good, that prize hog," the poet laughed. "Least irritation, least effort—a compromise of Nirvana and life. Least irritation, least effort, the ideal existence: a jellyfish floating in a tideless, tepid, twilight sea."

"But you're missin' all the good things," Billy objected.

"Name them," came the challenge.

Billy was silent a moment. To him life seemed a large and generous thing. He felt as if his arms ached from inability to compass it all, and he began, haltingly at first, to put his feeling into speech.

"If you'd ever stood up in the ring an' out-gamed an' out-fought a man as good as yourself for twenty rounds, you'd get what I'm drivin' at. Jim Hazard an' I get it when we swim out through the surf an' laugh in the teeth of the biggest breakers that ever pounded the beach, an' when we come out from the shower, rubbed down and dressed, our skin an' muscles like silk, our bodies an' brains all a-tinglin' like silk.. .."

He paused and gave up from sheer inability to express ideas that were nebulous at best and that in reality were remembered sensations.

"Silk of the body, can you beat it?" he concluded lamely, feeling that he had failed to make his point, embarrassed by the circle of listeners.

"We know all that," Hall retorted. "The lies of the flesh. Afterward come rheumatism and diabetes. The wine of life is heady, but all too quickly it turns to—"

"Uric acid," interpolated the wild Irish playwright.

"They's plenty more of the good things," Billy took up with a sudden rush of words. "Good things all the way up from juicy porterhouse and the kind of coffee Mrs. Hall makes to...." He hesitated at what he was about to say, then took it at a plunge. "To a woman you can love an' that loves you. Just take a look at Saxon there with the ukulele in her lap. There's where I got the jellyfish in the dishwater an' the prize hog skinned to death."

A shout of applause and great hand-clapping went up from the girls, and Billy looked painfully uncomfortable.

"But suppose the silk goes out of your body till you creak like a rusty wheelbarrow?" Hall pursued. "Suppose, just suppose, Saxon went away with another man. What then?"

Billy considered a space.

"Then it'd be me for the dishwater an' the jellyfish, I guess." He straightened up in his chair and threw back his shoulders unconsciously as he ran a hand over his biceps and swelled it. Then he took another look at Saxon. "But thank the Lord I still got a wallop in both my arms an' a wife to fill 'em with love."

Again the girls applauded, and Mrs. Hall cried:

"Look at Saxon! She blushing! What have you to say for yourself?"

"That no woman could be happier," she stammered, "and no queen as proud. And that—"

She completed the thought by strumming on the ukulele and singing:

"De Lawd move in er mischievous way His blunders to perform."

"I give you best," Hall grinned to Billy.

"Oh, I don't know," Billy disclaimed modestly. "You've read so much I guess you know more about everything than I do."

"Oh! Oh!" "Traitor!" "Taking it all back!" the girls cried variously.

Billy took heart of courage, reassured them with a slow smile, and said:

"Just the same I'd sooner be myself than have book indigestion. An' as for Saxon, why, one kiss of her lips is worth more'n all the libraries in the world."

CHAPTER X

"There must be hills and valleys, and rich land, and streams of clear water, good wagon roads and a railroad not too far away, plenty of sunshine, and cold enough at night to need blankets, and not only pines but plenty of other kinds of trees, with open spaces to pasture Billy's horses and cattle, and deer and rabbits for him to shoot, and lots and lots of redwood trees, and... and... well, and no fog," Saxon concluded the description of the farm she and Billy sought.

Mark Hall laughed delightedly.

"And nightingales roosting in all the trees," he cried; "flowers that neither fail nor fade, bees without stings, honey dew every morning, showers of manna betweenwhiles, fountains of youth and quarries of philosopher's stones—why, I know the very place. Let me show you."

She waited while he pored over road-maps of the state. Failing in them, he got out a big atlas, and, though all the countries of the world were in it, he could not find what he was after.

"Never mind," he said. "Come over to-night and I'll be able to show you."

That evening he led her out on the veranda to the telescope, and she found herself looking through it at the full moon.

"Somewhere up there in some valley you'll find that farm," he teased.

Mrs. Hall looked inquiringly at them as they returned inside.

"I've been showing her a valley in the moon where she expects to go farming," he laughed.

"We started out prepared to go any distance," Saxon said. "And if it's to the moon, I expect we can make it."

"But my dear child, you can't expect to find such a paradise on the earth," Hall continued. "For instance, you can't have redwoods without fog. They go together. The redwoods grow only in the fog belt."

Saxon debated a while.

"Well, we could put up with a little fog," she conceded, "—almost anything to have redwoods. I don't know what a quarry of philosopher's stones is like, but if it's anything like Mr. Hafler's marble quarry, and there's a railroad handy, I guess we could manage to worry along. And you don't have to go to the moon for honey dew. They scrape it off of the leaves of the bushes up in Nevada County. I know that for a fact, because my father told my mother about it, and she told me."

A little later in the evening, the subject of farming having remained uppermost, Hall swept off into a diatribe against the "gambler's paradise," which was his epithet for the United States.

"When you think of the glorious chance," he said. "A new country, bounded by the oceans, situated just right in latitude, with the richest land and vastest natural resources of any country in the world, settled by immigrants who had thrown off all the leading strings of the Old World and were in the humor for democracy. There was only one thing to stop them from perfecting the democracy they started, and that thing was greediness.

"They started gobbling everything in sight like a lot of swine, and while they gobbled democracy went to smash. Gobbling became gambling. It was a nation of tin horns. Whenever a man lost his stake, all he had to do was to chase the frontier west a few miles and get another stake. They moved over the face of the land like so many locusts. They destroyed everything—the Indians, the soil, the forests, just as they destroyed the buffalo and the passenger pigeon. Their morality in business and politics was gambler morality. Their laws were gambling laws—how to play the game. Everybody played. Therefore, hurrah for the game. Nobody objected, because nobody was unable to play. As I said, the losers chased the frontier for fresh stakes. The winner of to-day, broke to-morrow, on the day following might be riding his luck to royal flushes on five-card draws.

"So they gobbled and gambled from the Atlantic to the Pacific, until they'd swined a whole continent. When they'd finished with the lands and forests and mines, they turned back, gambling for any little stakes they'd overlooked, gambling for franchises and monopolies, using politics to protect their crooked deals and brace games. And democracy gone clean to smash.

"And then was the funniest time of all. The losers couldn't get any more stakes, while the winners went on gambling among themselves. The losers could only stand around with their hands in their pockets and look on. When they got hungry, they went, hat in hand, and begged the successful gamblers for a job. The losers went to work for the winners, and they've been working for them ever since, and democracy side-tracked up Salt Creek. You, Billy Roberts, have never had a hand in the game in your life. That's because your people were among the also-rans."

"How about yourself?" Billy asked. "I ain't seen you holdin' any hands."

"I don't have to. I don't count. I am a parasite."

"What's that?"

"A flea, a woodtick, anything that gets something for nothing. I batten on the mangy hides of the workingmen. I don't have to gamble. I don't have to work. My father left me enough of his winnings.—Oh, don't preen yourself, my boy. Your folks were just as bad as mine. But yours lost, and mine won, and so you plow in my potato patch."

"I don't see it," Billy contended stoutly. "A man with gumption can win out to-day—"

"On government land?" Hall asked quickly.

Billy swallowed and acknowledged the stab.

"Just the same he can win out," he reiterated.

"Surely—he can win a job from some other fellow? A young husky with a good head like yours can win jobs anywhere. But think of the handicaps on the fellows who lose. How many tramps have you met along the road who could get a job driving four horses for the Carmel Livery Stable? And some of them were as husky as you when they were young. And on top of it all you've got no shout coming. It's a mighty big come-down from gambling for a continent to gambling for a job."

"Just the same—" Billy recommenced.

"Oh, you've got it in your blood," Hall cut him off cavalierly. "And why not? Everybody in this country has been gambling for generations. It was in the air when you were born. You've breathed it all your life. You, who 've never had a white chip in the game, still go on shouting for it and capping for it."

"But what are all of us losers to do?" Saxon inquired.

"Call in the police and stop the game," Hall recommended. "It's crooked."

Saxon frowned.

"Do what your forefathers didn't do," he amplified. "Go ahead and perfect democracy."

She remembered a remark of Mercedes. "A friend of mine says that democracy is an enchantment."

"It is—in a gambling joint. There are a million boys in our public schools right now swallowing the gump of canal boy to President, and millions of worthy citizens who sleep sound every night in the belief that they have a say in running the country."

"You talk like my brother Tom," Saxon said, failing to comprehend. "If we all get into politics and work hard for something better maybe we'll get it after a thousand years or so. But I want it now." She clenched her hands passionately. "I can't wait; I want it now."

"But that is just what I've been telling you, my dear girl. That's what's the trouble with all the losers. They can't wait. They want it now —a stack of chips and a fling at the game. Well, they won't get it now. That's what's the matter with you, chasing a valley in the moon. That's what's the matter with Billy, aching right now for a chance to win ten cents from me at Pedro cussing wind-chewing under his breath."

"Gee! you'd make a good soap-boxer," commented Billy.

"And I'd be a soap-boxer if I didn't have the spending of my father's ill-gotten gains. It's none of my affair. Let them rot. They'd be just as bad if they were on top. It's all a mess—blind bats, hungry swine, and filthy buzzards—"

Here Mrs. Hall interfered.

"Now, Mark, you stop that, or you'll be getting the blues."

He tossed his mop of hair and laughed with an effort.

"No I won't," he denied. "I'm going to get ten cents from Billy at a game of Pedro. He won't have a look in."

Saxon and Billy flourished in the genial human atmosphere of Carmel. They appreciated in their own estimation. Saxon felt that she was something more than a laundry girl and the wife of a union teamster. She was no longer pent in the narrow working class environment of a Pine street neighborhood. Life had grown opulent. They fared better physically, materially, and spiritually; and all this was reflected in their features, in the carriage of their bodies. She knew Billy had never been handsomer nor in more splendid bodily condition. He swore he had a harem, and that she was his second wife— twice as beautiful as the first one he had married. And she demurely confessed to him that Mrs. Hall and several others of the matrons had enthusiastically admired her form one day when in for a cold dip in Carmel river. They had got around her, and called her Venus, and made her crouch and assume different poses.

Billy understood the Venus reference; for a marble one, with broken arms, stood in Hall's living room, and the poet had told him the world worshiped it as the perfection of female form.

"I always said you had Annette Kellerman beat a mile," Billy said; and so proud was his air of possession that Saxon blushed and trembled, and hid her hot face against his breast.

The men in the crowd were open in their admiration of Saxon, in an above-board manner. But she made no mistake. She did not lose her head. There was no chance of that, for her love for Billy beat more strongly than ever.

Nor was she guilty of over-appraisal. She knew him for what he was, and loved him with open eyes. He had no book learning, no art, like the other men. His grammar was bad; she knew that, just as she knew that he would never mend it. Yet she would not have exchanged him for any of the others, not even for Mark Hall with the princely heart whom she loved much in the same way that she loved his wife.

For that matter, she found in Billy a certain health and rightness, a certain essential integrity, which she prized more highly than all book learning and bank accounts. It was by virtue of this health, and rightness, and integrity, that he had beaten Hall in argument the night the poet was on the pessimistic rampage. Billy had beaten him, not with the weapons of learning, but just by being himself and by speaking out the truth that was in him. Best of all, he had not even known that he had beaten, and had taken the applause as good-natured banter. But Saxon knew, though she could scarcely tell why; and she would always remember how the wife of Shelley had whispered to her afterward with shining eyes: "Oh, Saxon, you must be so happy."

Were Saxon driven to speech to attempt to express what Billy meant to her, she would have done it with the simple word "man." Always he was that to her. Always in glowing splendor, that was his connotation—MAN. Sometimes, by herself, she would all but weep with joy at recollection of his way of informing some truculent male that he was standing on his foot. "Get off your foot. You're standin' on it." It was Billy! It was magnificently Billy. And it was this Billy who loved her. She knew it. She knew it by the pulse that only a woman knows how to gauge. He loved her less wildly, it was true; but more fondly, more maturely. It was the love that lasted—if only they did not go back to the city where the beautiful things of the spirit perished and the beast bared its fangs.

In the early spring, Mark Hall and his wife went to New York, the two Japanese servants of the bungalow were dismissed, and Saxon and Billy were installed as caretakers. Jim Hazard, too, departed on his yearly visit to Paris; and though Billy missed him, he continued his long swims out through the breakers. Hall's two saddle horses had been left in his charge, and Saxon made herself a pretty cross-saddle riding costume of tawny-brown corduroy that matched the glints in her hair. Billy no longer worked at odd jobs. As extra driver at the stable he earned more than they spent, and, in preference to cash, he taught Saxon to ride, and was out and away with her over the country on all-day trips. A favorite ride was around by the coast to Monterey, where he taught her to swim in the big Del Monte tank. They would come home in the evening across the hills. Also, she took to following him on his early morning hunts, and life seemed one long vacation.

"I'll tell you one thing," he said to Saxon, one day, as they drew their horses to a halt and gazed down into Carmel Valley. "I ain't never going to work steady for another man for wages as long as I live."

"Work isn't everything," she acknowledged.

"I should guess not. Why, look here, Saxon, what'd it mean if I worked teamin' in Oakland for a million dollars a day for a million years and just had to go on stayin' there an' livin' the way we used to? It'd mean work all day, three squares, an' movin' pictures for recreation. Movin' pictures! Huh! We're livin' movin' pictures these days. I'd sooner have one year like what we're havin' here in Carmel and then die, than a thousan' million years like on Pine street."

Saxon had warned the Halls by letter that she and Billy intended starting on their search for the valley in the moon as soon as the first of summer arrived. Fortunately, the poet was put to no inconvenience, for Bideaux, the Iron Man with the basilisk eyes, had abandoned his dreams of priesthood and decided to become an actor. He arrived at Carmel from the Catholic college in time to take charge of the bungalow.

Much to Saxon's gratification, the crowd was loth to see them depart. The owner of the Carmel stable offered to put Billy in charge at ninety dollars a month. Also, he received a similar offer from the stable in Pacific Grove.

"Whither away," the wild Irish playwright hailed them on the station platform at Monterey. He was just returning from New York.

"To a valley in the moon," Saxon answered gaily.

He regarded their business-like packs.

"By George!" he cried. "I'll do it! By George! Let me come along." Then his face fell. "And I've signed the contract," he groaned. "Three acts! Say, you're lucky. And this time of year, too."

CHAPTER XI

"We hiked into Monterey last winter, but we're ridin' out now, b 'gosh!" Billy said as the train pulled out and they leaned back in their seats.

They had decided against retracing their steps over the ground already traveled, and took the train to San Francisco. They had been warned by Mark Hall of the enervation of the south, and were bound north for their blanket climate. Their intention was to cross the Bay to Sausalito and wander up through the coast counties. Here, Hall had told them, they would find the true home of the redwood. But Billy, in the smoking car for a cigarette, seated himself beside a man who was destined to deflect them from their course. He was a keen-faced, dark-eyed man, undoubtedly a Jew; and Billy, remembering Saxon's admonition always to ask questions, watched his opportunity and started a conversation. It took but a little while to learn that Gunston was a commission merchant, and to realize that the content of his talk was too valuable for Saxon to lose. Promptly, when he saw that the other's cigar was finished, Billy invited him into the next car to meet Saxon. Billy would have been incapable of such an act prior to his sojourn in Carmel. That much at least he had acquired of social facility.

"He's just ben tellin' me about the potato kings, and I wanted him to tell you," Billy explained to Saxon after the introduction. "Go on and tell her, Mr. Gunston, about that fan tan sucker that made nineteen thousan' last year in celery an' asparagus."

"I was just telling your husband about the way the Chinese make things go up the San Joaquin river. It would be worth your while to go up there and look around. It's the good season now—too early for mosquitoes. You can get off the train at Black Diamond or Antioch and travel around among the big farming islands on the steamers and launches. The fares are cheap, and you'll find some of those big gasoline boats, like the Duchess and Princess, more like big steamboats."

"Tell her about Chow Lam," Billy urged.

The commission merchant leaned back and laughed.

"Chow Lam, several years ago, was a broken-down fan tan player. He hadn't a cent, and his health was going back on him. He had worn out his back with twenty years' work in the gold mines, washing over the tailings of the early miners. And whatever he'd made he'd lost at gambling. Also, he was in debt three hundred dollars to the Six Companies—you know, they're Chinese affairs. And, remember, this was only seven years ago—health breaking down, three hundred in debt, and no trade. Chow Lam blew into Stockton and got a job on the peat lands at day's wages. It was a Chinese company, down on Middle River, that farmed celery and asparagus. This was when he got onto himself and took stock of himself. A quarter of a century in the United States, back not so strong as it used to was, and not a penny laid by for his return to China. He saw how the Chinese in the company had done it—saved their wages and bought a share.

"He saved his wages for two years, and bought one share in a thirty-share company. That was only five years ago. They leased three hundred acres of peat land from a white man who preferred traveling in Europe. Out of the profits of that one share in the first year, he bought two shares in another company. And in a year more, out of the three shares, he organized a company of his own. One year of this, with bad luck, and he just broke even. That brings it up to three years ago. The following year, bumper crops, he netted four thousand. The next year it was five thousand. And last year he cleaned up nineteen thousand dollars. Pretty good, eh, for old broken-down Chow Lam?"

"My!" was all Saxon could say.

Her eager interest, however, incited the commission merchant to go on.

"Look at Sing Kee—the Potato King of Stockton. I know him well. I've had more large deals with him and made less money than with any man I know. He was only a coolie, and he smuggled himself into the United States twenty years ago. Started at day's wages, then peddled vegetables in a couple of baskets slung on a stick, and after that opened up a store in Chinatown in San Francisco. But he had a head on him, and he was soon onto the curves of the Chinese farmers that dealt at his store. The store couldn't make money fast enough to suit him. He headed up the San Joaquin. Didn't do much for a couple of years except keep his eyes peeled. Then he jumped in and leased twelve hundred acres at seven dollars an acre."

"My God!" Billy said in an awe-struck voice. "Eight thousan', four hundred dollars just for rent the first year. I know five hundred acres I can buy for three dollars an acre."

"Will it grow potatoes?" Gunston asked.

Billy shook his head. "Nor nothin' else, I guess."

All three laughed heartily and the commission merchant resumed:

"That seven dollars was only for the land. Possibly you know what it costs to plow twelve hundred acres?"

Billy nodded solemnly.

"And he got a hundred and sixty sacks to the acre that year," Gunston continued. "Potatoes were selling at fifty cents. My father was at the head of our concern at the time, so I know for a fact. And Sing Kee could have sold at fifty cents and made money. But did he? Trust a Chinaman to know the market. They can skin the commission merchants at it. Sing Kee held on. When 'most everybody else had sold, potatoes began to climb. He laughed at our buyers when we offered him sixty cents, seventy cents, a dollar. Do you want to know what he finally did sell for? One dollar and sixty-five a sack. Suppose they actually cost him forty cents. A hundred and sixty times twelve hundred... let me see... twelve times nought is nought and twelve times sixteen is a hundred and ninety-two... a hundred and ninety-two thousand sacks at a dollar and a quarter net... four into a hundred and ninety-two is forty-eight, plus, is two hundred and forty—there you are, two hundred and forty thousand dollars clear profit on that year's deal."

"An' him a Chink," Billy mourned disconsolately. He turned to Saxon. "They ought to be some new country for us white folks to go to. Gosh!—we're settin' on the stoop all right, all right."

"But, of course, that was unusual," Gunston hastened to qualify. "There was a failure of potatoes in other districts, and a corner, and in some strange way Sing Kee was dead on. He never made profits like that again. But he goes ahead steadily. Last year he had four thousand acres in potatoes, a thousand in asparagus, five hundred in celery and five hundred in beans. And he's running six hundred acres in seeds. No matter what happens to one or two crops, he can't lose on all of them."

"I've seen twelve thousand acres of apple trees," Saxon said. "And I'd like to see four thousand acres in potatoes."

"And we will," Billy rejoined with great positiveness. "It's us for the San Joaquin. We don't know what's in our country. No wonder we're out on the stoop."

"You'll find lots of kings up there," Gunston related. "Yep Hong Lee—they call him 'Big Jim,' and Ah Pock, and Ah Whang, and—then there's Shima, the Japanese potato king. He's worth several millions. Lives like a prince."

"Why don't Americans succeed like that?" asked Saxon.

"Because they won't, I guess. There's nothing to stop them except themselves. I'll tell you one thing, though—give me the Chinese to deal with. He's honest. His word is as good as his bond. If he says he'll do a thing, he'll do it. And, anyway, the white man doesn't know how to farm. Even the up-to-date white farmer is content with one crop at a time and rotation of crops. Mr. John Chinaman goes him one better, and grows two crops at one time on the same soil. I've seen it—radishes and carrots, two crops, sown at one time."

"Which don't stand to reason," Billy objected. "They'd be only a half crop of each."

"Another guess coming," Gunston jeered. "Carrots have to be thinned when they're so far along. So do radishes. But carrots grow slow. Radishes grow fast. The slow-going carrots serve the purpose of thinning the radishes. And when the radishes are pulled, ready for market, that thins the carrots, which come along later. You can't beat the Chink."

"Don't see why a white man can't do what a Chink can," protested Billy.

"That sounds all right," Gunston replied. "The only objection is that the white man doesn't. The Chink is busy all the time, and he keeps the ground just as busy. He has organization, system. Who ever heard of white farmers keeping books? The Chink does. No guess work with him. He knows just where he stands, to a cent, on any crop at any moment. And he knows the market. He plays both ends. How he does it is beyond me, but he knows the market better than we commission merchants.

"Then, again, he's patient but not stubborn. Suppose he does make a mistake, and gets in a crop, and then finds the market is wrong. In such a situation the white man gets stubborn and hangs on like a bulldog. But not the Chink. He's going to minimize the losses of that mistake. That land has got to work, and make money. Without a quiver or a regret, the moment he's learned his error, he puts his plows into that crop, turns it under, and plants something else. He has the savve. He can look at a sprout, just poked up out of the ground, and tell how it's going to turn out—whether it will head up or won't head up; or if it's going to head up good, medium, or bad. That's one end. Take the other end. He controls his crop. He forces it or holds it back with an eye on the market. And when the market is just right, there's his crop, ready to deliver, timed to the minute."

The conversation with Gunston lasted hours, and the more he talked of the Chinese and their farming ways the more Saxon became aware of a growing dissatisfaction. She did not question the facts. The trouble was that they were not alluring. Somehow, she could not find place for them in her valley of the moon. It was not until the genial Jew left the train that Billy gave definite statement to what was vaguely bothering her.

"Huh! We ain't Chinks. We're white folks. Does a Chink ever want to ride a horse, hell-bent for election an' havin' a good time of it? Did you ever see a Chink go swimmin' out through the breakers at Carmel?—or boxin', wrestlin', runnin' an' jumpin' for the sport of it? Did you ever see a Chink take a shotgun on his arm, tramp six miles, an' come back happy with one measly rabbit? What does a Chink do? Work his damned head off. That's all he's good for. To hell with work, if that's the whole of the game—an' I've done my share of work, an' I can work alongside of any of 'em. But what's the good? If they's one thing I've learned solid since you an' me hit the road, Saxon, it is that work's the least part of life. God!—if it was all of life I couldn't cut my throat quick enough to get away from it. I want shotguns an' rifles, an' a horse between my legs. I don't want to be so tired all the time I can't love my wife. Who wants to be rich an' clear two hundred an' forty thousand on a potato deal! Look at Rockefeller. Has to live on milk. I want porterhouse and a stomach that can bite sole-leather. An' I want you, an' plenty of time along with you, an' fun for both of us. What's the good of life if they ain't no fun?"

"Oh, Billy!" Saxon cried. "It's just what I've been trying to get straightened out in my head. It's been worrying me for ever so long. I was afraid there was something wrong with me—that I wasn't made for the country after all. All the time I didn't envy the San Leandro Portuguese. I didn't want to be one, nor a Pajaro Valley Dalmatian, nor even a Mrs. Mortimer. And you didn't either. What we want is a valley of the moon, with not too much work, and all the fun we want. And we'll just keep on looking until we find it. And if we don't find it, we'll go on having the fun just as we have ever since we left Oakland. And, Billy... we're never, never going to work our damned heads off, are we?"

"Not on your life," Billy growled in fierce affirmation.

They walked into Black Diamond with their packs on their backs. It was a scattered village of shabby little cottages, with a main street that was a wallow of black mud from the last late spring rain. The sidewalks bumped up and down in uneven steps and landings. Everything seemed un-American. The names on the strange dingy shops were unspeakably foreign. The one dingy hotel was run by a Greek. Greeks were everywhere—swarthy men in sea-boots and tam-o'-shanters, hatless women in bright colors, hordes of sturdy children, and all speaking in outlandish voices, crying shrilly and vivaciously with the volubility of the Mediterranean.

"Huh!—this ain't the United States," Billy muttered. Down on the water front they found a fish cannery and an asparagus cannery in the height of the busy season, where they looked in vain among the toilers for familiar American faces. Billy picked out the bookkeepers and foremen for Americans. All the rest were Greeks, Italians, and Chinese.

At the steamboat wharf, they watched the bright-painted Greek boats arriving, discharging their loads of glorious salmon, and departing. New York Cut-Off, as the slough was called, curved to the west and north and flowed into a vast body of water which was the united Sacramento and San Joaquin rivers.

Beyond the steamboat wharf, the fishing wharves dwindled to stages for the drying of nets; and here, away from the noise and clatter of the alien town, Saxon and Billy took off their packs and rested. The tall, rustling tules grew out of the deep water close to the dilapidated boat-landing where they sat. Opposite the town lay a long flat island, on which a row of ragged poplars leaned against the sky.

"Just like in that Dutch windmill picture Mark Hall has," Saxon said.

Billy pointed out the mouth of the slough and across the broad reach of water to a cluster of tiny white buildings, behind which, like a glimmering mirage, rolled the low Montezuma Hills.

"Those houses is Collinsville," he informed her. "The Sacramento river comes in there, and you go up it to Rio Vista an' Isleton, and Walnut Grove, and all those places Mr. Gunston was tellin' us about. It's all islands and sloughs, connectin' clear across an' back to the San Joaquin."

"Isn't the sun good," Saxon yawned. "And how quiet it is here, so short a distance away from those strange foreigners. And to think! in the cities, right now, men are beating and killing each other for jobs."

Now and again an overland passenger train rushed by in the distance, echoing along the background of foothills of Mt. Diablo, which bulked, twin-peaked, greencrinkled, against the sky. Then the slumbrous quiet would fall, to be broken by the far call of a foreign tongue or by a gasoline fishing boat chugging in through the mouth of the slough.

Not a hundred feet away, anchored close in the tules, lay a beautiful white yacht. Despite its tininess, it looked broad and comfortable. Smoke was rising for'ard from its stovepipe. On its stern, in gold letters, they read Roamer. On top of the cabin, basking in the sunshine, lay a man and woman, the latter with a pink scarf around her head. The man was reading aloud from a book, while she sewed. Beside them sprawled a fox terrier.

"Gosh! they don't have to stick around cities to be happy," Billy commented.

A Japanese came on deck from the cabin, sat down for'ard, and began picking a chicken. The feathers floated away in a long line toward the mouth of the slough.

"Oh! Look!" Saxon pointed in her excitement. "He's fishing! And the line is fast to his toe!"

The man had dropped the book face-downward on the cabin and reached for the line, while the woman looked up from her sewing, and the terrier began to bark. In came the line, hand under hand, and at the end a big catfish.

When this was removed, and the line rebaited and dropped overboard, the man took a turn around his toe and went on reading.

A Japanese came down on the landing-stage beside Saxon and Billy, and hailed the yacht. He carried parcels of meat and vegetables; one coat pocket bulged with letters, the other with morning papers. In response to his hail, the Japanese on the yacht stood up with the part-plucked chicken. The man said something to him, put aside the book, got into the white skiff lying astern, and rowed to the landing. As he came alongside the stage, he pulled in his oars, caught hold, and said good morning genially.

"Why, I know you," Saxon said impulsively, to Billy's amazement. "You are.. .."

Here she broke off in confusion.

"Go on," the man said, smiling reassurance.

"You are Jack Hastings, I 'm sure of it. I used to see your photograph in the papers all the time you were war correspondent in the Japanese-Russian War. You've written lots of books, though I've never read them."

"Right you are," he ratified. "And what's your name?"

Saxon introduced herself and Billy, and, when she noted the writer's observant eye on their packs, she sketched the pilgrimage they were on. The farm in the valley of the moon evidently caught his fancy, and, though the Japanese and his parcels were safely in the skiff, Hastings still lingered. When Saxon spoke of Carmel, he seemed to know everybody in Hall's crowd, and when he heard they were intending to go to Rio Vista, his invitation was immediate.

"Why, we're going that way ourselves, inside an hour, as soon as slack water comes," he exclaimed. "It's just the thing. Come on on board. We'll be there by four this afternoon if there's any wind at all. Come on. My wife's on board, and Mrs. Hall is one of her best chums. We've been away to South America—just got back; or you'd have seen us in Carmel. Hal wrote to us about the pair of you."

It was the second time in her life that Saxon had been in a small boat, and the Roamer was the first yacht she had ever been on board. The writer's wife, whom he called Clara, welcomed them heartily, and Saxon lost no time in falling in love with her and in being fallen in love with in return. So strikingly did they resemble each other, that Hastings was not many minutes in calling attention to it. He made them stand side by side, studied their eyes and mouths and ears, compared their hands, their hair, their ankles, and swore that his fondest dream was shattered—namely, that when Clara had been made the mold was broken.

On Clara's suggestion that it might have been pretty much the same mold, they compared histories. Both were of the pioneer stock. Clara's mother, like Saxon's, had crossed the Plains with ox-teams, and, like Saxon's, had wintered in Salt Intake City—in fact, had, with her sisters, opened the first Gentile school in that Mormon stronghold. And, if Saxon's father had helped raise the Bear Flag rebellion at Sonoma, it was at Sonoma that Clara's father had mustered in for the War of the Rebellion and ridden as far east with his troop as Salt Lake City, of which place he had been provost marshal when the Mormon trouble flared up. To complete it all, Clara fetched from the cabin an ukulele of boa wood that was the twin to Saxon's, and together they sang "Honolulu Tomboy."

Hastings decided to eat dinner—he called the midday meal by its old-fashioned name—before sailing; and down below Saxon was surprised and delighted by the measure of comfort in so tiny a cabin. There was just room for Billy to stand upright. A centerboard-case divided the room in half longitudinally, and to this was attached the hinged table from which they ate. Low bunks that ran the full cabin length, upholstered in cheerful green, served as seats. A curtain, easily attached by hooks between the centerboard-case and the roof, at night screened Mrs. Hastings' sleeping quarters. On the opposite side the two Japanese bunked, while for'ard, under the deck, was the galley. So small was it that there was just room beside it for the cook, who was compelled by the low deck to squat on his hands. The other Japanese, who had brought the parcels on board, waited on the table.

"They are looking for a ranch in the valley of the moon," Hastings concluded his explanation of the pilgrimage to Clara.

"Oh!—don't you know—" she cried; but was silenced by her husband.

"Hush," he said peremptorily, then turned to their guests. "Listen. There's something in that valley of the moon idea, but I won't tell you what. It is a secret. Now we've a ranch in Sonoma Valley about eight miles from the very town of Sonoma where you two girls' fathers took up soldiering; and if you ever come to our ranch you'll learn the secret. Oh, believe me, it's connected with your valley of the moon.—Isn't it, Mate?"

This last was the mutual name he and Clara had for each other.

She smiled and laughed and nodded her head.

"You might find our valley the very one you are looking for," she said.

But Hastings shook his head at her to check further speech. She turned to the fox terrier and made it speak for a piece of meat.

"Her name's Peggy," she told Saxon. "We had two Irish terriers down in the South Seas, brother and sister, but they died. We called them Peggy and Possum. So she's named after the original Peggy."

Billy was impressed by the ease with which the Roamer was operated. While they lingered at table, at a word from Hastings the two Japanese had gone on deck. Billy could hear them throwing down the halyards, casting off gaskets, and heaving the anchor short on the tiny winch. In several minutes one called down that everything was ready, and all went on deck. Hoisting mainsail and jigger was a matter of minutes. Then the cook and cabin-boy broke out anchor, and, while one hove it up, the other hoisted the jib. Hastings, at the wheel, trimmed the sheet. The Roamer paid off, filled her sails, slightly heeling, and slid across the smooth water and out the mouth of New York Slough. The Japanese coiled the halyards and went below for their own dinner.

"The flood is just beginning to make," said Hastings, pointing to a striped spar-buoy that was slightly tipping up-stream on the edge of the channel.

The tiny white houses of Collinsville, which they were nearing, disappeared behind a low island, though the Montezuma Hills, with their long, low, restful lines, slumbered on the horizon apparently as far away as ever.

As the Roamer passed the mouth of Montezuma Slough and entered the Sacramento, they came upon Collinsville close at hand. Saxon clapped her hands.

"It's like a lot of toy houses," she said, "cut out of cardboard. And those hilly fields are just painted up behind."

They passed many arks and houseboats of fishermen moored among the tules, and the women and children, like the men in the boats, were dark-skinned, black-eyed, foreign. As they proceeded up the river, they began to encounter dredges at work, biting out mouthfuls of the sandy river bottom and heaping it on top of the huge levees. Great mats of willow brush, hundreds of yards in length, were laid on top of the river-slope of the levees and held in place by steel cables and thousands of cubes of cement. The willows soon sprouted, Hastings told them, and by the time the mats were rotted away the sand was held in place by the roots of the trees.

"It must cost like Sam Hill," Billy observed.

"But the land is worth it," Hastings explained. "This island land is the most productive in the world. This section of California is like Holland. You wouldn't think it, but this water we're sailing on is higher than the surface of the islands. They're like leaky boats—calking, patching, pumping, night and day and all the time. But it pays. It pays."

Except for the dredgers, the fresh-piled sand, the dense willow thickets, and always Mt. Diablo to the south, nothing was to be seen. Occasionally a river steamboat passed, and blue herons flew into the trees.

"It must be very lonely," Saxon remarked.

Hastings laughed and told her she would change her mind later. Much he related to them of the river lands, and after a while he got on the subject of tenant farming. Saxon had started him by speaking of the land-hungry Anglo-Saxons.

"Land-hogs," he snapped. "That's our record in this country. As one old Reuben told a professor of an agricultural experiment station: 'They ain't no sense in tryin' to teach me farmin'. I know all about it. Ain't I worked out three farms?' It was his kind that destroyed New England. Back there great sections are relapsing to wilderness. In one state, at least, the deer have increased until they are a nuisance. There are abandoned farms by the tens of thousands. I've gone over the lists of them—farms in New York, New Jersey, Massachusetts, Connecticut. Offered for sale on easy payment. The prices asked wouldn't pay for the improvements, while the land, of course, is thrown in for nothing.

"And the same thing is going on, in one way or another, the same land-robbing and hogging, over the rest of the country—down in Texas, in Missouri, and Kansas, out here in California. Take tenant farming. I know a ranch in my county where the land was worth a hundred and twenty-five an acre. And it gave its return at that valuation. When the old man died, the son leased it to a Portuguese and went to live in the city. In five years the Portuguese skimmed the cream and dried up the udder. The second lease, with another Portuguese for three years, gave one-quarter the former return. No third Portuguese appeared to offer to lease it. There wasn't anything left. That ranch was worth fifty thousand when the old man died. In the end the son got eleven thousand for it. Why, I've seen land that paid twelve per cent., that, after the skimming of a five-years' lease, paid only one and a quarter per cent."

"It's the same in our valley," Mrs. Hastings supplemented. "All the old farms are dropping into ruin. Take the Ebell Place, Mate." Her husband nodded emphatic indorsement. "When we used to know it, it was a perfect paradise of a farm. There were dams and lakes, beautiful meadows, lush hayfields, red hills of grape-lands, hundreds of acres of good pasture, heavenly groves of pines and oaks, a stone winery, stone barns, grounds—oh, I couldn't describe it in hours. When Mrs. Bell died, the family scattered, and the leasing began. It's a ruin to-day. The trees have been cut and sold for firewood. There's only a little bit of the vineyard that isn't abandoned—just enough to make wine for the present Italian lessees, who are running a poverty-stricken milk ranch on the leavings of the soil. I rode over it last year, and cried. The beautiful orchard is a horror. The grounds have gone back to the wild. Just because they didn't keep the gutters cleaned out, the rain trickled down and dry-rotted the timbers, and the big stone barn is caved in. The same with part of the winery—the other part is used for stabling the cows. And the house!—words can't describe!"

"It's become a profession," Hastings went on. "The 'movers.' They lease, clean out and gut a place in several years, and then move on. They're not like the foreigners, the Chinese, and Japanese, and the rest. In the main they're a lazy, vagabond, poor-white sort, who do nothing else but skin the soil and move, skin the soil and move. Now take the Portuguese and Italians in our country. They are different. They arrive in the country without a penny and work for others of their countrymen until they've learned the language and their way about. Now they're not movers. What they are after is land of their own, which they will love and care for and conserve. But, in the meantime, how to get it? Saving wages is slow. There is a quicker way. They lease. In three years they can gut enough out of somebody else's land to set themselves up for life. It is sacrilege, a veritable rape of the land; but what of it? It's the way of the United States."

He turned suddenly on Billy.

"Look here, Roberts. You and your wife are looking for your bit of land. You want it bad. Now take my advice. It's cold, hard advice. Become a tenant farmer. Lease some place, where the old folks have died and the country isn't good enough for the sons and daughters. Then gut it. Wring the last dollar out of the soil, repair nothing, and in three years you'll have your own place paid for. Then turn over a new leaf, and love your soil. Nourish it. Every dollar you feed it will return you two. And have nothing scrub about the place. If it's a horse, a cow, a pig, a chicken, or a blackberry vine, see that it's thoroughbred."

"But it's wicked!" Saxon wrung out. "It's wicked advice."

"We live in a wicked age," Hastings countered, smiling grimly. "This wholesale land-skinning is the national crime of the United States to-day. Nor would I give your husband such advice if I weren't absolutely certain that the land he skins would be skinned by some Portuguese or Italian if he refused. As fast as they arrive and settle down, they send for their sisters and their cousins and their aunts. If you were thirsty, if a warehouse were burning and beautiful Rhine wine were running to waste, would you stay your hand from scooping a drink? Well, the national warehouse is afire in many places, and no end of the good things are running to waste. Help yourself. If you don't, the immigrants will."

"Oh, you don't know him," Mrs. Hastings hurried to explain. "He spends all his time on the ranch in conserving the soil. There are over a thousand acres of woods alone, and, though he thins and forests like a surgeon, he won't let a tree be chopped without his permission. He's even planted a hundred thousand trees. He's always draining and ditching to stop erosion, and experimenting with pasture grasses. And every little while he buys some exhausted adjoining ranch and starts building up the soil."

"Wherefore I know what I 'm talking about," Hastings broke in. "And my advice holds. I love the soil, yet to-morrow, things being as they are and if I were poor, I'd gut five hundred acres in order to buy twenty-five for myself. When you get into Sonoma Valley, look me up, and I'll put you onto the whole game, and both ends of it. I'll show you construction as well as destruction. When you find a farm doomed to be gutted anyway, why jump in and do it yourself."

"Yes, and he mortgaged himself to the eyes," laughed Mrs. Hastings, "to keep five hundred acres of woods out of the hands of the charcoal burners."

Ahead, on the left bank of the Sacramento, just at the fading end of the Montezuma Hills, Rio Vista appeared. The Roamer slipped through the smooth water, past steamboat wharves, landing stages, and warehouses. The two Japanese went for'ard on deck. At command of Hastings, the jib ran down, and he shot the Roomer into the wind, losing way, until he called, "Let go the hook!" The anchor went down, and the yacht swung to it, so close to shore that the skiff lay under overhanging willows.

"Farther up the river we tie to the bank," Mrs. Hastings said, "so that when you wake in the morning you find the branches of trees sticking down into the cabin."

"Ooh!" Saxon murmured, pointing to a lump on her wrist. "Look at that. A mosquito."

"Pretty early for them," Hastings said. "But later on they're terrible. I've seen them so thick I couldn't back the jib against them."

Saxon was not nautical enough to appreciate his hyperbole, though Billy grinned.

"There are no mosquitoes in the valley of the moon," she said.

"No, never," said Mrs. Hastings, whose husband began immediately to regret the smallness of the cabin which prevented him from offering sleeping accommodations.

An automobile bumped along on top of the levee, and the young boys and girls in it cried, "Oh, you kid!" to Saxon and Billy, and Hastings, who was rowing them ashore in the skiff. Hastings called, "Oh, you kid!" back to them; and Saxon, pleasuring in the boyishness of his sunburned face, was reminded of the boyishness of Mark Hall and his Carmel crowd.

CHAPTER XII

Crossing the Sacramento on an old-fashioned ferry a short distance above Rio Vista, Saxon and Billy entered the river country. From the top of the levee she got her revelation. Beneath, lower than the river, stretched broad, flat land, far as the eye could see. Roads ran in every direction, and she saw countless farmhouses of which she had never dreamed when sailing on the lonely river a few feet the other side of the willowy fringe.

Three weeks they spent among the rich farm islands, which heaped up levees and pumped day and night to keep afloat. It was a monotonous land, with an unvarying richness of soil and with only one landmark—Mt. Diablo, ever to be seen, sleeping in the midday azure, limping its crinkled mass against the sunset sky, or forming like a dream out of the silver dawn. Sometimes on foot, often by launch, they criss-crossed and threaded the river region as far as the peat lands of the Middle River, down the San Joaquin to Antioch, and up Georgiana Slough to Walnut Grove on the Sacramento. And it proved a foreign land. The workers of the soil teemed by thousands, yet Saxon and Billy knew what it was to go a whole day without finding any one who spoke English. They encountered—sometimes in whole villages—Chinese, Japanese, Italians, Portuguese, Swiss, Hindus, Koreans, Norwegians, Danes, French, Armenians, Slavs, almost every nationality save American. One American they found on the lower reaches of Georgiana who eked an illicit existence by fishing with traps. Another American, who spouted blood and destruction on all political subjects, was an itinerant bee-farmer. At Walnut Grove, bustling with life, the few Americans consisted of the storekeeper, the saloonkeeper, the butcher, the keeper of the drawbridge, and the ferryman. Yet two thriving towns were in Walnut Grove, one Chinese, one Japanese. Most of the land was owned by Americans, who lived away from it and were continually selling it to the foreigners.

A riot, or a merry-making—they could not tell which—was taking place in the Japanese town, as Saxon and Billy steamed out on the Apache, bound for Sacramento.

"We're settin' on the stoop," Billy railed. "Pretty soon they'll crowd us off of that."

"There won't be any stoop in the valley of the moon," Saxon cheered him.

But he was inconsolable, remarking bitterly:

"An' they ain't one of them damn foreigners that can handle four horses like me.

"But they can everlastingly farm," he added.

And Saxon, looking at his moody face, was suddenly reminded of a lithograph she had seen in her childhood. It was of a Plains Indian, in paint and feathers, astride his horse and gazing with wondering eye at a railroad train rushing along a fresh-made track. The Indian had passed, she remembered, before the tide of new life that brought the railroad. And were Billy and his kind doomed to pass, she pondered, before this new tide of life, amazingly industrious, that was flooding in from Asia and Europe?

At Sacramento they stopped two weeks, where Billy drove team and earned the money to put them along on their travels. Also, life in Oakland and Carmel, close to the salt edge of the coast, had spoiled them for the interior. Too warm, was their verdict of Sacramento and they followed the railroad west, through a region of swamp-land, to Davisville. Here they were lured aside and to the north to pretty Woodland, where Billy drove team for a fruit farm, and where Saxon wrung from him a reluctant consent for her to work a few days in the fruit harvest. She made an important and mystifying secret of what she intended doing with her earnings, and Billy teased her about it until the matter passed from his mind. Nor did she tell him of a money order inclosed with a certain blue slip of paper in a letter to Bud Strothers.

They began to suffer from the heat. Billy declared they had strayed out of the blanket climate.

"There are no redwoods here," Saxon said. "We must go west toward the coast. It is there we'll find the valley of the moon."

From Woodland they swung west and south along the county roads to the fruit paradise of Vacaville. Here Billy picked fruit, then drove team; and here Saxon received a letter and a tiny express package from Bud Strothers. When Billy came into camp from the day's work, she bade him stand still and shut his eyes. For a few seconds she fumbled and did something to the breast of his cotton work-shirt. Once, he felt a slight prick, as of a pin point, and grunted, while she laughed and bullied him to continue keeping his eyes shut.

"Close your eyes and give me a kiss," she sang, "and then I'll show you what iss."

She kissed him and when he looked down he saw, pinned to his shirt, the gold medals he had pawned the day they had gone to the moving picture show and received their inspiration to return to the land.

"You darned kid!" he exclaimed, as he caught her to him. "So that's what you blew your fruit money in on? An' I never guessed!—Come here to you."

And thereupon she suffered the pleasant mastery of his brawn, and was hugged and wrestled with until the coffee pot boiled over and she darted from him to the rescue.

"I kinda always been a mite proud of 'em," he confessed, as he rolled his after-supper cigarette. "They take me back to my kid days when I amateured it to beat the band. I was some kid in them days, believe muh.—But say, d'ye know, they'd clean slipped my recollection. Oakland's a thousan' years away from you an' me, an' ten thousan' miles."

"Then this will bring you back to it," Saxon said, opening Bud's letter and reading it aloud.

Bud had taken it for granted that Billy knew the wind-up of the strike; so he devoted himself to the details as to which men had got back their jobs, and which had been blacklisted. To his own amazement he had been taken back, and was now driving Billy's horses. Still more amazing was the further information he had to impart. The old foreman of the West Oakland stables had died, and since then two other foremen had done nothing but make messes of everything. The point of all which was that the Boss had spoken that day to Bud, regretting the disappearance of Billy.

"Don't make no mistake," Bud wrote. "The Boss is onto all your curves. I bet he knows every scab you slugged. Just the same he says to me—Strothers, if you ain't at liberty to give me his address, just write yourself and tell him for me to come a running. I'll give him a hundred and twenty-five a month to take hold the stables."

Saxon waited with well-concealed anxiety when the letter was finished. Billy, stretched out, leaning on one elbow, blew a meditative ring of smoke. His cheap workshirt, incongruously brilliant with the gold of the medals that flashed in the firelight, was open in front, showing the smooth skin and splendid swell of chest. He glanced around—at the blankets bowered in a green screen and waiting, at the campfire and the blackened, battered coffee pot, at the well-worn hatchet, half buried in a tree trunk, and lastly at Saxon. His eyes embraced her; then into them came a slow expression of inquiry. But she offered no help.

"Well," he uttered finally, "all you gotta do is write Bud Strothers, an' tell 'm not on the Boss's ugly tintype.—An' while you're about it, I'll send 'm the money to get my watch out. You work out the interest. The overcoat can stay there an' rot."

But they did not prosper in the interior heat. They lost weight. The resilience went out of their minds and bodies. As Billy expressed it, their silk was frazzled. So they shouldered their packs and headed west across the wild mountains. In the Berryessa Valley, the shimmering heat waves made their eyes ache, and their heads; so that they traveled on in the early morning and late afternoon. Still west they headed, over more mountains, to beautiful Napa Valley. The next valley beyond was Sonoma, where Hastings had invited them to his ranch. And here they would have gone, had not Billy chanced upon a newspaper item which told of the writer's departure to cover some revolution that was breaking out somewhere in Mexico.

"We'll see 'm later on," Billy said, as they turned northwest, through the vineyards and orchards of Napa Valley. "We're like that millionaire Bert used to sing about, except it's time that we've got to burn. Any direction is as good as any other, only west is best."

Three times in the Napa Valley Billy refused work. Past St. Helena, Saxon hailed with joy the unmistakable redwoods they could see growing up the small canyons that penetrated the western wall of the valley. At Calistoga, at the end of the railroad, they saw the six-horse stages leaving for Middletown and Lower Lake. They debated their route. That way led to Lake County and not toward the coast, so Saxon and Billy swung west through the mountains to the valley of the Russian River, coming out at Healdsburg. They lingered in the hop-fields on the rich bottoms, where Billy scorned to pick hops alongside of Indians, Japanese, and Chinese.

"I couldn't work alongside of 'em an hour before I'd be knockin' their blocks off," he explained. "Besides, this Russian River's some nifty. Let's pitch camp and go swimmin'."

So they idled their way north up the broad, fertile valley, so happy that they forgot that work was ever necessary, while the valley of the moon was a golden dream, remote, but sure, some day of realization. At Cloverdale, Billy fell into luck. A combination of sickness and mischance found the stage stables short a driver. Each day the train disgorged passengers for the Geysers, and Billy, as if accustomed to it all his life, took the reins of six horses and drove a full load over the mountains in stage time. The second trip he had Saxon beside him on the high boxseat. By the end of two weeks the regular driver was back. Billy declined a stable-job, took his wages, and continued north.

Saxon had adopted a fox terrier puppy and named him Possum, after the dog Mrs. Hastings had told them about. So young was he that he quickly became footsore, and she carried him until Billy perched him on top of his pack and grumbled that Possum was chewing his back hair to a frazzle.

They passed through the painted vineyards of Asti at the end of the grape-picking, and entered Ukiah drenched to the skin by the first winter rain.

"Say," Billy said, "you remember the way the Roamer just skated along. Well, this summer's done the same thing—gone by on wheels. An' now it's up to us to find some place to winter. This Ukiah looks like a pretty good burg. We'll get a room to-night an' dry out. An' to-morrow I'll hustle around to the stables, an' if I locate anything we can rent a shack an' have all winter to think about where we'll go next year."

CHAPTER XIII

The winter proved much less exciting than the one spent in Carmel, and keenly as Saxon had appreciated the Carmel folk, she now appreciated them more keenly than ever. In Ukiah she formed nothing more than superficial acquaintances. Here people were more like those of the working class she had known in Oakland, or else they were merely wealthy and herded together in automobiles. There was no democratic artist-colony that pursued fellowship disregardful of the caste of wealth.

Yet it was a more enjoyable winter than any she had spent in Oakland. Billy had failed to get regular employment; so she saw much of him, and they lived a prosperous and happy hand-to-mouth existence in the tiny cottage they rented. As extra man at the biggest livery stable, Billy's spare time was so great that he drifted into horse-trading. It was hazardous, and more than once he was broke, but the table never wanted for the best of steak and coffee, nor did they stint themselves for clothes.

"Them blamed farmers—I gotta pass it to 'em," Billy grinned one day, when he had been particularly bested in a horse deal. "They won't tear under the wings, the sons of guns. In the summer they take in boarders, an' in the winter they make a good livin' doin' each other up at tradin' horses. An' I just want to tell YOU, Saxon, they've sure shown me a few. An' I 'm gettin' tough under the wings myself. I'll never tear again so as you can notice it. Which means one more trade learned for yours truly. I can make a livin' anywhere now tradin' horses."

Often Billy had Saxon out on spare saddle horses from the stable, and his horse deals took them on many trips into the surrounding country. Likewise she was with him when he was driving horses to sell on commission; and in both their minds, independently, arose a new idea concerning their pilgrimage. Billy was the first to broach it.

"I run into an outfit the other day, that's stored in town," he said, "an' it's kept me thinkin' ever since. Ain't no use tryin' to get you to guess it, because you can't. I'll tell you—the swellest wagon-campin' outfit anybody ever heard of. First of all, the wagon's a peacherino. Strong as they make 'em. It was made to order, upon Puget Sound, an' it was tested out all the way down here. No load an' no road can strain it. The guy had consumption that had it built. A doctor an' a cook traveled with 'm till he passed in his checks here in Ukiah two years ago. But say—if you could see it. Every kind of a contrivance—a place for everything—a regular home on wheels. Now, if we could get that, an' a couple of plugs, we could travel like kings, an' laugh at the weather."

"Oh! Billy! it's just what I've been dreamin' all winter. It would be ideal. And... well, sometimes on the road I'm sure you can't help forgetting what a nice little wife you've got... and with a wagon I could have all kinds of pretty clothes along."

Billy's blue eyes glowed a caress, cloudy and warm; as he said quietly:

"I've ben thinkin' about that."

"And you can carry a rifle and shotgun and fishing poles and everything," she rushed along. "And a good big axe, man-size, instead of that hatchet you're always complaining about. And Possum can lift up his legs and rest. And—but suppose you can't buy it? How much do they want?"

"One hundred an' fifty big bucks," he answered. "But dirt cheap at that. It's givin' it away. I tell you that rig wasn't built for a cent less than four hundred, an' I know wagon-work in the dark. Now, if I can put through that dicker with Caswell's six horses—say, I just got onto that horse-buyer to-day. If he buys 'em, who d'ye think he'll ship 'em to? To the Boss, right to the West Oakland stables. I'm goin' to get you to write to him. Travelin', as we're goin' to, I can pick up bargains. An' if the Boss'll talk, I can make the regular horse-buyer's commissions. He'll have to trust me with a lot of money, though, which most likely he won't, knowin' all his scabs I beat up."

"If he could trust you to run his stable, I guess he isn't afraid to let you handle his money," Saxon said.

Billy shrugged his shoulders in modest dubiousness.

"Well, anyway, as I was sayin' if I can sell Caswell's six horses, why, we can stand off this month's bills an' buy the wagon."

"But horses!" Saxon queried anxiously.

"They'll come later—if I have to take a regular job for two or three months. The only trouble with that 'd be that it'd run us pretty well along into summer before we could pull out. But come on down town an' I'll show you the outfit right now."

Saxon saw the wagon and was so infatuated with it that she lost a night's sleep from sheer insomnia of anticipation. Then Caswell's six horses were sold, the month's bills held over, and the wagon became theirs. One rainy morning, two weeks later, Billy had scarcely left the house, to be gone on an all-day trip into the country after horses, when he was back again.

"Come on!" he called to Saxon from the street. "Get your things on an' come along. I want to show you something."

He drove down town to a board stable, and took her through to a large, roofed inclosure in the rear. There he led to her a span of sturdy dappled chestnuts, with cream-colored manes and tails.

"Oh, the beauties! the beauties!" Saxon cried, resting her cheek against the velvet muzzle of one, while the other roguishly nuzzled for a share.

"Ain't they, though?" Billy reveled, leading them up and down before her admiring gaze. "Thirteen hundred an' fifty each, an' they don't look the weight, they're that slick put together. I couldn't believe it myself, till I put 'em on the scales. Twenty-seven hundred an' seven pounds, the two of 'em. An' I tried 'em out—that was two days ago. Good dispositions, no faults, an' true-pullers, automobile broke an' all the rest. I'd back 'em to out-pull any team of their weight I ever seen.—Say, how'd they look hooked up to that wagon of ourn?"

Saxon visioned the picture, and shook her head slowly in a reaction of regret.

"Three hundred spot cash buys 'em," Billy went on. "An' that's bed-rock. The owner wants the money so bad he's droolin' for it. Just gotta sell, an' sell quick. An' Saxon, honest to God, that pair'd fetch five hundred at auction down in the city. Both mares, full sisters, five an' six years old, registered Belgian sire, out of a heavy standard-bred mare that I know. Three hundred takes 'em, an' I got the refusal for three days."

Saxon's regret changed to indignation.

"Oh, why did you show them to me? We haven't any three hundred, and you know it. All I've got in the house is six dollars, and you haven't that much."

"Maybe you think that's all I brought you down town for," he replied enigmatically. "Well, it ain't."

He paused, licked his lips, and shifted his weight uneasily from one leg to the other.

"Now you listen till I get all done before you say anything. Ready?"

She nodded.

"Won't open your mouth?"

This time she obediently shook her head.

"Well, it's this way," he began haltingly. "They's a youngster come up from Frisco, Young Sandow they call 'm, an' the Pride of Telegraph Hill. He's the real goods of a heavyweight, an' he was to fight Montana Red Saturday night, only Montana Red, just in a little trainin' bout, snapped his forearm yesterday. The managers has kept it quiet. Now here's the proposition. Lots of tickets sold, an' they'll be a big crowd Saturday night. At the last moment, so as not to disappoint 'em, they'll spring me to take Montana's place. I 'm the dark horse. Nobody knows me—not even Young Sandow. He's come up since my time. I'll be a rube fighter. I can fight as Horse Roberts.

"Now, wait a minute. The winner'll pull down three hundred big round iron dollars. Wait, I 'm tellin' you! It's a lead-pipe cinch. It's like robbin' a corpse. Sandow's got all the heart in the world—regular knock-down-an'-drag-out-an'-hang-on fighter. I've followed 'm in the papers. But he ain't clever. I 'm slow, all right, all right, but I 'm clever, an' I got a hay-maker in each arm. I got Sandow's number an' I know it.

"Now, you got the say-so in this. If you say yes, the nags is ourn. If you say no, then it's all bets off, an' everything all right, an' I'll take to harness-washin' at the stable so as to buy a couple of plugs. Remember, they'll only be plugs, though. But don't look at me while you're makin' up your mind. Keep your lamps on the horses."

It was with painful indecision that she looked at the beautiful animals.

"Their names is Hazel an' Hattie," Billy put in a sly wedge. "If we get 'em we could call it the 'Double H' outfit."

But Saxon forgot the team and could only see Billy's frightfully bruised body the night he fought the Chicago Terror. She was about to speak, when Billy, who had been hanging on her lips, broke in:

"Just hitch 'em up to our wagon in your mind an' look at the outfit. You got to go some to beat it."

"But you're not in training, Billy," she said suddenly and without having intended to say it.

"Huh!" he snorted. "I've been in half trainin' for the last year. My legs is like iron. They'll hold me up as long as I've got a punch left in my arms, and I always have that. Besides, I won't let 'm make a long fight. He's a man-eater, an' man-eaters is my meat. I eat 'm alive. It's the clever boys with the stamina an' endurance that I can't put away. But this young Sandow's my meat. I'll get 'm maybe in the third or fourth round—you know, time 'm in a rush an' hand it to 'm just as easy. It's a lead-pipe cinch, I tell you. Honest to God, Saxon, it's a shame to take the money."

"But I hate to think of you all battered up," she temporized. "If I didn't love you so, it might be different. And then, too, you might get hurt."

Billy laughed in contemptuous pride of youth and brawn.

"You won't know I've been in a fight, except that we'll own Hazel an' Hattie there. An' besides, Saxon, I just gotta stick my fist in somebody's face once in a while. You know I can go for months peaceable an' gentle as a lamb, an' then my knuckles actually begin to itch to land on something. Now, it's a whole lot sensibler to land on Young Sandow an' get three hundred for it, than to land on some hayseed an' get hauled up an' fined before some justice of the peace. Now take another squint at Hazel an' Hattie. They're regular farm furniture, good to breed from when we get to that valley of the moon. An' they're heavy enough to turn right into the plowin', too."

The evening of the fight at quarter past eight, Saxon parted from Billy. At quarter past nine, with hot water, ice, and everything ready in anticipation, she heard the gate click and Billy's step come up the porch. She had agreed to the fight much against her better judgment, and had regretted her consent every minute of the hour she had just waited; so that, as she opened the front door, she was expectant of any sort of a terrible husband-wreck. But the Billy she saw was precisely the Billy she had parted from.

"There was no fight?" she cried, in so evident disappointment that he laughed.

"They was all yellin' 'Fake! Fake!' when I left, an' wantin' their money back."

"Well, I've got YOU," she laughed, leading him in, though secretly she sighed farewell to Hazel and Hattie.

"I stopped by the way to get something for you that you've been wantin' some time," Billy said casually. "Shut your eyes an' open your hand; an' when you open your eyes you'll find it grand," he chanted.

Into her hand something was laid that was very heavy and very cold, and when her eyes opened she saw it was a stack of fifteen twenty-dollar gold pieces.

"I told you it was like takin' money from a corpse," he exulted, as he emerged grinning from the whirlwind of punches, whacks, and hugs in which she had enveloped him. "They wasn't no fight at all. D 'ye want to know how long it lasted? Just twenty-seven seconds—less 'n half a minute. An' how many blows struck? One. An' it was me that done it. Here, I'll show you. It was just like this—a regular scream."

Billy had taken his place in the middle of the room, slightly crouching, chin tucked against the sheltering left shoulder, fists closed, elbows in so as to guard left side and abdomen, and forearms close to the body.

"It's the first round," he pictured. "Gong's sounded, an' we've shook hands. Of course, seein' as it's a long fight an' we've never seen each other in action, we ain't in no rush. We're just feelin' each other out an' fiddlin' around. Seventeen seconds like that. Not a blow struck. Nothin'. An' then it's all off with the big Swede. It takes some time to tell it, but it happened in a jiffy, in less'n a tenth of a second. I wasn't expectin' it myself. We're awful close together. His left glove ain't a foot from my jaw, an' my left glove ain't a foot from his. He feints with his right, an' I know it's a feint, an' just hunch up my left shoulder a bit an' feint with my right. That draws his guard over just about an inch, an' I see my openin'. My left ain't got a foot to travel. I don't draw it back none. I start it from where it is, corkscrewin' around his right guard an' pivotin' at the waist to put the weight of my shoulder into the punch. An' it connects!—Square on the point of the chin, sideways. He drops deado. I walk back to my corner, an', honest to God, Saxon, I can't help gigglin' a little, it was that easy. The referee stands over 'm an' counts 'm out. He never quivers. The audience don't know what to make of it an' sits paralyzed. His seconds carry 'm to his corner an' set 'm on the stool. But they gotta hold 'm up. Five minutes afterward he opens his eyes—but he ain't seein' nothing. They're glassy. Five minutes more, an' he stands up. They got to help hold 'm, his legs givin' under 'm like they was sausages. An' the seconds has to help 'm through the ropes, an' they go down the aisle to his dressin' room a-helpin' 'm. An' the crowd beginning to yell fake an' want its money back. Twenty-seven seconds—one punch—n' a spankin' pair of horses for the best wife Billy Roberts ever had in his long experience."

All of Saxon's old physical worship of her husband revived and doubled on itself many times. He was in all truth a hero, worthy to be of that wing-helmeted company leaping from the beaked boats upon the bloody English sands. The next morning he was awakened by her lips pressed on his left hand.

"Hey!—what are you doin'?" he demanded.

"Kissing Hazel and Hattie good morning," she answered demurely. "And now I 'm going to kiss you good morning.. .. And just where did your punch land? Show me."

Billy complied, touching the point of her chin with his knuckles. With both her hands on his arm, she shoved it back and tried to draw it forward sharply in similitude of a punch. But Billy withstrained her.

"Wait," he said. "You don't want to knock your jaw off. I'll show you. A quarter of an inch will do."

And at a distance of a quarter of an inch from her chin he administered the slightest flick of a tap.

On the instant Saxon's brain snapped with a white flash of light, while her whole body relaxed, numb and weak, volitionless, sad her vision reeled and blurred. The next instant she was herself again, in her eyes terror and understanding.

"And it was at a foot that you struck him," she murmured in a voice of awe.

"Yes, and with the weight of my shoulders behind it," Billy laughed. "Oh, that's nothing.—Here, let me show you something else."

He searched out her solar plexus, and did no more than snap his middle finger against it. This time she experienced a simple paralysis, accompanied by a stoppage of breath, but with a brain and vision that remained perfectly clear. In a moment, however, all the unwonted sensations were gone.

"Solar Plexus," Billy elucidated. "Imagine what it's like when the other fellow lifts a wallop to it all the way from his knees. That's the punch that won the championship of the world for Bob Fitzsimmons."

Saxon shuddered, then resigned herself to Billy's playful demonstration of the weak points in the human anatomy. He pressed the tip of a finger into the middle of her forearm, and she knew excruciating agony. On either side of her neck, at the base, he dented gently with his thumbs, and she felt herself quickly growing unconscious.

"That's one of the death touches of the Japs," he told her, and went on, accompanying grips and holds with a running exposition. "Here's the toe-hold that Notch defeated Hackenschmidt with. I learned it from Farmer Burns.—An' here's a half-Nelson.—An' here's you makin' roughhouse at a dance, an' I 'm the floor manager, an' I gotta put you out."

One hand grasped her wrist, the other hand passed around and under her forearm and grasped his own wrist. And at the first hint of pressure she felt that her arm was a pipe-stem about to break.

"That's called the 'come along.'—An' here's the strong arm. A boy can down a man with it. An' if you ever get into a scrap an' the other fellow gets your nose between his teeth—you don't want to lose your nose, do you? Well, this is what you do, quick as a flash."

Involuntarily she closed her eyes as Billy's thumb-ends pressed into them. She could feel the fore-running ache of a dull and terrible hurt.

"If he don't let go, you just press real hard, an' out pop his eyes, an' he's blind as a bat for the rest of his life. Oh, he'll let go all right all right."

He released her and lay back laughing.

"How d'ye feel?" he asked. "Those ain't boxin' tricks, but they're all in the game of a roughhouse."

"I feel like revenge," she said, trying to apply the "come along" to his arm.

When she exerted the pressure she cried out with pain, for she had succeeded only in hurting herself. Billy grinned at her futility. She dug her thumbs into his neck in imitation of the Japanese death touch, then gazed ruefully at the bent ends of her nails. She punched him smartly on the point of the chin, and again cried out, this time to the bruise of her knuckles.

"Well, this can't hurt me," she gritted through her teeth, as she assailed his solar plexus with her doubled fists.

By this time he was in a roar of laughter. Under the sheaths of muscles that were as armor, the fatal nerve center remained impervious.

"Go on, do it some more," he urged, when she had given up, breathing heavily. "It feels fine, like you was ticklin' me with a feather."

"All right, Mister Man," she threatened balefully. "You can talk about your grips and death touches and all the rest, but that's all man's game. I know something that will beat them all, that will make a strong man as helpless as a baby. Wait a minute till I get it. There. Shut your eyes. Ready? I won't be a second."

He waited with closed eyes, and then, softly as rose petals fluttering down, he felt her lips on his mouth.

"You win," he said in solemn ecstasy, and passed his arms around her.

CHAPTER XIV

In the morning Billy went down town to pay for Hazel and Hattie. It was due to Saxon's impatient desire to see them, that he seemed to take a remarkably long time about so simple a transaction. But she forgave him when he arrived with the two horses hitched to the camping wagon.

"Had to borrow the harness," he said. "Pass Possum up and climb in, an' I'll show you the Double H Outfit, which is some outfit, I'm tellin' you."

Saxon's delight was unbounded and almost speechless as they drove out into the country behind the dappled chestnuts with the cream-colored tails and manes. The seat was upholstered, high-backed, and comfortable; and Billy raved about the wonders of the efficient brake. He trotted the team along the hard county road to show the standard-going in them, and put them up a steep earthroad, almost hub-deep with mud, to prove that the light Belgian sire was not wanting in their make-up.

When Saxon at last lapsed into complete silence, he studied her anxiously, with quick sidelong glances. She sighed and asked:

"When do you think we'll be able to start?"

"Maybe in two weeks... or, maybe in two or three months." He sighed with solemn deliberation. "We're like the Irishman with the trunk an' nothin' to put in it. Here's the wagon, here's the horses, an' nothin' to pull. I know a peach of a shotgun I can get, second-hand, eighteen dollars; but look at the bills we owe. Then there's a new '22 Automatic rifle I want for you. An' a 30-30 I've had my eye on for deer. An' you want a good jointed pole as well as me. An' tackle costs like Sam Hill. An' harness like I want will cost fifty bucks cold. An' the wagon ought to be painted. Then there's pasture ropes, an' nose-bags, an' a harness punch, an' all such things. An' Hazel an' Hattie eatin' their heads off all the time we're waitin'. An' I 'm just itchin' to be started myself."

He stopped abruptly and confusedly.

"Now, Billy, what have you got up your sleeve?—I can see it in your eyes," Saxon demanded and indicted in mixed metaphors.

"Well, Saxon, you see, it's like this. Sandow ain't satisfied. He's madder 'n a hatter. Never got one punch at me. Never had a chance to make a showin', an' he wants a return match. He's blattin' around town that he can lick me with one hand tied behind 'm, an' all that kind of hot air. Which ain't the point. The point is, the fight-fans is wild to see a return-match. They didn't get a run for their money last time. They'll fill the house. The managers has seen me already. That was why I was so long. They's three hundred more waitin' on the tree for me to pick two weeks from last night if you'll say the word. It's just the same as I told you before. He's my meat. He still thinks I 'm a rube, an' that it was a fluke punch."

"But, Billy, you told me long ago that fighting took the silk out of you. That was why you'd quit it and stayed by teaming."

"Not this kind of fightin'," he answered. "I got this one all doped out. I'll let 'm last till about the seventh. Not that it'll be necessary, but just to give the audience a run for its money. Of course, I'll get a lump or two, an' lose some skin. Then I'll time 'm to that glass jaw of his an' drop 'm for the count. An' we'll be all packed up, an' next mornin' we'll pull out. What d'ye say? Aw, come on."

Saturday night, two weeks later, Saxon ran to the door when the gate clicked. Billy looked tired. His hair was wet, his nose swollen, one cheek was puffed, there was skin missing from his ears, and both eyes were slightly bloodshot.

"I 'm darned if that boy didn't fool me," he said, as he placed the roll of gold pieces in her hand and sat down with her on his knees. "He's some boy when he gets extended. Instead of stoppin' 'm at the seventh, he kept me hustlin' till the fourteenth. Then I got 'm the way I said. It's too bad he's got a glass jaw. He's quicker'n I thought, an' he's got a wallop that made me mighty respectful from the second round—an' the prettiest little chop an' come-again I ever saw. But that glass jaw! He kept it in cotton wool till the fourteenth an' then I connected.

"—An', say. I 'm mighty glad it did last fourteen rounds. I still got all my silk. I could see that easy. I wasn't breathin' much, an' every round was fast. An' my legs was like iron. I could a-fought forty rounds. You see, I never said nothin', but I've been suspicious all the time after that beatin' the Chicago Terror gave me."

"Nonsense!—you would have known it long before now," Saxon cried. "Look at all your boxing, and wrestling, and running at Carmel."

"Nope." Billy shook his head with the conviction of utter knowledge. "That's different. It don't take it outa you. You gotta be up against the real thing, fightin' for life, round after round, with a husky you know ain't lost a thread of his silk yet—then, if you don't blow up, if your legs is steady, an' your heart ain't burstin', an' you ain't wobbly at all, an' no signs of queer street in your head—why, then you know you still got all your silk. An' I got it, I got all mine, d'ye hear me, an' I ain't goin' to risk it on no more fights. That's straight. Easy money's hardest in the end. From now on it's horsebuyin' on commish, an' you an' me on the road till we find that valley of the moon."

Next morning, early, they drove out of Ukiah. Possum sat on the seat between them, his rosy mouth agape with excitement. They had originally planned to cross over to the coast from Ukiah, but it was too early in the season for the soft earth-roads to be in shape after the winter rains; so they turned east, for Lake County, their route to extend north through the upper Sacramento Valley and across the mountains into Oregon. Then they would circle west to the coast, where the roads by that time would be in condition, and come down its length to the Golden Gate.

All the land was green and flower-sprinkled, and each tiny valley, as they entered the hills, was a garden.

"Huh!" Billy remarked scornfully to the general landscape. "They say a rollin' stone gathers no moss. Just the same this looks like some outfit we've gathered. Never had so much actual property in my life at one time—an' them was the days when I wasn't rollin'. Hell—even the furniture wasn't ourn. Only the clothes we stood up in, an' some old socks an' things."

Saxon reached out and touched his hand, and he knew that it was a hand that loved his hand.

"I've only one regret," she said. "You've earned it all yourself. I've had nothing to do with it."

"Huh!—you've had everything to do with it. You're like my second in a fight. You keep me happy an' in condition. A man can't fight without a good second to take care of him. Hell, I wouldn't a-ben here if it wasn't for you. You made me pull up stakes an' head out. Why, if it hadn't been for you I'd a-drunk myself dead an' rotten by this time, or had my neck stretched at San Quentin over hittin' some scab too hard or something or other. An' look at me now. Look at that roll of greenbacks"—he tapped his breast—"to buy the Boss some horses. Why, we're takin' an unendin' vacation, an' makin' a good livin' at the same time. An' one more trade I got—horse-buyin' for Oakland. If I show I've got the savve, an' I have, all the Frisco firms'll be after me to buy for them. An' it's all your fault. You're my Tonic Kid all right, all right, an' if Possum wasn't lookin', I'd—well, who cares if he does look?"

And Billy leaned toward her sidewise and kissed her.

The way grew hard and rocky as they began to climb, but the divide was an easy one, and they soon dropped down the canyon of the Blue Lakes among lush fields of golden poppies. In the bottom of the canyon lay a wandering sheet of water of intensest blue. Ahead, the folds of hills interlaced the distance, with a remote blue mountain rising in the center of the picture.

They asked questions of a handsome, black-eyed man with curly gray hair, who talked to them in a German accent, while a cheery-faced woman smiled down at them out of a trellised high window of the Swiss cottage perched on the bank. Billy watered the horses at a pretty hotel farther on, where the proprietor came out and talked and told him he had built it himself, according to the plans of the black-eyed man with the curly gray hair, who was a San Francisco architect.

"Goin' up, goin' up," Billy chortled, as they drove on through the winding hills past another lake of intensest blue. "D'ye notice the difference in our treatment already between ridin' an' walkin' with packs on our backs? With Hazel an' Hattie an' Saxon an' Possum, an' yours truly, an' this high-toned wagon, folks most likely take us for millionaires out on a lark."

The way widened. Broad, oak-studded pastures with grazing livestock lay on either hand. Then Clear Lake opened before them like an inland sea, flecked with little squalls and flaws of wind from the high mountains on the northern slopes of which still glistened white snow patches.

"I've heard Mrs. Hazard rave about Lake Geneva," Saxon recalled; "but I wonder if it is more beautiful than this."

"That architect fellow called this the California Alps, you remember," Billy confirmed. "An' if I don't mistake, that's Lakeport showin' up ahead. An' all wild country, an' no railroads."

"And no moon valleys here," Saxon criticized. "But it is beautiful, oh, so beautiful."

"Hotter'n hell in the dead of summer, I'll bet," was Billy's opinion. "Nope, the country we're lookin' for lies nearer the coast. Just the same it is beautiful... like a picture on the wall. What d'ye say we stop off an' go for a swim this afternoon?"

Ten days later they drove into Williams, in Colusa County, and for the first time again encountered a railroad. Billy was looking for it, for the reason that at the rear of the wagon walked two magnificent work-horses which he had picked up for shipment to Oakland.

"Too hot," was Saxon's verdict, as she gazed across the shimmering level of the vast Sacramento Valley. "No redwoods. No hills. No forests. No manzanita. No madronos. Lonely, and sad—"

"An' like the river islands," Billy interpolated. "Richer 'n hell, but looks too much like hard work. It'll do for those that's stuck on hard work—God knows, they's nothin' here to induce a fellow to knock off ever for a bit of play. No fishin', no huntin', nothin' but work. I'd work myself, if I had to live here."

North they drove, through days of heat and dust, across the California plains, and everywhere was manifest the "new" farming—great irrigation ditches, dug and being dug, the land threaded by power-lines from the mountains, and many new farmhouses on small holdings newly fenced. The bonanza farms were being broken up. However, many of the great estates remained, five to ten thousand acres in extent, running from the Sacramento bank to the horizon dancing in the heat waves, and studded with great valley oaks.

"It takes rich soil to make trees like those," a ten-acre farmer told them.

They had driven off the road a hundred feet to his tiny barn in order to water Hazel and Hattie. A sturdy young orchard covered most of his ten acres, though a goodly portion was devoted to whitewashed henhouses and wired runways wherein hundreds of chickens were to be seen. He had just begun work on a small frame dwelling.

"I took a vacation when I bought," he explained, "and planted the trees. Then I went back to work an' stayed with it till the place was cleared. Now I 'm here for keeps, an' soon as the house is finished I'll send for the wife. She's not very well, and it will do her good. We've been planning and working for years to get away from the city." He stopped in order to give a happy sigh. "And now we're free."

The water in the trough was warm from the sun.

"Hold on," the man said. "Don't let them drink that. I'll give it to them cool."

Stepping into a small shed, he turned an electric switch, and a motor the size of a fruit box hummed into action. A five-inch stream of sparkling water splashed into the shallow main ditch of his irrigation system and flowed away across the orchard through many laterals.

"Isn't it beautiful, eh?—beautiful! beautiful!" the man chanted in an ecstasy. "It's bud and fruit. It's blood and life. Look at it! It makes a gold mine laughable, and a saloon a nightmare. I know. I... I used to be a barkeeper. In fact, I've been a barkeeper most of my life. That's how I paid for this place. And I've hated the business all the time. I was a farm boy, and all my life I've been wanting to get back to it. And here I am at last."

He wiped his glasses the better to behold his beloved water, then seized a hoe and strode down the main ditch to open more laterals.

"He's the funniest barkeeper I ever seen," Billy commented. "I took him for a business man of some sort. Must a-ben in some kind of a quiet hotel."

"Don't drive on right away," Saxon requested. "I want to talk with him."

He came back, polishing his glasses, his face beaming, watching the water as if fascinated by it. It required no more exertion on Saxon's part to start him than had been required on his part to start the motor.

"The pioneers settled all this in the early fifties," he said. "The Mexicans never got this far, so it was government land. Everybody got a hundred and sixty acres. And such acres! The stories they tell about how much wheat they got to the acre are almost unbelievable. Then several things happened. The sharpest and steadiest of the pioneers held what they had and added to it from the other fellows. It takes a great many quarter sections to make a bonanza farm. It wasn't long before it was 'most all bonanza farms."

"They were the successful gamblers," Saxon put in, remembering Mark Hall's words.

The man nodded appreciatively and continued.

"The old folks schemed and gathered and added the land into the big holdings, and built the great barns and mansions, and planted the house orchards and flower gardens. The young folks were spoiled by so much wealth and went away to the cities to spend it. And old folks and young united in one thing: in impoverishing the soil. Year after year they scratched it and took out bonanza crops. They put nothing back. All they left was plow-sole and exhausted land. Why, there's big sections they exhausted and left almost desert.

"The bonanza farmers are all gone now, thank the Lord, and here's where we small farmers come into our own. It won't be many years before the whole valley will be farmed in patches like mine. Look at what we're doing! Worked-out land that had ceased to grow wheat, and we turn the water on, treat the soil decently, and see our orchards!

"We've got the water—from the mountains, and from under the ground. I was reading an account the other day. All life depends on food. All food depends on water. It takes a thousand pounds of water to produce one pound of food; ten thousand pounds to produce one pound of meat. How much water do you drink in a year? About a ton. But you eat about two hundred pounds of vegetables and two hundred pounds of meat a year— which means you consume one hundred tons of water in the vegetables and one thousand tons in the meat—which means that it takes eleven hundred and one tons of water each year to keep a small woman like you going."

"Gee!" was all Billy could say.

"You see how population depends upon water," the ex-barkeeper went on. "Well, we've got the water, immense subterranean supplies, and in not many years this valley will be populated as thick as Belgium."

Fascinated by the five-inch stream, sluiced out of the earth and back to the earth by the droning motor, he forgot his discourse and stood and gazed, rapt and unheeding, while his visitors drove on.

"An' him a drink-slinger!" Billy marveled. "He can sure sling the temperance dope if anybody should ask you."

"It's lovely to think about—all that water, and all the happy people that will come here to live—"

"But it ain't the valley of the moon!" Billy laughed.

"No," she responded. "They don't have to irrigate in the valley of the moon, unless for alfalfa and such crops. What we want is the water bubbling naturally from the ground, and crossing the farm in little brooks, and on the boundary a fine big creek—"

"With trout in it!" Billy took her up. "An' willows and trees of all kinds growing along the edges, and here a riffle where you can flip out trout, and there a deep pool where you can swim and high-dive. An' kingfishers, an' rabbits comin' down to drink, an', maybe, a deer."

"And meadowlarks in the pasture," Saxon added. "And mourning doves in the trees. We must have mourning doves—and the big, gray tree-squirrels."

"Gee!—that valley of the moon's goin' to be some valley," Billy meditated, flicking a fly away with his whip from Hattie's side. "Think we'll ever find it?"

Saxon nodded her head with great certitude.

"Just as the Jews found the promised land, and the Mormons Utah, and the Pioneers California. You remember the last advice we got when we left Oakland? 'Tis them that looks that finds.'"

CHAPTER XV

Ever north, through a fat and flourishing rejuvenated land, stopping at the towns of Willows, Red Bluff and Redding, crossing the counties of Colusa, Glenn, Tehama, and Shasta, went the spruce wagon drawn by the dappled chestnuts with cream-colored manes and tails. Billy picked up only three horses for shipment, although he visited many farms; and Saxon talked with the women while he looked over the stock with the men. And Saxon grew the more convinced that the valley she sought lay not there.

At Redding they crossed the Sacramento on a cable ferry, and made a day's scorching traverse through rolling foot-hills and flat tablelands. The heat grew more insupportable, and the trees and shrubs were blasted and dead. Then they came again to the Sacramento, where the great smelters of Kennett explained the destruction of the vegetation.

They climbed out of the smelting town, where eyrie houses perched insecurely on a precipitous landscape. It was a broad, well-engineered road that took them up a grade miles long and plunged down into the Canyon of the Sacramento. The road, rock-surfaced and easy-graded, hewn out of the canyon wall, grew so narrow that Billy worried for fear of meeting opposite-bound teams. Far below, the river frothed and flowed over pebbly shallows, or broke tumultuously over boulders and cascades, in its race for the great valley they had left behind.

Sometimes, on the wider stretches of road, Saxon drove and Billy walked to lighten the load. She insisted on taking her turns at walking, and when he breathed the panting mares on the steep, and Saxon stood by their heads caressing them and cheering them, Billy's joy was too deep for any turn of speech as he gazed at his beautiful horses and his glowing girl, trim and colorful in her golden brown corduroy, the brown corduroy calves swelling sweetly under the abbreviated slim skirt. And when her answering look of happiness came to him—a sudden dimness in her straight gray eyes—he was overmastered by the knowledge that he must say something or burst.

"O, you kid!" he cried.

And with radiant face she answered, "O, you kid!"

They camped one night in a deep dent in the canyon, where was snuggled a box-factory village, and where a toothless ancient, gazing with faded eyes at their traveling outfit, asked: "Be you showin'?"

They passed Castle Crags, mighty-bastioned and glowing red against the palpitating blue sky. They caught their first glimpse of Mt. Shasta, a rose-tinted snow-peak rising, a sunset dream, between and beyond green interlacing walls of canyon—a landmark destined to be with them for many days. At unexpected turns, after mounting some steep grade, Shasta would appear again, still distant, now showing two peaks and glacial fields of shimmering white. Miles and miles and days and days they climbed, with Shasta ever developing new forms and phases in her summer snows.

"A moving picture in the sky," said Billy at last.

"Oh,—it is all so beautiful," sighed Saxon. "But there are no moon-valleys here."

They encountered a plague of butterflies, and for days drove through untold millions of the fluttering beauties that covered the road with uniform velvet-brown. And ever the road seemed to rise under the noses of the snorting mares, filling the air with noiseless flight, drifting down the breeze in clouds of brown and yellow soft-flaked as snow, and piling in mounds against the fences, ever driven to float helplessly on the irrigation ditches along the roadside. Hazel and Hattie soon grew used to them though Possum never ceased being made frantic.

"Huh!—who ever heard of butterfly-broke horses?" Billy chaffed. "That's worth fifty bucks more on their price."

"Wait till you get across the Oregon line into the Rogue River Valley," they were told. "There's God's Paradise—climate, scenery, and fruit-farming; fruit ranches that yield two hundred per cent. on a valuation of five hundred dollars an acre."

"Gee!" Billy said, when he had driven on out of hearing; "that's too rich for our digestion."

And Saxon said, "I don't know about apples in the valley of the moon, but I do know that the yield is ten thousand per cent. of happiness on a valuation of one Billy, one Saxon, a Hazel, a Hattie, and a Possum."

Through Siskiyou County and across high mountains, they came to Ashland and Medford and camped beside the wild Rogue River.

"This is wonderful and glorious," pronounced Saxon; "but it is not the valley of the moon."

"Nope, it ain't the valley of the moon," agreed Billy, and he said it on the evening of the day he hooked a monster steelhead, standing to his neck in the ice-cold water of the Rogue and fighting for forty minutes, with screaming reel, ere he drew his finny prize to the bank and with the scalp-yell of a Comanche jumped and clutched it by the gills.

"'Them that looks finds,'" predicted Saxon, as they drew north out of Grant's Pass, and held north across the mountains and fruitful Oregon valleys.

One day, in camp by the Umpqua River, Billy bent over to begin skinning the first deer he had ever shot. He raised his eyes to Saxon and remarked:

"If I didn't know California, I guess Oregon'd suit me from the ground up."

In the evening, replete with deer meat, resting on his elbow and smoking his after-supper cigarette, he said:

"Maybe they ain't no valley of the moon. An' if they ain't, what of it? We could keep on this way forever. I don't ask nothing better."

"There is a valley of the moon," Saxon answered soberly. "And we are going to find it. We've got to. Why Billy, it would never do, never to settle down. There would be no little Hazels and little Hatties, nor little... Billies—"

"Nor little Saxons," Billy interjected.

"Nor little Possums," she hurried on, nodding her head and reaching out a caressing hand to where the fox terrier was ecstatically gnawing a deer-rib. A vicious snarl and a wicked snap that barely missed her fingers were her reward.

"Possum!" she cried in sharp reproof, again extending her hand.

"Don't," Billy warned. "He can't help it, and he's likely to get you next time."

Even more compelling was the menacing threat that Possum growled, his jaws close-guarding the bone, eyes blazing insanely, the hair rising stiffly on his neck.

"It's a good dog that sticks up for its bone," Billy championed. "I wouldn't care to own one that didn't."

"But it's my Possum," Saxon protested. "And he loves me. Besides, he must love me more than an old bone. And he must mind me.—Here, you, Possum, give me that bone! Give me that bone, sir!"

Her hand went out gingerly, and the growl rose in volume and key till it culminated in a snap.

"I tell you it's instinct," Billy repeated. "He does love you, but he just can't help doin' it."

"He's got a right to defend his bones from strangers but not from his mother," Saxon argued. "I shall make him give up that bone to me."

"Fox terriers is awful highstrung, Saxon. You'll likely get him hysterical."

But she was obstinately set in her purpose. She picked up a short stick of firewood.

"Now, sir, give me that bone."

She threatened with the stick, and the dog's growling became ferocious. Again he snapped, then crouched back over his bone. Saxon raised the stick as if to strike him, and he suddenly abandoned the bone, rolled over on his back at her feet, four legs in the air, his ears lying meekly back, his eyes swimming and eloquent with submission and appeal.

"My God!" Billy breathed in solemn awe. "Look at it!—presenting his solar plexus to you, his vitals an' his life, all defense down, as much as sayin': 'Here I am. Stamp on me. Kick the life outa me.' I love you, I am your slave, but I just can't help defendin' my bone. My instinct's stronger'n me. Kill me, but I can't help it."

Saxon was melted. Tears were in her eyes as she stooped and gathered the mite of an animal in her arms. Possum was in a frenzy of agitation, whining, trembling, writhing, twisting, licking her face, all for forgiveness.

"Heart of gold with a rose in his mouth," Saxon crooned, burying her face in the soft and quivering bundle of sensibilities. "Mother is sorry. She'll never bother you again that way. There, there, little love. See? There's your bone. Take it."

She put him down, but he hesitated between her and the bone, patently looking to her for surety of permission, yet continuing to tremble in the terrible struggle between duty and desire that seemed tearing him asunder. Not until she repeated that it was all right and nodded her head consentingly did he go to the bone. And once, a minute later, he raised his head with a sudden startle and gazed inquiringly at her. She nodded and smiled, and Possum, with a happy sigh of satisfaction, dropped his head down to the precious deer-rib.

"That Mercedes was right when she said men fought over jobs like dogs over bones," Billy enunciated slowly. "It's instinct. Why, I couldn't no more help reaching my fist to the point of a scab's jaw than could Possum from snappin' at you. They's no explainin' it. What a man has to he has to. The fact that he does a thing shows he had to do it whether he can explain it or not. You remember Hall couldn't explain why he stuck that stick between Timothy McManus's legs in the foot race. What a man has to, he has to. That's all I know about it. I never had no earthly reason to beat up that lodger we had, Jimmy Harmon. He was a good guy, square an' all right. But I just had to, with the strike goin' to smash, an' everything so bitter inside me that I could taste it. I never told you, but I saw 'm once after I got out—when my arms was mendin'. I went down to the roundhouse an' waited for 'm to come in off a run, an' apologized to 'm. Now why did I apologize? I don't know, except for the same reason I punched 'm—I just had to."

And so Billy expounded the why of like in terms of realism, in the camp by the Umpqua River, while Possum expounded it, in similar terms of fang and appetite, on the rib of deer.

CHAPTER XVI

With Possum on the seat beside her, Saxon drove into the town of Roseburg. She drove at a walk. At the back of the wagon were tied two heavy young work-horses. Behind, half a dozen more marched free, and the rear was brought up by Billy, astride a ninth horse. All these he shipped from Roseburg to the West Oakland stables.

It was in the Umpqua Valley that they heard the parable of the white sparrow. The farmer who told it was elderly and flourishing. His farm was a model of orderliness and system. Afterwards, Billy heard neighbors estimate his wealth at a quarter of a million.

"You've heard the story of the farmer and the white sparrow'" he asked Billy, at dinner.

"Never heard of a white sparrow even," Billy answered.

"I must say they're pretty rare," the farmer owned. "But here's the story: Once there was a farmer who wasn't making much of a success. Things just didn't seem to go right, till at last, one day, he heard about the wonderful white sparrow. It seems that the white sparrow comes out only just at daybreak with the first light of dawn, and that it brings all kinds of good luck to the farmer that is fortunate enough to catch it. Next morning our farmer was up at daybreak, and before, looking for it. And, do you know, he sought for it continually, for months and months, and never caught even a glimpse of it." Their host shook his head. "No; he never found it, but he found so many things about the farm needing attention, and which he attended to before breakfast, that before he knew it the farm was prospering, and it wasn't long before the mortgage was paid off and he was starting a bank account."

That afternoon, as they drove along, Billy was plunged in a deep reverie.

"Oh, I got the point all right," he said finally. "An' yet I ain't satisfied. Of course, they wasn't a white sparrow, but by getting up early an' attendin' to things he'd been slack about before—oh, I got it all right. An' yet, Saxon, if that's what a farmer's life means, I don't want to find no moon valley. Life ain't hard work. Daylight to dark, hard at it—might just as well be in the city. What's the difference? Al' the time you've got to yourself is for sleepin', an' when you're sleepin' you're not enjoyin' yourself. An' what's it matter where you sleep, you're deado. Might as well be dead an' done with it as work your head off that way. I'd sooner stick to the road, an' shoot a deer an' catch a trout once in a while, an' lie on my back in the shade, an' laugh with you an' have fun with you, an'... an' go swimmin'. An' I 'm a willin' worker, too. But they's all the difference in the world between a decent amount of work an' workin' your head off."

Saxon was in full accord. She looked back on her years of toil and contrasted them with the joyous life she had lived on the road.

"We don't want to be rich," she said. "Let them hunt their white sparrows in the Sacramento islands and the irrigation valleys. When we get up early in the valley of the moon, it will be to hear the birds sing and sing with them. And if we work hard at times, it will be only so that we'll have more time to play. And when you go swimming I 'm going with you. And we'll play so hard that we'll be glad to work for relaxation."

"I 'm gettin' plumb dried out," Billy announced, mopping the sweat from his sunburned forehead. "What d'ye say we head for the coast?"

West they turned, dropping down wild mountain gorges from the height of land of the interior valleys. So fearful was the road, that, on one stretch of seven miles, they passed ten broken-down automobiles. Billy would not force the mares and promptly camped beside a brawling stream from which he whipped two trout at a time. Here, Saxon caught her first big trout. She had been accustomed to landing them up to nine and ten inches, and the screech of the reel when the big one was hooked caused her to cry out in startled surprise. Billy came up the riffle to her and gave counsel. Several minutes later, cheeks flushed and eyes dancing with excitement, Saxon dragged the big fellow carefully from the water's edge into the dry sand. Here it threw the hook out and flopped tremendously until she fell upon it and captured it in her hands.

"Sixteen inches," Billy said, as she held it up proudly for inspection. "—Hey!—what are you goin' to do?"

"Wash off the sand, of course," was her answer.

"Better put it in the basket," he advised, then closed his mouth and grimly watched.

She stooped by the side of the stream and dipped in the splendid fish. It flopped, there was a convulsive movement on her part, and it was gone.

"Oh!" Saxon cried in chagrin.

"Them that finds should hold," quoth Billy.

"I don't care," she replied. "It was a bigger one than you ever caught anyway."

"Oh, I 'm not denyin' you're a peach at fishin'," he drawled. "You caught me, didn't you?"

"I don't know about that," she retorted. "Maybe it was like the man who was arrested for catching trout out of season. His defense was self defense."

Billy pondered, but did not see.

"The trout attacked him," she explained.

Billy grinned. Fifteen minutes later he said:

"You sure handed me a hot one."

The sky was overcast, and, as they drove along the bank of the Coquille River, the fog suddenly enveloped them.

"Whoof!" Billy exhaled joyfully. "Ain't it great! I can feel myself moppin' it up like a dry sponge. I never appreciated fog before."

Saxon held out her arms to receive it, making motions as if she were bathing in the gray mist.

"I never thought I'd grow tired of the sun," she said; "but we've had more than our share the last few weeks."

"Ever since we hit the Sacramento Valley," Billy affirmed. "Too much sun ain't good. I've worked that out. Sunshine is like liquor. Did you ever notice how good you felt when the sun come out after a week of cloudy weather. Well, that sunshine was just like a jolt of whiskey. Had the same effect. Made you feel good all over. Now, when you're swimmin', an' come out an' lay in the sun, how good you feel. That's because you're lappin' up a sun-cocktail. But suppose you lay there in the sand a couple of hours. You don't feel so good. You're so slow-movin' it takes you a long time to dress. You go home draggin' your legs an' feelin' rotten, with all the life sapped outa you. What's that? It's the katzenjammer. You've been soused to the ears in sunshine, like so much whiskey, an' now you're payin' for it. That's straight. That's why fog in the climate is best."

"Then we've been drunk for months," Saxon said. "And now we're going to sober up."

"You bet. Why, Saxon, I can do two days' work in one in this climate.—Look at the mares. Blame me if they ain't perkin' up already."

Vainly Saxon's eye roved the pine forest in search of her beloved redwoods. They would find them down in California, they were told in the town of Bandon.

"Then we're too far north," said Saxon. "We must go south to find our valley of the moon."

And south they went, along roads that steadily grew worse, through the dairy country of Langlois and through thick pine forests to Port Orford, where Saxon picked jeweled agates on the beach while Billy caught enormous rockcod. No railroads had yet penetrated this wild region, and the way south grew wilder and wilder. At Gold Beach they encountered their old friend, the Rogue River, which they ferried across where it entered the Pacific. Still wilder became the country, still more terrible the road, still farther apart the isolated farms and clearings.

And here were neither Asiatics nor Europeans. The scant population consisted of the original settlers and their descendants. More than one old man or woman Saxon talked with, who could remember the trip across the Plains with the plodding oxen. West they had fared until the Pacific itself had stopped them, and here they had made their clearings, built their rude houses, and settled. In them Farthest West had been reached. Old customs had changed little. There were no railways. No automobile as yet had ventured their perilous roads. Eastward, between them and the populous interior valleys, lay the wilderness of the Coast Range—a game paradise, Billy heard; though he declared that the very road he traveled was game paradise enough for him. Had he not halted the horses, turned the reins over to Saxon, and shot an eight-pronged buck from the wagon-seat?

South of Gold Beach, climbing a narrow road through the virgin forest, they heard from far above the jingle of bells. A hundred yards farther on Billy found a place wide enough to turn out. Here he waited, while the merry bells, descending the mountain, rapidly came near. They heard the grind of brakes, the soft thud of horses' hoofs, once a sharp cry of the driver, and once a woman's laughter.

"Some driver, some driver," Billy muttered. "I take my hat off to 'm whoever he is, hittin' a pace like that on a road like this.—Listen to that! He's got powerful brakes.—Zooie! That WAS a chuck-hole! Some springs, Saxon, some springs!"

Where the road zigzagged above, they glimpsed through the trees four sorrel horses trotting swiftly, and the flying wheels of a small, tan-painted trap.

At the bend of the road the leaders appeared again, swinging wide on the curve, the wheelers flashed into view, and the light two-seated rig; then the whole affair straightened out and thundered down upon them across a narrow plank-bridge. In the front seat were a man and woman; in the rear seat a Japanese was squeezed in among suit cases, rods, guns, saddles, and a typewriter case, while above him and all about him, fastened most intricately, sprouted a prodigious crop of deer- and elk-horns.

"It's Mr. and Mrs. Hastings," Saxon cried.

"Whoa!" Hastings yelled, putting on the brake and gathering his horses in to a stop alongside. Greetings flew back and forth, in which the Japanese, whom they had last seen on the Roamer at Rio Vista, gave and received his share.

"Different from the Sacramento islands, eh?" Hastings said to Saxon. "Nothing but old American stock in these mountains. And they haven't changed any. As John Fox, Jr., said, they're our contemporary ancestors. Our old folks were just like them."

Mr. and Mrs. Hastings, between them, told of their long drive. They were out two months then, and intended to continue north through Oregon and Washington to the Canadian boundary.

"Then we'll ship our horses and come home by train," concluded Hastings.

"But the way you drive you oughta be a whole lot further along than this," Billy criticized.

"But we keep stopping off everywhere," Mrs. Hastings explained.

"We went in to the Hoopa Reservation," said Mr. Hastings, "and canoed down the Trinity and Klamath Rivers to the ocean. And just now we've come out from two weeks in the real wilds of Curry County."

"You must go in," Hastings advised. "You'll get to Mountain Ranch to-night. And you can turn in from there. No roads, though. You'll have to pack your horses. But it's full of game. I shot five mountain lions and two bear, to say nothing of deer. And there are small herds of elk, too.—No; I didn't shoot any. They're protected. These horns I got from the old hunters. I'll tell you all about it."

And while the men talked, Saxon and Mrs. Hastings were not idle.

"Found your valley of the moon yet?" the writer's wife asked, as they were saying good-by.

Saxon shook her head.

"You will find it if you go far enough; and be sure you go as far as Sonoma Valley and our ranch. Then, if you haven't found it yet, we'll see what we can do."

Three weeks later, with a bigger record of mountain lions and bear than Hastings' to his credit, Billy emerged from Curry County and drove across the line into California. At once Saxon found herself among the redwoods. But they were redwoods unbelievable. Billy stopped the wagon, got out, and paced around one.

"Forty-five feet," he announced. "That's fifteen in diameter. And they're all like it only bigger. No; there's a runt. It's only about nine feet through. An' they're hundreds of feet tall."

"When I die, Billy, you must bury me in a redwood grove," Saxon adjured.

"I ain't goin' to let you die before I do," he assured her. "An' then we'll leave it in our wills for us both to be buried that way."

CHAPTER XVII

South they held along the coast, hunting, fishing, swimming, and horse-buying. Billy shipped his purchases on the coasting steamers. Through Del Norte and Humboldt counties they went, and through Mendocino into Sonoma—counties larger than Eastern states—threading the giant woods, whipping innumerable trout-streams, and crossing countless rich valleys. Ever Saxon sought the valley of the moon. Sometimes, when all seemed fair, the lack was a railroad, sometimes madrono and manzanita trees, and, usually, there was too much fog.

"We do want a sun-cocktail once in a while," she told Billy.

"Yep," was his answer. "Too much fog might make us soggy. What we're after is betwixt an' between, an' we'll have to get back from the coast a ways to find it."

This was in the fall of the year, and they turned their backs on the Pacific at old Fort Ross and entered the Russian River Valley, far below Ukiah, by way of Cazadero and Guerneville. At Santa Rosa Billy was delayed with the shipping of several horses, so that it was not until afternoon that he drove south and east for Sonoma Valley.

"I guess we'll no more than make Sonoma Valley when it'll be time to camp," he said, measuring the sun with his eye. "This is called Bennett Valley. You cross a divide from it and come out at Glen Ellen. Now this is a mighty pretty valley, if anybody should ask you. An' that's some nifty mountain over there."

"The mountain is all right," Saxon adjudged. "But all the rest of the hills are too bare. And I don't see any big trees. It takes rich soil to make big trees."

"Oh, I ain't sayin' it's the valley of the moon by a long ways. All the same, Saxon, that's some mountain. Look at the timber on it. I bet they's deer there."

"I wonder where we'll spend this winter," Saxon remarked.

"D'ye know, I've just been thinkin' the same thing. Let's winter at Carmel. Mark Hall's back, an' so is Jim Hazard. What d'ye say?"

Saxon nodded.

"Only you won't be the odd-job man this time."

"Nope. We can make trips in good weather horse-buyin'," Billy confirmed, his face beaming with self-satisfaction. "An' if that walkin' poet of the Marble House is around, I'll sure get the gloves on with 'm just in memory of the time he walked me off my legs—"

"Oh! Oh!" Saxon cried. "Look, Billy! Look!"

Around a bend in the road came a man in a sulky, driving a heavy stallion. The animal was a bright chestnut-sorrel, with cream-colored mane and tail. The tail almost swept the ground, while the mane was so thick that it crested out of the neck and flowed down, long and wavy. He scented the mares and stopped short, head flung up and armfuls of creamy mane tossing in the breeze. He bent his head until flaring nostrils brushed impatient knees, and between the fine-pointed ears could be seen a mighty and incredible curve of neck. Again he tossed his head, fretting against the bit as the driver turned widely aside for safety in passing. They could see the blue glaze like a sheen on the surface of the horse's bright, wild eyes, and Billy closed a wary thumb on his reins and himself turned widely. He held up his hand in signal, and the driver of the stallion stopped when well past, and over his shoulder talked draught-horses with Billy.

Among other things, Billy learned that the stallion's name was Barbarossa, that the driver was the owner, and that Santa Rosa was his headquarters.

"There are two ways to Sonoma Valley from here," the man directed. "When you come to the crossroads the turn to the left will take you to Glen Ellen by Bennett Peak—that's it there."

Rising from rolling stubble fields, Bennett Peak towered hot in the sun, a row of bastion hills leaning against its base. But hills and mountains on that side showed bare and heated, though beautiful with the sunburnt tawniness of California.

"The turn to the right will take you to Glen Ellen, too, only it's longer and steeper grades. But your mares don't look as though it'd bother them."

"Which is the prettiest way?" Saxon asked.

"Oh, the right hand road, by all means," said the man. "That's Sonoma Mountain there, and the road skirts it pretty well up, and goes through Cooper's Grove."

Billy did not start immediately after they had said good-by, and he and Saxon, heads over shoulders, watched the roused Barbarossa plunging mutinously on toward Santa Rosa.

"Gee!" Billy said. "I'd like to be up here next spring."

At the crossroads Billy hesitated and looked at Saxon.

"What if it is longer?" she said. "Look how beautiful it is—all covered with green woods; and I just know those are redwoods in the canyons. You never can tell. The valley of the moon might be right up there somewhere. And it would never do to miss it just in order to save half an hour."

They took the turn to the right and began crossing a series of steep foothills. As they approached the mountain there were signs of a greater abundance of water. They drove beside a running stream, and, though the vineyards on the hills were summer-dry, the farmhouses in the hollows and on the levels were grouped about with splendid trees.

"Maybe it sounds funny," Saxon observed; "but I 'm beginning to love that mountain already. It almost seems as if I'd seen it before, somehow, it's so all-around satisfying—oh!"

Crossing a bridge and rounding a sharp turn, they were suddenly enveloped in a mysterious coolness and gloom. All about them arose stately trunks of redwood. The forest floor was a rosy carpet of autumn fronds. Occasional shafts of sunlight, penetrating the deep shade, warmed the somberness of the grove. Alluring paths led off among the trees and into cozy nooks made by circles of red columns growing around the dust of vanished ancestors— witnessing the titanic dimensions of those ancestors by the girth of the circles in which they stood.

Out of the grove they pulled to the steep divide, which was no more than a buttress of Sonoma Mountain. The way led on through rolling uplands and across small dips and canyons, all well wooded and a-drip with water. In places the road was muddy from wayside springs.

"The mountain's a sponge," said Billy. "Here it is, the tail-end of dry summer, an' the ground's just leakin' everywhere."

"I know I've never been here before," Saxon communed aloud. "But it's all so familiar! So I must have dreamed it. And there's madronos!—a whole grove! And manzanita! Why, I feel just as if I was coming home... Oh, Billy, if it should turn out to be our valley."

"Plastered against the side of a mountain?" he queried, with a skeptical laugh.

"No; I don't mean that. I mean on the way to our valley. Because the way— all ways—to our valley must be beautiful. And this; I've seen it all before, dreamed it."

"It's great," he said sympathetically. "I wouldn't trade a square mile of this kind of country for the whole Sacramento Valley, with the river islands thrown in and Middle River for good measure. If they ain't deer up there, I miss my guess. An' where they's springs they's streams, an' streams means trout."

They passed a large and comfortable farmhouse, surrounded by wandering barns and cow-sheds, went on under forest arches, and emerged beside a field with which Saxon was instantly enchanted. It flowed in a gentle concave from the road up the mountain, its farther boundary an unbroken line of timber. The field glowed like rough gold in the approaching sunset, and near the middle of it stood a solitary great redwood, with blasted top suggesting a nesting eyrie for eagles. The timber beyond clothed the mountain in solid green to what they took to be the top. But, as they drove on, Saxon, looking back upon what she called her field, saw the real summit of Sonoma towering beyond, the mountain behind her field a mere spur upon the side of the larger mass.

Ahead and toward the right, across sheer ridges of the mountains, separated by deep green canyons and broadening lower down into rolling orchards and vineyards, they caught their first sight of Sonoma Valley and the wild mountains that rimmed its eastern side. To the left they gazed across a golden land of small hills and valleys. Beyond, to the north, they glimpsed another portion of the valley, and, still beyond, the opposing wall of the valley—a range of mountains, the highest of which reared its red and battered ancient crater against a rosy and mellowing sky. From north to southeast, the mountain rim curved in the brightness of the sun, while Saxon and Billy were already in the shadow of evening. He looked at Saxon, noted the ravished ecstasy of her face, and stopped the horses. All the eastern sky was blushing to rose, which descended upon the mountains, touching them with wine and ruby. Sonoma Valley began to fill with a purple flood, laving the mountain bases, rising, inundating, drowning them in its purple. Saxon pointed in silence, indicating that the purple flood was the sunset shadow of Sonoma Mountain. Billy nodded, then chirruped to the mares, and the descent began through a warm and colorful twilight.

On the elevated sections of the road they felt the cool, delicious breeze from the Pacific forty miles away; while from each little dip and hollow came warm breaths of autumn earth, spicy with sunburnt grass and fallen leaves and passing flowers.

They came to the rim of a deep canyon that seemed to penetrate to the heart of Sonoma Mountain. Again, with no word spoken, merely from watching Saxon, Billy stopped the wagon. The canyon was wildly beautiful. Tall redwoods lined its entire length. On its farther rim stood three rugged knolls covered with dense woods of spruce and oak. From between the knolls, a feeder to the main canyon and likewise fringed with redwoods, emerged a smaller canyon. Billy pointed to a stubble field that lay at the feet of the knolls.

"It's in fields like that I've seen my mares a-pasturing," he said.

They dropped down into the canyon, the road following a stream that sang under maples and alders. The sunset fires, refracted from the cloud-driftage of the autumn sky, bathed the canyon with crimson, in which ruddy-limbed madronos and wine-wooded manzanitas burned and smoldered. The air was aromatic with laurel. Wild grape vines bridged the stream from tree to tree. Oaks of many sorts were veiled in lacy Spanish moss. Ferns and brakes grew lush beside the stream. From somewhere came the plaint of a mourning dove. Fifty feet above the ground, almost over their heads, a Douglas squirrel crossed the road—a flash of gray between two trees; and they marked the continuance of its aerial passage by the bending of the boughs.

"I've got a hunch," said Billy.

"Let me say it first," Saxon begged.

He waited, his eyes on her face as she gazed about her in rapture.

"We've found our valley," she whispered. "Was that it?"

He nodded, but checked speech at sight of a small boy driving a cow up the road, a preposterously big shotgun in one hand, in the other as preposterously big a jackrabbit. "How far to Glen Ellen?" Billy asked.

"Mile an' a half," was the answer.

"What creek is this?" inquired Saxon.

"Wild Water. It empties into Sonoma Creek half a mile down."

"Trout?"—this from Billy.

"If you know how to catch 'em," grinned the boy.

"Deer up the mountain?"

"It ain't open season," the boy evaded.

"I guess you never shot a deer," Billy slyly baited, and was rewarded with:

"I got the horns to show."

"Deer shed their horns," Billy teased on. "Anybody can find 'em."

"I got the meat on mine. It ain't dry yet—"

The boy broke off, gazing with shocked eyes into the pit Billy had dug for him.

"It's all right, sonny," Billy laughed, as he drove on. "I ain't the game warden. I 'm buyin' horses."

More leaping tree squirrels, more ruddy madronos and majestic oaks, more fairy circles of redwoods, and, still beside the singing stream, they passed a gate by the roadside. Before it stood a rural mail box, on which was lettered "Edmund Hale." Standing under the rustic arch, leaning upon the gate, a man and woman composed a picture so arresting and beautiful that Saxon caught her breath. They were side by side, the delicate hand of the woman curled in the hand of the man, which looked as if made to confer benedictions. His face bore out this impression—a beautiful-browed countenance, with large, benevolent gray eyes under a wealth of white hair that shone like spun glass. He was fair and large; the little woman beside him was daintily wrought. She was saffron-brown, as a woman of the white race can well be, with smiling eyes of bluest blue. In quaint sage-green draperies, she seemed a flower, with her small vivid face irresistibly reminding Saxon of a springtime wake-robin.

Perhaps the picture made by Saxon and Billy was equally arresting and beautiful, as they drove down through the golden end of day. The two couples had eyes only for each other. The little woman beamed joyously. The man's face glowed into the benediction that had trembled there. To Saxon, like the field up the mountain, like the mountain itself, it seemed that she had always known this adorable pair. She knew that she loved them.

"How d'ye do," said Billy.

"You blessed children," said the man. "I wonder if you know how dear you look sitting there."

That was all. The wagon had passed by, rustling down the road, which was carpeted with fallen leaves of maple, oak, and alder. Then they came to the meeting of the two creeks.

"Oh, what a place for a home," Saxon cried, pointing across Wild Water. "See, Billy, on that bench there above the meadow."

"It's a rich bottom, Saxon; and so is the bench rich. Look at the big trees on it. An' they's sure to be springs."

"Drive over," she said.

Forsaking the main road, they crossed Wild Water on a narrow bridge and continued along an ancient, rutted road that ran beside an equally ancient worm-fence of split redwood rails. They came to a gate, open and off its hinges, through which the road led out on the bench.

"This is it—I know it," Saxon said with conviction. "Drive in, Billy."

A small, whitewashed farmhouse with broken windows showed through the trees.

"Talk about your madronos—"

Billy pointed to the father of all madronos, six feet in diameter at its base, sturdy and sound, which stood before the house.

They spoke in low tones as they passed around the house under great oak trees and came to a stop before a small barn. They did not wait to unharness.

Tying the horses, they started to explore. The pitch from the bench to the meadow was steep yet thickly wooded with oaks and manzanita. As they crashed through the underbrush they startled a score of quail into flight.

"How about game?" Saxon queried.

Billy grinned, and fell to examining a spring which bubbled a clear stream into the meadow. Here the ground was sunbaked and wide open in a multitude of cracks.

Disappointment leaped into Saxon's face, but Billy, crumbling a clod between his fingers, had not made up his mind.

"It's rich," he pronounced; "—the cream of the soil that's been washin' down from the hills for ten thousan' years. But—"

He broke off, stared all about, studying the configuration of the meadow, crossed it to the redwood trees beyond, then came back.

"It's no good as it is," he said. "But it's the best ever if it's handled right. All it needs is a little common sense an' a lot of drainage. This meadow's a natural basin not yet filled level. They's a sharp slope through the redwoods to the creek. Come on, I'll show you."

They went through the redwoods and came out on Sonoma Creek. At this spot was no singing. The stream poured into a quiet pool. The willows on their side brushed the water. The opposite side was a steep bank. Billy measured the height of the bank with his eye, the depth of the water with a driftwood pole.

"Fifteen feet," he announced. "That allows all kinds of high-divin' from the bank. An' it's a hundred yards of a swim up an' down."

They followed down the pool. It emptied in a riffle, across exposed bedrock, into another pool. As they looked, a trout flashed into the air and back, leaving a widening ripple on the quiet surface.

"I guess we won't winter in Carmel," Billy said. "This place was specially manufactured for us. In the morning I'll find out who owns it."

Half an hour later, feeding the horses, he called Saxon's attention to a locomotive whistle.

"You've got your railroad," he said. "That's a train pulling into Glen Ellen, an' it's only a mile from here."

Saxon was dozing off to sleep under the blankets when Billy aroused her.

"Suppose the guy that owns it won't sell?"

"There isn't the slightest doubt," Saxon answered with unruffled certainty. "This is our place. I know it."

CHAPTER XVIII

They were awakened by Possum, who was indignantly reproaching a tree squirrel for not coming down to be killed. The squirrel chattered garrulous remarks that drove Possum into a mad attempt to climb the tree. Billy and Saxon giggled and hugged each other at the terrier's frenzy.

"If this is goin' to be our place, they'll be no shootin' of tree squirrels," Billy said.

Saxon pressed his hand and sat up. From beneath the bench came the cry of a meadow lark.

"There isn't anything left to be desired," she sighed happily.

"Except the deed," Billy corrected.

After a hasty breakfast, they started to explore, running the irregular boundaries of the place and repeatedly crossing it from rail fence to creek and back again. Seven springs they found along the foot of the bench on the edge of the meadow.

"There's your water supply," Billy said. "Drain the meadow, work the soil up, and with fertilizer and all that water you can grow crops the year round. There must be five acres of it, an' I wouldn't trade it for Mrs. Mortimer's."

They were standing in the old orchard, on the bench where they had counted twenty-seven trees, neglected but of generous girth.

"And on top the bench, back of the house, we can grow berries." Saxon paused, considering a new thought. "If only Mrs. Mortimer would come up and advise us!—Do you think she would, Billy?"

"Sure she would. It ain't more 'n four hours' run from San Jose. But first we'll get our hooks into the place. Then you can write to her."

Sonoma Creek gave the long boundary to the little farm, two sides were worm fenced, and the fourth side was Wild Water.

"Why, we'll have that beautiful man and woman for neighbors," Saxon recollected. "Wild Water will be the dividing line between their place and ours."

"It ain't ours yet," Billy commented. "Let's go and call on 'em. They'll be able to tell us all about it."

"It's just as good as," she replied. "The big thing has been the finding. And whoever owns it doesn't care much for it. It hasn't been lived in for a long time. And—Oh, Billy—are you satisfied!"

"With every bit of it," he answered frankly, "as far as it goes. But the trouble is, it don't go far enough."

The disappointment in her face spurred him to renunciation of his particular dream.

"We'll buy it—that's settled," he said. "But outside the meadow, they's so much woods that they's little pasture—not more 'n enough for a couple of horses an' a cow. But I don't care. We can't have everything, an' what they is is almighty good."

"Let us call it a starter," she consoled. "Later on we can add to it—maybe the land alongside that runs up the Wild Water to the three knolls we saw yesterday."

"Where I seen my horses pasturin'," he remembered, with a flash of eye. "Why not? So much has come true since we hit the road, maybe that'll come true, too.

"We'll work for it, Billy."

"We'll work like hell for it," he said grimly.

They passed through the rustic gate and along a path that wound through wild woods. There was no sign of the house until they came abruptly upon it, bowered among the trees. It was eight-sided, and so justly proportioned that its two stories made no show of height. The house belonged there. It might have sprung from the soil just as the trees had. There were no formal grounds. The wild grew to the doors. The low porch of the main entrance was raised only a step from the ground. "Trillium Covert," they read, in quaint carved letters under the eave of the porch.

"Come right upstairs, you dears," a voice called from above, in response to Saxon's knock.

Stepping back and looking up, she beheld the little lady smiling down from a sleeping-porch. Clad in a rosy-tissued and flowing house gown, she again reminded Saxon of a flower.

"Just push the front door open and find your way," was the direction.

Saxon led, with Billy at her heels. They came into a room bright with windows, where a big log smoldered in a rough-stone fireplace. On the stone slab above stood a huge Mexican jar, filled with autumn branches and trailing fluffy smoke-vine. The walls were finished in warm natural woods, stained but without polish. The air was aromatic with clean wood odors. A walnut organ loomed in a shallow corner of the room. All corners were shallow in this octagonal dwelling. In another corner were many rows of books. Through the windows, across a low couch indubitably made for use, could be seen a restful picture of autumn trees and yellow grasses, threaded by wellworn paths that ran here and there over the tiny estate. A delightful little stairway wound past more windows to the upper story. Here the little lady greeted them and led them into what Saxon knew at once was her room. The two octagonal sides of the house which showed in this wide room were given wholly to windows. Under the long sill, to the floor, were shelves of books. Books lay here and there, in the disorder of use, on work table, couch and desk. On a sill by an open window, a jar of autumn leaves breathed the charm of the sweet brown wife, who seated herself in a tiny rattan chair, enameled a cheery red, such as children delight to rock in.

"A queer house," Mrs. Hale laughed girlishly and contentedly. "But we love it. Edmund made it with his own hands even to the plumbing, though he did have a terrible time with that before he succeeded."

"How about that hardwood floor downstairs?—an' the fireplace?" Billy inquired.

"All, all," she replied proudly. "And half the furniture. That cedar desk there, the table—with his own hands."

"They are such gentle hands," Saxon was moved to say.

Mrs. Hale looked at her quickly, her vivid face alive with a grateful light.

"They are gentle, the gentlest hands I have ever known," she said softly. "And you are a dear to have noticed it, for you only saw them yesterday in passing."

"I couldn't help it," Saxon said simply.

Her gaze slipped past Mrs. Hale, attracted by the wall beyond, which was done in a bewitching honeycomb pattern dotted with golden bees. The walls were hung with a few, a very few, framed pictures.

"They are all of people," Saxon said, remembering the beautiful paintings in Mark Hall's bungalow.

"My windows frame my landscape paintings," Mrs. Hale answered, pointing out of doors. "Inside I want only the faces of my dear ones whom I cannot have with me always. Some of them are dreadful rovers."

"Oh!" Saxon was on her feet and looking at a photograph. "You know Clara Hastings!"

"I ought to. I did everything but nurse her at my breast. She came to me when she was a little baby. Her mother was my sister. Do you know how greatly you resemble her? I remarked it to Edmund yesterday. He had already seen it. It wasn't a bit strange that his heart leaped out to you two as you came drilling down behind those beautiful horses."

So Mrs. Hale was Clara's aunt—old stock that had crossed the Plains. Saxon knew now why she had reminded her so strongly of her own mother.

The talk whipped quite away from Billy, who could only admire the detailed work of the cedar desk while he listened. Saxon told of meeting Clara and Jack Hastings on their yacht and on their driving trip in Oregon. They were off again, Mrs. Hale said, having shipped their horses home from Vancouver and taken the Canadian Pacific on their way to England. Mrs. Hale knew Saxon's mother or, rather, her poems; and produced, not only "The Story of the Files," but a ponderous scrapbook which contained many of her mother's poems which Saxon had never seen. A sweet singer, Mrs. Hale said; but so many had sung in the days of gold and been forgotten. There had been no army of magazines then, and the poems had perished in local newspapers.

Jack Hastings had fallen in love with Clara, the talk ran on; then, visiting at Trillium Covert, he had fallen in love with Sonoma Valley and bought a magnificent home ranch, though little enough he saw of it, being away over the world so much of the time. Mrs. Hale talked of her own Journey across the Plains, a little girl, in the late Fifties, and, like Mrs. Mortimer, knew all about the fight at Little Meadow, and the tale of the massacre of the emigrant train of which Billy's father had been the sole survivor.

"And so," Saxon concluded, an hour later, "we've been three years searching for our valley of the moon, and now we've found it."

"Valley of the Moon?" Mrs. Hale queried. "Then you knew about it all the time. What kept you so long?"

"No; we didn't know. We just started on a blind search for it. Mark Hall called it a pilgrimage, and was always teasing us to carry long staffs. He said when we found the spot we'd know, because then the staffs would burst into blossom. He laughed at all the good things we wanted in our valley, and one night he took me out and showed me the moon through a telescope. He said that was the only place we could find such a wonderful valley. He meant it was moonshine, but we adopted the name and went on looking for it."

"What a coincidence!" Mrs. Hale exclaimed. "For this is the Valley of the Moon."

"I know it," Saxon said with quiet confidence. "It has everything we wanted."

"But you don't understand, my dear. This is the Valley of the Moon. This is Sonoma Valley. Sonoma is an Indian word, and means the Valley of the

Moon. That was what the Indians called it for untold ages before the first white men came. We, who love it, still so call it."

And then Saxon recalled the mysterious references Jack Hastings and his wife had made to it, and the talk tripped along until Billy grew restless. He cleared his throat significantly and interrupted.

"We want to find out about that ranch acrost the creek—who owns it, if they'll sell, where we'll find 'em, an' such things."

Mrs. Hale stood up.

"We'll go and see Edmund," she said, catching Saxon by the hand and leading the way.

"My!" Billy ejaculated, towering above her. "I used to think Saxon was small. But she'd make two of you."

"And you're pretty big," the little woman smiled; "but Edmund is taller than you, and broader-shouldered."

They crossed a bright hall, and found the big beautiful husband lying back reading in a huge Mission rocker. Beside it was another tiny child's chair of red-enameled rattan. Along the length of his thigh, the head on his knee and directed toward a smoldering log in a fireplace, clung an incredibly large striped cat. Like its master, it turned its head to greet the newcomers. Again Saxon felt the loving benediction that abided in his face, his eyes, his hands— toward which she involuntarily dropped her eyes. Again she was impressed by the gentleness of them. They were hands of love. They were the hands of a type of man she had never dreamed existed. No one in that merry crowd of Carmel had prefigured him. They were artists. This was the scholar, the philosopher. In place of the passion of youth and all youth's mad revolt, was the benignance of wisdom. Those gentle hands had passed all the bitter by and plucked only the sweet of life. Dearly as she loved them, she shuddered to think what some of those Carmelites would be like when they were as old as he—especially the dramatic critic and the Iron Man.

"Here are the dear children, Edmund," Mrs. Hale said. "What do you think! They want to buy the Madrono Ranch. They've been three years searching for it—I forgot to tell them we had searched ten years for Trillium Covert. Tell them all about it. Surely Mr. Naismith is still of a mind to sell!"

They seated themselves in simple massive chairs, and Mrs. Hale took the tiny rattan beside the big Mission rocker, her slender hand curled like a tendril in Edmund's. And while Saxon listened to the talk, her eyes took in the grave rooms lined with books. She began to realize how a mere structure of wood and stone may express the spirit of him who conceives and makes it. Those gentle hands had made all this—the very furniture, she guessed as her eyes roved from desk to chair, from work table to reading stand beside the bed in the other room, where stood a green-shaded lamp and orderly piles of magazines and books.

As for the matter of Madrono Ranch, it was easy enough he was saying. Naismith would sell. Had desired to sell for the past five years, ever since he had engaged in the enterprise of bottling mineral water at the springs lower down the valley. It was fortunate that he was the owner, for about all the rest of the surrounding land was owned by a Frenchman—an early settler. He would not part with a foot of it. He was a peasant, with all the peasant's love of the soil, which, in him, had become an obsession, a disease. He was a land-miser. With no business capacity, old and opinionated, he was land poor, and it was an open question which would arrive first, his death or bankruptcy.

As for Madrono Ranch, Naismith owned it and had set the price at fifty dollars an acre. That would be one thousand dollars, for there were twenty acres. As a farming investment, using old-fashioned methods, it was not worth it. As a business investment, yes; for the virtues of the valley were on the eve of being discovered by the outside world, and no better location for a summer home could be found. As a happiness investment in joy of beauty and climate, it was worth a thousand times the price asked. And he knew Naismith would allow time on most of the amount. Edmund's suggestion was that they take a two years' lease, with option to buy, the rent to apply to the purchase if they took it up. Naismith had done that once with a Swiss, who had paid a monthly rental of ten dollars. But the man's wife had died, and he had gone away.

Edmund soon divined Billy's renunciation, though not the nature of it; and several questions brought it forth—the old pioneer dream of land spaciousness; of cattle on a hundred hills; one hundred and sixty acres of land the smallest thinkable division.

"But you don't need all that land, dear lad," Edmund said softly. "I see you understand intensive farming. Have you thought about intensive horse-raising?"

Billy's jaw dropped at the smashing newness of the idea. He considered it, but could see no similarity in the two processes. Unbelief leaped into his eyes.

"You gotta show me!" he cried.

The elder man smiled gently.

"Let us see. In the first place, you don't need those twenty acres except for beauty. There are five acres in the meadow. You don't need more than two of them to make your living at selling vegetables. In fact, you and your wife, working from daylight to dark, cannot properly farm those two acres. Remains three acres. You have plenty of water for it from the springs. Don't be satisfied with one crop a year, like the rest of the old-fashioned farmers in this valley. Farm it like your vegetable plot, intensively, all the year, in crops that make horse-feed, irrigating, fertilizing, rotating your crops. Those three acres will feed as many horses as heaven knows how huge an area of unseeded, uncared for, wasted pasture would feed. Think it over. I'll lend you books on the subject. I don't know how large your crops will be, nor do I know how much a horse eats; that's your business. But I am certain, with a hired man to take your place helping your wife on her two acres of vegetables, that by the time you own the horses your three acres will feed, you will have all you can attend to. Then it will be time to get more land, for more horses, for more riches, if that way happiness lie."

Billy understood. In his enthusiasm he dashed out:

"You're some farmer."

Edmund smiled and glanced toward his wife.

"Give him your opinion of that, Annette."

Her blue eyes twinkled as she complied.

"Why, the dear, he never farms. He has never farmed. But he knows." She waved her hand about the booklined walls. "He is a student of good. He studies all good things done by good men under the sun. His pleasure is in books and wood-working."

"Don't forget Dulcie," Edmund gently protested.

"Yes, and Dulcie." Annette laughed. "Dulcie is our cow. It is a great question with Jack Hastings whether Edmund dotes more on Dulcie, or Dulcie dotes more on Edmund. When he goes to San Francisco Dulcie is miserable. So is Edmund, until he hastens back. Oh, Dulcie has given me no few jealous pangs. But I have to confess he understands her as no one else does."

"That is the one practical subject I know by experience," Edmund confirmed. "I am an authority on Jersey cows. Call upon me any time for counsel."

He stood up and went toward his book-shelves; and they saw how magnificently large a man he was. He paused a book in his hand, to answer a question from Saxon. No; there were no mosquitoes, although, one summer when the south wind blew for ten days—an unprecedented thing— a few mosquitoes had been carried up from San Pablo Bay. As for fog, it was the making of the valley. And where they were situated, sheltered behind Sonoma Mountain, the fogs were almost invariably high fogs. Sweeping in from the ocean forty miles away, they were deflected by Sonoma Mountain and shunted high into the air. Another thing, Trillium Covert and Madrono Ranch were happily situated in a narrow thermal belt, so that in the frosty mornings of winter the temperature was always several degrees higher than in the rest of the valley. In fact, frost was very rare in the thermal belt, as was proved by the successful cultivation of certain orange and lemon trees.

Edmund continued reading titles and selecting books until he had drawn out quite a number. He opened the top one, Bolton Hall's "Three Acres and Liberty," and read to them of a man who walked six hundred and fifty miles a year in cultivating, by old-fashioned methods, twenty acres, from which he harvested three thousand bushels of poor potatoes; and of another man, a "new" farmer, who cultivated only five acres, walked two hundred miles, and produced three thousand bushels of potatoes, early and choice, which he sold at many times the price received by the first man.

Saxon received the books from Edmund, and, as she heaped them in Billy's arms, read the titles. They were: Wickson's "California Fruits," Wickson's "California Vegetables," Brooks' "Fertilizers," Watson's "Farm Poultry," King's "Irrigation and Drainage," Kropotkin's "Fields, Factories and Workshops," and Farmer's Bulletin No. 22 on "The Feeding of Farm Animals."

"Come for more any time you want them," Edmund invited. "I have hundreds of volumes on farming, and all the Agricultural Bulletins... . And you must come and get acquainted with Dulcie your first spare time," he called after them out the door.

CHAPTER XIX

Mrs. Mortimer arrived with seed catalogs and farm books, to find Saxon immersed in the farm books borrowed from Edmund. Saxon showed her around, and she was delighted with everything, including the terms of the lease and its option to buy.

"And now," she said. "What is to be done? Sit down, both of you. This is a council of war, and I am the one person in the world to tell you what to do. I ought to be. Anybody who has reorganized and recatalogued a great city library should be able to start you young people on in short order. Now, where shall we begin?"

She paused for breath of consideration.

"First, Madrono Ranch is a bargain. I know soil, I know beauty, I know climate. Madrono Ranch is a gold mine. There is a fortune in that meadow. Tilth—I'll tell you about that later. First, here's the land. Second, what are you going to do with it? Make a living? Yes. Vegetables? Of course. What are you going to do with them after you have grown them? Sell. Where?—Now listen. You must do as I did. Cut out the middle man. Sell directly to the consumer. Drum up your own market. Do you know what I saw from the car windows coming up the valley, only several miles from here? Hotels, springs, summer resorts, winter resorts—population, mouths, market. How is that market supplied? I looked in vain for truck gardens.—Billy, harness up your horses and be ready directly after dinner to take Saxon and me driving. Never mind everything else. Let things stand. What's the use of starting for a place of which you haven't the address. We'll look for the address this afternoon. Then we'll know where we are—at."—The last syllable a smiling concession to Billy.

But Saxon did not accompany them. There was too much to be done in cleaning the long-abandoned house and in preparing an arrangement for Mrs. Mortimer to sleep. And it was long after supper time when Mrs. Mortimer and Billy returned.

"You lucky, lucky children," she began immediately. "This valley is just waking up. Here's your market. There isn't a competitor in the valley. I thought those resorts looked new—Caliente, Boyes Hot Springs, El Verano, and all along the line. Then there are three little hotels in Glen Ellen, right next door. Oh, I've talked with all the owners and managers."

"She's a wooz," Billy admired. "She'd brace up to God on a business proposition. You oughta seen her."

Mrs. Mortimer acknowledged the compliment and dashed on.

"And where do all the vegetables come from? Wagons drive down twelve to fifteen miles from Santa Rosa, and up from Sonoma. Those are the nearest truck farms, and when they fail, as they often do, I am told, to supply the increasing needs, the managers have to express vegetables all the way from San Francisco. I've introduced Billy. They've agreed to patronize home industry. Besides, it is better for them. You'll deliver just as good vegetables just as cheap; you will make it a point to deliver better, fresher vegetables; and don't forget that delivery for you will be cheaper by virtue of the shorter haul.

"No day-old egg stunt here. No jams nor jellies. But you've got lots of space up on the bench here on which you can't grow vegetables. To-morrow morning I'll help you lay out the chicken runs and houses. Besides, there is the matter of capons for the San Francisco market. You'll start small. It will be a side line at first. I'll tell you all about that, too, and send you the literature. You must use your head. Let others do the work. You must understand that thoroughly. The wages of superintendence are always larger than the wages of the laborers. You must keep books. You must know where you stand. You must know what pays and what doesn't and what pays best. Your books will tell that. I'll show you all in good time."

"An' think of it—all that on two acres!" Billy murmured.

Mrs. Mortimer looked at him sharply.

"Two acres your granny," she said with asperity. "Five acres. And then you won't be able to supply your market. And you, my boy, as soon as the first rains come will have your hands full and your horses weary draining that meadow. We'll work those plans out to-morrow Also, there is the matter of berries on the bench here—and trellised table grapes, the choicest. They bring the fancy prices. There will be blackberries—Burbank's, he lives at Santa Rosa—Loganberries, Mammoth berries. But don't fool with strawberries. That's a whole occupation in itself. They're not vines, you know. I've examined the orchard. It's a good foundation. We'll settle the pruning and grafts later."

"But Billy wanted three acres of the meadow," Saxon explained at the first chance.

"What for?"

"To grow hay and other kinds of food for the horses he's going to raise."

"Buy it out of a portion of the profits from those three acres," Mrs. Mortimer decided on the instant.

Billy swallowed, and again achieved renunciation.

"All right," he said, with a brave show of cheerfulness. "Let her go. Us for the greens."

During the several days of Mrs. Mortimer's visit, Billy let the two women settle things for themselves. Oakland had entered upon a boom, and from the West Oakland stables had come an urgent letter for more horses. So Billy was out, early and late, scouring the surrounding country for young work animals. In this way, at the start, he learned his valley thoroughly. There was also a clearing out at the West Oakland stables of mares whose feet had been knocked out on the hard city pavements, and he was offered first choice at bargain prices. They were good animals. He knew what they were because he knew them of old time. The soft earth of the country, with a preliminary rest in pasture with their shoes pulled off, would put them in shape. They would never do again on hard-paved streets, but there were years of farm work in them. And then there was the breeding. But he could not undertake to buy them. He fought out the battle in secret and said nothing to Saxon.

At night, he would sit in the kitchen and smoke, listening to all that the two women had done and planned in the day. The right kind of horses was hard to buy, and, as he put it, it was like pulling a tooth to get a farmer to part with one, despite the fact that he had been authorized to increase the buying sum by as much as fifty dollars. Despite the coming of the automobile, the price of heavy draught animals continued to rise. From as early as Billy could remember, the price of the big work horses had increased steadily. After the great earthquake, the price had jumped; yet it had never gone back.

"Billy, you make more money as a horse-buyer than a common laborer, don't you?" Mrs. Mortimer asked. "Very well, then. You won't have to drain the meadow, or plow it, or anything. You keep right on buying horses. Work with your head. But out of what you make you will please pay the wages of one laborer for Saxon's vegetables. It will be a good investment, with quick returns."

"Sure," he agreed. "That's all anybody hires any body for—to make money outa 'm. But how Saxon an' one man are goin' to work them five acres, when Mr. Hale says two of us couldn't do what's needed on two acres, is beyond me."

"Saxon isn't going to work," Mrs. Mortimer retorted.

"Did you see me working at San Jose? Saxon is going to use her head. It's about time you woke up to that. A dollar and a half a day is what is earned by persons who don't use their heads. And she isn't going to be satisfied with a dollar and a half a day. Now listen. I had a long talk with Mr. Hale this afternoon. He says there are practically no efficient laborers to be hired in the valley."

"I know that," Billy interjected. "All the good men go to the cities. It's only the leavin's that's left. The good ones that stay behind ain't workin' for wages."

"Which is perfectly true, every word. Now listen, children. I knew about it, and I spoke to Mr. Hale. He is prepared to make the arrangements for you. He knows all about it himself, and is in touch with the Warden. In short, you will parole two good-conduct prisoners from San Quentin; and they will be gardeners. There are plenty of Chinese and Italians there, and they are the best truck-farmers. You kill two birds with one stone. You serve the poor convicts, and you serve yourselves."

Saxon hesitated, shocked; while Billy gravely considered the question.

"You know John," Mrs. Mortimer went on, "Mr. Hale's man about the place? How do you like him?"

"Oh, I was wishing only to-day that we could find somebody like him," Saxon said eagerly. "He's such a dear, faithful soul. Mrs. Hale told me a lot of fine things about him."

"There's one thing she didn't tell you," smiled Mrs. Mortimer. "John is a paroled convict. Twenty-eight years ago, in hot blood, he killed a man in a quarrel over sixty-five cents. He's been out of prison with the Hales three years now. You remember Louis, the old Frenchman, on my place? He's another. So that's settled. When your two come—of course you will pay them fair wages—and we'll make sure they're the same nationality, either Chinese or Italians—well, when they come, John, with their help, and under Mr. Hale's guidance, will knock together a small cabin for them to live in. We'll select the spot. Even so, when your farm is in full swing you'll have to have more outside help. So keep your eyes open, Billy, while you're gallivanting over the valley."

The next night Billy failed to return, and at nine o'clock a Glen Ellen boy on horseback delivered a telegram. Billy had sent it from Lake County. He was after horses for Oakland.

Not until the third night did he arrive home, tired to exhaustion, but with an ill concealed air of pride.

"Now what have you been doing these three days?" Mrs. Mortimer demanded.

"Usin' my head," he boasted quietly. "Killin' two birds with one stone; an', take it from me, I killed a whole flock. Huh! I got word of it at Lawndale, an' I wanta tell you Hazel an' Hattie was some tired when I stabled 'm at Calistoga an' pulled out on the stage over St. Helena. I was Johnny-on-the-spot, an' I nailed 'm—eight whoppers—the whole outfit of a mountain teamster. Young animals, sound as a dollar, and the lightest of 'em over fifteen hundred. I shipped 'm last night from Calistoga. An', well, that ain't all.

"Before that, first day, at Lawndale, I seen the fellow with the teamin' contract for the pavin'-stone quarry. Sell horses! He wanted to buy 'em. He wanted to buy 'em bad. He'd even rent 'em, he said."

"And you sent him the eight you bought!" Saxon broke in.

"Guess again. I bought them eight with Oakland money, an' they was shipped to Oakland. But I got the Lawndale contractor on long distance, and he agreed to pay me half a dollar a day rent for every work horse up to half a dozen. Then I telegraphed the Boss, tellin' him to ship me six sore-footed mares, Bud Strothers to make the choice, an' to charge to my commission. Bud knows what I 'm after. Soon as they come, off go their shoes. Two weeks in pasture, an' then they go to Lawndale. They can do the work. It's a down-hill haul to the railroad on a dirt road. Half a dollar rent each—that's three dollars a day they'll bring me six days a week. I don't feed 'em, shoe 'm, or nothin', an' I keep an eye on 'm to see they're treated right. Three bucks a day, eh! Well, I guess that'll keep a couple of dollar-an '-a-half men goin' for Saxon, unless she works 'em Sundays. Huh! The Valley of the Moon! Why, we'll be wearin' diamonds before long. Gosh! A fellow could live in the city a thousan' years an' not get such chances. It beats China lottery."

He stood up.

"I 'm goin' out to water Hazel an' Hattie, feed 'm, an' bed 'm down. I'll eat soon as I come back."

The two women were regarding each other with shining eyes, each on the verge of speech when Billy returned to the door and stuck his head in.

"They's one thing maybe you ain't got," he said. "I pull down them three dollars every day; but the six mares is mine, too. I own 'm. They're mine. Are you on?"

CHAPTER XX

"I'm not done with you children," had been Mrs. Mortimer's parting words; and several times that winter she ran up to advise, and to teach Saxon how to calculate her crops for the small immediate market, for the increasing spring market, and for the height of summer, at which time she would be able to sell all she could possibly grow and then not supply the demand. In the meantime, Hazel and Hattie were used every odd moment in hauling manure from Glen Ellen, whose barnyards had never known such a thorough cleaning. Also there were loads of commercial fertilizer from the railroad station, bought under Mrs. Mortimer's instructions.

The convicts paroled were Chinese. Both had served long in prison, and were old men; but the day's work they were habitually capable of won Mrs. Mortimer's approval. Gow Yum, twenty years before, had had charge of the vegetable garden of one of the great Menlo Park estates. His disaster had come in the form of a fight over a game of fan tan in the Chinese quarter at Redwood City. His companion, Chan Chi, had been a hatchet-man of note, in the old fighting days of the San Francisco tongs. But a quarter of century of discipline in the prison vegetable gardens had cooled his blood and turned his hand from hatchet to hoe. These two assistants had arrived in Glen Ellen like precious goods in bond and been receipted for by the local deputy sheriff, who, in addition, reported on them to the prison authorities each month. Saxon, too, made out a monthly report and sent it in.

As for the danger of their cutting her throat, she quickly got over the idea of it. The mailed hand of the State hovered over them. The taking of a single drink of liquor would provoke that hand to close down and jerk them back to prison-cells. Nor had they freedom of movement. When old Gow Yum needed to go to San Francisco to sign certain papers before the Chinese Consul, permission had first to be obtained from San Quentin. Then, too, neither man was nasty tempered. Saxon had been apprehensive of the task of bossing two desperate convicts; but when they came she found it a pleasure to work with them. She could tell them what to do, but it was they who knew how to do. From them she learned all the ten thousand tricks and quirks of artful gardening, and she was not long in realizing how helpless she would have been had she depended on local labor.

Still further, she had no fear, because she was not alone. She had been using her head. It was quickly apparent to her that she could not adequately oversee the outside work and at the same time do the house work. She wrote to Ukiah to the energetic widow who had lived in the adjoining house and taken in washing. She had promptly closed with Saxon's offer. Mrs. Paul was forty, short in stature, and weighed two hundred pounds, but never wearied on her feet. Also she was devoid of fear, and, according to Billy, could settle the hash of both Chinese with one of her mighty arms. Mrs. Paul arrived with her son, a country lad of sixteen who knew horses and could milk Hilda, the pretty Jersey which had successfully passed Edmund's expert eye. Though Mrs. Paul ably handled the house, there was one thing Saxon insisted on doing—namely, washing her own pretty flimsies.

"When I 'm no longer able to do that," she told Billy, "you can take a spade to that clump of redwoods beside Wild Water and dig a hole. It will be time to bury me."

It was early in the days of Madrono Ranch, at the time of Mrs. Mortimer's second visit, that Billy drove in with a load of pipe; and house, chicken yards, and barn were piped from the second-hand tank he installed below the house-spring.

"Huh! I guess I can use my head," he said. "I watched a woman over on the other side of the valley, packin' water two hundred feet from the spring to the house; an' I did some figurin'. I put it at three trips a day and on wash days a whole lot more; an' you can't guess what I made out she traveled a year packin' water. One hundred an' twenty-two miles. D'ye get that? One hundred and twenty-two miles! I asked her how long she'd been there. Thirty-one years. Multiply it for yourself. Three thousan', seven hundred an' eighty-two miles—all for the sake of two hundred feet of pipe. Wouldn't that jar you?"

"Oh, I ain't done yet. They's a bath-tub an' stationary tubs a-comin' soon as I can see my way. An', say, Saxon, you know that little clear flat just where Wild Water runs into Sonoma. They's all of an acre of it. An' it's mine! Got that? An' no walkin' on the grass for you. It'll be my grass. I 'm goin' up stream a ways an' put in a ram. I got a big second-hand one staked out that I can get for ten dollars, an' it'll pump more water'n I need. An' you'll see alfalfa growin' that'll make your mouth water. I gotta have another horse to travel around on. You're usin' Hazel an' Hattie too much to give me a chance; an' I'll never see 'm as soon as you start deliverin' vegetables. I guess that alfalfa'll help some to keep another horse goin'."

But Billy was destined for a time to forget his alfalfa in the excitement of bigger ventures. First, came trouble. The several hundred dollars he had arrived with in Sonoma Valley, and all his own commissions since earned, had gone into improvements and living. The eighteen dollars a week rental for his six horses at Lawndale went to pay wages. And he was unable to buy the needed saddle-horse for his horse-buying expeditions. This, however, he had got around by again using his head and killing two birds with one stone. He began breaking colts to drive, and in the driving drove them wherever he sought horses.

So far all was well. But a new administration in San Francisco, pledged to economy, had stopped all street work. This meant the shutting down of the Lawndale quarry, which was one of the sources of supply for paving blocks. The six horses would not only be back on his hands, but he would have to feed them. How Mrs. Paul, Gow Yum, and Chan Chi were to be paid was beyond him.

"I guess we've bit off more'n we could chew," he admitted to Saxon.

That night he was late in coming home, but brought with him a radiant face. Saxon was no less radiant.

"It's all right," she greeted him, coming out to the barn where he was unhitching a tired but fractious colt. "I've talked with all three. They see the situation, and are perfectly willing to let their wages stand a while. By another week I start Hazel and Hattie delivering vegetables. Then the money will pour in from the hotels and my books won't look so lopsided. And—oh, Billy—you'd never guess. Old Gow Yum has a bank account. He came to me afterward—I guess he was thinking it over—and offered to lend me four hundred dollars. What do you think of that?"

"That I ain't goin' to be too proud to borrow it off 'm, if he IS a Chink. He's a white one, an' maybe I'll need it. Because, you see—well, you can't guess what I've been up to since I seen you this mornin'. I've been so busy I ain't had a bite to eat."

"Using your head?" She laughed.

"You can call it that," he joined in her laughter. "I've been spendin' money like water."

"But you haven't got any to spend," she objected.

"I've got credit in this valley, I'll let you know," he replied. "An' I sure strained it some this afternoon. Now guess."

"A saddle-horse?"

He roared with laughter, startling the colt, which tried to bolt and lifted him half off the ground by his grip on its frightened nose and neck.

"Oh, I mean real guessin'," he urged, when the animal had dropped back to earth and stood regarding him with trembling suspicion.

"Two saddle-horses?"

"Aw, you ain't got imagination. I'll tell you. You know Thiercroft. I bought his big wagon from 'm for sixty dollars. I bought a wagon from the Kenwood blacksmith—so-so, but it'll do—for forty-five dollars. An' I bought Ping's wagon—a peach—for sixty-five dollars. I could a-got it for fifty if he hadn't seen I wanted it bad."

"But the money?" Saxon questioned faintly. "You hadn't a hundred dollars left."

"Didn't I tell you I had credit? Well, I have. I stood 'm off for them wagons. I ain't spent a cent of cash money to-day except for a couple of long-distance switches. Then I bought three sets of work-harness—they're chain harness an' second-hand—for twenty dollars a set. I bought 'm from the fellow that's doin' the haulin' for the quarry. He don't need 'm any more. An' I rented four wagons from 'm, an' four span of horses, too, at half a dollar a day for each horse, an' half a dollar a day for each wagon—that's six dollars a day rent I gotta pay 'm. The three sets of spare harness is for my six horses. Then... lemme see... yep, I rented two barns in Glen Ellen, an' I ordered fifty tons of hay an' a carload of bran an' barley from the store in Glenwood—you see, I gotta feed all them fourteen horses, an' shoe 'm, an' everything.

"Oh, sure Pete, I've went some. I hired seven men to go drivin' for me at two dollars a day, an'—ouch! Jehosaphat! What you doin'!"

"No," Saxon said gravely, having pinched him, "you're not dreaming." She felt his pulse and forehead. "Not a sign of fever." She sniffed his breath. "And you've not been drinking. Go on, tell me the rest of this... whatever it is."

"Ain't you satisfied?"

"No. I want more. I want all."

"All right. But I just want you to know, first, that the boss I used to work for in Oakland ain't got nothin' on me. I 'm some man of affairs, if anybody should ride up on a vegetable wagon an' ask you. Now, I 'm goin' to tell you, though I can't see why the Glen Ellen folks didn't beat me to it. I guess they was asleep. Nobody'd a-overlooked a thing like it in the city. You see, it was like this: you know that fancy brickyard they're gettin' ready to start for makin' extra special fire brick for inside walls? Well, here was I worryin' about the six horses comin' back on my hands, earnin' me nothin' an' eatin' me into the poorhouse. I had to get 'm work somehow, an' I remembered the brickyard. I drove the colt down an' talked with that Jap chemist who's been doin' the experimentin'. Gee! They was foremen lookin' over the ground an' everything gettin' ready to hum. I looked over the lay an' studied it. Then I drove up to where they're openin' the clay pit—you know, that fine, white chalky stuff we saw 'em borin' out just outside the hundred an' forty acres with the three knolls. It's a down-hill haul, a mile, an' two horses can do it easy. In fact, their hardest job'll be haulin' the empty wagons up to the pit. Then I tied the colt an' went to figurin'.

"The Jap professor'd told me the manager an' the other big guns of the company was comin' up on the mornin' train. I wasn't shoutin' things out to anybody, but I just made myself into a committee of welcome; an', when the train pulled in, there I was, extendin' the glad hand of the burg—likewise the glad hand of a guy you used to know in Oakland once, a third-rate dub prizefighter by the name of—lemme see—yep, I got it right—Big Bill Roberts was the name he used to sport, but now he's known as William Roberts, E. S. Q.

"Well, as I was sayin', I gave 'm the glad hand, an' trailed along with 'em to the brickyard, an' from the talk I could see things was doin'. Then I watched my chance an' sprung my proposition. I was scared stiff all the time for maybe the teamin' was already arranged. But I knew it wasn't when they asked for my figures. I had 'm by heart, an' I rattled 'm off, and the top-guy took 'm down in his note-book.

"'We're goin' into this big, an' at once,' he says, lookin' at me sharp. 'What kind of an outfit you got, Mr. Roberts?'"

"Me!—with only Hazel an' Hattie, an' them too small for heavy teamin'.

"'I can slap fourteen horses an' seven wagons onto the job at the jump,' says I. 'An' if you want more, I'll get 'm, that's all.'

"'Give us fifteen minutes to consider, Mr. Roberts,' he says.

"'Sure,' says I, important as all hell—ahem—me!—'but a couple of other things first. I want a two year contract, an' them figures all depends on one thing. Otherwise they don't go.'

"'What's that,' he says.

"'The dump,' says I. 'Here we are on the ground, an' I might as well show you.'

"An' I did. I showed 'm where I'd lose out if they stuck to their plan, on account of the dip down an' pull up to the dump. 'All you gotta do,' I says, 'is to build the bunkers fifty feet over, throw the road around the rim of the hill, an' make about seventy or eighty feet of elevated bridge.'

"Say, Saxon, that kind of talk got 'em. It was straight. Only they'd been thinkin' about bricks, while I was only thinkin' of teamin'.

"I guess they was all of half an hour considerin', an' I was almost as miserable waitin' as when I waited for you to say yes after I asked you. I went over the figures, calculatin' what I could throw off if I had to. You see, I'd given it to 'em stiff—regular city prices; an' I was prepared to trim down. Then they come back.

"'Prices oughta be lower in the country,' says the top-guy.

"'Nope,' I says. 'This is a wine-grape valley. It don't raise enough hay an' feed for its own animals. It has to be shipped in from the San Joaquin Valley. Why, I can buy hay an' feed cheaper in San Francisco, laid down, than I can here an' haul it myself.'

"An' that struck 'm hard. It was true, an' they knew it. But—say! If they'd asked about wages for drivers, an' about horse-shoein' prices, I'd a-had to come down; because, you see, they ain't no teamsters' union in the country, an' no horseshoers' union, an' rent is low, an' them two items come a whole lot cheaper. Huh! This afternoon I got a word bargain with the blacksmith across from the post office; an' he takes my whole bunch an' throws off twenty-five cents on each shoein', though it's on the Q. T. But they didn't think to ask, bein' too full of bricks."

Billy felt in his breast pocket, drew out a legal-looking document, and handed it to Saxon.

"There it is," he said, "the contract, full of all the agreements, prices, an' penalties. I saw Mr. Hale down town an' showed it to 'm. He says it's O.K. An' say, then I lit out. All over town, Kenwood, Lawndale, everywhere, everybody, everything. The quarry teamin' finishes Friday of this week. An' I take the whole outfit an' start Wednesday of next week haulin' lumber for the buildin's, an' bricks for the kilns, an' all the rest. An' when they're ready for the clay I 'm the boy that'll give it to them.

"But I ain't told you the best yet. I couldn't get the switch right away from Kenwood to Lawndale, and while I waited I went over my figures again. You couldn't guess it in a million years. I'd made a mistake in addition somewhere, an' soaked 'm ten per cent. more'n I'd expected. Talk about findin' money! Any time you want them couple of extra men to help out with the vegetables, say the word. Though we're goin' to have to pinch the next couple of months. An' go ahead an' borrow that four hundred from Gow Yum. An' tell him you'll pay eight per cent. interest, an' that we won't want it more 'n three or four months."

When Billy got away from Saxon's arms, he started leading the colt up and down to cool it off. He stopped so abruptly that his back collided with the colt's nose, and there was a lively minute of rearing and plunging. Saxon waited, for she knew a fresh idea had struck Billy.

"Say," he said, "do you know anything about bank accounts and drawin' checks?"

CHAPTER XXI

It was on a bright June morning that Billy told Saxon to put on her riding clothes to try out a saddle-horse.

"Not until after ten o'clock," she said. "By that time I'll have the wagon off on a second trip."

Despite the extent of the business she had developed, her executive ability and system gave her much spare time. She could call on the Hales, which was ever a delight, especially now that the Hastings were back and that Clara was often at her aunt's. In this congenial atmosphere Saxon burgeoned. She had begun to read—to read with understanding; and she had time for her books, for work on her pretties, and for Billy, whom she accompanied on many expeditions.

Billy was even busier than she, his work being more scattered and diverse. And, as well, he kept his eye on the home barn and horses which Saxon used. In truth he had become a man of affairs, though Mrs. Mortimer had gone over his accounts, with an eagle eye on the expense column, discovering several minor leaks, and finally, aided by Saxon, bullied him into keeping books. Each night, after supper, he and Saxon posted their books. Afterward, in the big morris chair he had insisted on buying early in the days of his brickyard contract, Saxon would creep into his arms and strum on the ukulele; or they would talk long about what they were doing and planning to do. Now it would be:

"I'm mixin' up in politics, Saxon. It pays. You bet it pays. If by next spring I ain't got a half a dozen teams workin' on the roads an' pullin' down the county money, it's me back to Oakland an' askin' the Boss for a job."

Or, Saxon: "They're really starting that new hotel between Caliente and Eldridge. And there's some talk of a big sanitarium back in the hills."

Or, it would be: "Billy, now that you've piped that acre, you've just got to let me have it for my vegetables. I'll rent it from you. I'll take your own estimate for all the alfalfa you can raise on it, and pay you full market price less the cost of growing it."

"It's all right, take it." Billy suppressed a sigh. "Besides, I 'm too busy to fool with it now."

Which prevarication was bare-faced, by virtue of his having just installed the ram and piped the land.

"It will be the wisest, Billy," she soothed, for she knew his dream of land-spaciousness was stronger than ever. "You don't want to fool with an acre. There's that hundred and forty. We'll buy it yet if old Chavon ever dies.

Besides, it really belongs to Madrono Ranch. The two together were the original quarter section."

"I don't wish no man's death," Billy grumbled. "But he ain't gettin' no good out of it, over-pasturin' it with a lot of scrub animals. I've sized it up every inch of it. They's at least forty acres in the three cleared fields, with water in the hills behind to beat the band. The horse feed I could raise on it'd take your breath away. Then they's at least fifty acres I could run my brood mares on, pasture mixed up with trees and steep places and such. The other fifty's just thick woods, an' pretty places, an' wild game. An' that old adobe barn's all right. With a new roof it'd shelter any amount of animals in bad weather. Look at me now, rentin' that measly pasture back of Ping's just to run my restin' animals. They could run in the hundred an' forty if I only had it. I wonder if Chavon would lease it."

Or, less ambitious, Billy would say: "I gotta skin over to Petaluma tomorrow, Saxon. They's an auction on the Atkinson Ranch an' maybe I can pick up some bargains."

"More horses!"

"Ain't I got two teams haulin' lumber for the new winery? An' Barney's got a bad shoulder-sprain. He'll have to lay off a long time if he's to get it in shape. An' Bridget ain't ever goin' to do a tap of work again. I can see that stickin' out. I've doctored her an' doctored her. She's fooled the vet, too. An' some of the other horses has gotta take a rest. That span of grays is showin' the hard work. An' the big roan's goin' loco. Everybody thought it was his teeth, but it ain't. It's straight loco. It's money in pocket to take care of your animals, an' horses is the delicatest things on four legs. Some time, if I can ever see my way to it, I 'm goin' to ship a carload of mules from Colusa County—big, heavy ones, you know. They'd sell like hot cakes in the valley here—them I didn't want for myself."

Or, in lighter vein, Billy: "By the way, Saxon, talkin' of accounts, what d'you think Hazel an' Hattie is worth?—fair market price?"

"Why?"

"I 'm askin' you."

"Well, say, what you paid for them—three hundred dollars."

"Hum." Billy considered deeply. "They're worth a whole lot more, but let it go at that. An' now, gettin' back to accounts, suppose you write me a check for three hundred dollars."

"Oh! Robber!"

"You can't show me. Why, Saxon, when I let you have grain an' hay from my carloads, don't you give me a check for it? An' you know how you're stuck on keepin' your accounts down to the penny," he teased. "If you're any kind of a business woman you just gotta charge your business with them two horses. I ain't had the use of 'em since I don't know when."

"But the colts will be yours," she argued. "Besides, I can't afford brood mares in my business. In almost no time, now, Hazel and Hattie will have to be taken off from the wagon—they're too good for it anyway. And you keep your eyes open for a pair to take their place. I'll give you a check for THAT pair, but no commission."

"All right," Billy conceded. "Hazel an' Hattie come back to me; but you can pay me rent for the time you did use 'em."

"If you make me, I'll charge you board," she threatened.

"An' if you charge me board, I'll charge you interest for the money I've stuck into this shebang."

"You can't," Saxon laughed. "It's community property."

He grunted spasmodically, as if the breath had been knocked out of him.

"Straight on the solar plexus," he said, "an' me down for the count. But say, them's sweet words, ain't they—community property." He rolled them over and off his tongue with keen relish. "An' when we got married the top of our ambition was a steady job an' some rags an' sticks of furniture all paid up an' half-worn out. We wouldn't have had any community property only for you."

"What nonsense! What could I have done by myself? You know very well that you earned all the money that started us here. You paid the wages of Gow Yum and Chan Chi, and old Hughie, and Mrs. Paul, and—why, you've done it all."

She drew her two hands caressingly across his shoulders and down along his great biceps muscles.

"That's what did it, Billy."

"Aw hell! It's your head that done it. What was my muscles good for with no head to run 'em,—sluggin' scabs, beatin' up lodgers, an' crookin' the elbow over a bar. The only sensible thing my head ever done was when it run me into you. Honest to God, Saxon, you've been the makin' of me."

"Aw hell, Billy," she mimicked in the way that delighted him, "where would I have been if you hadn't taken me out of the laundry? I couldn't take myself out. I was just a helpless girl. I'd have been there yet if it hadn't been for you. Mrs. Mortimer had five thousand dollars; but I had you."

"A woman ain't got the chance to help herself that a man has," he generalized. "I'll tell you what: It took the two of us. It's been team-work. We've run in span. If we'd a-run single, you might still be in the laundry; an', if I was lucky, I'd be still drivin' team by the day an' sportin' around to cheap dances."

Saxon stood under the father of all madronos, watching Hazel and Hattie go out the gate, the full vegetable wagon behind them, when she saw Billy ride in, leading a sorrel mare from whose silken coat the sun flashed golden lights.

"Four-year-old, high-life, a handful, but no vicious tricks," Billy chanted, as he stopped beside Saxon. "Skin like tissue paper, mouth like silk, but kill the toughest broncho ever foaled—look at them lungs an' nostrils. They call her Ramona—some Spanish name: sired by Morellita outa genuine Morgan stock."

"And they will sell her?" Saxon gasped, standing with hands clasped in inarticulate delight.

"That's what I brought her to show you for."

"But how much must they want for her?" was Saxon's next question, so impossible did it seem that such an amazement of horse-flesh could ever be hers.

"That ain't your business," Billy answered brusquely. "The brickyard's payin' for her, not the vegetable ranch. She's yourn at the word. What d'ye say?"

"I'll tell you in a minute."

Saxon was trying to mount, but the animal danced nervously away.

"Hold on till I tie," Billy said. "She ain't skirt-broke, that's the trouble."

Saxon tightly gripped reins and mane, stepped with spurred foot on Billy's hand, and was lifted lightly into the saddle.

"She's used to spurs," Billy called after. "Spanish broke, so don't check her quick. Come in gentle. An' talk to her. She's high-life, you know."

Saxon nodded, dashed out the gate and down the road, waved a hand to Clara Hastings as she passed the gate of Trillium Covert, and continued up Wild Water canyon.

When she came back, Ramona in a pleasant lather, Saxon rode to the rear of the house, past the chicken houses and the flourishing berry-rows, to join Billy on the rim of the bench, where he sat on his horse in the shade, smoking a cigarette. Together they looked down through an opening among the trees to the meadow which was a meadow no longer. With mathematical accuracy it was divided into squares, oblongs, and narrow strips, which displayed sharply the thousand hues of green of a truck garden. Gow Yum and Chan Chi, under enormous Chinese grass hats, were planting green onions. Old Hughie, hoe in hand, plodded along the main artery of running water, opening certain laterals, closing others. From the work-shed beyond the barn the strokes of a hammer told Saxon that Carlsen was wire-binding vegetable boxes. Mrs. Paul's cheery soprano, lifted in a hymn, floated through the trees, accompanied by the whirr of an egg-beater. A sharp barking told where Possum still waged hysterical and baffled war on the Douglass squirrels. Billy took a long draw from his cigarette, exhaled the smoke, and continued to look down at the meadow. Saxon divined trouble in his manner. His rein-hand was on the pommel, and her free hand went out and softly rested on his. Billy turned his slow gaze upon her mare's lather, seeming not to note it, and continued on to Saxon's face.

"Huh!" he equivocated, as if waking up. "Them San Leandro Porchugeeze ain't got nothin' on us when it comes to intensive farmin'. Look at that water runnin'. You know, it seems so good to me that sometimes I just wanta get down on hands an' knees an' lap it all up myself."

"Oh, to have all the water you want in a climate like this!" Saxon exclaimed.

"An' don't be scared of it ever goin' back on you. If the rains fooled you, there's Sonoma Creek alongside. All we gotta do is install a gasolene pump."

"But we'll never have to, Billy. I was talking with 'Redwood' Thompson. He's lived in the valley since Fifty-three, and he says there's never been a failure of crops on account of drought. We always get our rain."

"Come on, let's go for a ride," he said abruptly. "You've got the time."

"All right, if you'll tell me what's bothering you."

He looked at her quickly.

"Nothin'," he grunted. "Yes, there is, too. What's the difference? You'd know it sooner or later. You ought to see old Chavon. His face is that long he can't walk without bumpin' his knee on his chin. His gold-mine's peterin' out."

"Gold mine!"

"His clay pit. It's the same thing. He's gettin' twenty cents a yard for it from the brickyard."

"And that means the end of your teaming contract." Saxon saw the disaster in all its hugeness. "What about the brickyard people?"

"Worried to death, though they've kept secret about it. They've had men out punchin' holes all over the hills for a week, an' that Jap chemist settin' up nights analyzin' the rubbish they've brought in. It's peculiar stuff, that clay, for what they want it for, an' you don't find it everywhere. Them experts that reported on Chavon's pit made one hell of a mistake. Maybe they was lazy with their borin's. Anyway, they slipped up on the amount of clay they was in it. Now don't get to botherin'. It'd come out somehow. You can't do nothin'."

"But I can," Saxon insisted. "We won't buy Ramona."

"You ain't got a thing to do with that," he answered. "I 'm buyin' her, an' her price don't cut any figure alongside the big game I 'm playin'. Of course, I can always sell my horses. But that puts a stop to their makin' money, an' that brickyard contract was fat."

"But if you get some of them in on the road work for the county?" she suggested.

"Oh, I got that in mind. An' I 'm keepin' my eyes open. They's a chance the quarry will start again, an' the fellow that did that teamin' has gone to Puget Sound. An' what if I have to sell out most of the horses? Here's you and the vegetable business. That's solid. We just don't go ahead so fast for a time, that's all. I ain't scared of the country any more. I sized things up as we went along. They ain't a jerk burg we hit all the time on the road that I couldn't jump into an' make a go. An' now where d'you want to ride?"

CHAPTER XXII

They cantered out the gate, thundered across the bridge, and passed Trillium Covert before they pulled in on the grade of Wild Water Canyon. Saxon had chosen her field on the big spur of Sonoma Mountains as the objective of their ride.

"Say, I bumped into something big this mornin' when I was goin' to fetch Ramona," Billy said, the clay pit trouble banished for the time. "You know the hundred an' forty. I passed young Chavon along the road, an'—I don't know why—just for ducks, I guess—I up an' asked 'm if he thought the old man would lease the hundred an' forty to me. An' what d 'you think! He said the old man didn't own it. Was just leasin' it himself. That's how we was always seein' his cattle on it. It's a gouge into his land, for he owns everything on three sides of it.

"Next I met Ping. He said Hilyard owned it an' was willin' to sell, only Chavon didn't have the price. Then, comin' back, I looked in on Payne. He's quit blacksmithin'—his back's hurtin' 'm from a kick—an' just startin' in for real estate. Sure, he said, Hilyard would sell, an' had already listed the land with 'm. Chavon's over-pastured it, an' Hilyard won't give 'm another lease."

When they had climbed out of Wild Water Canyon they turned their horses about and halted on the rim where they could look across at the three densely wooded knolls in the midst of the desired hundred and forty.

"We'll get it yet," Saxon said.

"Sure we will," Billy agreed with careless certitude. "I've ben lookin' over the big adobe barn again. Just the thing for a raft of horses, an' a new roof'll be cheaper 'n I thought. Though neither Chavon or me'll be in the market to buy it right away, with the clay pinchin' out."

When they reached Saxon's field, which they had learned was the property of Redwood Thompson, they tied the horses and entered it on foot. The hay, just cut, was being raked by Thompson, who hallo'd a greeting to them. It was a cloudless, windless day, and they sought refuge from the sun in the woods beyond. They encountered a dim trail.

"It's a cow trail," Billy declared. "I bet they's a teeny pasture tucked away somewhere in them trees. Let's follow it."

A quarter of an hour later, several hundred feet up the side of the spur, they emerged on an open, grassy space of bare hillside. Most of the hundred and forty, two miles away, lay beneath them, while they were level with the tops of the three knolls. Billy paused to gaze upon the much-desired land, and Saxon joined him.

"What is that?" she asked, pointing toward the knolls. "Up the little canyon, to the left of it, there on the farthest knoll, right under that spruce that's leaning over."

What Billy saw was a white scar on the canyon wall.

"It's one on me," he said, studying the scar. "I thought I knew every inch of that land, but I never seen that before. Why, I was right in there at the head of the canyon the first part of the winter. It's awful wild. Walls of the canyon like the sides of a steeple an' covered with thick woods."

"What is it?" she asked. "A slide?"

"Must be—brought down by the heavy rains. If I don't miss my guess—" Billy broke off, forgetting in the intensity with which he continued to look.

"Hilyard'll sell for thirty an acre," he began again, disconnectedly. "Good land, bad land, an' all, just as it runs, thirty an acre. That's forty-two hundred. Payne's new at real estate, an' I'll make 'm split his commission an' get the easiest terms ever. We can re-borrow that four hundred from Gow Yum, an' I can borrow money on my horses an' wagons—"

"Are you going to buy it to-day?" Saxon teased.

She scarcely touched the edge of his thought. He looked at her, as if he had heard, then forgot her the next moment.

"Head work," he mumbled. "Head work. If I don't put over a hot one—"

He started back down the cow trail, recollected Saxon, and called over his shoulder:

"Come on. Let's hustle. I wanta ride over an' look at that."

So rapidly did he go down the trail and across the field, that Saxon had no time for questions. She was almost breathless from her effort to keep up with him.

"What is it?" she begged, as he lifted her to the saddle.

"Maybe it's all a joke—I'll tell you about it afterward," he put her off.

They galloped on the levels, trotted down the gentler slopes of road, and not until on the steep descent of Wild Water canyon did they rein to a walk. Billy's preoccupation was gone, and Saxon took advantage to broach a subject which had been on her mind for some time.

"Clara Hastings told me the other day that they're going to have a house party. The Hazards are to be there, and the Halls, and Roy Blanchard...."

She looked at Billy anxiously. At the mention of Blanchard his head had tossed up as to a bugle call. Slowly a whimsical twinkle began to glint up through the cloudy blue of his eyes.

"It's a long time since you told any man he was standing on his foot," she ventured slyly.

Billy began to grin sheepishly.

"Aw, that's all right," he said in mock-lordly fashion. "Roy Blanchard can come. I'll let 'm. All that was a long time ago. Besides, I 'm too busy to fool with such things."

He urged his horse on at a faster walk, and as soon as the slope lessened broke into a trot. At Trillium Covert they were galloping.

"You'll have to stop for dinner first," Saxon said, as they neared the gate of Madrono Ranch.

"You stop," he answered. "I don't want no dinner."

"But I want to go with you," she pleaded. "What is it?"

"I don't dast tell you. You go on in an' get your dinner."

"Not after that," she said. "Nothing can keep me from coming along now."

Half a mile farther on, they left the highway, passed through a patent gate which Billy had installed, and crossed the fields on a road which was coated thick with chalky dust. This was the road that led to Chavon's clay pit. The hundred and forty lay to the west. Two wagons, in a cloud of dust, came into sight.

"Your teams, Billy," cried Saxon. "Think of it! Just by the use of the head, earning your money while you're riding around with me."

"Makes me ashamed to think how much cash money each one of them teams is bringin' me in every day," he acknowledged.

They were turning off from the road toward the bars which gave entrance to the one hundred and forty, when the driver of the foremost wagon hallo'd and waved his hand. They drew in their horses and waited.

"The big roan's broke loose," the driver said, as he stopped beside them. "Clean crazy loco—bitin', squealin', strikin', kickin'. Kicked clean out of the harness like it was paper. Bit a chunk out of Baldy the size of a saucer, an' wound up by breakin' his own hind leg. Liveliest fifteen minutes I ever seen."

"Sure it's broke?" Billy demanded sharply.

"Sure thing."

"Well, after you unload, drive around by the other barn and get Ben. He's in the corral. Tell Matthews to be easy with 'm. An' get a gun. Sammy's got one. You'll have to see to the big roan. I ain't got time now.—Why couldn't Matthews a-come along with you for Ben? You'd save time."

"Oh, he's just stickin' around waitin'," the driver answered. "He reckoned I could get Ben."

"An' lose time, eh? Well, get a move on."

"That's the way of it," Billy growled to Saxon as they rode on. "No savve. No head. One man settin' down an' holdin his hands while another team drives outa its way doin what he oughta done. That's the trouble with two-dollar-a-day men."

"With two-dollar-a-day heads," Saxon said quickly. "What kind of heads do you expect for two dollars?"

"That's right, too," Billy acknowledged the hit. "If they had better heads they'd be in the cities like all the rest of the better men. An' the better men are a lot of dummies, too. They don't know the big chances in the country, or you couldn't hold 'm from it."

Billy dismounted, took the three bars down, led his horse through, then put up the bars.

"When I get this place, there'll be a gate here," he announced. "Pay for itself in no time. It's the thousan' an' one little things like this that count up big when you put 'm together." He sighed contentedly. "I never used to think about such things, but when we shook Oakland I began to wise up. It was them San Leandro Porchugeeze that gave me my first eye-opener. I'd been asleep, before that."

They skirted the lower of the three fields where the ripe hay stood uncut. Billy pointed with eloquent disgust to a break in the fence, slovenly repaired, and on to the standing grain much-trampled by cattle.

"Them's the things," he criticized. "Old style. An' look how thin that crop is, an' the shallow plowin'. Scrub cattle, scrub seed, scrub farmin'. Chavon's worked it for eight years now, an' never rested it once, never put anything in for what he took out, except the cattle into the stubble the minute the hay was on."

In a pasture glade, farther on, they came upon a bunch of cattle.

"Look at that bull, Saxon. Scrub's no name for it. They oughta be a state law against lettin' such animals exist. No wonder Chavon's that land poor he's had to sink all his clay-pit earnin's into taxes an' interest. He can't make his land pay. Take this hundred an forty. Anybody with the savve can just rake silver dollars offen it. I'll show 'm."

They passed the big adobe barn in the distance.

"A few dollars at the right time would a-saved hundreds on that roof," Billy commented. "Well, anyway, I won't be payin' for any improvements when I buy. An I'll tell you another thing. This ranch is full of water, and if Glen Ellen ever grows they'll have to come to see me for their water supply."

Billy knew the ranch thoroughly, and took short-cuts through the woods by way of cattle paths. Once, he reined in abruptly, and both stopped. Confronting them, a dozen paces away, was a half-grown red fox. For half a minute, with beady eyes, the wild thing studied them, with twitching sensitive nose reading the messages of the air. Then, velvet-footed, it leapt aside and was gone among the trees.

"The son-of-a-gun!" Billy ejaculated.

As they approached Wild Water; they rode out into a long narrow meadow. In the middle was a pond.

"Natural reservoir, when Glen Ellen begins to buy water," Billy said. "See, down at the lower end there?—wouldn't cost anything hardly to throw a dam across. An' I can pipe in all kinds of hill-drip. An' water's goin' to be money in this valley not a thousan' years from now.—An' all the ginks, an' boobs, an' dubs, an' gazabos poundin' their ear deado an' not seein' it comin.—An' surveyors workin' up the valley for an electric road from Sausalito with a branch up Napa Valley."

They came to the rim of Wild Water canyon. Leaning far back in their saddles, they slid the horses down a steep declivity, through big spruce woods, to an ancient and all but obliterated trail.

"They cut this trail 'way back in the Fifties," Billy explained. "I only found it by accident. Then I asked Poppe yesterday. He was born in the valley. He said it was a fake minin' rush across from Petaluma. The gamblers got it up, an' they must a-drawn a thousan' suckers. You see that flat there, an' the old stumps. That's where the camp was. They set the tables up under the trees. The flat used to be bigger, but the creek's eaten into it. Poppe said they was a couple of killin's an' one lynchin'."

Lying low against their horses' necks, they scrambled up a steep cattle trail out of the canyon, and began to work across rough country toward the knolls.

"Say, Saxon, you're always lookin' for something pretty. I'll show you what'll make your hair stand up... soon as we get through this manzanita."

Never, in all their travels, had Saxon seen so lovely a vista as the one that greeted them when they emerged. The dim trail lay like a rambling red shadow cast on the soft forest floor by the great redwoods and over-arching oaks. It seemed as if all local varieties of trees and vines had conspired to weave the leafy roof—maples, big madronos and laurels, and lofty tan-bark oaks, scaled and wrapped and interwound with wild grape and flaming poison oak. Saxon drew Billy's eyes to a mossy bank of five-finger ferns. All slopes seemed to meet to form this basin and colossal forest bower. Underfoot the floor was spongy with water. An invisible streamlet whispered under broad-fronded brakes. On every hand opened tiny vistas of enchantment, where young redwoods grouped still and stately about fallen giants, shoulder-high to the horses, moss-covered and dissolving into mold.

At last, after another quarter of an hour, they tied their horses on the rim of the narrow canyon that penetrated the wilderness of the knolls. Through a rift in the trees Billy pointed to the top of the leaning spruce.

"It's right under that," he said. "We'll have to follow up the bed of the creek. They ain't no trail, though you'll see plenty of deer paths crossin' the creek. You'll get your feet wet."

Saxon laughed her joy and held on close to his heels, splashing through pools, crawling hand and foot up the slippery faces of water-worn rocks, and worming under trunks of old fallen trees.

"They ain't no real bed-rock in the whole mountain," Billy elucidated, "so the stream cuts deeper'n deeper, an' that keeps the sides cavin' in. They're as steep as they can be without fallin' down. A little farther up, the canyon ain't much more'n a crack in the ground—but a mighty deep one if anybody should ask you. You can spit across it an' break your neck in it."

The climbing grew more difficult, and they were finally halted, in a narrow cleft, by a drift-jam.

"You wait here," Billy directed, and, lying flat, squirmed on through crashing brush.

Saxon waited till all sound had died away. She waited ten minutes longer, then followed by the way Billy had broken. Where the bed of the canyon became impossible, she came upon what she was sure was a deer path that skirted the steep side and was a tunnel through the close greenery. She caught a glimpse of the overhanging spruce, almost above her head on the opposite side, and emerged on a pool of clear water in a clay-like basin. This basin was of recent origin, having been formed by a slide of earth and trees. Across the pool arose an almost sheer wall of white. She recognized it for what it was, and looked about for Billy. She heard him whistle, and looked up. Two hundred feet above, at the perilous top of the white wall, he was holding on to a tree trunk. The overhanging spruce was nearby.

"I can see the little pasture back of your field," he called down. "No wonder nobody ever piped this off. The only place they could see it from is that speck of pasture. An' you saw it first. Wait till I come down and tell you all about it. I didn't dast before."

It required no shrewdness to guess the truth. Saxon knew this was the precious clay required by the brickyard. Billy circled wide of the slide and came down the canyon-wall, from tree to tree, as descending a ladder.

"Ain't it a peach?" he exulted, as he dropped beside her. "Just look at it— hidden away under four feet of soil where nobody could see it, an' just waitin' for us to hit the Valley of the Moon. Then it up an' slides a piece of the skin off so as we can see it."

"Is it the real clay?" Saxon asked anxiously.

"You bet your sweet life. I've handled too much of it not to know it in the dark. Just rub a piece between your fingers.—Like that. Why, I could tell by the taste of it. I've eaten enough of the dust of the teams. Here's where our fun begins. Why, you know we've been workin' our heads off since we hit this valley. Now we're on Easy street."

"But you don't own it," Saxon objected.

"Well, you won't be a hundred years old before I do. Straight from here I hike to Payne an' bind the bargain—an option, you know, while title's searchin' an' I 'm raisin' money. We'll borrow that four hundred back again from Gow Yum, an' I'll borrow all I can get on my horses an' wagons, an' Hazel and Hattie, an' everything that's worth a cent. An' then I get the deed with a mortgage on it to Hilyard for the balance. An' then—it's takin' candy from a baby—I'll contract with the brickyard for twenty cents a yard— maybe more. They'll be crazy with joy when they see it. Don't need any borin's. They's nearly two hundred feet of it exposed up an' down. The whole knoll's clay, with a skin of soil over it."

"But you'll spoil all the beautiful canyon hauling out the clay," Saxon cried with alarm.

"Nope; only the knoll. The road'll come in from the other side. It'll be only half a mile to Chavon's pit. I'll build the road an' charge steeper teamin', or the brickyard can build it an' I'll team for the same rate as before. An' twenty cents a yard pourin' in, all profit, from the jump. I'll sure have to buy more horses to do the work."

They sat hand in hand beside the pool and talked over the details.

"Say, Saxon," Billy said, after a pause had fallen, "sing 'Harvest Days,' won't you?"

And, when she had complied: "The first time you sung that song for me was comin' home from the picnic on the train—"

"The very first day we met each other," she broke in. "What did you think about me that day?"

"Why, what I've thought ever since—that you was made for me.—I thought that right at the jump, in the first waltz. An' what'd you think of me?

"Oh, I wondered, and before the first waltz, too, when we were introduced and shook hands—I wondered if you were the man. Those were the very words that flashed into my mind.—IS HE THE MAN?"

"An' I kinda looked a little some good to you?" he queried. "I thought so, and my eyesight has always been good."

"Say!" Billy went off at a tangent. "By next winter, with everything hummin' an' shipshape, what's the matter with us makin' a visit to Carmel? It'll be slack time for you with the vegetables, an' I'll be able to afford a foreman."

Saxon's lack of enthusiasm surprised him.

"What's wrong?" he demanded quickly.

With downcast demurest eyes and hesitating speech, Saxon said:

"I did something yesterday without asking your advice, Billy."

He waited.

"I wrote to Tom," she added, with an air of timid confession.

Still he waited—for he knew not what.

"I asked him to ship up the old chest of drawers—my mother's, you remember—that we stored with him."

"Huh! I don't see anything outa the way about that," Billy said with relief. "We need the chest, don't we? An' we can afford to pay the freight on it, can't we?"

"You are a dear stupid man, that's what you are. Don't you know what is in the chest?"

He shook his head, and what she added was so soft that it was almost a whisper:

"The baby clothes."

"No!" he exclaimed.

"True."

"Sure?"

She nodded her head, her cheeks flooding with quick color.

"It's what I wanted, Saxon, more'n anything else in the world. I've been thinkin' a whole lot about it lately, ever since we hit the valley," he went on, brokenly, and for the first time she saw tears unmistakable in his eyes. "But after all I'd done, an' the hell I'd raised, an' everything, I... I never urged you, or said a word about it. But I wanted it... oh, I wanted it like ... like I want you now."

His open arms received her, and the pool in the heart of the canyon knew a tender silence.

Saxon felt Billy's finger laid warningly on her lips. Guided by his hand, she turned her head back, and together they gazed far up the side of the knoll where a doe and a spotted fawn looked down upon them from a tiny open space between the trees.

Milton Keynes UK
Ingram Content Group UK Ltd.
UKHW040833071024
449371UK00007B/775

9 789362 928016